DEATH & DESIRE

in Shakespeare's Sonnets

P. D. McIntosh

Copyright © 2023 Peter D. McIntosh

All rights reserved. Apart from any fair dealing for the purpose of private study, research, criticism or review, no part of this publication may be reproduced, stored in a retrieval system, or transmitted in any form or by any means, without the prior permission in writing of the publisher.

Otakou Press, Hobart, 2023

otakoupress@gmail.com

Typeface: Bookman Old Style and Georgia

ISBN: 978-0-646-87632-0

To Mr Egford, an extraordinary teacher.

Verses are not feelings, as people imagine – those one has early enough; they are experiences.

Rainer Maria Rilke, *The Notebooks of Malte Laurids Brigge*, translated by Michael Hulse

Our job is to cut through the myths and the lies, and do the best we can to get to the truth. Follow . . . the evidence and be prepared to meet a lot of resistance from the establishment.

Nick Brodie, historian, *The Weekend Australian*, September 2–3, 2017

A collusion of scholars had for over three centuries created a universe.

Michelle Cahill, *Borges and I*

It takes some hard work first to understand the evidence properly, and second to try to disable psychological biases.

William Easterly, *The Tyranny of Experts*

Contents

PART ONE. ENIGMAS IN THE SONNETS 1
1. "The Darling Buds of May" 1
2. "The Ashes of his Youth" 4
3. The "Upstart Crow" 8
4. "My Lovely Boy" 12
5. The Elusive Shakespeare 16
6. The Dedication Puzzle 30

PART TWO. THE SONNETS 37
7. First Acquaintance 37
8. Shakespeare gets Intimate 42
9. "Loathsome Canker" 48
10. A New Look at the Dedication 53
11. "The Perfect Rhythms of her Speech" 59
12. Who was the Fair Youth? 67
13. The Royal Male? 73
14. Youth travels 83
15. Roses and Courtly Imagery 93
16. Wasteful war 100
17. Adventures at Sea 108
18. "The Rank Smell of Weeds" 112
19. The Rival Poets 121
20. A Relationship on the Rocks 126
21. Laughing Saturn and the Irish Campaign 133
22. Paradise Lost 141
23. A Backward Look 149

PART THREE. THE PLAYS 162
24. Dating the Plays 162
25. The Tempest – Shakespeare's last play? 172
26. The Tempest – the Spanish-American connection 189
27. The 'late' Roman plays: Anthony and Cleopatra and Coriolanus 201
28. Troilus and Cressida 215
29. Measure for Measure 220
30. More Fantasies: Cymbeline and The Winter's Tale 230
31. All's Well that Ends Well 237
32. Macbeth 241
33. Timon of Athens and Pericles 251
34. The Two Noble Kinsmen 261
35. Henry VIII 265
36. The Royal Hand in Hamlet 271
37. Othello and King Lear 276
38. Two early plays: Romeo and Juliet and The Taming of the Shrew 283

PART FOUR. NEW LIGHT ON THE DARK LADY 288
39. Are We There Yet? 288
40. The Dark Lady Sonnets 290
41. Heart of Darkness 299
42. Psychoanalysis, Elizabethan Style 307
43. Flirting sonnets 311

PART FIVE. THE BIG PICTURE 317
44. The "Heaven-Born Goddess" 317
45. A Lover's Complaint 330
46. The Phoenix and the Turtle 335
47. The Royal Poet 339
48. Epilogue 345

Acknowledgements 349
Literature cited 350
Appendix 1 360
Appendix 2 364
Appendix 3 366

Preface

The great early twentieth century biographer Lytton Strachey challenged the literary world to find "the key which shall unlock the mystery of *Shakespeare's Sonnets*" and commented that the quest for the key "seems to offer hopes of a prize of extraordinary value – nothing less than a true insight into the most secret recesses of the thoughts and feelings of perhaps the greatest man who ever lived".

One hundred years after Strachey wrote these hopeful words finding keys to unlock mysteries and seeking prizes of extraordinary value has become unfashionable. Scholarly books on *Sonnets* like John Kerrigan's apparently comprehensive analysis (published by Penguin in 1986), and the equally thorough later book by Colin Burrow (published by Oxford University Press in 2002 and revised in 2008) seem to offer all the answers to curious readers. They certainly present a wealth of fascinating detail but neither of these books nor other standard works seriously consider fundamental issues relating to the *Sonnets*' historical or biographical context.

For example, while there is an abundance of academic speculation about the identity of fair youth of the earlier sonnets and the 'Dark Lady' of the later poems, there is no independent evidence whatsoever that Shakespeare ever expressed an interest a fair young man or that he was attracted to a woman of dark complexion. Indeed, nothing in the poems can be related with any certainty to William Shakespeare's private life. Another unresolved issue is that numerous sonnets refer to the advanced age of the poet. For example, in sonnet 45 the poet writes "My life . . . Sinks down to death, oppressed with melancholy". But Shakespeare was only in his mid-thirties when most of the sonnets were written.

These issues and many others demand serious attention and resolution. While some commentators explain away difficult problems of interpretation by arguing that the sonnets are works of the imagination, such an explanation is not only impossible to substantiate but seems unlikely to be true, given the emotional intensity portrayed in the poems, ranging from joy on first acquaintance, loneliness and anxiety during times of separation, frustration after disagreements, jealousy when the youth is attracted to someone else, and distress following the deaths of friends. The expression of these emotions in relatively modern terms, without the customary classical allusions and conventional vocabulary of a lover pursuing his unattainable beloved, radiates authenticity and points to the existence of a real youth with a real and active career – a youth with whom the poet had a complex relationship which was often loving but sometimes strained to breaking point.

The account of the relationship in *Sonnets* seems to be the poet's way of resolving mental turmoil arising from the troubled liaison. At least this is a reasonable hypothesis that must be considered when searching for meaning in the poems. In this search we need to remind ourselves that speculation, even when couched in scholarly terms, is not evidence; and possibilities do not become probabilities, or probabilities facts, by virtue of being repeated. Establishing the facts requires evidence. New evidence relevant to "the key which shall unlock the mystery of *Shakespeare's Sonnets*" is unlikely to come from a single source such as a newly discovered manuscript or historical document. It is more likely to come from a careful reconsideration and reinterpretation of existing knowledge, and analysis of observations made and conclusions reached by historians and literary scholars in the four hundred years or so since *Sonnets* was published.

Our approach should be to search for answers not only within the sonnets themselves, but also in the historical record, in what other authors were saying at the time, in Shakespeare's other works, and in the biographies of those people whose persons or activities may be alluded to in the poems. While marshalling this information we must scrupulously separate evidence from speculation. Only the evidence matters. Individual observations, considered in isolation, are unlikely to be sufficiently convincing to give us new insights for interpreting the sonnets. It is the *cumulative* evidence of many observations that will be definitive.

This book follows the approach outlined above and summarises my research over several years. The argument presented is a long one, since there is so much ground to cover and there are so many strands of evidence to present. But I have written the book in a style as popular as the subject matter permits, so that the book will appeal to general readers with an interest in Shakespeare and Elizabethan history as well as to open-minded members of the academic community.

Enjoy the journey into the "undiscovered country" of *Shakespeare's Sonnets*!

Peter D. McIntosh
Hobart

A note on the texts of the sonnets

In the sonnets quoted I have generally followed the punctuation of the first edition of the sonnets entitled "*Shake-speares Sonnets. Never before Imprinted.*" published in 1609, but in a few instances where the 1609 punctuation distorts or obscures meaning for a present-day reader, I have made changes. In the quoted sonnets and Elizabethan and Jacobean documents I have updated most spelling to conform to modern British usage. Typesetting errors in the 1609 edition and the curious substitution of "their" for "thy" in several sonnets have been corrected, following the minimally edited version of *Sonnets* prepared by Seymour-Smith (1963). I refer to the 1609 publication as *Sonnets* and the poems themselves as the sonnets (not italicised).

PART ONE. ENIGMAS IN THE SONNETS

1. "The Darling Buds of May"

Shall I compare thee to a Summer's day?
Thou art more lovely and more temperate
— Sonnet 18

With these immortal lines Shakespeare begins his most famous sonnet and perhaps the most famous love poem of all time. This poem and over one hundred others, first published over 400 years ago in a slim volume entitled *Shake-speares Sonnets*[1], was written by Shakespeare not about a beautiful young woman, but a beautiful young man[2].

> *Sonnet 18*
> Shall I compare thee to a Summer's day?
> Thou art more lovely and more temperate:
> Rough winds do shake the darling buds of May,
> And Summer's lease hath all too short a date:
> Sometime too hot the eye of heaven shines,
> And often is his gold complexion dimm'd,
> And every fair from fair some-time declines,
> By chance, or nature's changing course untrim'd:
> But thy eternal Summer shall not fade,
> Nor lose possession of that fair thou ow'st,
> Nor shall death brag thou wandr'st in his shade,
> When in eternal lines to time thou grow'st,
>   So long as men can breathe or eyes can see,
>   So long lives this, and this gives life to thee.

In sonnet (126) Shakespeare addresses this young man as "my lovely Boy" He was apparently infatuated this young man, but who was he? Shakespeare did not keep a diary and the sonnets are the closest he comes to telling us about his personal relationships, but what do they actually tell us?

Did the lovely boy and Shakespeare have an intimate physical relationship? If so, what do we make of the 'Dark Lady' of the later sonnets?

If the lovely boy was a rich aristocrat, as the poems seem to suggest, how did Shakespeare, a young man from the country who started his career on the fringes of respectability, living in lodgings in London, make his acquaintance? And what about *Sonnets*' enigmatic dedication that refers to a mysterious "M^r.W.H." – is M^r.W.H. a clue to the identity of the lovely boy or do these initials refer to someone else? And if M^r.W.H. is someone else, who is he, why is he mentioned at all, and how does he relate to what we read in *Sonnets*?

We have almost no knowledge of Shakespeare's day to day activities, other than those that can be gleaned from records of financial transactions in Stratford and London. Consequently, relating the sonnets to Shakespeare's personal experiences is difficult, to say the least. A number of the sonnets contain sexual references and innuendoes which even by the far-from-prudish standards of the time must have been considered daring, especially as Shakespeare was still alive in 1609, when *Sonnets* was published.

Although collectively the sonnets can be described as love poems, they do not follow the Elizabethan convention for this genre – "the adoring lover and the unresponsive mistress"[3]. Shakespeare has broken with this tradition of lusty yearning. Instead he writes from the heart and the head about a close but often unstable relationship, using the sonnet form to analyse complex and nuanced intimate feelings.

Shakespeare's sonnets undoubtedly describe very personal issues and contain glimpses of the poet's friends, and references to amorous affairs, rivals, and current events. However, despite analyses in scores of academic volumes and hundreds of research papers, the world's best literary minds have not reached a happy consensus concerning to which friends, relationships, rivals and current events Shakespeare refers. As one group of commentators stated: "The study of the relationship between *Sonnets* and its author's lived experience is . . . hamstrung by our inability to say what part of Shakespeare's life we are talking about when we discuss this work"[4]. The writer and editor Martin Seymour-Smith was more critical and more succinct: "Shakespeare's Sonnets have had much learned ink wasted upon them"[5].

Some analyses of the sonnets have been concerned with historical issues and some with literary and artistic qualities, others with unravelling the personal entanglements described and unlocking what the great Edwardian writer and biographer Lytton Strachey grandly and romantically called "the mystery of Shakespeare's Sonnets"[6]. In his inimitable prose Strachey warned that the paths trodden by those in search for the key to the mystery was "already white with the bones of innumerable commentators" but added that the quest "seems to offer hopes of a prize of extraordinary value – nothing less than a true insight into the most secret recesses of the thoughts and feelings of perhaps the greatest man who ever lived".

Times have changed since Strachey wrote these challenging words. In our more cynical literary world it is unfashionable to believe in "true insights", or mysteries that can be unlocked, or prizes of extraordinary value not denominated in dollars, or even to question orthodox literary opinions. For example, in stark contrast to Strachey's open-minded comment, and A. L. Rowse's conclusion[7] that the sonnets are "markedly autobiographical", the Cambridge scholar John Kerrigan was categorical: "The Sonnets are not autobiographical in a psychological mode"[8]. Colin Burrow was slightly less definite: while admitting that the "poems seem to have their roots in experience rather than in literary experimentation" he also speculated that there is no reason to suppose that the first group of sonnets (1–126) are addressed to one man[9]. He then followed this unsupported assertion with another: that it is impossible to link the varieties of possible meanings in the sonnets "to particular characters, or . . . to a known set of events"[10]. Despite suggesting that the poems have their roots in experience he ended his essay with the dismissive generalisation that the sonnets "do not give any insights into the heart of Shakespeare"[11], seemingly implying that they are, after all, just make-believe literary exercises. I beg to differ.

For centuries the issue of how what we read in *Sonnets* relates to Shakespeare's life and the people he knew has perplexed people who love reading the poems, scholars included. Perhaps there is simply not enough evidence to gain "a true insight into the most secret recesses of the thoughts and feelings of perhaps the greatest man who ever lived". Alternatively, is it possible that learned researchers have missed crucial evidence indispensable for correctly interpreting the poems?

I believe they have, which is why I have written this book.

---

[1] In the text I refer to the 1609 publication as *Sonnets* and the poems themselves as the sonnets (not italicised).
[2] Although sonnet 18 does not mention a male subject, sonnets 2, 3, 9, 11, 15, 16 and 19 in this early sequence contain references to a male, as do numerous later sonnets.
[3] Evans (1977, p. viii). In the Introduction to his book *Elizabethan Sonnets* Evans traced the development of the conventional love sonnet, which he describes as the "poetry of frustration", from its origin in the works of Ovid.
[4] Hieatt et al. (1991, p. 70).
[5] Seymour-Smith (1963).
[6] Strachey (1905).
[7] Rowse (1974, p. 191).
[8] Kerrigan (1986, p. 11).
[9] Burrow (2002, p. 118).
[10] Burrow (2002, p. 119).
[11] Burrow (2002, p. 138).

2. "The Ashes of his Youth"

My love looks fresh, and death to me subscribes
— Sonnet 107

In the London of the late 1500s and early 1600s books were sold from stalls and shops close to the major churches. Sometime in 1609 a London literary gentleman (or gentlewoman), browsing through the latest publications at John Wright's bookstall at Christ Church Gate during his or her lunchtime, might have noticed a new book entitled "SHAKE-SPEARES SONNETS. Never before Imprinted." published by Thomas Thorpe. The book included a narrative poem entitled "A Lover's Complaint". Perhaps he or she bought one of the thirteen copies that have survived to the present day and took it home to read by the fireside.

If this literary person had the habit of looking at the first and last sonnets to help him (or her) decide whether to purchase the volume, he or she would have noted nothing particularly surprising: the first poems make the unoriginal suggestion, apparently to a young man, that he should father an heir. The last appear to be conventional sonnets on the theme of Cupid's charms. Nothing *risqué* or confronting here apparently – let us assume he or she buys the volume.

On reaching home and reading further our Elizabethan poetry buff might have raised an eyebrow. Scattered among the 154 poems are daring references and sexual innuendoes showing that the poet was taking more than a general interest in the future of the young man's family name. The youth proves to be the poet's primary subject and seems to have a relationship with the poet that we could describe politely as intimate. Our mythical purchaser might have found it remarkable that the great actor/playwright William Shakespeare, still alive and apparently living in respectable semi-retirement in Stratford, was so careless about his reputation that he dared to publicise his unusual relationship with the youth in print. (In 1609 homosexuality was still a capital offence.) We can call this problem number one.

Let us now look at problem number two. Reading sonnet 22 and later poems our perceptive reader would have noticed repeated references to the age of the poet. Statements about melancholy, old age, forthcoming death, mourning, a feeling of being crushed by life's cares, and of being past the best pervade the sonnets. Not only does the poet describe himself as older than the young man (the subject of his incessant attention), but also as old in absolute terms – in fact so old as to be near death.

A few examples (see below) show that the poet isn't just complaining of being weary after tedious rehearsals in the theatre. (The italics in these sixteen examples are mine, and sonnet numbers are shown in brackets, as they are throughout this book.)

My glass shall not persuade me *I am old* (22)

Then look I *death my days should expiate* [finish] (22)

If thou survive my well contented day,
When *that churl death my bones with dust shall cover* (32)

My life . . . Sinks down *to death, oppressed with melancholy* (45)

My *grief lies onward and my joy behind* (50)

But when my glass shows me my self indeed
Beated and chopped with tanned antiquity (62)

I am now With time's injurious hand *crushed and o'er-worn* (63)

Tir'd with all these *for restful death I cry* (66)

No Longer mourn for me *when I am dead* (71)

After my death (dear love) forget me quite (72)

In me thou see'st *the twi-light of such day* (73)

In me thou see'st the glowing of such fire,
That on *the ashes of his youth* doth lie,
As the death bed, whereon *it must expire* (73)

The *prey of worms, my body being dead* (74)

Or shall I live your Epitaph to make,
Or you survive *when I in earth am rotten* (81)

My love looks fresh, and *death to me subscribes* (107)

My days are past the best (138)

It is true that Elizabethan writers sometimes posed as world-weary, and following poetic conventions, feigned age and wisdom[1], but in the sonnets the words death, die (and their derivatives) and old are used seventy-two times. Surely a poet who consistently writes about being crushed by time, dusty bones, oppressive melancholy, being past his best, a future full of grief, being in his twilight years and looking forward to restful death cannot simply be adopting a pose for poetic effect? The writer must be someone who has lost his youthful *joie de vivre*, has a lifetime of experience behind him, is physically frail, and troubled about further inevitable decline. As the youth is addressed as "sweet boy" (108) and "my lovely Boy" (126), and the author of *Sonnets* complains of his great age, the age gap between the two must have been considerable.

Living until one's sixties or seventies is nowadays unremarkable but in Elizabethan England it was unusual. The very limited statistics available indicate that prosperous men often survived into their fifties but seldom into their sixties[2]; most people in their late fifties or sixties would have considered themselves old and on the way out.

An anecdote concerning Sir Henry Lee, Master of the Armoury, is revealing. In his youth Sir Henry had been a superb horseman and in his middle age organised the annual Accession Day Tilts in honour of Elizabeth I's accession to the throne on 17 November 1558. By the 1580s the Accession Day Tilts, an anachronism carried over from the Middle Ages, had evolved into elaborate displays of pageantry in which knights, literally in shining armour, competed with each other to display their manliness and flatter the Queen in stage-managed demonstrations of jousting and horsemanship. In 1590 the fifty-seven-year-old Sir Henry gave a spectacular display celebrating Elizabeth as one of the four vestal virgins. But shortly afterwards he resigned his administrative post of master of ceremonies, "being by age overtaken"[3].

Our reader would have reasonably deduced from the references to age, decay and death in the sonnets listed above, that the writer of *Sonnets*, like Sir Henry, was probably older than fifty, and perhaps close to sixty years old. But this conclusion, strongly supported by the internal evidence of the sonnets and by what we know about Elizabethan demographics, is extremely puzzling, for some of the sonnets were already written by 1599, when Shakespeare was only thirty-five[4], and he was only forty-five years old when *Sonnets* was published.

The difficulty is obvious: far from being old and near death when the sonnets were written, Shakespeare was probably in his thirties and in his creative prime. Some of his most famous plays had recently been performed and published (*Romeo and Juliet*, *Richard III* and *Love's Labours Lost*) and he still had to write his masterpieces like *Hamlet*, *Othello* and *King Lear*. He was on his way up in the theatrical business, looking to the future and driven by entrepreneurial spirit: in 1599 he bought a ten percent shareholding in the new Globe theatre; in 1602 he bought 107 acres of land near Stratford. These are the actions of a man of vigour and ambition, not of a melancholy world-weary person in his twilight years.

We know nothing about Shakespeare's life that can explain the references to age, decay and death by the author of *Sonnets*. Although the Cambridge scholar C. Burrow recognised a problem and was clearly puzzled by it when he wrote "Shakespeare would still have counted as a youth by this date" (meaning 1599, when he was thirty-five years old)[5], he offered no explanation. Like Shakespearean colleagues in academia before him he studiously ignored the problem and had nothing further to say on the discrepancy between Shakespeare's age as implied in his writing and his actual age. How can this discrepancy be explained?

[1] Burrow (2002, p. 424).
[2] Picard (2003, p. 89).
[3] Strong (1987, p. 151).
[4] In sonnet 138 of Thomas Thorpe's 1609 edition the author complains "Although she knows my days are past the best". This sonnet appeared in print with slightly different wording in 1599 when it was published as part of a miscellany entitled *The Passionate Pilgrim*. In the variant the line reads "Although I know my years be past the best".
[5] Burrow (2002, p. 656).

3. The "Upstart Crow"

an upstart Crow, beautified with our feathers
— Robert Greene, *A Groatsworth of Wit*

Shakespeare's introduction to the public did not begin with legendary rave reviews of a blockbuster performance. Nor did it begin quietly. It began with a virulent attack by an envious fellow author.

In September 1592 the penniless author Robert Greene, only thirty-four years old, lay dying in the house of a poor shoemaker. He was one of the first Elizabethans to write in an autobiographical and journalistic style, but he never made an adequate or respectable living from writing. Three of his books describe London's low life. He was probably too intimate with his seamy subject matter for his own good.

Greene's original poems and writings are all but forgotten today, and only read by Elizabethan specialists. He is known today for another reason — he made the first published reference to Shakespeare. Greene's reference is ambiguous and provocative. It generated controversy when it was first published more than four hundred years ago (as it was probably intended to do), and still generates debate today.

The offending lines are contained in a pamphlet entitled *A Groatsworth of Wit*[1], published in 1592 by Henry Chettle, a writer and publisher whose admirable but unprofitable aim in life seems to have been to annoy the establishment. In his preface to *Groatsworth* Chettle described the pamphlet as the last creation of the dying Robert Greene. But a 1969 report penned by the researcher W. B. Austin, intriguingly published by the U.S. Department of Health, Education and Welfare, argued that it was likely that Chettle himself wrote the entire pamphlet, and presented it as Greene's work[2].

In *Groatsworth* an embittered Greene attacks those whom he considers to have treated him badly. He singles out an actor/author whom he names an "upstart Crow" and a Jack-of-all-trades who thinks he can write plays without the assistance of established authors (probably meaning university-educated people like Greene himself). He warns three of his fellow writers against this unwelcome newcomer:

> Base-minded men all three of you, if by my misery you be not warned ... for there is an upstart Crow, beautified with our feathers, that with his *Tiger's heart wrapped in a Player's hide*, supposes he is as well able to bombast out a blank verse as the best of you: and being an absolute *Johannes factotum* [Jack-of-all-trades], is in his own conceit the only Shake-scene in a country.

If "Shake-scene" is taken to be a thinly veiled reference to Shakespeare (which seems highly probable as it was not a colloquial expression of the times), this is the first surviving published reference to Shakespeare by any of his theatrical or literary colleagues. It is also the first time that Shakespeare's work was quoted: the words *Tiger's heart wrapped in a Player's hide* appear to be a deliberate misquote of Shakespeare's line *Tiger's heart wrapped in a woman's hide* from the play we now know as *Henry VI Part 3*, which Greene (or Chettle, if we accept Austin's analysis) must have heard on the stage, unless he had access to a manuscript, as the play was not published until 1595.

But why did Greene choose to misquote this line of Shakespeare's? Greene's text is unmistakably derogatory, and undoubtedly it was intended to be. Firstly, there is the reference "beautified with our feathers", implying that Shakespeare has dressed himself up as someone literary. The words "Tiger's heart wrapped in a Player's hide" also imply that a powerful and/or menacing person is play-acting. Then there is the Jack-of-all-trades slur on Shakespeare's reputation. Finally, there is the accusation that the "upstart Crow" thinks he is the "only Shake-scene in a country", implying there is another Shake-scene (Shake-speare) lurking somewhere.

Greene's *Groatsworth* caused quite a stir when it was published. Gossips must have alleged that it was written by Thomas Nashe, the brilliant and provocative Elizabethan pamphleteer, for Nashe felt obliged to refute the allegation by publishing a statement making clear that he had nothing to do with the writing of it. Perhaps influential people were pointing accusing fingers at him. Discounting Greene's *Groatsworth* as a "trivial lying pamphlet" Nashe wrote "God never have care of my soul, but utterly renounce me, if the least word or syllable in it proceeded from my pen"[3].

Nashe's concern to disassociate himself from Greene's comments is surprising, as actors did not have high social standing in Elizabethan England. Nor did writers, with the exception of those who were members of the aristocracy (for example Sir Philip Sidney), or lucky enough to be noticed and patronised by aristocratic benefactors (for example Edmund Spenser, who received a pension from the Queen). No one would have expected the published rantings of a disgruntled and dissolute minor author to have offended anyone of importance, particularly as the offending individual was now permanently silent (Greene died before *Groatsworth* was published). Why did Nashe have to defend himself against suspicion of being the pamphlet's author?

Chettle himself became as nervous as Nashe. In December 1592, two months after the publication of *A Groatsworth of Wit*, he published *Kind-Heart's Dream*, in which he apologised to one of the unnamed "play-makers" who apparently were offended by Greene's words. *Kind-Heart's Dream* repeated the statement that Thomas Nashe had nothing to do with Greene's assertions. We cannot be absolutely sure that Chettle was referring to Shakespeare when he made his apology, but it seems likely that he was referring to Greene's "upstart Crow" jibe, and therefore a reference to Shakespeare[4] is probable:

> I am as sorry as if the original fault had been my fault, because myself have seen his [i.e. the "upstart Crow['s]"] demeanour no less civil than he excellent in the quality he professes: besides divers of worship [titled gentlemen] have reported his uprightness of dealing, which argues his honesty, and his facetious grace in writing, that approves his Art.[5]

Chettle's apology provides some clues as to who had complained about the "upstart Crow" insult: Greene's invective had provoked a response from "divers of worship" who vouched for the integrity of the unnamed "play-maker". Chettle is acknowledging concern from powerful people, probably rich gentlemen or aristocrats at the Elizabethan court. It seems likely that their worships made it clear to Chettle, in no uncertain terms, that the implication that Shakespeare was a hack writer/actor or fraud should be corrected. Probably in response to pressure, Chettle published a retraction describing the play-maker as an honest man with great writing ability ("a facetious grace in writing"), undeserving of Greene's slanderous comments.

The sequence of events is apparently logical: a dying man slanders an author in oblique terms, the slander is published, a complaint is lodged, and the publisher of the comments issues a retraction. But the apology raises several issues. It is restrained. It looks like the sort of apology you make when you don't want to apologise, and it is interesting to note what Chettle does not say. He does not identify the "play-maker" who has complained. He does not wholeheartedly admit that the slandered author (probably Shakespeare) is honest; he writes that Shakespeare is *reported* to be upright in his dealings, which in turn supports the supposition that he is honest; and he writes that the author is *reported* to have writing ability. He is doing the minimum required to quieten criticism and neutralise a complaint (and it probably worked). However, these questions have never been satisfactorily answered:

- What made Chettle so nervous that he felt he had to apologise for *Groatsworth*'s contents?
- Why did Chettle not identify the "play-maker" who complained? The playwright Ben Jonson not only identified his adversaries, but also fought a duel with one of them.
- Why did Nashe feel obliged to make strong denials of his authorship of *Groatsworth*?
- Why would anyone important have bothered to take note of the bitter last words and insults of a recently deceased poet, who while living had few friends and no influence?
- Why did Greene choose to misquote Shakespeare's line from *Henry VI Part 3*? (The play was not in print at the time, so only Shakespeare and his colleagues, and a few very attentive members of the public who had heard the play performed and were expert at writing rapid notes, would have recognised the source.)

- How did William Shakespeare, a recent arrival from the provinces, gain influential and protective friends so soon after arriving in London?

The sequence of events is all the more curious because at the time of Robert Greene's attack Shakespeare's name had never appeared in print. Some of his plays had appeared on the stage but he had published nothing. Very few people in the London of 1592 are likely to have known his name. He was just another young man from the provinces, hoping to make his fortune in the rapidly expanding capital by tapping into the market of young and educated professionals with money to spend and time on their hands (the yuppies of the age). He made his first appearance in print the following year, but as a poet, not a "play-maker".

---

[1] Greene (1923; first published 1592).
[2] Austin (1969). Austin's conclusions were supported by the research of J. Jowett published in 1993 and that of D. A. Carrol published in 1994 (Vickers 2002, p. 14).
[3] Steane (1972, p. 50).
[4] Potter (2012) wrote that the person addressed in the apology was "probably Shakespeare"; Dutton (1996) assumed the person was Shakespeare.
[5] Chettle (1841; first published 1592).

4. "My Lovely Boy"

O thou my lovely Boy

– Sonnet 126

The sonnets describe a relationship. Even a cursory reading of the poems will reveal that the relationship was not the type normally described by poets of the time. We do not read about a passionate male pursuing an attractive and beautiful woman, often physically unobtainable, as so typically portrayed by Sir Philip Sidney in his sonnet sequence *Astrophel and Stella* or by Samuel Daniel in his *Delia* sonnets. Instead the author seems chiefly concerned about working out complex and ambiguous emotions about a male friend or lover.

The observations in the sonnets are intensely personal. The sexual innuendo in some and the introverted reflections in others indicate that they were not written for public entertainment or edification. They seem to be a private record – something their author wrote to clarify his thoughts on an affair of the heart. Their author is unlikely to have begun writing them with publication in mind.

Sonnets 1–126 can be loosely grouped under the headings of first acquaintance (1–19), infatuation (20–33), difficulties (34–65) and increasing disillusion (66–126). But such headings oversimplify the subject matter – many sonnets are hard to categorise. The later sonnets (127–154) contain the references to the so-called Dark Lady, and do not fall into any obvious pattern, chronological or otherwise.

Some researchers who doubt that Shakespeare wrote *Sonnets* have taken the liberty of reordering the sonnets to suit their pet theories about who wrote them and why[1], but there is no general agreement among academics that such reordering is justified. The arguments in favour of reordering are generally circular: so-and-so fell in love with so-and-so, and these are the known events of their respective lives; if the sonnets are reordered the revised sequence matches these events and the history of the relationship of these two people; therefore, these two people must be the author and subject of the sonnets. QED!

There is, in fact, no strong independent evidence that the sonnets should be reordered. The internal evidence (derived from the sonnets themselves) is rather to the contrary. There are references to clocks and time in sonnet 12 and to minutes and time in sonnet 60. These references are surely not coincidental – we can be almost certain that at least these two sonnets have retained their numbered place in the sequence, as defined by the author.

With this established, and taking into account that the entire sequence of sonnets 1–126 follows the natural progress of a relationship (first acquaintance, infatuation, doubts etc.), it seems probable that the sonnets as printed are in the sequence presented to the publisher by the author. At least this assumption should be the starting point for further investigations.

Likewise, since there is no incontrovertible evidence that sonnets 1–126 are addressed to more than one person, we must assume (at least in our initial studies) that they concern one person: the fair youth mentioned in the early sonnets.

If we are to have a chance of identifying the young man with whom Shakespeare was obsessed, it would help to know when the sonnets were written. If the young man was a public figure (as several sonnets indicate) some likely dates of composition might also enable us to put together a short list of handsome young men as candidates.

We know that some sonnets were circulating in 1598 because in this year the Elizabethan literary critic Francis Meres tantalisingly mentioned the circulation of Shakespeare's "sugar'd sonnets among his private friends" and listed him among other poets as "the most passionate amongst us to bewail and bemoan the perplexities of love"[2]. Unfortunately, we have no way of telling whether the "sugar'd sonnets" mentioned by Meres were among those printed in 1609, but Meres' comment does confirm that by 1598 Shakespeare had written sonnets.

A comparison of the vocabulary and subject matter of *Sonnets* and *Love's Labours Lost*, which contains sonnets and was probably written in 1594–1595[3], and of *Sonnets* and Shakespeare's earlier poems *Venus and Adonis* (1593) and *The Rape of Lucrece* (1594), indicates that some sonnets had probably been written by 1595. The earliest dates of composition suggested have been the late 1580s[4].

It is noteworthy that in sonnet 16 Shakespeare refers to his "pupil pen". This would have been a strangely modest comment to make after the publication and sales success of the highly polished erotic poem *Venus and Adonis* in 1593, and supports the notion that the early sonnets (at least sonnets 1–19, which form a distinct subject-matter sequence) were written before this date. The inclusion of the words "pupil pen" in the 1609 edition of *Sonnets* also indicates that sonnet 16 was probably not revised before publication.

Dating the later sonnets is harder. Sonnet 107 seems to refer to contemporary historical events (I consider the options in chapter 21) so is potentially important for dating. Unfortunately, commentators can't agree on the events to which the sonnet refers. Some favour the year of the Armada (1588) or shortly afterwards; some favour the year of James I's accession to the throne (1603); others favour events between these two dates[5]. This fifteen-year range tells us only what we already know – that Shakespeare was writing sonnets in the last 15 years of Elizabeth's reign.

Sonnets 138 and 144 were certainly written by 1599, since in this year William Jaggard published versions of these two poems that differ only slightly from the versions published by Thomas Thorpe ten years later.

More sophisticated analyses are possible. Scholars have compared the use of rarely used words and styles of writing in *Sonnets* and the plays, and then, by linking sequences of sonnets with plays, have postulated when the sonnets were written and, in some cases, revised. Their analyses have resulted in two schools of thought. The first believes that sonnets 1–60 were written c. 1591–5 and then revised; sonnets 61–103 were written in the same period but were not revised; sonnets 104–126 were written later (1597–1603); and the final group (127–154), containing no "late" rarely-used words, was written early (1591–5)[6]. The second retains this relative chronology but prefers later dates for some sequences[7].

Analyses like these have weaknesses. Firstly, the date of first publication, which is known for several plays, may not correspond to the year of first performance or year of composition, which may be some years earlier. Secondly, for several plays the date of first performance is not known. Thirdly, although the presence of rarely used words can be useful for relative dating of Shakespeare's texts, their absence in certain sonnets may be simply because they were not appropriate in the context, or Shakespeare may have experimented with different styles, or he may have deliberately written some sonnets in an earlier style[8]. Lastly, a handful of the sonnets may not in fact have been written by Shakespeare – the simple language and rhymes of some have aroused suspicion concerning their authorship. For all the above reasons chronologies based on word use and style must be treated cautiously.

The upshot of all this analysis is that we can be reasonably confident that Shakespeare wrote *Sonnets* between the late 1580s and the early years of the new century; that he didn't write the second group of sonnets (127–154) after the first (1–126) but at about the same time; that we must be cautious assigning firm dates to sonnets on the basis of stylistic criteria; and the entire sonnet sequence was completed by 1603, or thereabouts.

Let's now return to the all-important identity question. If we search in the sonnets for a physical description of the young man who caught the poet's attention, we will be disappointed. As mentioned above, Shakespeare is more concerned with sorting out his own emotions than with praising the physical attributes of his subject. He does not reveal the colour of his eyes, his height or his build. His appearance is only described in general terms, but he is consistently described as fair (which meant good looking in Elizabethan times, rather than blonde) and as younger than Shakespeare. However, his hair is compared to the golden buds of marjoram (sonnet 99), so he was probably good-looking and had light brown hair. Who might this young man be?

In contrast to the Adonis described in Shakespeare's 1593 poem *Venus and Adonis*, who is obviously an invention and does crazy things like resisting the passionate advances of Venus, the youth of the sonnets has the attributes of a real person. The young man charms, he disappoints, he absents himself, he travels, he reappears, his affections stray, he seeks other lovers, he is praised by other poets, and he exasperates his poet-lover and is forgiven, only to disappoint the poet again. In other words, his behaviour is that of a normal but spoilt and self-centred human being – someone we might call a rich playboy in today's parlance. Theories that the youth is a poetic invention must surely be nonsense – the emotions expressed and events described are clearly authentic and were keenly felt by the author. There is also no evidence that the youth is a composite image. All the actions and feelings described are consistent with an attachment of the poet to a single person.

As we have few direct clues to the youth's identity, we are entitled to explore indirect ways of establishing whom he might be. For example, if we list the personal and apparently historical events described in the sonnets in the order in which they occur in the poems, we may have a prospect of matching at least some of these events with the documented biographies of known people in Elizabethan and early Jacobean England, and events occurring in society at the time. In scientific terms we would be attempting a correlation, or test of goodness-of-fit, between events described in the sonnets and those in a person's life.

There are 126 sonnets in the first sequence, so, in order to follow this line of investigation, the first job to do is something that will make poetry lovers cringe: we must strip away the poetic language of eternal love and other emotions and make a list of all the personal and apparently historical events described in the sonnets. I begin making this list in Part 2.

---

[1] For example, Ogburn (1988) and Padel (1981).
[2] Meres (1598).
[3] David (1994, p. xxviii).
[4] Hotson (1949).
[5] See Kerrigan (1986) and Burrow (2002) for a discussion.
[6] Hieatt et al. (1991, p. 98).
[7] Burrow (2002, pp. 104–105) summarised the more recent research.
[8] However, where rarely-used words are absent from a long sequence of sonnets, such as the absence of 'late' rarely-used words in sonnets 127–154 (Hieatt et al. 1991, p. 89), we can be sure that it is not context which is controlling word choice (i.e., the absence of 'late' rarely-used words), but some other factor.

5. The Elusive Shakespeare

Some glory in their birth, some in their skill

– Sonnet 91

A great and witty writer is usually good company – the sort of person who enlivens a dinner party. A professional actor like Shakespeare, whose plays abound in original verbal exchanges, must have been an outstanding conversationalist and never at a loss for words. His contemporaries must surely have noticed his sparkling humour and remarked on the brilliance of the man who displayed unparalleled penetrating insights into human nature, loved bawdy jokes, relished sexual innuendoes, created unforgettable characters like Falstaff and Malvolio, displayed an extraordinary knowledge of history and the classics, and expressed such heartfelt personal experiences in his sonnets.

Wouldn't a man with his originality, personality and wit have been the leading speaker at literary gatherings, been idolised by admirers, been the central figure at post-performance visits to the tavern, and been in demand as a guest of honour at court occasions?

But here we draw a blank. Although people today regard Shakespeare as a literary giant and the most talented writer of the English renaissance and possibly of all time, in his lifetime none of Shakespeare's contemporaries seem to have considered him to be in any way remarkable. There is no record that anyone *ever* made an appointment to see him, lent him a book, recorded a witty conversation with him, wrote him a letter on literary matters, congratulated him on writing a play, had a riotous party with him, or invited him to give an after-dinner speech. Nor is there a record of his attendance at court or a visit to the house of an aristocrat in a personal capacity. Only one letter addressed to Shakespeare has survived. It concerns mundane monetary matters and was never sent. Isn't this very odd?

All the verifiable facts about William Shakespeare are sparse and can be summarised in a few paragraphs[1]. We know more about Geoffrey Chaucer, who lived two hundred years earlier, than we know about Shakespeare, and the Chaucer record reveals a literary life parallel to, and in harmony with, his rise in status from page to trusted court official, emissary and senior administrator.

There are several references to Shakespeare's *works* by Elizabethan and Jacobean writers. But during Shakespeare's lifetime there were only a couple of ambiguous references to the character of Shakespeare himself: a fellow author criticised him as an "upstart Crow" (see chapter 3); a student play lampooned him as "sweet Mr. Shakespeare"[2] and the publisher Henry Chettle described him as honest by repute, as having a civil demeanour and a "facetious grace in writing"[3]. Slim pickings indeed.

Of Shakespeare's personal papers only his will and documents relating to property, land trading and legal proceedings have survived. He left behind no signed literary manuscripts, no letters, no notebooks, and no library[4]. Although his works indicate that he read hundreds of publications, there is no evidence that he ever owned a single volume, or ever borrowed one.

When Shakespeare died in 1616 there were no great outpourings of grief for England's greatest writer and poet. No one except the Stratford parish clerk seems to have noted his departure. The clerk simply recorded the death of "Will. Shakspere, gent". Shakespeare's will is a prosaic business document. It contains no mention of books, manuscripts, plays, or anything pertaining to a literary career. We may justifiably ask why Shakespeare was largely unnoticed in life as well as in death, and why the usual literary paraphernalia associated with a lifetime of writing seems to have disappeared completely.

Several literary and artistic giants, among them Henry James, Charles Chaplin and Mark Twain, have had strong doubts about the traditional story of the young man of Stratford becoming the greatest of all English poets and playwrights. In his autobiography Charles Chaplin eloquently expressed his reservations, which crystallised after being shown around the house purporting to be 'Shakespeare's Cottage' by the then Mayor of Stratford-upon-Avon:

> I can by no means associate the Bard with it; that such a mind ever dwelt or had its beginning there, seems incredible. It is easy to imagine a farmer's boy emigrating to London and becoming a successful actor and theatre-owner; but for him to have become the great poet and dramatist, and to have had such knowledge of foreign courts, cardinals and kings, is inconceivable to me. I am not concerned with who wrote the works of Shakespeare . . . but I can hardly think it was the Stratford boy. Whoever wrote them had an aristocratic attitude. His utter disregard for grammar could only have been the attitude of a princely, gifted mind. In the work of the greatest of geniuses humble beginnings will reveal themselves somewhere – but one cannot trace the slightest sign of them in Shakespeare.[5]

Several years after Shakespeare's death the playwright Ben Jonson wrote prefatory remarks introducing the first collected edition of Shakespeare's plays – what we now call the 'First Folio' of 1623. Shakespeare was born eight years earlier than Ben Jonson. Their careers overlapped and Shakespeare is known to have acted in Jonson's plays[6] so it is likely they knew each other. This was probably why Jonson was asked to write the prefatory remarks, although whether he and Shakespeare were close friends we don't know.

Readers might have expected Jonson's remarks to have sketched Shakespeare's life from his humble beginnings to his exalted status as England's finest author, referring to his most famous works, noting his wit, erudition and human qualities – the usual advertising blurb for an expensive book. We are all familiar with the format. What Jonson actually wrote is unexpected and rather surprising.

Jonson begins with 16 lines of doggerel, warning readers that comments in praise of Shakespeare should not be born out of "Ignorance," "blind Affection" or "crafty Malice". He writes that comments of the last-mentioned kind would be akin to those of a whore praising a matron and could hurt Shakespeare (presumably meaning Shakespeare's reputation). He then counters this curious stray thought (where did that come from?) with the assurance that Shakespeare is "proof" [immune] against all such ignorant, foolish or malicious praise.

Then, abruptly changing his style from irreverent humour to fervent adulation, he begins the sales pitch in earnest, in what can only be described as 'over-the-top' marketing: Shakespeare is the "Sweet swan of Avon" and "the Soul of the Age! The applause! delight! the wonder of our Stage!"

> O draw no envy (Shakespeare) on thy name,
>   Am I thus ample to thy Book, and Fame:
> While I confess thy writings to be such,
>   As neither Man, nor Muse, can praise too much.
> 'Tis true, and all men's suffrage. But these wayes
> Were not the paths I meant unto thy praise:
> For seeliest [blind] ignorance on these may light,
> Which when it sounds at best, but echo's right;
> [at best only sounds like an imitation]
> Or blind Affection, which doth ne're advance
> The truth, but gropes, and urgeth all by chance.
> Or crafty Malice, might pretend this praise,
> And thinke [aim] to ruine, where it seem'd to raise.
> These are, as some infamous Bawd, or whore,
> Should praise a Matron. What could hurt her more?
> But thou art proofe against them, and indeed
> Above th'ill fortune of them, or the need.
> I, therefore will begin. Soule of the Age!
> The applause! delight! the wonder of our Stage!

But in the middle of this effusive eulogy Jonson pauses. A few more stray thoughts require attention. He informs the reader that Shakespeare had "small Latin, and less Greek", which is surprising to learn, given Shakespeare's profound knowledge of classical texts which is so evident in his works. And when Shakespeare is wearing his buskins (riding boots covering the calf) he (Jonson) will call forth Aeschylus, Euripides and Sophocles to hear him. But when he is only wearing his socks he will leave him alone! So it goes on – in light-hearted superficial commentary – for another 42 lines.

Like his contemporaries, Jonson has chosen to reflect on Shakespeare's *works* and not on Shakespeare the *man*. In 80 lines the *only* biographical detail revealed is that Shakespeare knew little Latin and less Greek (and this can hardly be true) and that he was gentle. The whole preface reminds one of a cheeky best-man speech at a wedding reception: 'I could tell you all these fascinating stories about this guy's past life, including salacious gossip of how he did this and that in his mis-spent youth, but it could be embarrassing, so I won't, I'll keep it very clean and simple, and just remind you of his good points, especially as he's now the chairperson of the local golf club'. His mixed message combining praise and ridicule should put us on our guard. There is no precedent for such flippant treatment of a great author.

Jonson wasn't the first or last person to make fun of Shakespeare. Anonymous student plays lampooned him as "sweet Mr. Shakespeare" and accused him of gathering together "shreds of poetry" at the theatres[7]. When an anthology of Shakespeare's poetry was published in 1640 with a frontispiece engraving of Shakespeare, its caption[8] questioned the image's authenticity by asking "This Shadowe is renowned Shakespear's [sic]?" In this volume Ben Jonson's exaggerated praises "The applause! Delight!" were repeated and re-punctuated as "The applause? delight?" So, twenty-four years after Shakespeare's death people were still poking fun at him.

The documentary record tells us very little about Shakespeare's human qualities. There are accounts of Shakespeare's land dealings and investments in Stratford, including tedious detail about negotiations with another Stratford landowner concerning land enclosures[9], but such transactions are typical of the activities of the small-town land-grabbing gentry at the time and tell us nothing personal – nothing about his opinions, views on current affairs, love life, literary activity, friendships, religion, or his hopes and fears.

The only image of Shakespeare that has any valid claim to authenticity is the lifeless and mask-like engraving by Martin Droeshout published in the First Folio. Whether this engraving is a good likeness of the playwright and poet is doubtful, for Ben Jonson tells us that the artist had a "strife with nature" to portray Shakespeare, a comment unique in Elizabethan publishing. Other authors were routinely portrayed in frontispiece engravings, presumably as lifelike images, without comment.

The shelves of our public and university libraries contain countless volumes purporting to be Shakespeare biographies. These tomes invariably contain numerous quotes from the plays, and so-called facts preceded by qualifiers such as 'probably', 'almost certainly' and 'most likely'; photographs of the so-called birthplace; desks in the Stratford Grammar School; the Shakespeare monument in Holy Trinity Church; and nicely engraved views of Stratford and London[10]. However, Shakespeare's life, when stripped of such padding, can be summarised very briefly[11].

* * *

William was the third child of John Shakespeare, a glover of Stratford-upon-Avon, and Mary Arden, daughter of a prosperous farmer. His date of birth is unknown, but he was baptised on 26 April 1564. John was probably illiterate as he signed his name with a mark, but he seems to have been a man of initiative and something of an entrepreneur. He is recorded as a buyer and seller of property, and as a trader in wool, timber and barley. He was also a dumper of illegal rubbish: in 1552 he was fined for making an unauthorised "dunghill" in Henley Street in his home town. Putting dunghills behind him, John grew in public stature, taking on civic duties in Stratford, eventually becoming Bailiff, with responsibilities similar to those of a mayor. Prospects for the three-year-old William must have appeared promising. However, by 1576 John Shakespeare's fortunes had declined and he stopped attending town council meetings. In the 1590s he no longer attended church for fear of being sued for debt.

Contrary to what popular biographers and Stratford tourist companies would have us believe, Shakespeare's birthplace in the town is not known. We know nothing about William's upbringing, education or early professional training. Adulatory comments like "At this time [the time of John Shakespeare's money worries] the Alderman's eldest son was a sharp and observant lad of thirteen"[12] are pure invention.

We do know that on 27 November 1582, when he was aged eighteen, the church issued a licence for the marriage of "William Shaxspere" to an Anne Whatley of Temple Grafton. However, records show that on the very next day "William Shagspere" and "Anne Hathwey of Stratford" were given permission to marry after only one reading of the marriage banns, instead of the usual three[13]. Anne Hathwey (now usually spelt as Hathaway) was eight years older than Shakespeare and already pregnant with his first child, which explains the hurry to marry. Whether the earlier Anne Whatley entry in the parish register was a clerical error, or Shaxspere and Shagspere were different men, or the Hathwey parents enforced Shakespeare's marriage to their pregnant daughter against William's wishes is not known.

The only Stratford records of William Shakespeare in the next fifteen years are the registration of the baptism of his daughter in 1583, his twins in 1585, a mention in legal papers in 1587, the registration of the death of his son Hamnet in 1596, and his purchase of a large house called New Place in 1597.

The first indication we have that Shakespeare was writing plays in the 1590s comes from Robert Greene's 1592 pamphlet entitled *A Groatsworth of Wit* (see chapter 3). This pamphlet contains the oblique and critical reference to Jack-of-all-trades actors who think they can do without the services of cultured intellectuals like Robert Greene, a university-educated poet. In the same year William Shakespeare apparently loaned £7 to a John Clayton[14] so he was probably already reasonably well off. Shakespeare made his first appearance in print the following year, but as a poet not a playwright. It was in April 1593 that *Venus and Adonis*, his immensely popular erotic narrative poem on a classical theme, was published by fellow Stratfordian Richard Field. The poem was reprinted nine times in William's lifetime.

In 1594 Shakespeare followed this outstanding success with another titillating poem on a classical theme, *The Rape of Lucrece*. Both *Venus and Adonis* and *The Rape of Lucrece* were dedicated to the rich aristocrat Henry Wriothesley, Earl of Southampton. In his dedications Shakespeare used the usual flowery language of the times and essentially asked Southampton to send a cheque in the mail. There is no evidence that Southampton responded or that they ever met.

Shakespeare joined the acting company the Chamberlain's Men in 1594. There are records of payments to him and fellow actors, but whether Shakespeare actually acted at this time is unclear – he may have been only an investor. Between 1594 and 1598 several plays that later appeared under his name were published anonymously. This was rather strange restraint on Shakespeare's part, given the fame and success he had recently achieved with his two long poems. Surely he would have been well aware that including his name on publications would boost sales? The first printed plays to bear his name were published in 1598 and 1599 and included *Love's Labours Lost* – a full five years after *Venus and Adonis* appeared.

Shakespeare appears to have taken pride in the professional presentation of his two early poems, which are immaculately printed. But for some reason he seems to have been quite indifferent to the quality of the first printings of his early plays, some of which were published from texts cobbled together from the deficient memories of his fellow-actors[15].

Painstaking research by scholars has established whether these early editions were based on authorial texts, the playhouse copy used by the prompter, or recollections of actors in Shakespeare's company. But they have ignored the big question: why would Shakespeare passively allow his own colleagues (whom he was probably meeting daily when the theatres were open) to exploit his brilliance and put his reputation at risk by publishing substandard texts of his creations, not once but several times? And if he did agree in principle to his plays being published, why did he not offer his own manuscripts, or reputable copies of them, to the publisher, instead of leaving it to his colleagues to re-create texts from faulty manuscript copies or unreliable memories?

In 1594 Shakespeare received his first mention as an author of note when he and his narrative poem *The Rape of Lucrece* were alluded to in a curious and satirical anonymous book of cryptic poems entitled *Willobie his Avisa*:

> *Though* Collatine *have dearly bought,*
> *To have renown, a lasting life,*
> *And found, that most in vain have sought,*
> *To have a* Faire, *and* Constant *wife,*
> *Yet* Tarquin *plucked his glistering grape,*
> *And* Shakespeare, *paints poor* Lucrece's *rape.*[16]

The book purportedly recounts how a strong-minded inn-keeper's wife named Avisa, living in the west of England, rejects several courtly suitors, both before and after she marries. Avisa is remarkably well educated for an innkeeper's wife: instead of refusing to serve ale to her unwanted suitors and shutting the inn door behind them she writes them carefully crafted poems (a total of 155 hexameter verses!) firmly rejecting their advances. That she found 155 ways to say 'no' invites the comment "The lady doth protest too much, methinks"[17]. Perhaps the author of the book intended its readers to think a similar thought. Perhaps Avisa was not as chaste as her incessant claims extolling virtue and rejecting male attention seem to indicate.

The stylised illustrations in the volume at first sight seem conventional and ornamental. They portray classically robed people and symbols. On closer inspection they reveal Tudor roses, a crown, symbols of cuckolded husbands (animals with horns), rabbits, and men and women teasingly lifting clothing and baring flesh. This daring combination of royal symbols and symbols of sexual hanky-panky, and the fact that Avisa signs off with Queen Elizabeth I's motto "Alway[s] the Same" (*semper eadem*), strongly suggests that the poem is actually a mischievous commentary on the Queen's imagined or actual sexual habits. For Elizabethan readers the primary entertainment value of the book may have been reading between the lines and browsing the titillating detail of the illustrations. As G. B. Harrison wrote in his introductory commentary in the 1996 edition: "the Elizabethan reader was accustomed to look for a hidden meaning in most of the books which he [sic] read".

For modern readers the main interest of *Willobie his Avisa* has been 'Who wrote it?' In an essay[18] G. B. Harrison argued strong that the author was the poet Mathew Roydon, an associate of the courtier/adventurer/poet Sir Walter Ralegh, who fell from royal grace so spectacularly in 1592 for the triple crime of seducing Elizabeth Throckmorton in the Queen's chambers, secretly marrying her without the Queen's permission, and then lying to the Queen about his new liaison. However, the author may have been Ralegh himself. Being an intellectual, with time on his hands while banished to the family seat near Sherbourne in the west country, Ralegh had both the ability and a motive for writing poems poking fun not only at his rivals who were still in favour at Court, but also at the woman who banished him: the Virgin Queen.

The book has additional interest for those who like speculating about Shakespeare's private life and connections. It contains two curious characters identified by the initials W. S. and H. W. The W. S. character is described by the author as having "tried the courtesy of the like passion" (i.e., the seduction of Avisa), but having failed, he led his friend (H. W.) on so that he could enjoy the spectacle of H. W. attempting the same impossible task. W. S.'s plotting is described in theatrical terms:

Thus this miserable comforter comforting his friend with an impossibility, either that he would secretly laugh at his friend's folly, that had given occasion not long before unto other to laugh at his own, or he would see that another could play his part better than himself, and in viewing afar off the course of this loving Comedy, he determined to see whether it would sort to a happier end for this new actor, than it did for the old player. But at length this Comedy was like to have grown to a Tragedy, by the weak and feeble estate that H.W. was brought unto, by a desperate view of an impossibility of obtaining his purpose, till Time and Necessity, being his best Physicians, brought him a plaster, if not to heal, yet in part to ease his malady.

One interpretation is that W. S. represents William Shakespeare and that H. W. represents Henry Wriothesley, Earl of Southampton. But H. W. most probably stands for the author, who calls himself Henry Willobie (almost certainly an invented name). The doubt about H. W. representing Henry Wriothesley weakens the case for W. S. representing William Shakespeare.

Shakespeare received more conventional recognition in 1598 when Francis Meres, a schoolmaster and self-appointed literary critic, mentioned him as "the most excellent" of English dramatists in *Palladis Tamia*, a book comparing the works of contemporary English authors and classical writers. Meres went on to list twelve Shakespeare plays. Tantalisingly, he also referred to Shakespeare's "sugar'd sonnets among his private friends". Whether these sonnets were some of those later published in Thomas Thorpe's 1609 collection we cannot tell.

There is no evidence in the form of letters or contemporary accounts that Shakespeare ever met the Earl of Southampton or received the patronage he requested in the dedications to *Venus and Adonis* and *The Rape of Lucrece*. Supposedly factual assertions such as "Shakespeare made the acquaintance of Southampton in the winter of 1591–2, when the young Earl had just come of age"[19] are myths. Nor is there any hint in any historical record that Shakespeare enjoyed a courtly life or associated with the aristocracy. The evidence is rather to the contrary. In 1596 he was the subject of a judicial restraining order for threatening a William Wayte "for fear of death and so forth". In both the years 1598 and 1599 Shakespeare was listed as a tax-evader and in 1599 he was living in lodgings near the new Globe theatre, in which he was a shareholder. We can conclude that at this time the actor/author Shakespeare was living on the margin of respectability, and sometimes on the wrong side of the margin. Indeed, circumstantial evidence[20] suggests that in the early 1590s Shakespeare was associated with a furtive group of characters that included the playwright Christopher Marlowe and a William Wayte (perhaps the same William Wayte referred to above) periodically employed as government informants or spies, although standard biographies ignore this evidence.

In London Shakespeare was acting, evading tax and possibly working for the government, but his activities in Stratford seem to have been those of a canny middle-aged businessman: he was hoarding grain during times of shortage and building up a property portfolio. After buying New Place for £60 in 1597 he acquired other land and properties worth more than £320 (a huge sum) in the early years of the new century. Stratford business records never mention his name in connection with writing or acting.

In 1599 William Jaggard published a miscellany of poems by Shakespeare, Christopher Marlowe, Sir Walter Ralegh and minor poets in a volume entitled "*The Passionate Pilgrim* by William Shakespeare". This book included two poems that later appeared (with slightly different wording) as sonnets 138 and 144[21] in Thomas Thorpe's 1609 edition of *Sonnets*, and three poems from *Love's Labours Lost*. Jaggard incorrectly and probably knowingly attributed all the poems in this collection to Shakespeare. Adding Shakespeare's name to a collection was probably a good marketing ploy. This was cheeky, considering that the litigious Shakespeare was still alive. But Shakespeare cannot have objected, for in 1612 Jaggard published another edition of *The Passionate Pilgrim*, this time including an extra nine poems by the author Thomas Heywood under Shakespeare's name. Again, there is no record that Shakespeare protested.

In 1601 a poem of Shakespeare's appeared in a miscellany entitled *Love's Martyr* published by the minor writer Robert Chester. Shakespeare's untitled poem, known as *The Phoenix and the Turtle*, is a tightly written piece about love and constancy between a turtle dove and a queen living in "married chastity". The love affair ends tragically with disappointment and death. The simplest explanation of the poem is almost certainly the correct one: it is an allegory on the love between Elizabeth I and her impetuous and emotionally unstable favourite, the Earl of Essex[22]. The date of publication of the poem supports this interpretation, for Essex was executed in 1601 and his fall from grace, from court favourite to traitor, would have been the talk of the town for months. But just how Shakespeare was able to publish a poem on a highly personal and sensitive subject concerning Queen Elizabeth and her favourite without incurring a severe penalty has never been explained.

By 1603 many of Shakespeare's plays had appeared in print: *Henry VI Part 2* (1594); *Titus Andronicus* (1594); *Henry VI Part 3* (1595); *Romeo and Juliet* (1597); *Richard II* (1597); *Richard III* (1597); *Love's Labours Lost* (1598); *Henry IV Part 1* (1598); *Henry IV Part 2* (1600); *A Midsummer Night's Dream* (1600); *Henry V* (1600); *The Merchant of Venice* (1600); *Much Ado about Nothing* (1600); *The Merry Wives of Windsor* (1602); and *Hamlet* (1603). As mentioned earlier, several of these first printings (referred to as quartos because of their small page size) were put together from actors' memories and are not regarded as definitive. *Edward III*, the authorship of which is disputed, was published in 1596. Between 1603 and 1623 (when the First Folio appeared) the only new plays to be published were *King Lear* (1608), *Pericles* (1609), *Troilus and Cressida* (1609) and *Othello* (1622). Why

Shakespeare refrained from publishing anything for about five years after his masterpiece *Hamlet* appeared in 1603 has never been explained.

Although Shakespeare was England's most famous poet and playwright in 1603, he failed to write a eulogy about his sovereign when she died. His silence did not pass unnoticed: Henry Chettle, who had earlier published Greene's *A Groatsworth of Wit* and never missed a chance to needle the establishment, commented on Shakespeare's sin of omission. In London Shakespeare headed the list of players on the occasion of King James I's coronation. In Stratford at about the same time he was selling malt and suing a resident for a debt of 2 shillings. In 1604 he was lodging with a wigmaker in Silver Street, Cripplegate. In 1605 he invested the huge amount of £440 in tithes. In 1608 he sued to recover a £6 debt and damages.

In 1609, when Shakespeare was forty-five years old, Thomas Thorpe published *Shake-speares Sonnets*, possibly the most famous book of English poetry ever written. It broke with tradition by expressing in frank and modern terms the love between Shakespeare and a fair male friend. Later poems in the publication refer to a woman having dark characteristics. The sequence is uncluttered by customary classical allusions and archaisms. The spelling mistakes, missing lines, misplaced words and careless punctuation suggest that both the printer (George Eld) and publisher (Thomas Thorpe) treated the publication of the *Sonnets* as a rush job. Thorpe's volume included the long poem *A Lover's Complaint* which follows a traditional pastoral formula: a wronged maid sits on a riverbank complaining about being deceived and seduced by her lover. While throwing his letters (and the jewels he gave her) into the stream she is comforted by a clergyman (from a respectable distance of course). Their conversation is overheard and narrated by a third person who must have been hiding in the bushes with a pen and notebook.

This curious poem is deliberately written in a formal and antiquated style[23] and is commonly regarded as being of lesser quality and less interest than the preceding *Sonnets*. Consequently, it has received less attention. Although some scholars believe that *A Lover's Complaint* was not written by Shakespeare, it is now accepted as one of his works[24]. In chapter 45 I look at this poem's relationship to *Sonnets*.

In contrast to the earlier poems formally dedicated to the Earl of Southampton, Shakespeare does not mention a potential sponsor in his *Sonnets* volume but does include a strangely worded inscription (Figure 1), usually referred to as the *Sonnets*' Dedication. This purports to be written by the publisher, Thomas Thorpe, whose initials are printed at the bottom of the page. It cites a "M[r].W.H." as being the "onlie begetter of these insuing sonnets". Most scholars agree that the Dedication is relevant to the interpretation of the sonnets, but don't agree on what its relevance is. The scholar C. Burrow observed that Thomas Thorpe only signed prefaces or dedications "if the author of the work was dead or out of the country"[25]. In a strange *non sequitur* he followed this interesting observation with the inference "This makes it very probable that Shakespeare was not in London while the sequence [*Sonnets*] was being set [in type]".

> TO.THE.ONLIE.BEGETTER.OF.
> THESE.INSVING.SONNETS.
> Mr. W. H. ALL.HAPPINESSE.
> AND.THAT.ETERNITIE.
> PROMISED.
>
> BY.
>
> OVR.EVER-LIVING.POET.
>
> WISHETH.
>
> THE.WELL-WISHING.
> ADVENTVRER.IN.
> SETTING.
> FORTH.
>
> **T. T.**

Figure 1. The Dedication page in Thomas Thorpe's first edition of *Shake-speare's Sonnets*, published in 1609.

At the time of *Sonnets*' publication Shakespeare was probably spending much of his time in Stratford, for town records for the period after 1602 refer to several of his dealings in land, houses and grain, and to his litigation. By 1609 Shakespeare appears to have lost interest in the publication of *Sonnets*. If he approved publication, he evidently took no interest in the quality of the final product. Alternatively, if *Sonnets* was printed from a stolen manuscript, there is no evidence that Shakespeare attempted legal redress, despite his readiness to use the courts to retrieve small debts owed to him. He seems to have been as casual about the publication of *Sonnets* as he was with the publication of his early plays.

On 10 March 1613 records show that "William Shakespeare, of Stratford-upon-Avon, in the county of Warwick, gentleman" bought a house near the Blackfriars Theatre in London and mortgaged the property back to its previous owner. This is the last record of Shakespeare's investments in the capital. Apart from a minor business transaction in the same year and an ownership document of 1615 which records his name, this is also the last we hear of Shakespeare in London.

In March 1616 Shakespeare amended his will that he himself had penned[26] earlier in the year. The register of Stratford-upon-Avon's Holy Trinity church records the burial of "Will. Shakspere, gent." on 25 April 1616. We do not know how he died. His will contains no hint of literary genius or personal warmth. It does not mention any books or manuscripts, nor does it provide funds for publication of the First Folio. It includes the famous line in which he left his wife his second-best bed. As an afterthought (written between the lines) he left money to his three theatrical colleagues, John Heminges, Richard Burbage and Henry Condell, so that they could buy rings in his memory. A monument in Holy Trinity church was erected after Shakespeare's death. Later an effigy of a figure holding a quill may have been substituted for an earlier figure holding a sack of commodities[27].

No one of any importance in London or in Stratford remarked on Shakespeare's departure from this world. Seven years after his death the collection of his plays we now refer to as the First Folio was published. The financier behind this expensive venture is not known, although the Earl of Pembroke, the dedicatee, must be a suspect. The First Folio of 1623 included eighteen plays not previously published, and all the plays previously mentioned except *Pericles*. *Two Noble Kinsmen* (a collaborative effort with John Fletcher) was published in 1634.

In summary, our knowledge of Shakespeare the writer is scant. He may have attended grammar school. He may have owned books. He may have conversed with the rich and famous. He may have travelled overseas. He may have learned foreign languages including Italian. He may have been sponsored by aristocrats. He may have had access to the greatest libraries of Elizabethan England. But there is absolutely no hard evidence for any of these possibilities.

During his lifetime contemporaries mentioned his plays and publications, but only Robert Greene and Henry Chettle referred to his personal qualities: Greene's reference was uncomplimentary and Chettle's comments were studiously conventional and may well have been made under duress, as they formed part of an apology. Even in 1623, seven years after Shakespeare's death, his erstwhile colleague Ben Jonson revealed remarkably little about Shakespeare's character when writing his introduction to the First Folio. In Stratford Shakespeare was known only as a dealer in land, houses and agricultural commodities, as a lender of money and as a litigant – typical concerns of a successful middle-class landowner – but not as a writer or as a man of exceptional abilities. His will is a business document with no literary style and no literary references.

It is informative to contrast what we know about Shakespeare with what we know about his contemporary Ben Jonson. Jonson's biography is consistent with his literary output. He was a bricklayer by trade (like his stepfather before him) and was occasionally teased about his origins. He won a scholarship to Westminster School, where he made acquaintance with the great historian William Camden, who taught there. We know that he associated with other playwrights and cooperated with them (probably out of financial necessity) in writing plays, many of which have not survived. He spent time in Marshalsea prison for offending the establishment with a play (written with Thomas Nashe) called *The Isle of Dogs*. He combined a quarrelsome nature with good swordsmanship, which led him to kill actor Gabriel Spenser in a duel in 1598. This altercation was recorded by theatre owner Philip Henslowe when writing to his son-in-law Edward Alleyn, an actor. Jonson's adventures with the English army sent to help Dutch rebels provided source material for one of his most famous plays *Every man in his Humour*. From these and other examples we build up a picture of an intelligent and adventurous character who is always 'up to' something. He is not only an intellectual but gets noticed, sometimes for the wrong reasons. He has human qualities other than his ability to write. He interacts with his peers – his life is part of their lives, and their lives (and deaths) are part of his – and they become source material for his writings[28].

Shakespeare, by contrast, is a ghost-like figure. He is present but not present. His writings seem a world apart from the rather humdrum person who was investing, living in lodgings, buying property, possibly mixing with the wrong sort, evading tax, shrewdly getting ahead financially and taking people to court for amounts of a few shillings or pounds.

It is remarkable that we know almost nothing about the poet and playwright Shakespeare through letters, accounts written by friends, diaries, records of the royal court and the like. Credible evidence linking Shakespeare the careful and litigious middle-class social climber, actor, theatre investor and landowner to Shakespeare the wise, effervescent, humorous, world-embracing great author is totally absent. Nowhere is this absence of a link between his life and work more obvious than in *Shakespeare's Sonnets*.

---

[1] Price (2001, p. 14–19), presents all the verifiable facts about Shakespeare's life in six pages.

[2] The Parnassus plays, *The Return from Parnassus Part 1, The Pilgrimage to Parnassus* and *The Return from Parnassus Part 2*, were staged at Cambridge University between 1598 and 1602.

[3] Chettle (1841). First published in 1592. The reference occurs in the introductory epistle "to the Gentlemen Readers".

[4] The historian and rare books expert Stuart Kells wrote a book entitled *Shakespeare's Library* (Kells 2018) in which he provides readers with an entertaining tour of the world of forgers, thieves and rogues associated with the rare book trade. Despite impeccable connections to rare book collectors the world over, he uncovered no evidence that a Shakespeare library ever existed.

[5] Chaplin (2003, p. 359). First published in 1964.

6 In the 1616 folio of Ben Jonson's works Shakespeare appears in the list of actors for *Every Man in his Humour*, first performed in 1598, and *Sejanus*, first performed in 1603.
7 *The Return from Parnassus Part 1*. There is no doubt that the reference to Shakespeare is irreverent and sarcastic, as several other authors, including Ovid, are lampooned in this and two other Parnassus plays, *The Pilgrimage to Parnassus* and *The Return from Parnassus Part 2*, which were staged in Cambridge University between 1598 and 1602.
8 The frontispiece of Benson's 1640 edition "Poems written by Wil. Shake-speare. Gent." The image is reproduced by Price (2001, p. 192).
9 Schoenbaum (1981).
10 The biography by Rowse (1973) is a good example.
11 For a summary of Shakespeare's historical record see Price (2001, pp. 14–19).
12 Rowse (1973, p. 21).
13 Mabillard, A. *Shakespeare of Stratford: Shakespeare's Marriage. Shakespeare Online*. 20 Aug. 2000. http://www.shakespeare-online.com/biography/shakespearemarriage.html. Accessed 12 April 2022.
14 Price (2001) points out that the record for this transaction mentioning "Willelmus Shackspere" does not mention the lender's profession or town of origin and that "Shackspere" and the Shakespeare from Stratford may be different persons.
15 The research by Pollard (1909) established that several early-published plays (Quartos) were derived from faultily remembered texts. Pollard's pioneering work has been corroborated and expanded by many other researchers.
16 Harrison (1966). Spelling has been modernised. In his essay Harrison discussed the book's likely author and the references to Shakespeare.
17 *Hamlet*, Act 1, scene 2.
18 Harrison (1966, pp. 222–231).
19 Rowse (1973, p. 63).
20 Phillips and Keatman (1995).
21 Burrow (2002, p. 103; 2008, p. 103) mistakenly identifies the pair of sonnets as 128 and 144.
22 Hyland (2003); the idea was first put forward by Grosart (1878).
23 Kerrigan (1986).
24 Jackson (2008) summarised the debate and presented the crucial evidence for authorship by Shakespeare.
25 Burrow (2002, p. 99).
26 Although most Shakespeare biographers assert that Francis Collins, a lawyer's clerk, wrote Shakespeare's will, detailed handwriting analysis by Hamilton (1985) demonstrated that the will was written by the same person who penned the Shakespeare signature appended to the will, i.e. William Shakespeare himself. Even to a non-expert eye Francis Collins' signature in the will, in spidery italic text, is clearly quite different in style to the main text of the will, written in the secretary hand. (The 'secretary hand' is the name given to the informal writing generally used in personal documents, in contrast to the italic hand generally used in official documents, and by the aristocracy.)
27 Phillips and Keatman (1995, p. 43).
28 Donaldson (2011).

6. The Dedication Puzzle

thy records, and what we see doth lie

– Sonnet 123

One needs only to read the introduction of any scholarly edition of *Sonnets* to see that the puzzle of the identity of the fair youth in the first group of sonnets, along with others like the identity of the 'Dark Lady' in the second group, has kept a small army of Shakespeare academics employed. One could be excused the fleeting thought that the academic literary world would rather *not* solve the mystery of *Shakespeare's Sonnets*.

Some scholars distance themselves from identity questions and choose to analyse the sonnets' artistic qualities – their ethereal characteristics of balance, tone, colour and structure[1]. These lucky people are untroubled by the actual subject matter of the poems or their historical context – Art is what matters. One distinguished commentator even confidently asserted that "in reading Shakespeare's Sonnets, biography need not impinge"[2]. One wonders how he came to this conclusion – it is akin to saying that John Masefield's early life as a sailor on tall ships had no relevance to his poems and ballads describing the sea and sailing.

Despite research and speculation spanning more than three centuries, the puzzle of identity persists, and actually begins in *Sonnets'* Dedication (Figure 1). (The text on this page of the *Sonnets* volume has no title, but traditionally is referred to as the Dedication.)

Shakespeare's *Venus and Adonis* and *The Rape of Lucrece* were dedicated to the Earl of Southampton. However, the Dedication of *Sonnets* makes no appeal to the generosity of this aristocrat, or any other member of the nobility, or any named person. It appears to be an acknowledgement of sorts: it confers happiness on a certain "M^r.W.H." (Master W.H.) who is described as the "onlie begetter" of the sonnets.

We now have three identity questions to consider. Not only do we not know the identity of the beautiful young man of the first group of sonnets, or that of the mysterious 'Dark Lady' of the second, but we now also have the mystery of Mr.W.H. to ponder over. What kind of relationship, professional or otherwise, did this man have with the author, the fair youth, the 'Dark Lady', and with that almost invisible person, Shakespeare's wife Anne Hathwey? And in what sense did he 'beget' the sonnets?

How should we interpret the Dedication? Should we take it seriously as a rather obtuse piece of writing? Should we treat it as a word puzzle? Or should we, as some have done, treat it as a mathematical or geometrical exercise?

Before I venture where angels fear to tread, I would like to draw attention to some rather odd features in the printing of the Dedication. These features can be categorised under five headings: typography, layout, custom or convention, grammar, and word choice.

The *typographical* oddity is the most obvious (Figure 1). Every complete word in the Dedication is separated from the next by a full stop. It could be argued that this unusual use of full stops is purely decorative. But full stops occur at ends of lines, where demands of symmetry suggest that stops are not required. There is only one instance of a full stop being followed by a space, and that is after the initials W.H. Of course, this unusual spacing may have no significance at all. It could be an accident of typesetting. But I think we should take note of it, particularly as the preceding initials W.H. are universally accepted by Shakespeare scholars as being important (although they don't agree on *why* they are important).

The *layout* oddities are often overlooked because scholars puzzling over the meaning of the Dedication often treat its text as continuous prose, or have been concerned only with the initials W.H. in isolation, or do not reproduce the Dedication as it was originally typeset. There are three odd layout features. The first concerns lines 6–8:

BY.

OUR.EVER-LIVING.POET.

WISHETH.

These are given special prominence by the extra spacing around them (Figure 1). Secondly, the verb **WISHETH** is isolated in a line of its own, as if it has some importance. Thirdly, **WISHETH** appears exactly where we might expect the author's name. For example, if the Dedication's text was written as follows:

BY.

OUR.EVER-LIVING.POET.

WILLIAM.SHAKESPEARE.

we would regard it as logical and unremarkable – what we would expect. Unfortunately, the text does not read like this. But why should the word WISHETH appear where we expect the author's name?

The oddity relating to *custom* or *convention* is the use of the words OUR.EVER-LIVING.POET to describe a poet who was still very much alive in 1609, the year of publication. At this time Shakespeare was semi-retired in Stratford-upon-Avon, engaging in commodity trading and property deals. (He died in 1616.) The convention in Elizabethan and Jacobean times, and in

Shakespeare's plays, was to describe great people as 'ever-living' or 'immortal' only after their death[2]. We still maintain this convention. We might speak of the immortal speeches of Winston Churchill, but just imagine how odd it would be in 2023, to refer to 'the greatest speeches of the ever-living Joe Biden' or to describe Vladimir Putin as 'immortal'.

The oddity relating to *grammar* has been ignored by most commentators. The problem lies with the word WISHETH in line 8. If lines 1–7 are a self-contained sentence ending at OUR.EVER-LIVING.POET (a reading that makes reasonable sense), then the word WISHETH is left in limbo without a subject, and makes no sense[3]. If, however, OUR.EVER-LIVING.POET is the subject of the second sentence, this sentence contains no object; what exactly is being wished on the well-wishing adventurer? Furthermore, the preceding lines 1–6 then have to end with the word BY. The grammatical conundrum is insoluble.

Finally, there is the oddity of *word choice*. Shakespeare *always* uses the word beget or begot in the biblical sense of a person brought into the world by a woman's labour, or in the closely related sense of a person who has created or produced something. He *never* uses the word to mean simply getting something, in the sense of acquiring. So presumably the creative meaning is the one to apply to BEGETTER in the Dedication. But if this is the meaning of BEGETTER we strike another problem: if Mr.W.H. is the person who produced the sonnets (i.e. brought them into the world by his labour, by his writing), where does that leave the EVER-LIVING POET, who surely must be Shakespeare?

At this point we could give up and conclude that the Dedication is indecipherable mumbo-jumbo and dismiss it as unimportant. But one has the nagging feeling that it is important, if only we could find the key for which people have been searching for about 400 years.

It has been suggested that Mr.W.H. is simply a typographical error for Mr.W.S., i.e. that Mr.W.H. refers to Mr. **W**illiam **S**hakespeare[4]. It is, however, unlikely that a typesetter would make a mistake like this on such a prominent page, especially as the letter H looks nothing like the letter S – surely a typesetter would have spotted a misplaced "H" in the "S" type box. Putting aside the unlikely possibility of a typographical error, if we do substitute Shakespeare's initials in Mr.W.H. the paraphrased Dedication would read 'all happiness to Shakespeare (the begetter of these sonnets), and that eternity promised by the ever-living poet [who presumably is Shakespeare again]' – a meaningless circular construction and surely not what the publisher or writer intended. Furthermore, if we do accept the improbable solution of Mr.W.H. denoting Mr. William Shakespeare, the problem of EVER-LIVING referring to a living poet remains unresolved.

Another theory is that BEGETTER is the person who 'got' or procured the *Sonnets* manuscript for the publisher Thomas Thorpe. But if Thorpe acquired the manuscript by straightforward means, presumably it came from

Shakespeare himself. In which case the intricate word game of the Dedication would be pointless, since the begetter's (Shakespeare's) name is emblazoned across the *Sonnets*' title page. If, on the other hand, Thomas Thorpe acquired the manuscript surreptitiously via an intermediary of dubious character, Thorpe would be most unlikely to advertise the initials of the rogue who relieved Shakespeare of his priceless poems, especially as the litigious poet was still alive.

Despite these seemingly fatal objections to the begetter-equals-procurer theory, candidates for the intermediary who obtained the *Sonnets*' manuscript for Thomas Thorpe have been suggested, among them being Sir William Hervey, third husband of the Earl of Southampton's mother. (The distant connection with the Earl of Southampton supposedly favours this theory.) But apart from the complete lack of evidence to support Sir William's candidacy for the doubtful honour of being M^r.W.H. the thief, there is another problem: in an age when rank and due deference were considered extremely important, who would dare address a knight as Mr. (Master)? And why would they take the risk?

A third M^r.W.H. theory is that BEGETTER means neither the writer nor the procurer of the sonnets but refers to the person who *inspired* them. Despite the drawback that Shakespeare never uses the word begetter in this sense (which is conveniently ignored), this theory has become a gold mine for academic speculators, for it allows them to use personal references in the sonnets to support the identity they attribute to M^r.W.H. For if M^r.W.H. inspired the sonnets, then arguably he must also be the fair youth with whom Shakespeare was infatuated. The two main contenders for the honour of M^r.W.H. doubling as the fair youth are Henry Wriothesley, Earl of Southampton and William Herbert, Earl of Pembroke.

The Earl of Southampton was the dedicatee of Shakespeare's poems *Venus and Adonis* (1593) and *The Rape of Lucrece* (1594). It is therefore possible that he had some prior personal association with Shakespeare, although there is no evidence whatsoever that they met or corresponded. Southampton apparently had some good qualities in his early bachelor days, for in 1595 he was described by the contemporary poet, George Peele, as "gentle and debonair"[5]. Such comment may of course have been conventional flattery by a poet eager to gain the recognition and patronage of an aristocrat. Southampton briefly attracted the attention of Elizabeth I but, lacking the charm and flair of the Earl of Essex, made no lasting impact on her affections. Elizabeth later damningly dismissed him as "such a one whose counsel can be of so little, and experience of less use"[6].

Despite Southampton's possible link to Shakespeare through the dedications of the latter's two early poems, the theory that Southampton was both M^r.W.H. and the fair youth has several fatal flaws, all of which are ignored by those who favour the M^r.W.H.-equals-Southampton theory[7]. Firstly, a painting of Southampton dating from 1601–1602 shows a gaunt long-faced man with dark brown hair and a darker beard – hardly attributes that would lead a poet to describe him as one of nature's fairest creatures. Secondly, why should Southampton's initials H.W. be reversed? Thirdly, who would dare address an earl as Mr. (Master)? And lastly, why would a publisher, unless he was suicidal, risk annoying a living earl by issuing a book that included poems indicating the earl had an intimate and probably homosexual relationship with a commoner (Shakespeare), and go so far as making *risqué* comments about the inspirer's genitalia (sonnets 20 and 151)? Publication of the comment describing the earl as "the Master Mistress of my passion" (20) would have been audacious beyond belief.

The argument for M^r.W.H. being William Herbert, the Earl of Pembroke is even weaker than the argument for M^r.W.H. being the Earl of Southampton. It depends heavily on the fact that in 1623, fourteen years after the publication of *Sonnets*, Pembroke, as a patron of the theatre, had the First Folio of Shakespeare's plays dedicated to him. However, no evidence for anything but a formal relationship of Pembroke to his theatrical colleagues has emerged. In any case he was born in 1580, and therefore far too young to have been the subject of exhortations to produce an heir in the late 1580s or early 1590s (sonnets 1–17). In addition, the objections relating to addressing an earl as "Mr." also count against Lord Pembroke's candidacy, and there is no evidence that he was a homosexual.

An intriguing solution to the M^r.W.H. identity question was canvassed by journalists G. Phillips and M. Keatman[8]. They proposed that a government spy named William Hall was actually William Shakespeare working under an assumed name, and in their book *The Shakespeare Conspiracy* wrote that from 1593 onwards a William Hall is mentioned sporadically in the official accounts of Secretary William Cecil (and after Cecil's death in 1598, in the accounts of his son Robert) as receiving payments for courier services. Phillips and Keatman proposed that the words M^r.W.H. ALL.HAPPINESSE etc. in the Dedication are a cipher for M^r.W. HALL.HAPPINESSE etc.

The theory sounds plausible, but the independent researcher Donna Murphy discredited Phillips' and Keatman's argument. She wrote[9] that the official accounts of Secretary William Cecil and his son Robert do not in fact support the existence of a courier or spy named William Hall. She also pointed out that Phillips and Keatman seem to have mis-referenced a work of Elizabethan astronomer Thomas Harriot in which (Phillips and Keatman argued) full stops and spaces are used in a similar way to their use in the *Sonnets*' Dedication. In summary, the research of Phillips and Keatman does not support their conclusions.

Apart from the issue of whether William Hall the courier actually existed, the William Hall-equals-M^r.W.H. theory suffers from two serious flaws concerning motive: what possible reason would Thomas Thorpe have to reveal the alias of a secret service spy in a book of romantic poems, and why would he take the risk?

Similarly weak are arguments that Mr.W.H. stands for William Hall, a printer known to Thomas Thorpe, who just possibly passed on the *Sonnets'* manuscript to him: what advantage would Thorpe gain by referring to an obscure printer colleague of his, in the dedication page of a book of poems?

It is no surprise that Elizabethan documents record a great number of people with the initials W.H. and from among these amateur and academic sleuths have selected several who seem to have plausible credentials for being the object of Shakespeare's affection. Oscar Wilde may or may not have been convinced that Mr.W.H. referred to the Elizabethan boy actor and singer Will Hewes. But convinced or not, in 1889 he wrote a charming novella to support his argument[10]. There may indeed be a pun on the name Hewes in sonnet 20, but we cannot be sure, because Elizabethan spelling was so variable. As with other theories that appear plausible on first reading, Oscar Wilde's case is based on very slender evidence, and neither historical analysis nor the texts of other sonnets support his entertaining theory.

The Shakespeare scholar Leslie Hotson was convinced that Mr.W.H. referred to William Hatcliffe of Lincolnshire, who studied at Cambridge and then at Gray's Inn in London[11]. He supported his argument with dubious discoveries of hidden messages in the text of the sonnets. Although couched in scholarly terms, his speculation had no more basis in evidence than Oscar Wilde's.

In summary we can say that no Elizabethan or Jacobean can be confidently identified as Mr.W.H. Should researchers forget the struggle and join that happy and select band of readers who enjoy the sonnets purely for their artistic qualities, without worrying about to whom most are addressed[12]? Or should we heed the frightening warning of Shakespeare's biographer Anthony Burgess who wrote "if we play the scholar's game and puzzle over the identity of a Mr.W.H. in Shakespeare's life, or come out confidently with an assertion as to who he was, then we enter a dangerous world of time-wasting dissension, where monomania thumps and lunacy beckons"[13]?

For anyone curious about historical context, and an interest in why Shakespeare wrote the words he did, biography *does* matter and biography *does* impinge. Like me, these persistent souls are probably prepared to risk beckoning lunacy while they puzzle over the meaning of the sonnets, in an attempt to find what Lytton Strachey described as the prize of "extraordinary value".

Is it possible that in trying to establish the identities of the primary subject of the sonnets and of Mr.W.H. we have underestimated the brilliance, deviousness and complexity of Shakespeare's mind? Should we reconsider the assumption that the Dedication is a basically straightforward piece of English? Could Mr.W.H. be a literary red herring? Have scholars have been asking the wrong questions for the last four hundred years? Does the Dedication require a different analytical approach?

[1] Vendler (1977).
[2] Although in Covell's book *Polimanteia* published during her lifetime Queen Elizabeth was referred to as "ever-living", the context of Covell's reference was a plea that writers should write in such a way as to confer immortality on the aged monarch. We must therefore conclude that this reference is not proof that the term "ever-living" was a normal descriptor of living people.
[3] Some commentators have suggested that the initials T.T. are the subject of the verb WISHETH, but the separation of T.T. from the rest of the text and the different type size used for T.T. make this unlikely.
[4] Foster (1987).
[5] Akrigg (1968, p. 48).
[6] In a letter to Essex dated 19 July 1599, while he was campaigning in Ireland (Marcus et al. 2002, p. 394).
[7] For example, Akrigg (1968) and Rowse (1973).
[8] Phillips and Keatman (1995).
[9] Murphy (2015) wrote "I looked for any occurrences of William or W. Hall with various spellings and abbreviations from 1580–1620 which could in any way be interpreted as related to intelligence activities. I also checked the Public Records Office Calendar of State Papers, Domestic, 1580–1610, and List and Analysis of State Papers Foreign, only available for 1589–1596. I did not have access to SP Hamburg III. I found none of the instances that Phillips and Keatman cited."
[10] Wilde (1958).
[11] Hotson (1964).
[12] For example, Vendler (1997).
[13] Burgess (1972, p. 125).

PART TWO. THE SONNETS

7. First Acquaintance

*If I could write the beauty of your eyes,
And in fresh numbers number all your graces*
— Sonnet 17

In Part One I cite some of the curious inconsistencies and puzzles concerning the traditional story of William Shakespeare and his works. It is now appropriate to have a look at the sonnets themselves. As I mentioned in chapter 1, no other work of Shakespeare's resembles a diary as much as his *Sonnets*. So, like Alice, let's start at the beginning.

In the first sonnets Shakespeare addresses a beautiful youth with a fair complexion. In these early poems the impressions are all visual – it's not the young man's voice or his intellect or his bravery or the way he moves that impress the poet, it's his appearance. The young man is one of nature's "fairest creatures"; he has "bright eyes"; he's the "world's fresh ornament" and the "herald to the gaudy spring". Some concepts and even some of the actual words of these early sonnets are derived from Marlowe's *Hero and Leander* which was circulating in manuscript in the early 1590s[1].

The formal 'thou' is used more frequently than the informal 'you'. The poems suggest interest from a respectful distance rather than intimacy. But even in the first sonnet ("From fairest creatures we desire increase") there is an undertone of physical desire. One suspects that the poet's concern for the young man's beautiful features to be passed on to an heir ("His tender heir might bear his memory") is code for sexual fascination rather than an expression of genuine concern that future generations might be deprived of the young man's features.

The first seventeen sonnets pursue the sexual theme. They urge the youth to father an heir and pass on his good looks and qualities to a child.

Sonnet 1
From fairest creatures we desire increase,
That thereby beauty's *Rose* might never die,
But as the riper should by time decease,
His tender heir might bear his memory:
But thou contracted to thine own bright eyes,
Feed'st thy light's flame with self substantial fuel,
Making a famine where abundance lies,
Thy self thy foe, to thy sweet self too cruel:
Thou that art now the world's fresh ornament,
And only herald to the gaudy spring,
Within thine own bud buriest thy content,
And tender churl mak'st waste in niggarding:
[Being a nice but miserly guy you waste your good qualities on yourself:]
    Pity the world, or else this glutton be,
    To eat the world's due, by the grave and thee[2].

The respectable goal of marriage receives passing mention only in sonnet 8 but the reference is indirect: the poet alludes to music (and specifically to the paired strings of the lute) as an analogy for the harmony of married life ("Mark how one string, sweet husband to another . . ."). The message conveyed is not the trite one that the young man should marry to achieve happiness. It is more subtle: the young man's thoughts are discordant, even when he listens to music, and that the concordant sounds of the lute are singing him a song: "thou single wilt prove none [nothing]". With its suggestive analogies of "sweet husband to another" and "well tuned sounds, By unions married" this sonnet is the closest Shakespeare comes to recommending that the youth should find a wife.

Sonnet 8
Music to hear, why hear'st thou music sadly?
Sweets with sweets war not, joy delights in joy:
Why lov'st thou that which thou receiv'st not gladly,
Or else receiv'st with pleasure thine annoy?
If the true concord of well tuned sounds,
By unions married do offend thine ear,
They do but sweetly chide thee, who confounds
In singleness the parts that thou should'st bear:
Mark how one string, sweet husband to another,
Strikes each in each by mutual ordering;
Resembling sire, and child, and happy mother,
Who all in one, one pleasing note do sing:
    Whose speechless song being many, seeming one,
    Sings this to thee: thou single wilt prove none.

The recommendation is touched upon again in sonnet 9, which accuses the youth of consuming himself in his single life. Then the poet writes more aggressively, claiming that the youth doesn't love others and is possessed by "murd'rous shame". By not producing a child and remaining single the self-centred youth is murdering his own beauty.

> *Sonnet 9*
> Is it for fear to wet a widow's eye,
> That thou consum'st thy self in single life?
> Ah; if thou issueless shalt hap to die,
> The world will wail thee like a makeless [childless] wife,
> The world will be thy widow and still weep,
> That thou no form of thee hast left behind,
> When every private widow may well keep,
> By children's eyes, her husband's shape in mind:
> Look what an unthrift in the world doth spend
> Shifts but his place, for still the world enjoys it
> But beauty's waste hath in the world an end [beauty eventually fades],
> And kept unused the user so destroys it:
> > No love toward others in that bosom sits
> > That on himself such murd'rous shame commits.

In sonnet 10 the poet uses strong words again ("murd'rous hate") and seems exasperated. The subject matter is still the poet's disquiet about the youth's resistance to procreation. But why should one of two recently acquainted gay men express such an insistent desire that the other has sex with an unspecified woman in order to produce a child? Surely two such men meeting for the first time would be more concerned with establishing their own relationship than worrying about what the world will miss if the lovely boy wastes his beauty. An alternative explanation, not raised or dealt with in the standard commentaries, is that all this talk about producing an heir is simply the poet's polite expression of a desire for sex or love-making.

> *Sonnet 10*
> For shame deny that thou bear'st love to any
> Who for thy self art so unprovident;
> Grant if thou wilt, thou art belov'd of many,
> But that thou none lov'st is most evident:
> For thou art so possessed with murd'rous hate,
> That 'gainst thy self thou stick'st not to conspire,
> Seeking that beauteous roof to ruinate
> Which to repair should be thy chief desire:
> O change thy thought, that I may change my mind,
> Shall hate be fairer lodg'd than gentle love?
> Be as thy presence is, gracious and kind,
> Or to thy self at least kind hearted prove,
> > Make thee another self for love of me,
> > That beauty still may live in thine or thee.

In the above sonnet, for the first time, Shakespeare mentions love, twice in a general sense (lines 1 and 10) but then in a personal (but restrained) sense in line 13's command: "Make thee another self for love of me". This is a curious line – Shakespeare is saying: 'Because you love me, reproduce yourself'.

It is clear in this initial sequence that Shakespeare has rejected the sentimental and courtly conventions of his predecessors. We are not reading anything remotely resembling the decorous sentiments of Sidney or Daniel. This is truly 'early modern' poetry. The youth's negative as well as positive qualities have been noticed. The poet has progressed from being bowled over by the youth's beauty and is trying to understand his psychology. He is certainly besotted with the youth, but whether the youth is besotted with Shakespeare is unclear.

By the time he writes sonnet 13 it is clear that the poet is emotionally committed to his young man. He is (at last) addressed as "love" and "dear my love" (lines 1 and 13). The informal 'you' and 'your' are used for the first time, in preference to 'thou', 'thine' and 'thy'.

Sonnet 13
O that you were your self, but love you are
No longer yours, then you your self here live,
Against this coming end you should prepare,
And your sweet semblance to some other give.
So should that beauty which you hold in lease
Find no determination, then you were
Your self again after your self's decease,
When your sweet issue your sweet form should bear.
Who lets so fair a house fall to decay,
Which husbandry in honour might uphold,
Against the stormy gusts of winter's day
And barren rage of death's eternal cold?
    O none but unthrifts, dear my love you know,
    You had a Father, let your Son say so.

The biographical gem in this poem is in the last line: "You had a Father, let your Son say so." Undoubtedly the youth's father is dead. If he had been still alive the poet would have written 'You *have* a Father . . .'.

The gloriously positive and joyful sonnet 18 "Shall I compare thee to a Summer's day?" (see chapter 1) that devotees of Shakespeare the world over learn by heart begins a new theme derived from the classical poet Ovid – the threat to beauty posed by the unstoppable ravages of time, and the way in which the poet's lines will survive. The "eternal summer" of the man's youthful looks will not fade and the poet's happy state of mind will live on in the sonnet as long as men on earth can breathe and eyes can see.

Sonnet 19 on the effects of "Devouring time" revisits this theme. The poet first asks time to refrain from marking the youth with signs of ageing but then, realising the futility of such a request, settles for the comforting thought that the youth's features will always appear young in the poet's verses:

> *Sonnet 19, lines 9–14.*
> O carve not with thy hours my love's fair brow,
> Nor draw no lines there with thine antique pen,
> Him in thy course untainted do allow,
> For beauty's pattern to succeeding men.
>   Yet do thy worst old Time despite thy wrong,
>   My love shall in my verse ever live young.

After all this naïve adoration and romantic philosophising, the relationship gradually becomes more complex as the poet and his subject get to know each other better. The following poems reflect a more realistic attitude – glorious summers do fade, time does assert itself, and differences as well as similarities have to be recognised and dealt with.

---

[1] Kerrigan (1986, pp. 175–176). Compare Marlowe's "Who builds a place and rams up the gate/Shall see it ruinous and desolate" with Shakespeare's accusation (10, line 7) that the young man is "seeking that beauteous roof [his lovely body] to ruinate". Also Marlowe's "One is no number; maids are nothing then/Without the sweet society of men" with Shakespeare's plea to the young man (8, line 14): "thou single wilt prove none." One could argue that the links to Marlowe's *Hero and Leander* support a post-1590 date for these early sonnets. But if Marlowe and Shakespeare were acquainted, they may have exchanged ideas, so the apparent reference to Marlowe's work is not useful for dating the poem precisely.

[2] The last three lines develop an argument about the world not benefiting from the young man's beauty: he's a "tender churl" [lovable miser] who makes "waste" where there should be plenty by being "niggarding" [restrained] in not passing on his qualities to the world by producing a child. The poet is accusing him of being a glutton by keeping his good qualities to himself, and for the grave.

8. Shakespeare gets Intimate

But since she pricked thee out for women's pleasure,
Mine be thy love and thy loves use their treasure
— Sonnet 20

Until now the poet has viewed the "lovely Boy" from a distance. It was his good looks, and perhaps his conversation, which stimulated the poet to write the beautifully eloquent first 19 poems, ending with the optimistic last line of sonnet 19 "My love shall in my verse ever live young", which follows lines cataloguing the "heinous" effects of "swift-footed time".

Up until this point the sonnets reflect a beautiful friendship between two persons of unequal age, perhaps similar to that between a doting father and a son, although the accusation of "murd'rous hate" in sonnet 10 is a warning to gentle readers that the personal story related in *Sonnets* will not follow conventional lines. More surprising to the reader are the words of sonnet 20, in which Shakespeare writes about his passion in intimate sexual terms.

In this sonnet the young man is described as an object of Shakespeare's sexual desire and is ambiguously and daringly described as the "Master Mistress of my passion." (Let us not forget that Shakespeare was still alive when *Sonnets* was published and that homosexuality was a capital offence in Elizabethan England.)

Not only does the poet intentionally mystify the young man's gender (or perhaps his gender role in the relationship), but he also makes an extraordinary reference to the young man's genitalia. It seems that the age difference between the youth and Shakespeare (chapter 2) was no barrier to physical intimacy.

Sonnet 20
A woman's face with nature's own hand painted,
Hast thou the Master Mistress of my passion,
A woman's gentle heart but not acquainted
With shifting change as is false women's fashion,
An eye more bright than theirs, less false in rolling [roving]:
Gilding the object where-upon it gazeth,
A man in hue all *Hews*[1] in his controlling,
Which steals men's eyes and women's souls amazeth.
And for a woman wert thou first created,
Till nature as she wrought thee fell a-doting,
And by addition me of thee defeated,
By adding one thing to my purpose nothing.
    But since she pricked thee out for women's pleasure,
    Mine be thy love and thy loves use their treasure.

Joyful thoughts and adoration have been replaced by something more animal. There seems to have been some pretty close contact – so close in fact that the last lines of the sonnet have been politely referred to as causing "acute scholarly and critical discomfort"[2] and, more disparagingly, as "filthy"[3].

The most straightforward reading of the last five lines is: 'Nature added something to your body/Which is useless to me/But since you have a penis for women's pleasure/I'll love you while other lovers enjoy sex with you'. The fact that Shakespeare makes such intimate references to the young man's private parts hints strongly that Shakespeare and the youth had a homosexual relationship. But the lines are not explicit and are open to different interpretations.

If a Jacobean first-time reader of the sonnets expected the subsequent sonnets to expand on sonnet 20 and provide titillating sexual details like those in *Venus and Adonis*, he or she would have been disappointed. The poet changes the subject. In sonnet 21 the poet writes that he will not, like some poets, compare his love to spring flowers and nature's other beautiful objects – the sun and moon and the stars. He is content to say that his love "is as fair as any mother's child" – a hint of the poet's realism and a marked change of tone from the pastoral romanticism of sonnet 18.

In sonnet 22 Shakespeare begins to tell us about his worries about becoming old and dying. As noted in chapter 2, this is a theme he returns to often.

Sonnet 22, lines 1–8
My glass shall not persuade me I am old,
So long as youth and thou are of one date,
But when in thee time's furrows I behold,
Then look I death my days should expiate [death will be my remedy].
For all that beauty that doth cover thee,
Is but the seemly raiment of my heart.
Which in thy breast doth live, as thine in me,
How can I then be elder than thou art?

In sonnet 24 Shakespeare reflects on a painting of the youth. Not a painting hanging on a wall, but one "which in my bosom's shop is hanging still . . . where-through the Sun Delights to peep, to gaze therein on thee".

Sonnet 24
Mine eye hath play'd the painter and hath steel'd [drawn],
Thy beauty's form in table [notebook] of my heart,
My body is the frame wherein 'tis held,
And perspective it is best Painter's art.
For through the Painter must you see his skill,
To find where your true Image pictur'd lies,
Which in my bosom's shop [on my chest] is hanging still,
That hath his windows glazed with thine eyes:

Now see what good-turns eyes for eyes have done,
Mine eyes have drawn thy shape, and thine for me
Are windows to my breast, where-through the Sun
Delights to peep, to gaze therein on thee.
    Yet eyes this cunning want to grace [are deficient in] their art
    They draw but what they see, know not the heart.

The most straightforward interpretation of these lines is that Shakespeare has a miniature painting of the youth hanging around his neck. This is another biographical clue: the miniaturist artist Nicholas Hilliard and his pupil Isaac Oliver painted many exquisite images of aristocratic Elizabethans and Jacobeans and one of these could be the youth.

The next two sonnets seem to imply a difficulty in the relationship. Sonnet 25 compares those in favour with princes and those out of favour, and the plight of famous warriors, who after suffering one defeat, are deleted from "the book of honour" despite being highly regarded previously. The fact that the subject matter is about exclusion and disregard must surely indicate that the young man has misbehaved or committed some indiscretion. But although the poet seems to have some misgivings about the youth's behaviour, the last two lines indicate that he is confident that the relationship will continue and that he has not been shunned by his young lover.

Sonnet 25
Let those who are in favour with their stars,
Of public honour and proud titles boast,
Whilst I whom fortune of such triumph bars
Unlooked for joy in that I honour most;
Great Princes' favourites their fair leaves spread,
But as the Marigold at the sun's eye,
And in them-selves their pride lies buried,
For at a frown they in their glory die.
The painful warrior famoused for worth,
After a thousand victories once foiled
Is from the book of honour razed quite,
And all the rest forgot for which he toiled:
    Then happy I that love and am beloved
    Where I may not remove, nor be removed.

In contrast sonnet 26 is a supplication. The meek poet emphasises his low status: he is a vassal, he is writing out of duty, not to show his cleverness. He is waiting for his guiding star to shine on him with a "fair aspect" (i.e. he is down on his luck, at least in this relationship) and he is hoping for the "sweet respect" his lover can provide. And until he receives this sweet respect, he is not going to show his head (line 14). The sonnet has particularly simple (one could say basic and plodding) rhymes. The first 4 lines are almost doggerel:

Sonnet 26
Lord of my love, to whom in vassalage
Thy merit hath my duty strongly knit;
To thee I send this written ambassage
To witness duty, not to show my wit [cleverness].
Duty so great, which wit so poor as mine
May make seem bare, in wanting words to shew it;
But that I hope some good conceit of thine
In thy soul's thought (all naked [pure]) will bestow it:
Till whatsoever star that guides my moving,
Points on me graciously with fair aspect,
And puts apparel on my tattered loving,
To show me worthy of thy sweet respect,
    Then may I dare to boast how I do love thee,
    Till then, not show my head where thou may'st prove me.

The poet then changes the subject matter. Instead of writing about intimacy, love and miniature paintings (sonnet 24) he writes about feeling lonely. Why this change? The reason is clear – the youth is no longer around. Sonnets 27 and 28 tell us that Shakespeare imagines his loving thoughts travelling "from far where I abide" and "still farther off from thee" making "a zealous pilgrimage" to the faraway youth (27).

Sonnet 27
Weary with toil, I haste me to my bed,
The dear repose for limbs with travail tired,
But then begins a journey in my head
To work my mind, when body's work's expired.
For then my thoughts (from far where I abide)
Intend [Imagine] a zealous pilgrimage to thee,
And keep my drooping eye-lids open wide,
Looking on darkness which the blind do see.
Save that my soul's imaginary sight
Presents thy shadow [image] to my sightless view,
Which like a jewel (hung in ghastly night)
Makes black night beauteous, and her old face new.
    Lo, thus by day my limbs, by night my mind,
    For thee, and for myself, no quiet find.

Then Shakespeare suffers misfortune, complains he has no friends and feels desperately lonely, but writes that remembering the "sweet love" of the youth raises his spirits.

Sonnet 29
When in disgrace with Fortune and men's eyes,
I all alone beweep my out-cast state,
And trouble deaf heaven with my bootless [useless] cries,

And look upon my self and curse my fate,
Wishing me like to one more rich in hope,
Featur'd like him, like him with friends possessed,
Desiring this man's art, and that man's scope,
With what I most enjoy contented least,
Yet in these thoughts my self almost despising,
Hap'ly I think on thee, and then my state,
(Like to the Lark at break of day arising)
From sullen earth sings hymns at Heaven's gate,
    For thy sweet love remembered such wealth brings,
    That then I scorn to change my state with Kings.

Sonnets 30 and 31 make it clear that the reason for Shakespeare's melancholy is not only the deaths of friends ("precious friends hid in death's dateless night") and past lovers ("the trophies of my lovers gone") but also the youth's absence.

Sonnet 31
Thy bosom is endeared with all hearts,
Which I by lacking have supposed dead,
And there reigns Love and all Love's loving parts,
And all those friends which I thought buried.
How many a holy and obsequious tear
Hath dear religious love stol'n from mine eye,
As interest of the dead, which now appear,
But things remov'd that hidden in there lie.
Thou art the grave where buried love doth live
[You contain the spirits of the friends I loved],
Hung with the trophies of my lovers gone,
Who all their parts of me to thee did give,
That due of many, now is thine alone.
    Their [Those] images I lov'd, I view in thee,
    And thou (all they) hast all the all of me.

This sonnet is further evidence that Shakespeare is really quite old – many of his friends and lovers have passed away, but his Indian summer of friendship with the youth has raised his spirits, for in the youth he sees the qualities of those he has lost. But his change of mood is only temporary – in sonnet 32 he seems really depressed again and foresees his forthcoming death and a time when the youth will remember him only by reading his sonnets.

Sonnet 32
If thou survive my well contented day,
When that churl death my bones with dust shall cover
And shalt by fortune once more re-survey:
These poor rude lines of thy deceased Lover:
Compare them with the bett'ring of the time,

> And though they be out-stripped by every pen,
> Reserve them [my lines] for my love, not for their rhyme,
> Exceeded by the height [achievement or status] of happier men.
> O then vouchsafe me but this loving thought:
> Had my friend's Muse grown with this growing age,
> A dearer birth than this his love had brought
> To march in ranks of better equipage [company]:
> > But since he died and Poets better prove,
> > Theirs for their style I'll read, his for his love.

In the last five lines Shakespeare invents a thought that he would like the young man to adopt: 'If my friend Shakespeare had developed his skills he would be seen as equal to other esteemed poets, but since he hasn't achieved this standard, I'll read his poems for his loving thoughts, and if I want to admire style, I'll read the poems of others'.

In these last five lines and in lines four to six ("These poor rude lines . . . be out-stripped by every pen") Shakespeare is charmingly modest about his skills in relation to other poets. This expression of modesty gives us a clue as to when the sonnet was written, for the comment would be very puzzling if it came from the author's pen after publication of his immensely popular poems *Venus and Adonis* and *The Rape of Lucrece*. This sonnet (like sonnet 16, discussed in chapter 4) must surely have been written *before* the publication in 1593 of *Venus and Adonis* (i.e. when Shakespeare was 29 years old or younger) and not after. But this conclusion concerning Shakespeare's age is incompatible with the references to forthcoming death and dust-covered bones in line 2. Shakespeare's biographers have a problem – there are not many successful men or up-and-coming authors who, in their late twenties, dwell on the subjects of losing their dearest friends and lovers, and dust covering their bones.

---

[1] As this word may be a pun on a proper name, the spelling has not been changed to *Hues*. For further discussion see Kerrigan (1986).

[2] Hyland (2003, p. 160). Even the normally restrained Seymour-Smith (1963) contrives to explain (in 24 lines of notes!) that Shakespeare's reference to the young man's private parts is quite normal for heterosexuals who have a friendship with an attractive man; he writes coyly that it appears that Shakespeare "is unable to consummate his passion by the means available to homosexuals" but he does not elaborate on why this should be so.

[3] Rollins (1944).

9. "Loathsome Canker"

loathsome canker lives in sweetest bud
— Sonnet 35

In sonnet 33 the theme of jealousy first appears because the youth has been attracted to another lover: "Even so my Sun one early morn did shine . . . But . . . he was but one hour mine" [I only had the pleasure of your company for a short time, then you deserted me for someone else]. The bright sunshine of first meetings has been obscured by cloud as the relationship has become increasingly complex. But Shakespeare's desire is unabated (line 13). He excuses the youth for his misdemeanours: line 14 can be paraphrased 'we can allow suns (sons?) of this world to have faults, because the sun itself is not always as perfect as we expect'.

> *Sonnet 33*
> Full many a glorious morning have I seen,
> Flatter the mountain tops with sovereign eye,
> Kissing with golden face the meadows green;
> Gilding pale streams with heavenly alchemy:
> Anon permit the basest clouds to ride,
> With ugly rack on his celestial face,
> And from the forlorn world his visage hide
> Stealing unseen to west with this disgrace:
> Even so my Sun one early morn did shine,
> With all triumphant splendour on my brow,
> But out alack, he was but one hour mine,
> The region [regional] cloud hath mask'd him from me now.
> >   Yet him for this, my love no whit disdaineth,
> >   Suns of the world may stain, when heaven's sun staineth.

But Shakespeare is putting a brave face on an unsatisfactory situation. In fact, he's pretty annoyed. In the next sonnet (34) which begins with the accusation "Why did'st thou promise such a beauteous day?" he accuses the youth of committing an offence. They have had an argument that ended in tears (line 6). Shakespeare blames him for disappointing him badly. Although the youth has apologised, Shakespeare still feels the hurt (line 10). However, in this sonnet, and many others to follow, he gives the youth the benefit of the doubt and forgives him for his offence – as is evident in the words of the last two lines.

> *Sonnet 34*
> Why didst thou promise such a beauteous day,
> And make me travel forth without my cloak,
> To let base clouds o'er-take me in my way,

Hiding thy brav'ry in their rotten smoke.
'Tis not enough that through the cloud thou break,
To dry the rain on my storm-beaten face,
For no man well of such a salve can speak,
That heals the wound, and cures not the disgrace:
Nor can thy shame give physic to my grief,
Though thou repent, yet I have still the loss,
Th'offender's sorrow lends but weak relief
To him that bears the strong offence's loss.
    Ah but those tears are pearl which thy love sheds,
    And they are rich, and ransom all ill deeds.

The youth must be associating with (and possibly bedding) someone other than Shakespeare, for sonnet 35 describes the youth's fault as "sensual", no doubt an Elizabethan euphemism for 'sexual'. Shakespeare goes to great lengths to excuse the youth: "Roses have thorns, and silver fountains mud . . . Loathsome canker lives in sweetest bud". Then we get an obscure clue to the identity of the interloper creating the *ménage à trois*: the youth's new amour is named a "sweet thief". The adjective "sweet" indicates that Shakespeare has some personal regard for this competitor. At this point we do not know whether the youth's new love is male or female.

Because of the youth's new liaison, the relationship between Shakespeare and the youth is strained to breaking point. Shakespeare writes that "we two must be twain" and "I may not ever-more acknowledge thee". He and the youth will no longer be able to show kindness to each other in public: "Nor thou with public kindness honour me" (36).

Sonnet 36
Let me confess that we two must be twain,
Although our undivided loves are one:
So shall those blots that do with me remain,
Without thy help, by me be borne alone.
In our two loves there is but one respect,
Though in our lives a separable spite [a force driving us apart],
Which though it alter not love's sole effect [the fundamental bond between us],
Yet doth it steal sweet hours from love's delight,
I may not ever-more acknowledge thee,
Lest my bewailed guilt should do thee shame,
Nor thou with public kindness honour me,
Unless thou take that honour from thy name:
[Because this would dishonour you:]
    But do not so, I love thee in such sort,
    As thou being mine, mine is thy good report.

This mention of care to avoid a public show of intimacy shows that Shakespeare and his friend had a public image to protect. We can conclude that either Shakespeare or the youth, or both, must have been widely known and recognisable. Notice that it is Shakespeare who fears being seen as guilty (line 10): displaying love for the youth in public would dishonour the youth (line 12). This suggests that the youth's association with the "sweet thief" is honourable, i.e., it has resulted in marriage, which would make Shakespeare the guilty party if he persisted in pursuing an intimate relationship with his young man. This information could help us identify the youth – he probably married shortly after meeting Shakespeare.

The estrangement makes Shakespeare reflective. As usual when he and the youth are separated he refers to his "muse" (38). Despite his previous conclusion that "we two must be twain" he thinks lovingly about the youth again – absence certainly made his heart grow fonder. In sonnet 39, although he comes to the conclusion "let us divided live", he tries to convince himself that there are positive aspects to their separation, noting that his unwelcome ("sour") leisure allows him "to entertain the time with thoughts of love":

Sonnet 39, lines 9–12
Oh absence what a torment would'st thou prove,
Were it not thy sour leisure [unwelcome leisure] gave sweet leave,
To entertain the time with thoughts of love,
Which time and thoughts so sweetly dost deceive
[Thoughts of love help to pass the time].

Despite these hopeful words, the rocky relationship continues. Intellectual arguments haven't helped – Shakespeare can't suppress his true feelings. He writes sarcastically: "Take all my loves, my love, yea take them all" although he still hopes for reconciliation: "Kill me with spites [malicious thoughts] yet we must not be foes" (40).

Sonnet 40
Take all my loves, my love, yea take them all,
What hast thou then more than thou had'st before?
No love, my love, that thou may'st true love call,
All mine was thine, before thou had'st this more [had your new lover's love]:
Then if for my love, thou my love receivest,
I cannot blame thee, for my love thou usest,
But yet be blam'd, if thou this self deceivest
By wilful taste of what thy self refusest.
I do forgive thy robb'ry gentle thief
Although thou steal thee all my poverty [what little I have]:
And yet love knows it is a greater grief
To bear love's wrong, than hate's known injury.
    Lascivious grace, in whom all ill well shows,
    Kill me with spites yet we must not be foes.

Note that contrary to some interpretations[1], this sonnet does not support the contention that the poet is referring to a female mistress. Lines 1–8 express the poet's attempt to come to terms with the fact that the youth loves someone else: in line 6 he develops the poetic conceit that the youth is using Shakespeare's love (stolen from him) elsewhere: "for my love thou usest". In lines 9–12 Shakespeare forgives the youth for robbing him of his love. In the final couplet Shakespeare addresses the youth as "Lascivious grace". In Elizabethan times the word "grace" was habitually used to describe aristocrats, so this is a clue to the youth's social status.

In sonnet 41 we read that Shakespeare has become reconciled to the fact that the youth's "pretty wrongs" are just a natural consequence of his physical beauty (sex appeal): "Beauteous thou art, therefore to be assailed, And when a woman woos, what woman's son, Will sourly leave her till he have prevailed". The cause of the rift between Shakespeare and the youth is now clear – the youth has been attracted to a beautiful woman, with whom he has "prevailed" (i.e. with whom he has achieved sexual satisfaction).

> *Sonnet 41*
> Those pretty wrongs that liberty commits,
> When I am some-time absent from thy heart,
> Thy beauty, and thy years full well befits,
> For still temptation follows where thou art.
> Gentle thou art, and therefore to be won,
> Beauteous thou art, therefore to be assailed.
> And when a woman woos, what woman's son,
> Will sourly leave her [leave her with regret] till he[2] have prevailed.
> Aye me, but yet thou might'st my seat[3] forbear [abandon interest in me],
> And chide thy beauty, and thy straying youth [and control your youthful urges],
> Who lead thee in their riot [sexual dissipation] even there [to places]
> Where thou art forced to break a two-fold truth
> > Hers by thy beauty tempting her to thee,
> > Thine by thy beauty being false to me.

Then in sonnet 42 we have another useful biographical clue. The woman with whom the youth is having sexual relations is known to Shakespeare and has been his close friend: "and yet it may be said I lov'd her dearly" (line 2). We can infer that Shakespeare, the youth and the youth's new female lover moved in the same social circle. This information could help us to identify the youth and his woman friend.

> *Sonnet 42*
> That thou hast her it is not all my grief,
> And yet it may be said I lov'd her dearly,
> That she hath thee is of my wailing chief [the prime cause of my unhappiness],
> A loss in love that touches me more nearly [that I feel deeply].
> Loving offenders thus will I excuse ye,
> Thou dost love her, because thou know'st I love her,
> And for my sake even so doth she abuse me,

> Suff'ring [Allowing] my friend for my sake to approve her,
> If I lose thee, my loss is my love's gain,
> And losing her, my friend hath found that loss [what I have lost],
> Both find each other, and I lose both twaine,
> And both for my sake lay on me this cross,
>> But here's the joy, my friend and I are one,
>> Sweet flattery, then she loves but me alone.

Shakespeare is up to his self-deceiving intellectual tricks again. The argument he presents is convoluted: you love her because you know that I love her, and she loves you for my sake, but you and I are one (because of our love for each other), so she actually loves me. So everything is OK after all!

Contrary to assumptions made by scholars who should know better, this sonnet provides no justification for concluding that the youth's lover is the 'Dark Lady' of the later sonnets, or indeed a mistress of Shakespeare's of any other complexion, blonde, brunette, or freckled.

---

[1] Kerrigan (1986, p. 223–224); Burrow (2002, p. 461).

[2] Kerrigan (1986, p. 225), changes "he" in line 8 to "she". This type of editorial amendment requires strong justification, and Kerrigan does not provide it. The sonnet is about a good-looking youth ("Beauteous thou art") being tempted and seduced by a woman. In modern English lines 7 and 8 might read "When a woman woos, what man could leave her until he has achieved sexual satisfaction?" which makes good sense in the context. Therefore no amendment is necessary.

[3] "my seat" could also be interpreted as 'my private parts'.

10. A New Look at the Dedication

every word doth almost tell my name
– Sonnet 76

In the last three chapters I looked at the relationship of Shakespeare to his young man, as recounted in examples from the first 42 sonnets. In these sonnets there are several biographical clues which may help us identify the youth. As there are over one hundred more sonnets to look at, I will pause at this point and resume examination of the unconventional features identified in the *Sonnets*' Dedication (chapter 6) that make it unique among dedications and inscriptions in English literature. Does the Dedication also hold some biographical clues?

Allow me to recapitulate. The odd features of the Dedication are: (1) the unusual use of full stops and spaces; (2) the peculiar layout, particularly the prominence given to the word WISHETH; (3) the perplexing and indeed nonsensical grammar; (4) the strange use of EVER-LIVING, which apparently refers to a living person; and (5) the unusual use of the word BEGETTER. I should add that the letters W and H which make up the intriguing initials of the elusive Mr.W.H. also occur in the prominently placed word WISHETH.

I argued that it is unlikely that Mr.W.H. refers to a real historical character having these initials, since none of the possible candidates seems to be convincing when all the available evidence is taken into account, and there is no consensus among scholars as to who or what the initials W.H. represent. Attempts to explain the Dedication as a straightforward piece of prose that has somehow become slightly garbled have not produced a logically defensible interpretation.

As no conventional attempt to make sense of the Dedication has been satisfactory, we must consider the possibility that it is a contrived piece of writing, deliberately written to be obscure. If Shakespeare made it so, he probably intended to keep certain information temporarily 'under wraps', or at least deniable, while also revealing to posterity something important. Perhaps (in Lytton Strachey's words) the Dedication will help us in our quest to find a "true insight into the most secret recesses of the thoughts and feelings of perhaps the greatest man who ever lived"[1].

As the Dedication precedes highly personal poems containing sexual innuendoes, it is reasonable to assume that the motive for writing these obscure (but possibly decipherable) lines of text may have been the protection of a person's reputation – most probably that of the author or his friend.

At this point we encounter a psychological obstacle, for the idea that hidden messages can be found in Shakespeare's works has been derided as undeserving of scholarly attention ever since amateur sleuths using computerised analyses purported to find proof of Francis Bacon's authorship in the bard's masterpieces. Such general dismissal of the possibility of ciphers being present in Shakespeare's works of course suits those with orthodox literary views. But it is unfair, because propositions ought to be judged on their own merits, and discredited hare-brained explanations should not influence our judgment concerning others that are better researched.

We must remember that Elizabethans were exceedingly fond of word games, puns and hidden meanings. We need look no further than *Love's Labours Lost*, a veritable Elizabethan Goon Show of clever repartee, containing line after line of word play, double entendre, and oblique comments on current events, not all of which are readily interpretable in the twenty-first century. An example of a poem with a hidden (but easily found) reading is the following anonymous epitaph containing an acrostic, published after Sir Francis Walsingham's death in 1590.

> Shall honour, fame and titles of renown,
> In clods of clay be thus enclosed still?
> Rather will I, though wiser wits may frown,
> For to enlarge his frame extend my skill.
> Right, gentle reader, be it known to thee,
> A famous knight doth here interred lie,
> Noble by birth, renowned for policy,
> Confounding foes, which wrought our jeopardy.
> In foreign countries their intents he knew,
> Such was his zeal to do his country good,
> When dangers would by enemies ensure,
> As well as they themselves he understood.
> Launch forth ye muses into streams of praise,
> Sing, and sound forth praise-worthy harmony;
> In England death cut off his dismal days,
> Not wronged by death, but by false treachery.
> Grudge not at this imperfect epitaph;
> Herein I have expressed my simple skill,
> As first-fruits proceeding from a graft:
> Make then a better whosoever will.

Reading vertically, the first letters of each line spell Sir Francis Walsingham. This is an amusing and elegant example of a simple word game in which the solution is easily discovered. However, government professionals of the time developed complex codes designed to stay secret if the coded texts fell into the wrong hands. Francis Walsingham, Mary Queen of Scots, William Cecil, Robert Cecil, Essex and the Queen herself routinely used codes to convey diplomatic, military and highly personal messages. The ever-curious Francis Bacon was intrigued by codes and invented one of his own which in 1623 he published in his book *De Augmentis Scientarium*. Codes were part of everyday life for the ruling class.

Taking into account the Elizabethans' love of word games and codes, I suggest that we should not rule out the possibility that the Dedication is deliberately contrived and ambiguous. Perhaps we should treat it as a word puzzle resembling a modern-day cryptic crossword clue. It will have internal logic, but not that of a normal text. As with cryptic crossword clues, we may need to regard the Dedication as a literary contraption in which a 'true' reading is hidden. Finding the true reading will involve some mental gymnastics.

Taking this novel approach, let's have a closer look at the first odd feature, the overall layout. What would we expect in a present-day title page? An Australian reading a book of poems by A. B. "Banjo" Paterson, of *Waltzing Matilda* fame, would not be surprised if a present-day title page read something like this:

BY

THE EVER-POPULAR POET

BANJO PATERSON

The layouts of title pages in the early 17th century were similar to layouts today. In 1609 a bibliophile, picking up *Shake-speares Sonnets* while browsing the books for sale at Christchurch Gate, might reasonably have expected lines 6 to 8 of the Dedication to have contained the name of the poet whose name is printed so prominently on the *Sonnets*' title page. For example, if lines 6 to 8 had appeared as follows:

BY.

OUR.EVER-LIVING.POET.

WILLIAM.SHAKESPEARE.

our 1609 bookstore browser would have considered the Dedication to be standard for the times, except that he or she might have vaguely wondered why M^r.W.H. was mentioned and what he had to do with the sonnets. He or she might also have considered Thomas Thorpe's choice of the phrase EVER-LIVING to describe a distinguished living writer to be rather premature and presumptuous.

If we could replace the word WISHETH with the poet's name, both the isolation of the word WISHETH and the prominence given to lines 6 to 8 by their extra line spacing would be explained. There would no longer be anything particularly odd about the layout. WISHETH therefore appears to be a key word – the riddle of the Dedication would be solved if we could find justification for replacing WISHETH with Shakespeare's name.

Shakespeare's name here would also make the Dedication grammatical. It would neatly finish the sentence that begins TO THE ONLIE BEGETTER. The lines (9–12) following WISHETH that read THE WELL-WISHING ADVENTURER IN SETTING FORTH TT then become self-contained: they can be read as Thomas Thorpe's humorous signing off, punning on the meanings of SETTING FORTH as applied to both setting type and setting out on a journey, and playing on the occurrence of his initials in SETTING.

If we accept that the word WISHETH should be substituted by the author's name, how do we make further headway? The obvious place to start is with the three people mentioned in the Dedication before we encounter the word WISHETH: the BEGETTER, M^r.W.H. and the POET. Are any of these relevant for sorting out the WISHETH puzzle?

The unique space after W.H. (Fig. 1) may be significant. I suggest that if the initials W.H. were intended to represent a person's *complete* name they would have had the same treatment as other complete words, i.e. a full stop and *no following space*. We can infer that the space after W.H. has been inserted to indicate that the initials W.H. do *not* represent a complete name and that the rest of the name, i.e. a surname of sorts, follows.

A logical choice for the surname is the next person mentioned, the POET. So W.H. becomes W.H.POET. We can speculate that the platitude "ALL HAPPINESSE AND THAT ETERNITIE PROMISED BY OUR EVER-LIVING" has been inserted to separate W.H. and POET and to obfuscate their connection.

Summarising progress so far, the Dedication mentions three people, each of whom, arguably, represents the writer of *Sonnets*:

BEGETTER
W.H. POET
WISHETH

The occurrence of W and H both as isolated initials in M^r.W.H. and in WISHETH is suggestive. Could the letters W and H be some sort of code? If W and H are a code and require substitution by other letters, should we pay attention to the word BEGETTER? It is certainly a most unusual word to use in relation to poetry. People talk of writers of poems, authors of poems, readers of poems, or even scribblers of poems. They never talk of begetters of poems. Is the writer of the Dedication, like the writer of a crossword clue, asking for a synonym to be substituted, and if so, what synonym is appropriate?

To answer this question, we must think like someone who lived a little over 400 years ago. In Elizabethan and Jacobean times 'to beget' meant the same as it does now: 'to procreate' or 'to produce a child' by a woman's labour. As mentioned in chapter 6, this, or the closely related meaning 'to make' or 'to produce' is always the meaning of 'to beget' in Shakespeare's plays. We should note that Shakespeare *never* uses the word in the sense of 'inspirer' or to indicate someone who acquired and delivered an item.

We need to look for begetter synonyms among the books that were to be found in Elizabethan or Jacobean libraries. In the early seventeenth century dictionaries were coming into vogue. In Randle Cotgrave's 1611 dictionary 'to elaborate' means to "labour painfully" and in Minsheus' slightly later (1617) dictionary the verb simply means "to produce by labour". Robert Cawdry's dictionary of the same date gives the meaning as "done curiously or diligently". (The present-day Spanish *elaborar* has the same meaning; the present-day English meaning 'to express in great detail' evolved later than 1617.) So, strange as it may seem to our 21st century minds, for an Elizabethan or Jacobean reader 'elaborator' would have been a synonym for 'begetter'. As an experiment we are therefore justified in substituting the synonym ELABORATOR for BEGETTER. Our list of the three 'people' previously identified now becomes:

ELABORATOR
W.H. POET
WISHETH

This looks interesting: ORATOR in ELABORATOR can be paired with POET. This coincidence is remarkable, and surely indicates intent. If we pair off ORATOR and POET, what are we left with? ELAB and W.H. So we can postulate that **EL** should be paired with **W**, and **AB** with **H**, as shown below:

EL / AB / ORATOR
W. / H. / POET
WISH / ETH

When we substitute these letter pairs for W and H in WISH (and dispense with the full stops), the intricate word game reveals its extraordinary outcome. Lines 6 to 8 of the Dedication now read:

BY.

OUR.EVER-LIVING.POET.

ELISABETH.

It seems that WISHETH does not stand for SHAKESPEARE after all. Nor does it stand for other candidates commonly put forward as the 'real' Shakespeare, for example, Edward de Vere, the seventeenth Earl of Oxford; or

Francis Bacon; or Christopher Marlowe; or Mary Sidney. WISHETH stands for ELISABETH.

The only person who could have used the name Elisabeth on its own in early seventeenth century England and be recognised throughout the realm was Elizabeth I. The spelling of Elisabeth with an 's' is not an issue as Elizabethans and Jacobeans used both the s and z spellings of the name. For example, a portrait of Elizabeth now in the Folger Shakespeare Library spells her name Elisabeth, as does the frontispiece of the first edition of the Bishop's Bible published in 1568. Queen Elizabeth I died in 1603; in 1609 "OUR EVER-LIVING POET" would have been the appropriate compliment for a recently deceased distinguished writer, so this apparently odd usage of "ever-living" is also explained.

This solution to the Dedication word puzzle, if correct, would of course be highly significant, not to mention controversial. In chapter 12 I reconsider the sonnets discussed in chapters 7–9, because, if Elizabeth I wrote these sonnets, we should be able to detect some relationship of what is described in the sonnets to the events in Elizabeth I's life in the late sixteenth century.

If the above analysis of the Dedication is correct, it follows that William Shakespeare's function was to serve as a 'front' man for the distinguished author, who, naturally enough, did not want her carefully cultivated virgin queen image to be tarnished by revelations that she was just as capable of other women of experiencing carnal desire and of falling in love with a handsome young man half her age. An actor, well-practiced in the art of dissimulation, was an ideal choice for the role of front man. He was probably paid handsomely for keeping his mouth shut.

In order to be sure that the Elizabeth-Essex hypothesis is correct, we need to find more evidence from within *Sonnets*, and from Shakespeare's other works. We also need to investigate whether Elizabeth had the skills of a great writer. So before returning to *Sonnets*, I will examine Elizabeth's educational and literary credentials.

---

[1] Strachey (1905).

11. "The Perfect Rhythms of her Speech"

– Lytton Strachey, *Elizabeth and Essex*

Elizabeth I was a freethinker. She distrusted dogma, whether it came from what we would now call the conservative right, which in her times meant the extreme Catholics and Jesuits, or from the radical left, the politically dangerous democratic Puritan faction of the Protestant church. She shared with her father Henry VIII an ability to think for herself, to weigh up opposites, and to see solutions and courses of action other than those presented in relatively simple terms by her advisers. She often prevaricated when pressured by others to make bold decisions likely to lead to uncertain outcomes. She was expert in using her femininity and charm to achieve political aims, for example, by pretending interest in marriage to foreign suitors.

Elizabeth could have played the part of the Protestant Queen who rallied northern Europe against the excesses of the Catholic Spanish monarch, but she did not. Her natural tolerance, parsimony, aversion to risk and waste, and mistrust of simplistic approaches to complex issues made her temperamentally unsuitable for the role of crusader. She also had a limited ability to raise taxes and simply could not afford a sustained interventionist role. Thus, Lytton Strachey remarked: "it was her destiny to be the champion, not of the Reformation, but of something greater – the Renaissance"[1].

Although there is no doubt that she was personally religious, and that prayers and devotions were a great comfort to her, her outlook was essentially secular. Unlike her father Henry VIII she had no interest in the finer points of theology. She considered a person's beliefs to be their own private affair and she had no wish to impose her religious views on others. However, she acted decisively when organised religion took on a political dimension and threatened her own powers or the state's stability.

We see in Elizabeth the full expression of the Renaissance woman – a woman with an active mind, a warm affectionate heart, a vivacious personality, and a cool head. She was probably one of the most intelligent monarchs ever to sit on an English throne and she was also one of the best educated. She combined feminine charisma, manipulative ability and imaginative thought with rational decision-making. Her abilities were sharpened by an upbringing best described as emotionally turbulent, which made her precociously wary and wise.

Her father, for whom she always expressed great admiration, had married Anne Boleyn not only because he was passionately attracted to her but also because his first wife, Catherine of Aragon, seemed incapable of producing a male heir (she gave birth to six children including two sons, but only Mary, later Queen Mary, survived). The birth of Elizabeth was a great disappointment to the King – he quickly lost interest in Anne and she was disposed of by a process best described as judicial murder when Elizabeth was just two years and eight months old. We do not know how the loss of her mother affected the young Elizabeth, but her deep attachment to Anne is indicated by the fact that when she reached adulthood she had a jeweller make a pearl and ruby ring (which reportedly she always wore) containing hidden miniature portraits of her mother and herself.

When fourteen years old she was sexually harassed by Thomas Seymour, who had married her stepmother Catherine Parr soon after Henry VIII's death in 1547. Seymour had access to her bedroom and used to play games with her while in his nightgown. Elizabeth seems to have felt some attraction to Seymour. Perhaps she just enjoyed high-spirited flirting – a natural response to the novelty of being the object of a man's attention for the first time. Their rumoured relationship became dangerous for her after Catherine Parr's death in 1548. Elizabeth's half–brother Edward was king, but as he was only a boy the Duke of Somerset (Thomas Seymour's older brother) held the position of Lord Protector.

Talk circulated that Elizabeth had been a willing participant in a plot by Thomas Seymour to ally himself with Elizabeth by marriage. Seymour had probably calculated that marriage to Elizabeth would increase his standing and influence and might enable him to usurp power from his brother, whom he detested. In early 1549 she was cross–examined about the supposed marriage plot but bore herself with dignity throughout her interrogation – no mean feat for a fifteen-year-old. She later wrote to the Lord Protector protesting against the malicious gossip being circulated about her being pregnant as a result of a supposed sexual dalliance with Seymour:

> Master Tyrwhitt [her interrogator] and others have told me that there goeth rumours abroad which be greatly both against mine honour and honesty, which above all other things I esteem, which be these: that I am in the Tower and with child by my Lord Admiral [Seymour]. My Lord, these are shameful slanders, for the which, besides the great desire I have to see the King's Majesty, I shall most heartily desire your Lordship that I may come to the court after your first determination, that I may show myself there as I am.[2]

Elizabeth survived this ordeal, but more trouble lay ahead. Her half-sister Mary succeeded to the throne when Edward died in 1553. Mary was a devout Catholic and no intellectual. She had the simple and distorted world view of the religious fanatic. Her mission was to return England to the true faith, and gradually it became an absorbing passion, fomenting hatred among her subjects.

This hatred intensified when Mary insisted on marrying King Philip of Spain. Her marriage was a disastrous political error that lost her any remaining sympathy among her non-Catholic subjects. For most of the population the marriage added the fear of foreign domination to their dislike of papal authority. Again, Elizabeth found herself in a dangerous position because she was the natural focus of Protestant opposition to Mary. Suspected of intrigue with the instigators of the unsuccessful Wyatt rebellion, she was interrogated in the Tower of London. No case was found against her and she was transferred to house arrest.

However much she disliked her half-sister, or thought her policies mistaken, Elizabeth recognised that Mary had a legitimate right to rule. She would not intrigue against her. But this is as far as her allegiance went. To Mary's frustration she always remained her own person – she would not be commanded. Elizabeth gave Mary the respect due to a ruler, but no more. She paid lip service to the Catholic religion, but refused to marry the Duke of Savoy, an ally of King Philip, whom Philip wanted her to marry in order to secure the friendship of England should Mary die.

In these early experiences Elizabeth's natural courage and integrity shine through. At an early age she had learned lessons about the nature of power, the intrigues of politicians, and the opposition and indeed hatred engendered in the public by implementation of policies based on dogma rather than tolerance. When she came to power her political and personal shrewdness were already well developed. G. B. Harrison described her as having "the keenest political mind in Europe . . . and an uncanny power of estimating character"[3].

So much for her formidable informal schooling in worldly affairs before she became Queen. What about her formal education? This was no less thorough. Henry VIII, for all his faults, including his propensity for ridding himself of inconvenient wives, ensured that his daughters Mary and Elizabeth as well as his son Edward received the best instruction his scholars could offer. Mary did not have the natural ability to absorb intellectual concepts or acquire the wisdom that would have equipped her for her future role, and which might have prevented her rapid decline from popular monarch to hated bigot. Elizabeth, by contrast, absorbed all she was taught. Her religious views were tempered by reason, which largely explains her secular and pragmatic outlook. During her early career and throughout her life Elizabeth continued to study literature. One suspects that, rather like Miranda in Shakespeare's *The Tempest*, who is found playing chess while Prospero manipulates his island's inhabitants with magical charms, Elizabeth found the world of the intellect to be a peaceful haven of ordered thought to which she could retreat while political, religious and personal squalls buffeted her and the realm.

We know something about Elizabeth's literary background, for there are records of her early tutoring, and letters to her family have survived. The author J. Dunn[4] provides an excellent summary of her strong grounding in the classics. By the time she was ten years old Elizabeth was fluent in Latin, was writing letters to her stepmother in Italian, and translating French poems. She studied Latin and Greek with the Cambridge scholar William Grindal, a pupil of the renowned teacher and educationalist Roger Ascham. She devoted mornings to the study of Greek (the Bible, Isocrates, Sophocles and

Demosthenes) and the afternoons to Latin. After Grindal's death in 1548 Roger Ascham himself took over the task of teaching the royal pupil.

The tradition of educating the royal womenfolk had begun with Henry's grandmother, Lady Margaret Beaufort. It continued under the influence of Henry's first wife, Catherine of Aragon, who brought Spanish scholars to England to teach her daughter Mary. Henry's second wife and Elizabeth's mother, Anne Boleyn, also had a broad and international education. Anne was brought up at the French court, before being recalled to England in 1521. She appreciated French poetry and, like her husband Henry and her daughter Elizabeth, was high-spirited and loved music and dancing.

By the age of sixteen Elizabeth could not only converse in Latin and Greek, but also in French and Italian. Her tutor Ascham remarked:

> No apprehension can be quicker than hers, no memory more retentive. French and Italian she speaks like English; Latin with fluency, propriety and judgement; she also spoke Greek with me, fluently, willingly and moderately well. Nothing can be more elegant than her handwriting, whether in the Greek or Roman character.[5]

She later learned Spanish, Welsh and German. In 1598 the Swiss visitor Paul Hentzner noted that she conversed "in English, French, and Italian; for, besides being well skilled in Greek, Latin, and the languages I have mentioned, she is mistress of Spanish, Scotch and Dutch"[6]. She continued to read Greek and Latin daily with her beloved tutor Ascham until her late twenties. In 1562 Ascham remarked that she read more Greek in a day than some clergymen read Latin in a year. When older she translated Greek and Latin texts for fun, sometimes at great speed but, one has to say, not with scholarly attention to detail[7].

Elizabeth's prose style, command of words and ability to express ideas metaphorically were already well developed by the time she was aged eleven. At this tender age, no doubt with some help from a tutor, she wrote a letter to her stepmother Catherine Parr that anticipated her ability throughout life to project an image of herself that suited the occasion (in this case the image of a serious and studious pupil); the letter also shows her propensity for writing in long and involved sentences, contrasting opposing ideas or actions:

> ... knowing that pusillanimity and idleness are most repugnant unto a reasonable creature and that (as the philosopher sayeth) even as an instrument of iron or of other metal waxeth soon rusty unless it be continually occupied, even so shall the wit of a man or a woman wax dull and unapt to do or understand anything perfectly unless it be always occupied upon some manner of study.[8]

Her habit of contrasting opposites was remarked on by her tutor Ascham: "She admires, above all, modest metaphors and comparisons of contraries well put together and contrasting felicitously with one another"[9]. Elizabeth's use of such juxtapositions is also evident in the beautifully composed letter she wrote to her brother King Edward in 1553, on the occasion of a planned but aborted meeting. The rhythms in this piece of prose conjure up images of the sea and sailing:

> Like as a shipman in stormy weather plucks down the sails, tarrying for better wind, so did I, most noble King, in my unfortunate chance a Thursday pluck down the high sails of my joy and comfort, and do trust one day that as troublesome waves have repulsed me backward, so a gentle wind will bring me forward to my haven.[10]

Elizabeth's formal handwriting, in the Italian style, was astoundingly beautiful. No one would describe her cursive hand in the same terms, but it is instantly recognisable as hers, and its bold and flowing form and liberal use of capitals indicate a strong character and rapid thinking.

Although she loved study and the world of the intellect, she was no bluestocking. She delighted in hunting and physical activity, especially dancing. She had what Lytton Strachey called "out-of-doors manners". She could swear like a man, and abuse a listener in Latin if the occasion demanded. In 1597 when the Polish ambassador insolently advised her how she should conduct her country's affairs she gave him a crushing rebuke in an impromptu Latin speech, ending with the words *"valeas et quiescas"* (goodbye and be quiet). She was so proud of her achievement she arranged for the absent Earl of Essex to receive a transcription.

In private her imaginative turn of phrase could be combined with impish humour, studied condescension and calculated lack of tact, as illustrated by her letter to the young James VI of Scotland concerning the political disunity in his country:

> I find in many ways your state so unjointed, that it needs a skilfuller bonesetter than I to join each part in his right place.[11]

Elizabeth's biographer A. Somerset, paraphrasing the words of J. E. Neale, described her masterful use of language:

> ... she did not see language simply as a means of communication, but as an artistic medium, and it was this that inspired the singular cadences and ornate phraseology of her mature speech.[12]

But perhaps Lytton Strachey's accolade, which revels in the exuberance of his own verbosity, is the finest:

> Elizabeth's accomplishments were many and dazzling. She was mistress of six languages besides her own, a student of Greek, a superb calligraphist, an excellent musician. She was a connoisseur of painting and poetry. She danced,

after the Florentine style, with a high magnificence that astonished beholders. Her conversation, full, not only of humour, but of elegance and wit, revealed an unerring social sense, a charming delicacy of personal perception. It was this spiritual versatility which made her one of the supreme diplomatists of history. Her protean mind, projecting itself with extreme rapidity into every sinuous shape conceivable, perplexed the most clear-sighted of her antagonists and deluded the most wary. But her crowning virtuosity was her command over the resources of words. When she wished, she could drive in her meaning up to the hilt with hammer blows of speech, and no one ever surpassed her in the elaborate confection of studied ambiguities. Her letters she composed in a regal mode of her own, full of apophthegm and insinuation . . . but her greatest moments came when, in public audience, she made known her wishes, her opinions, and her meditations to the world. Then the splendid sentences, following one another in a steady volubility, proclaimed the curious working of her intellect with enthralling force; while the woman's inward passion vibrated magically through the loud high uncompromising utterance and the perfect rhythms of her speech.[13]

We must take these comments with a proverbial pinch of salt. Lytton Strachey seems to have been in love with the image of the Virgin Queen. He is embellishing a legend, albeit a legend with some firm foundations in fact. But who has written in such terms about William Shakespeare?

In what has become known as the Queen's Golden Speech of November 1601, Elizabeth made known to Parliament (and to posterity, for she was a Master-Mistress of public relations) her devotion to her people, in words that have no parallel:

> I do assure you, there is no prince that loveth his subjects better, or whose love can countervail our love. There is no jewel, be it of never so rich a price, which I set before this jewel – I mean your loves. For I do esteem it more than any treasure or riches, for that we know how to prize, but love and thanks I count unvaluable [invaluable], and though God hath raised me high, yet this I count the glory of my crown; that I have reigned with your loves.[14]

Authors have remarked on the remarkable linguistic abilities of both Queen Elizabeth and Shakespeare, but if they ever suspected a link between the two, they have kept very quiet about it. Just how close some authors have come to making the link is illustrated by Jane Dunn's remarkable comment on Elizabeth's education:

> If Cicero was Elizabeth's brilliant companion then it was Plutarch who helped teach her how to govern. In his masterpiece, *Parallel Lives*, read by Elizabeth and quoted often, she read of the lives of great men, written not so much as factual biographies but more to explore character and exemplify individual virtue. Shakespeare was to use them as source material for *Julius Caesar*, *Anthony and Cleopatra*, *Timon of Athens* and *Coriolanus*, and Elizabeth quoted from them [Plutarch's biographies] on various occasions . . .[15]

It is remarkable that, having made a connection between Elizabeth's reading habits and Shakespeare's writing, it didn't occur to Jane Dunn that Elizabeth and the playwright/poet might possibly be the same person. Imagine if Elizabeth's tutor Ascham had made the following statement about the young William Shakespeare:

> I am very often astonished at seeing him so ably understand . . . the feeling and spirit of the speaker, the struggle of the whole debate, the decrees and inclinations of the people, the manners and institutions of every state, and all other matters of this kind . . .[16]

Had Ascham made these comments about Shakespeare we would regard them as remarkably prescient. The comments would be proof that the young Shakespeare possessed an analytical and receptive mind precociously aware of the driving forces governing human interactions at both the personal and societal level in real life, and proof that he had the potential for constructing dramas in which these forces played out on the stage. However, Ascham did not make these comments about Shakespeare – he made them about the young Elizabeth. (I have substituted 'him' for the original 'her' in the first line of the extract.)

Elizabeth's speeches and letters show how beautifully composed and balanced was her prose style. But surprisingly it was not for the writing of her public and parliamentary speeches that a contemporary commentator, Francis Meres, praised Elizabeth, it was for her poetry, and not for just one form of poetry, but five:

> So Elizabeth, our dread sovereign and gracious queen, is not only a liberal patron unto poets, but an excellent poet herself, whose learned, delicate and noble muse surmounteth, be it in ode, elegy, epigram, or in any other kind of poem heroic or lyric.[17]

We can't dismiss these comments as mere flattery (excuse the pun) – Meres' observations are too specific. We may well ask, how did Meres, who was not a member of the court, find out about Elizabeth's poetry? And to which particular poems is he referring?

Clearly Elizabeth had the intellect, background and education to enable her to write poems, and we know that she did write poems – a few known to be written by her have survived. (I discuss these in chapter 47.) As she was intellectually inclined, we can imagine that writing poems was a way of organising her thoughts and feelings during times of personal elation, uncertainty, distress or political commotion. But most of the sonnets concern the relationship of the poet to a young man, so the big question is not whether she could have written poems of the quality of those in *Sonnets* (she could) but who might her young man be?

[1] Strachey (1971, p. 15).
[2] Marcus et al. (2002, p. 24).
[3] Harrison (1937, p. 131).
[4] Dunn (2003, chapter 3).
[5] Mumby (1909), quoted by Dunn (2003, p. 121).
[6] Walpole (1797).
[7] Mueller and Scodel (2009, p. 54).
[8] Marcus et al. (2002, p. 6).
[9] Neale (1961, p. 22).
[10] Marcus et al. (2002, p. 38).
[11] Neale (1958, p. 90).
[12] Somerset (1991, p. 15).
[13] Strachey (1971, pp. 17–18).
[14] Marcus et al. (2002, p. 337).
[15] Dunn (2003, p. 121), quoting from Mumby (1909).
[16] Mumby (1914), quoted by Dunn (2003, p. 123).
[17] Meres (1598).

12. Who was the Fair Youth?

Thou that art now the world's fresh ornament
— Sonnet 1

Let's briefly recapitulate what the sonnets tell us about the fair youth's character and activities. Even without any in-depth analysis we can conclude that he is young and handsome. He is described both as a youth and a "lovely Boy", so he is likely to have been in his late teens or early twenties when the poet first met him. He was childless and single when he first came to the attention of the author of *Sonnets*. Sonnet 13 informs us that his father is dead. The youth is attracted to a woman known to the poet and the evidence suggests that the youth marries her. As a consequence the poet and the youth become estranged.

The sonnets tell us repeatedly that the poet is much older than the youth and contemplating death (chapter 2), so the poet is probably older than fifty and possibly in his/her sixties. This deduction conflicts with Shakespeare's known age at the time *Sonnets* was written. The conflict has never been resolved (or indeed seriously considered) by scholars. However, the deduction fits perfectly with Elizabeth's age — in late 1595 she was 62 years old.

The sonnets also tell us that the youth was a public figure, so a promising line of research could be to compare the biographies of prominent Elizabethans with the events described in the sonnets. Such a comparison is worth trying, but needs to be made cautiously and should cover a long period because many Elizabethan nobles travelled abroad, fought in wars and had affairs, and it is not difficult to match isolated events in their lives with events mentioned in individual sonnets. For example, commentators commonly assume that William Cecil's attempt to marry off Elizabeth de Vere to the Earl of Southampton is reflected in the words of the early sonnets that urge the fair youth to produce an heir, or that the reference to lameness in sonnet 89 refers to the lameness of Edward de Vere, the seventeenth Earl of Oxford. In isolation these propositions seem reasonable, but more than one corresponding pair of observations is required to prove a significant connection to *Sonnets*.

What is important is to match a *sequence* of events in someone's life with a *sequence* of events described in the sonnets, in the same order. If such a match could be demonstrated statisticians would describe it as 'a good correlation between two datasets' and would rank the correlation based on the likelihood of it occurring purely by chance. For example, twenty events in common, in the right chronological order, have a much lower probability of occurring by chance than (say) three. If we were able to establish that a candidate's life had forty to fifty events in common with those mentioned in a sonnet sequence, in the correct historical order, we would have to conclude that the sonnet sequence was indeed describing events in this candidate's life.

To be able to use this matching or correlation technique we first need to make a shortlist of possible candidates and then examine their brief biographies. Whom should we consider?

Of the eligible men at the Elizabethan court qualifying as possible candidates for the young man of the sonnets there are seven who caught the eye of Elizabeth: Robert Dudley the Earl of Leicester, Elizabeth I's early favourite and possibly her lover, who died in 1588; Sir Philip Sidney, who died in heroic fashion soon after the Battle of Zutphen in 1586; Sir Walter Ralegh who dramatically fell out of favour in 1592; Lord Howard of Effingham of Armada fame; Robert Devereux, Earl of Essex, who became Elizabeth's favourite after Robert Dudley's death in 1588, and was executed in 1601; Sir Charles Blount, who fought with the Earl of Essex in Ireland, and succeeded where Essex failed; and the Earl of Southampton, who belonged to the same generation as the Earl of Essex, fought with him in Ireland and narrowly escaped execution for his part in the Essex rebellion.

Robert Dudley, Earl of Leicester, was the son of the Earl of Northumberland, who in 1572 was executed as a traitor for supporting the northern rebellion of 1569. The athletic and handsome Robert was Master of the Horse, a great judge of horseflesh and of women, an excellent jouster and rider, and almost the same age as Elizabeth I. The two had known each other since childhood. They were undoubtedly in love and may have been lovers. He possessed the important talent of being able to make Elizabeth laugh. Unfortunately for them both, Robert was already married, but this fact did not prevent some rather indiscreet intimacy between the two. In April 1559 the Spanish ambassador wrote: "During the last few days Lord Robert has come so much into favour that he does whatever he likes with affairs and it is even said that her majesty visits him in his chamber day and night. People talk of this so freely that they go so far as to say that his wife has a malady in one of her breasts and the Queen is only waiting for her to die to marry Lord Robert"[1]. (Whether we can take this statement seriously is doubtful: the ambassador was probably just reporting gossip.)

In September 1560 Robert Dudley's wife Amy Robsart did die, but not from a disease of the breasts. She was found dead with a broken neck at the foot of the stairs in her country home near Oxford. Although the official verdict was suicide, rumours abounded that Dudley had arranged for her to be pushed. Dudley's image was tainted. The Queen's sober judgment prevailed. By 1561 the romance between the two was over; it gradually cooled to a sentimental friendship. In 1585–1586 Dudley led campaigns in the Netherlands to support the Protestant Dutch in their revolt against the Spanish. He died in 1588, the year of the Armada, while travelling to take the waters at Buxton.

Dudley's career was too early to fit the events described in the sonnets, which were most probably written from the late 1580s onwards (chapter 4), unless we consider the entire sequence to have been retrospectively written. But there are also biographical problems – the early sonnets urging a single young man to produce an heir cannot be matched in any way to Dudley's life history.

Similar objections apply to Sir Walter Ralegh and Lord Howard of Effingham – they were simply too old to be the *Sonnets*' fair youth. Sir Philip Sidney can also be ruled out as he died in 1586. Sir Charles Blount, later Lord Mountjoy, was a highly competent professional soldier but his personal life bears no relationship to what we read in *Sonnets*. He fell in love with Penelope, the Earl of Essex's sister and wife of Lord Rich, and had six children by her. Elizabeth showed great respect for his professional abilities in her letters written during the Irish campaign[2] but these letters, although sometimes playful in tone[3], contain no hint that either was in love with the other.

The Earl of Southampton was the dedicatee of Shakespeare's narrative poems *Venus and Adonis* and *The Rape of Lucrece*. This literary connection to Shakespeare's works has prompted many commentators to suggest that he was the sonnets' fair youth. He had auburn hair, as can be seen in a Nicholas Hilliard miniature portrait in the Fitzwilliam Museum Cambridge[4], so could probably be described as 'fair'. Some events in his life have been linked to what we read in the sonnets. For example, when Southampton was still a young man his guardian William Cecil urged him to marry the Earl of Oxford's daughter (Cecil's granddaughter), whom Cecil had selected as an eminently suitable bride for him. Southampton had other ideas and was reluctant to oblige. Consequently, some scholars have inferred that the first seventeen poems (the so-called 'procreation sonnets') were written to persuade him to change his mind. Such an inference is not supported by the texts of these sonnets. Only sonnet 8 actually mentions marriage, and even in this sonnet the allusion is oblique (chapter 7). The subject matter of these sonnets is not marriage[5], it is something more earthy: they urge the youth to produce an heir by sexual intercourse. For example, in sonnet 16 the poet writes:

> And many maiden gardens yet unset,
> With virtuous wish would bear your living flowers.

The poet doesn't seem to care whom the youth beds – there are *many maidens* willing to spread their legs and let the youth plant flowers in their gardens. Forget about marriage – sex and reproduction are what is required. The virtues and good qualities of the Earl of Oxford's daughter are not mentioned. A similar image of an "un-ear'd womb" (womb without planted ears of corn) requiring the youth's tillage appears in sonnet 3:

> For where is she so fair whose un-ear'd womb
> Disdains the tillage of thy husbandry?

In less flowery language (excuse the pun) we might say today: 'Which attractive young lady could resist your sexual advances?' Clearly, if one pays attention to detail rather than try to fit the sonnets to a theory, it is apparent that the parallels to Southampton's early life are not as close as some commentators have chosen to portray.

Putting aside the exhortation-to-marry argument, Southampton, born on 6 October 1573, was the right age; it is possible that Elizabeth (or Shakespeare) could have addressed him as "my lovely Boy" and "sweet boy." But here we strike a major problem concerning Elizabethan and Jacobean etiquette: the printing of such common terms of endearment (apparently expressed between two men) in a book for public sale, while the earl and Shakespeare were alive, would be most surprising and dangerous for both William Shakespeare (the assumed author) and Thomas Thorpe (the publisher), and it is inconceivable that in 1609 Southampton would have permitted publication of *Sonnets* to proceed.

Elizabeth's disdain for Southampton clinches the argument. There is no evidence that he and Elizabeth I were close. As mentioned in chapter 6, Elizabeth had little regard for him. Southampton fell in love with the Earl of Essex's cousin, Elizabeth Vernon, who was a Maid of Honour at court. Despite the young lady's lack of a fortune (her father was the undistinguished John Vernon of Shropshire) he secretly married her in August 1598 when she was aged twenty-five. Their affectionate correspondence during a marriage that was tested both by Southampton's brief detention in Fleet prison and his longer stay in the Tower of London is a joy to read and indicates that their marriage was a true love match.

A scurrilous note addressed to Robert Cecil by an informer at the time of Southampton's disgrace and trial for his part in the Essex rebellion alleged that while campaigning in Ireland in 1599 Southampton shared a tent with a Captain Pearce Edmonds whom he would embrace, hug and "play wantonly with"[3]. However, this unsubstantiated anecdote from a source of doubtful integrity proves neither that Southampton was a homosexual nor that he was the fair youth of the sonnets.

In fact, the much-touted theory of a relationship between Shakespeare and Southampton is based only on the slender evidence that Shakespeare's earliest poems were dedicated to him. These formal dedications use the standard phraseology of a supplicant seeking a favour from a superior. They contain no hint of intimacy. There is no record of a response by Southampton. There is certainly no justification for unauthenticated fantasies, from authors who should know better, such as "Southampton would swiftly have discovered dangerous matters of mutual concern to discuss in discreet corners"[6].

Sonnets following the early procreation sequence also have little, if any, relationship to Southampton's life. Lacking the flair of Essex for flamboyant gestures (and possibly lacking Essex's good looks) he did not catch the public's imagination. Although he was the subject of conventional expressions of esteem by writers he was not praised by poets. As mentioned above, he took part in the Irish campaign alongside the Earl of Essex. He supported Essex in the 1601 rebellion, was imprisoned but then pardoned by James I. He lived for many years after the publication of *Sonnets* in 1609, so sonnet 112 and the sonnets that seem to be written retrospectively about the poet's relationship (many of those in the sequence 113–126; see chapter 23) cannot be matched to his life history. Nor do these sonnets make any reference to the addressee being in prison – they seem to be about a person who has died.

Although the argument for Southampton being the fair youth has been propounded by G. Akrigg[7] and others, it has not been accepted as proven. We therefore need to look elsewhere.

Robert Devereux, Earl of Essex is someone who has to be considered as a candidate for the fair youth. He was described by his biographer P. Hammer as "the man who alternately enchanted and infuriated her [the Queen] until, in the end, he lost his head, both metaphorically and literally"[8]. He was born on 10 November 1565[9], at Netherwood, Herefordshire. He was the first son of Walter Devereux, the first Earl of Essex, and Lettice Knollys, daughter of the Queen's cousin Sir Francis Knollys, who was a Privy Councillor.

Robert Devereux was certainly good looking and fair. He had a reddish beard. His secretary Sir Henry Wotton described "the incomparable fairness and fine shape of his hands"[10] and a Venetian described him as "fair-skinned, tall but wiry"[11]. He became the Queen's favourite after the death of his stepfather Robert Dudley in 1588. He often travelled on military campaigns on land and by sea (to the low countries, France, Spain, Portugal, the Azores and Ireland). He married (against Queen Elizabeth's wishes) and also had affairs. He was praised by many poets and after the brilliant Cadiz raid was idolised by the London public. After leading an unsuccessful military campaign in Ireland, he abandoned his army against orders, returned to England and was received coolly by the Queen. He unsuccessfully tried to seize power, was detained, tried and then executed.

Essex's life as sketched above seems to parallel several references in the sonnets and therefore deserves further attention. In the next chapter I consider how well the early sonnets (1–42) considered in chapters 7–9 parallel the lives of Elizabeth and Essex, and their somewhat precarious relationship.

---

[1] Neale (1961, p. 83).
[2] Letter to Lord Mountjoy, 17 February 1603, published by Marcus et al. (2002, pp. 405–408).

3 In a letter Elizabeth addressed Mountjoy as her "kitchenmaid" (Marcus et al. 2002, p. 399).
4 Doran (2003, p. 112).
5 It is surprising how uncritically the standard Shakespeare editions repeat this claim. For example, the Oxford Shakespeare *Complete Works* (Wells et al. 2005, p. 777), referring to the sonnets, states "all the first seventeen ... exhort a young man to marry". Similarly, Burrow (2002, p. 115) writes "the first seventeen poems, which urge the friend to marry, are a crucial part of the design of the whole sequence".
6 Holden (1999, p. 112).
7 Akrigg (1968).
8 Hammer (1999, p. 4).
9 The year of Robert Devereux's birth is uncertain; some historians prefer 1566. For a discussion see Margetts (1988).
10 Wotton (1651).
11 Strong (1987, p. 64).

13. The Royal Male?

O how I faint when I of you do write
— Sonnet 80

Robert Devereux inherited the title of second Earl of Essex, but no fortune, on the death of his father in Dublin in 1576, following the first earl's militarily and financially disastrous Irish campaign. Robert's star began its ascendancy soon after the Queen's favourite Robert Dudley, Earl of Leicester, secretly married Essex's mother Lettice Knollys (already pregnant with Leicester's child), on 21 September 1578, almost two years after the death of Lettice's first husband.

Elizabeth hated having attractive wives at court. Four months after she heard of the marriage of Leicester and Lettice Knollys, she barred the unfortunate Lettice from her company, only relenting ungraciously in her old age. She referred to Lettice as a "she-wolf"[1]. Her intense dislike of Lettice was no doubt coloured by her realisation that Lettice enjoyed something that she could only crave: a satisfying sex life with her court favourite, Leicester. But she was more lenient towards Leicester than Lettice. Her old friend, who was possibly her lover, soon returned to favour. With Leicester back at court his stepson Essex had an opportunity to shine: he had access to the Queen.

Essex delighted in intellectual studies. In November 1576 Edward Waterhouse reported to Essex's guardian, Lord Burghley, that the eleven-year-old Essex was able to "express his mind in Latin and French as well as in English"[2]. He later learnt Greek, Italian and some Spanish. In July 1581 he graduated with an M.A. from Trinity College, Cambridge. After spending time on his estates in Pembrokeshire the young Essex was formally presented to the Queen in September 1585.

Essex was not content to be an ornament at court. On 8 December 1585 he sailed with his stepfather to join a military campaign in the Netherlands, in which the English forces under Leicester's ineffective leadership were assisting the Dutch against a vastly superior Spanish occupation army. In September 1586 he distinguished himself in the so-called Battle of Zutphen, which was really a skirmish, and was made a knight banneret for his gallantry.

In this engagement he was upstaged by the poet-soldier-courtier Sir Philip Sidney, who was mortally wounded in the thigh by a Spanish musket shot. Sidney secured a place in the annals of romantic chivalry and in public esteem by selflessly offering his water flask to an injured comrade while he himself was bleeding profusely. One biographer rather cynically remarked that, with the exception of his literary creations, "the greatest success of Sidney's life was in the manner of his dying"[3]. His heroic actions at Zutphen would certainly have made a good newspaper story today – 'mortally wounded poet-soldier offers succour to injured colleague on the battlefield' – but another biographer has noted that the water-flask anecdote was written down by Sidney's friend Fulke Greville at least thirty-five years after Sidney's death and may have been a legend invented by Greville to immortalise his comrade.

Sidney's death was opportune for Essex – a brilliant intellectual and a competitor for public and royal attention was out of the way. He was able to don Sidney's mantle of the noble knight fighting for a just cause: Protestantism and freedom from Spanish repression. (Despite his early Catholic sympathies, Sidney had adopted the politically safer new religion.) The dying Sidney recognised Essex as his successor by symbolically bequeathing to Essex his best sword. In 1590, in another act not without symbolism, Essex married his widow Frances Walsingham.

Despite Sir Philip Sidney's heroics, the Netherlands campaign was a failure. In October 1586 Essex was back at court, having proved his virility and fearlessness in battle. On 17 November he took part in the Queen's Accession Day tilts for the first time – his first appearance in jousts before the Queen. The Queen's serious and reciprocated interest in Essex probably dates from around this time.

By May 1587 Essex was the Queen's frequent companion. He could certainly turn on the charm: a contemporary remarked that "his goodly person, and a kind of urbanity and innate courtesy, combined with the recollection of his father's misfortunes, won him the hearts of both Queen and people"[4].

Later in the year the Queen made him Master of the Horse, worth £1500 a year[5]. This was a magnificent promotion after so short a period of royal service. In this position he oversaw all her travel and ceremonial arrangements. It required frequent communication with his mistress and entitled him to accompany her on her travels, in public engagements and during processions. However, although the position recognised his high personal standing with the Queen it did not give Essex political influence.

The evidence of surviving letters and observations of other courtiers recorded around this time indicates mutual infatuation, and perhaps love. "When she is abroad," Essex's servant Anthony Bagot wrote proudly to his father in Shropshire, "nobody near her but my L. of Essex; and, at night, my Lord is at cards, or one game or another with her, that he cometh not to his own lodging till birds sing in the morning"[6]. The phrase "at . . . one game or another with her" can of course be interpreted innocently or otherwise and may have been intended to be ambiguous.

At about this time the artist Nicholas Hilliard painted his famous miniatures of handsome young courtiers and some of these are thought to be of Essex[7]. Essex was certainly well acquainted with Hilliard, for in 1595 he gave him the princely sum of £140 to repair his collapsing house[8].

The sonnets describing the first acquaintance of the poet with the youth and encouraging the youth to procreate (1–17) could be based on observations of Essex's attendance at court in 1586/7: this singularly attractive young man must have turned heads. The references to a painting of the youth in sonnet 24 could be related to Hilliard's miniature portraits, thought to be of Essex, painted around 1587 to 1588. If the earliest sonnets do relate to Essex's attendance at court, then they were probably written in the late 1580s and Hotson's chronology[9] for the early sonnets is correct.

The reference to the youth's mother in sonnet 3 provides an important clue to the youth's identity: "Thou art thy mother's glass and she in thee Calls back the lovely April of her prime". The lines are distinctly catty. The poet is saying 'you are as beautiful as your mother was when she was young and in her prime' – a complimentary comment with a bite. As the subject matter of the first sonnets relates well to the appearance of Essex at court, this comment may reflect Elizabeth I's animosity towards Essex's mother, Lettice Knollys.

The parallels continue. Sonnet 20 suggesting intimacy ("the Master Mistress of my passion") may have been written at the same time that Anthony Bagot mentioned the night-time games played by the Queen and Essex.

Essex's facility with words must have enthralled the ageing Queen. Absent from court for a few days, he addressed himself to her in terms designed to enchant:

> Madam, the delights of this place cannot make me unmindful of one in whose sweet company I have joyed as much as the happiest man doth in his highest contentment; and if my horse could run as fast as my thoughts do fly, I would as often make mine eyes rich in beholding the treasure of my love as my desires do triumph when I seem to myself in a strong imagination to conquer your resisting will.[10]

However, it was ominous that even in this seductively charming early address Essex perceived his relationship with the Queen in terms of a clash of wills. Or does Essex's word "will" in this letter have a bawdy meaning[11] consistent with Essex playing night-time games with his distinguished female companion? There is no way of telling. As with Bagot's letter to his father, Essex's words may have been carefully chosen, to allow an alternative but deniable second meaning.

In July 1587 Essex had the first of many tiffs with the Queen, involving a bout of over-confidence in which his less admirable and potentially dangerous qualities were displayed. The reason for the disagreement was the presence of his sister, Lady Dorothy Perrott, at Lord Warwick's house (Northaw) while Elizabeth was visiting.

Lady Perrott, formerly one of the Queen's ladies in waiting, had been banned from court for her clandestine marriage to Thomas Perrott, a soldier and courtier. Elizabeth, on hearing that Lady Perrott was present in the same house as herself, ordered the unfortunate woman to be confined to her rooms. Essex was furious. Suspecting that his rival, Sir Walter Ralegh, had had a word in Elizabeth's ear, Essex said as much to Elizabeth. When Elizabeth defended Walter Ralegh and said nasty things about Essex's mother (whom she had never forgiven for marrying Leicester), the furious Essex left in a huff and rode to Sandwich on the Kent coast, where he planned to take a boat to join in the defence of the Dutch town of Sluis. He was intercepted by Robert Carey, fourth son of Lord Hunsdon, who had been sent to retrieve him. It has been suggested that Essex may have arranged for his own interception, with the intention of ensuring his return to court[12].

> *Although sonnets 9 and 10 are purportedly about procreation, the harsh words they contain ("murd'rous shame", "murd'rous hate", "that thou none lov'st is most evident") and their admonition "Be as thy presence is, gracious and kind" seem inappropriately strong commentary on a good-looking bachelor whose only failing is that he hasn't produced an heir. The comments make one suspect that some disagreement has occurred. The poems may have been prompted by Essex's impetuous behaviour following his first semi-public disagreement with the Queen at Lord Warwick's house.*

Within a month the disagreement was put aside and in 1588 the Queen invested Essex with the honour of Knight of the Garter, England's highest and most coveted order of chivalry. He was only twenty-two. Essex certainly knew how to ingratiate himself with his sovereign.

Essex's short temper and sharp tongue were proverbial. Although the Queen could excuse his behaviour on account of his youth, she was clearly irritated by it. When Sir Charles Blount, a young knight, was awarded a gold chess-queen for his performance in the tilts, Essex exclaimed "Now, I perceive, every fool must wear a favour"[13]. In the ensuing duel in Marylebone Park Charles injured Essex in the thigh with a rapier, prompting the Queen to remark "By God's death, it were fitting someone should take him down, and teach him better manners, or there were no rule with him"[14]. But despite this comment she remained infatuated with her hot-headed courtier, who seemed to rule her heart.

In early April 1589 the restless and impatient Essex, tiring of court life and eager for military glory, rode to Plymouth without leave of absence from court, and against the Queen's wishes, to participate in the Corunna and Lisbon raids led by Sir John Norris and Sir Francis Drake. The aim of the expedition was ambitious – none other than to install the pretender to the Portuguese throne, Dom Antonio, as king. Essex avoided both his pursuers and letters from the Queen demanding his return. He sailed from Falmouth with the popular Welsh soldier Sir Roger Williams, who had secretly fitted out his ship the *Swiftsure* for instant departure once Essex arrived. However, the ship was damaged in a storm and had to return to port. It sailed again, with Essex on board, on 18 April.

On 16 May the forces led by Williams and Essex overran the castle of Peniche, north of Lisbon. Other successes eluded the expedition and the main objective of encouraging the Portuguese to rise against their Spanish masters was not achieved. The fleet returned to England at the end of June after suffering huge losses: eight thousand of the fifteen thousand men who had set out had died.

> *The sonnets mentioning love and separation (25–28) from the youth (the poet's thoughts travel "far from where I abide") correspond to Essex's unofficial absence from court in 1589 to take part in the Corunna and Lisbon raids. Sonnet 26 is widely regarded as being of mediocre quality. The rhythm is plodding. It uses the "commonplace literary language of courtly love"[15] and is apparently addressed to someone of higher social standing, the "Lord of my love" to whom the poet is bound by "vassalage". The unsophisticated schoolboy rhymes, conventional concepts expressed, and simple construction indicate that this poem was written by a competent but unimaginative writer.*
>
> *We know that contemporary courtiers remarked on Essex's abilities as a poet. His poetic skills were praised by the poets John Mundy and Thomas Watson, and his surviving poems[16] include a humorous one about the joys of smoking the newly discovered American tobacco. His secretary Sir Henry Wotton recorded that it was Essex's "common way" when addressing the Queen "to evaporate his thoughts in a sonnet", which he would then have sung before the Queen by her favourite singer[17].*
>
> *Essex's letters to the Queen habitually ended with the words "your Majesty's humblest and most affectionate vassal"[18], so the mention of "vassalage" in line 1 of sonnet 26 supports authorship of this sonnet by Essex.*
>
> *Essex knew that he was breaking the rules by absenting himself from court without permission, in order to take part in the Portugal expedition. Consequently he had to communicate carefully with Elizabeth, as he could expect a stern reprimand, or at worst, a complete loss of her favour, if she chose to impose a sanction on him. Sonnet 26 (chapter 8) may be his attempt to appease the annoyed Queen – we know that Essex was nervous about how he would be received on his return, for before re-appearing at court he sent his*

brother Walter ahead 'to test the water'[19]. *The writer of sonnet 26 is on the defensive and using all his charm to coax Elizabeth to treat him kindly. He asks her to bestow upon him her good opinion ("fair aspect") and to look upon him graciously like a guiding star so that he can show himself worthy of her respect. The last line of the sonnet can be paraphrased neatly in modern slang: 'Until I hear something positive from you, I'll keep my head down'. Perhaps Essex sent this sonnet to London when his damaged ship briefly returned to port for refitting after the April 1589 storm.*

The failure of the Portugal expedition did not prevent Essex glorifying his part in it. In London on his return he had printed a self-congratulatory broadsheet entitled *An Eclogue Gratulatory: To the right honourable and renowned Shepherd of Arcadia: Robert Earl of Essex and Ewe, for his welcome into England from Portugal.* This publication was a best seller in a city eager to create and welcome heroes. Essex had caught the public eye and he had established himself as a popular militarist[20].

At about this time the Queen was troubled by the death of friends and trusted officials who had been her steadfast companions and advisors since her childhood and accession to the throne. Among those who died in the 1588–1590 period were Robert Dudley, Earl of Leicester (1588); Sir Walter Mildmay, Chancellor of the Exchequer (1589); Blanche Parry, Chief Gentlewoman of the Privy Chamber (1590); Sir Francis Walsingham, Secretary of State and Lord Treasurer (1590); Sir James Croft, Comptroller of the Queen's Household (1590); Ambrose Dudley, Earl of Warwick (1590); and the Earl of Shrewsbury (1590).

The loss of Elizabeth's closest friends and advisors between 1588 and 1590 matches the description of the poet's distress at the loss of friends and lovers in sonnets 29–31 and supports the proposition that Elizabeth wrote these sonnets. In contrast, nothing in these sonnets matches what we know about Shakespeare's social life (which admittedly is very little). The death in 1588 of the Earl of Leicester, shortly after the defeat of the Armada is especially relevant as he and Elizabeth were almost certainly in love when young, and may have been lovers, and sonnet 31 mentions "lovers gone".

It would be natural for the Queen to see in Essex the qualities of Leicester (Essex's stepfather) and her other deceased courtiers and officials who had given her loyal service and moral support during her difficult years as Princess and her early years as Queen: "Their images I lov'd, I view in thee" (31).

Table 1. Essex's early life compared to the sequence of events described in sonnets 1–42.

Date	Events in Essex's life and at court	Sonnet number	Subject matter	Interpretation
7 Sep 1533	Elizabeth born			
10 Nov 1565	Robert Devereux born			
1577	Presented at court			
1581	Graduates from Cambridge			
1585	Formal presentation to Queen			
Dec 1585	Joins Netherlands campaign			
Sep 1586	Battle of Zutphen			
Oct 1586	Back at court	1–9	First expression of interest in fair youth by poet	Elizabeth's attention captured by Essex's good looks, charm and grace.
Jun 1587	Made Master of the Horse			
		3	Mentions youth's mother being lovely when young	Catty comment about Lettice Knollys, whom Elizabeth disliked
Jul 1587	1st argument with Queen	10	Youth is capable of "murd'rous hate"	Elizabeth detects flaw in youth's character
Aug 1587	Reconciliation	11–23	Restated love	
	Late night games with the Queen	20	Bawdy sonnet implying intimacy	Elizabeth and Essex become intimate?
Late 1587		22	First mention of death and poet being old	Elizabeth is 53 or 54 years old
1587/88	Miniatures, probably of Essex, by Nicholas Hilliard	24	Mention of picture of youth; youth absent	Essex probably commissioning miniatures by Hilliard for himself and the Queen
Early Apr 1589	Rides to Plymouth; departs from Falmouth for Corunna and Lisbon raids	25	Disregard for military honours	Love more important than honours
18 Apr – June 1589	Re-embarks from Plymouth; fleet returns	27, 28	Youth "from far where I abide"	Essex absent from court

1588–1590	Seven friends of the Queen die: Earl of Leicester; Sir Walter Mildmay, Chancellor of the Exchequer; Blanche Parry, Chief Gentlewoman of the Privy Chamber; Sir Francis Walsingham, Secretary of State and Lord Treasurer; Sir James Croft, Comptroller of the Queen's Household 1590; Ambrose Dudley, Earl of Warwick; Earl of Shrewsbury	29, 30	Poet refers to misfortune and deaths of friends and past lovers	Elizabeth devastated by the deaths of so many of her friends and courtiers and particularly by the death of (her lover?) Robert Dudley, Earl of Leicester
		31	Youth considered to be a reminder of a past love	Essex reminds Elizabeth of Leicester
		32	Love poem; poet refers to his/her own death	Elizabeth is depressed
Oct 1590	Marriage to Frances Walsingham, widow of Sir Philip Sidney revealed at court; Queen's displeasure	33	Poet is jealous	Elizabeth is jealous
		34–36	Youth has committed an offence; his straying affections	
	Essex banned from court	37, 38	Reflective poems	Essex banned from court temporarily
		39	Poet and youth separated	
	Affair with Elizabeth Southwell	40, 41	Youth has another lover	Elizabeth Southwell was the Queen's Maid of Honour and Frances was known to the Queen
		42	Youth attracted to a woman who is known to the poet	

In the spring of 1590 Essex married Frances Walsingham, widow of Sir Philip Sidney and daughter of Sir Francis Walsingham. The secret marriage was revealed to the Queen in October. It was a measure of Essex's charm and influence that on hearing the news of her favourite's marriage, Elizabeth was angry for a fortnight but then accepted Essex back at court. (For similar breaches of court rules Sir Walter Ralegh, Sir Thomas Perrott and the Earl of Southampton were imprisoned.)

However, it did not take long for the delights of matrimony and of bedding Frances to pall, for within months of his marriage Essex had an affair with Elizabeth Southwell, the Queen's Maid of Honour, and in 1591 had a son by her, born within a month of his wife Frances bearing him a son[21].

Sonnets 33–34 can be linked to Essex's marriage to Frances Walsingham. Frances was well known to the Queen, both as Francis Walsingham's daughter and as Sidney's wife and widow. The Queen's affection for Frances explains both the comment in sonnet 42 that "I lov'd her dearly" and the reference to the young man's lover (Frances) as a "sweet thief" – the sweet Frances had stolen Essex's affection. After her initial anger on hearing of Essex's marriage, Elizabeth must have come to the conclusion that her close relationship with Essex was finished: "Let me confess that we two must be twain" (36) and that continuing a relationship with the newly wed Essex might affect his reputation: "I may not ever-more acknowledge thee, Lest my bewailed guilt should do thee shame" (36). So, again, the words of the sonnets exactly match the personal events in the lives of the Queen and Essex.

Elizabeth Southwell, Elizabeth's Maid of Honour, by whom Essex had a son, could be the woman referred to in sonnets 41 and 42 as having experienced Essex's "pretty wrongs". Maids of Honour were essentially the Queen's property; the line in sonnet 40 "Take all my loves, my love, yea take them all" appears to be the Queen's sarcastic comment on Essex's lustful interest in her attractive female assistants.

In Table 1 I have summarised the synopsis given above. There is clearly a close correlation between what we read in sonnets 1 to 42 and what we know about the relationship of Queen Elizabeth and the Earl of Essex in the period 1586 to 1590. We read about their first meeting. There is a catty comment about Essex's mother, whom Elizabeth disliked. The bawdy sonnet 20 which implies intimacy between them has parallels with the comments in Anthony Bagot's letter revealing that Essex and the Queen played games with each other late into the night. Sonnets mentioning Essex being far away correspond to his absence on the Corunna and Lisbon raids.

Those about loneliness and death of friends correspond to the period 1588–1590 when Elizabeth lost several friends and trusted advisors whom she had known since before her coronation. Sonnets expressing jealousy seem to reflect Elizabeth's unhappiness at Essex's decision to marry Frances Walsingham. The seduction of Elizabeth Southwell by Essex is arguably the event which made the poet complain of the youth's "pretty wrongs".

The fact that for this short period of four years events in Essex's and Elizabeth's lives can be exactly matched with events described in the early sonnets (1–42) is strong evidence that these sonnets (except for sonnet 26) were indeed written by the Queen and refer to Essex. A sonnet is long enough to define a subject, consider it from various angles, and come to a conclusion (usually in the final couplet). It is an ideal verse format for isolating problematic issues and discussing solutions. It seems that the sonnet form provided Elizabeth with a literary mechanism that enabled her to clarify her thoughts about the complex and sometimes troublesome relationship she had with her favourite.

---

[1] Guy (2016, p. 51 and endnote 46).
[2] Hammer (1999, p. 23).
[3] Hammer (1999, p. 53).
[4] Duncan-Jones (1991, p. 304).
[5] Hammer (1999, p. 60). The post of General of the Horse (supreme commander of the cavalry), followed in 1588 (Hammer 1999, p. 72).
[6] Devereux (1853a, p. 186).
[7] Strong (1987).
[8] Hammer (1999, p. 208).
[9] Hotson (1949).
[10] Devereux (1853a, p. 292).
[11] Partridge (1969).
[12] Hammer (1999, p. 62).
[13] Devereux (1853a, p. 194).
[14] Devereux (1853a, p. 194).
[15] Kerrigan (1986, p. 207).
[16] May (1980).
[17] Strong (1987, p. 81).
[18] Devereux (1853a, chapters XIV and XV) cites several examples of Essex signing letters with the word "vassal". This habit continued for years. For example, when responding to the Queen, after she had delayed Star Chamber proceedings that would have tried him for misdemeanours associated with his failed 1599 military campaign against Tyrone's rebels in Ireland, Essex wrote "I shall live and die your most humble vassal" (Guy, 2016, p. 326).
[19] Hammer (1999, p. 65).
[20] Hammer (1999, chapter 6) argues that many of Essex's actions in the late 1580s and 1590s resulted from his belief that he had a mission to fulfil – his life should be an expression of military virtue and unwavering support of Protestantism. He persisted in extolling these ideas even when they did not coincide with Elizabeth's more pragmatic approach to foreign policy. Because his idealistic mission did not fit well with his duty to be his monarch's loyal subject, conflict with Elizabeth was inevitable.
[21] Hammer (1999, pp. 95–96). Elizabeth may only have found out in 1595 that Essex was the boy's father (Hammer 1999, p. 320).

14. Youth travels

So either by thy picture or my love,
Thy self away, are present still with me

– Sonnet 47

Let's summarise what the last three chapters tell us. Firstly, Elizabeth was one of the best educated people in England: she studied literature and languages with the best tutors and had a masterly command of words. Secondly the 'events' mentioned in sonnets 1–42 match perfectly with what we know about the interactions between Queen Elizabeth and the Earl of Essex between late 1586 and late 1590. Thirdly, an analysis of the Dedication puzzle reveals Elizabeth's name exactly where we expect the author's name. And fourthly, the imagery used in *Sonnets* matches that preferred and used by the Queen and her courtiers.

In contrast, any attempt to relate Shakespeare's social interactions to the early sonnets fails miserably. There is no independent historical evidence that he had a relationship to a young man, or that the details recorded in sonnets 1–42 match anything we know about Shakespeare's life. In addition, the Dedication does not point to Shakespeare as *Sonnets*' author and there is no evidence at all that Shakespeare's education included tuition in foreign languages or studies of classical literature.

But we need to be aware that the good correlation between the subject matter of 42 sonnets and the real lives of two Elizabethan individuals could, just possibly, have arisen by chance. For this reason the test we have begun needs to be extended: if we assume that all the sonnets in the first group (1–126) are in chronological order, is the correspondence between their subject matter and the lives of Elizabeth and Essex noted for sonnets 1–42 sustained?

Sonnets 43–52 are immensely relevant to the Elizabeth-Essex hypothesis. They describe a relationship between two separated friends or lovers. As is often the case with lovers, we learn more about their lives during their times of separation, when they have to communicate by the technology available, than we learn during their times of living close to each other.

In sonnet 43 the poet describes how the image of the youth is so clear in her dreams that she hardly needs to see him in the "living day" (lines 9–10). But days are like nights because the youth is absent (lines 13–14).

Sonnet 43
When most I wink [close my eyes] then do mine eyes best see,
For all the day they view things unrespected,
But when I sleep, in dreams they look on thee,
And darkly bright, are bright in dark directed.
Then thou whose shadow shadows doth make bright,
How would thy shadows form, form happy show,

To the clear day with thy much clearer light,
When to un-seeing eyes thy shade shines so?
How would (I say) mine eyes be blessed made,
By looking on thee in the living day?
When in dead night thy fair imperfect shade,
Through heavy sleep on sightless eyes doth stay?
    All days are nights to see till I see thee,
    And nights bright days when dreams do show thee me [thee to me].

This sonnet tells us about the poet's night-time reaction to the youth's absence. In the next we learn some crucial details about the kind of journey the youth has undertaken. He has journeyed to a place "far remote" (44) separated from the poet by "large lengths of miles" and "earth and water", but the poet is confident that her thoughts "can jump both sea and land". This is a useful clue to the youth's identity – presumably he has an occupation in which he journeys overseas, and at this point in time actually is overseas.

Sonnet 44
If the dull substance of my flesh were thought [If I was made of thoughts],
Injurious distance should not stop my way [distance would be no barrier],
For then despite of space I would be brought,
From limits far remote, where thou dost stay,
No matter then although my foot did stand
Upon the farthest earth remov'd from thee,
For nimble thought can jump both sea and land,
As soon as think the place where he would be.
But ah, thought kills me that I am not thought
To leap large lengths of miles when thou art gone,
But that so much of earth and water wrought,
I must attend, time's leisure with my moan.
    Receiving naught by elements so slow,
    But heavy tears, badges of either's woe.

The last couplet tells us that at this point in time the poet has received no news from the young man. But sonnet 45 makes clear that, despite their separation, the poet and the youth *are* still communicating – the youth sends "swift messengers" and the poet answers in kind: "I send them back again". We can guess that the youth has travelled to Ireland, France, or the Low Countries, all places within reach of English or Welsh ports in a day or two by fast sailing boats called pinnaces[1].

Sonnet 45
The other two, slight air, and purging fire,
Are both with thee, where ever I abide,
The first my thought, the other my desire,
These present absent with swift motion slide.
For when these quicker Elements are gone

> In tender Embassy of love to thee,
> My life being made of four, with two alone,
> Sinks down to death, oppressed with melancholy.
> Until life's composition be re-cured [restored],
> By those swift messengers return'd from thee,
> Who even but now come back again assured,
> Of thy fair health, recounting it to me.
>   This told, I joy, but then no longer glad,
>   I send them back again and straight grow sad.

The only people in Elizabethan England who had the financial means and social connections to enable them to communicate to overseas countries in this way were high-ranking soldiers, diplomats or travelling aristocrats, like the young Philip Sidney while on his grand tour of Europe (1572–1575). The youth (and the poet, by merit of association with the youth) must have belonged to one of these privileged groups. Both were able to make use of diplomatic channels and ships to send communications – another useful clue to the youth's status and identity.

We know of no letters sent by travelling aristocrats (or other high-ranking persons) to Shakespeare, nor is there any record of Shakespeare sending letters to travelling aristocrats. But if we look at Essex's activities in 1591, we find that the references in sonnets 44 and 45 to separation by sea and land, and to two persons communicating despite being separated, match with events in Essex's life that follow seamlessly from those referred to sonnets 1–42 (Table 1).

Essex, still fancying himself as a great commander, and longing for military fame, saw opportunities for glory in northern France, where King Henri IV, in theory a Protestant ally against the Spanish, was fighting a civil war. Essex urged the Queen to let him lead the English forces sent to Normandy to support Henri. Initially she refused to let him go, but on 21 July 1591 she relented.

Essex landed at Dieppe on 3 August 1591 with an army of 4000 men. Elizabeth took an intense personal interest in the campaign. She was unhappy with Essex's flamboyant tactics, the unnecessary personal danger to which he exposed himself by his recklessness, and his propensity for knighting officers against her orders. (Despite a lacklustre campaign he created twenty-four knights.) She communicated her displeasure in curt correspondence forwarded to Essex across the English Channel. Naturally, Essex replied. He knew how to respond: he switched on the flow of charm, and did it in bucketloads, in this case writing what can be considered either as the greatest expression in the English language of love of a sovereign by a subject, or a magnificent example of insincere syrupy flattery. (Incidentally the letter predicts the catastrophic effect on him should she withdraw her affection. But this was several years away.)

> The two windows of your privy chamber shall be the poles of my sphere, where, as long as your Majesty will please to have me, I am fixed and unmoveable. When your Majesty thinks that heaven too good for me, I will not fall like a star, but be consumed like a vapour by the sun that drew me up to such a height. While your Majesty gives me leave to say I love you, my fortune is as my affection, unmatchable. If ever you deny me that liberty, you may end my life, but never shake my constancy, for were the sweetness of your nature turned into the greatest bitterness that could be, it is not in your power, as great a Queen as you are, to make me love you less.[2]

Essex returned to England briefly on 8 October but the worsening military situation in Normandy required him to resume duties there on 19 October. He returned to England at the end of November 1591, then resumed campaign duties in early December[3]. On 8 January 1592 he finally left France for good, leaving his old friend Sir Roger Williams in charge.

While in Normandy Essex was kept on a close leash. He was originally asked to send reports home once a week, but it is documented that William Cecil (Lord Burghley) specified that he report daily via Sir Henry Unton[4], who was officially in Normandy as the Queen's ambassador, but whose chief function seems to have been to keep a watchful eye on Essex's performance during his first command. Pinnaces must have been crossing the English Channel daily, carrying Essex's news and campaign reports to the court, and no doubt returning with court news, personal letters and formal notices regarding the military operation[5].

While he was away Elizabeth was travelling on one of her regular summer progresses in the south of England. She stayed at Portsmouth for a couple of days hoping that Henri IV and possibly Essex would cross the Channel to meet her and discuss the French campaign[6].

The historical record supports the deduction that these sonnets about separation (43–52) concern Elizabeth's fears and unsettled state of mind while her young man was fighting overseas. She uses metaphors based on the four elements of earth, water, air and fire to express her thoughts – these elements were thought by Elizabethans to be the fundamental constituents of all matter.

The distance of sea and land separating the two lovers brings to her mind the slow and heavy elements of earth and water, and induces tears (44, line 14). But messages ("messengers") containing air and fire (thought and desire) (45, line 3) received from Essex generate feelings of joy, restoring the royal poet's happiness. These messages are replied to by the Queen in a "tender Embassy of love to thee" (45, line 6). But once she has sent her reply she becomes despondent while awaiting a response, resulting in her thoughts once again being dominated by the two heavy elements of earth and water, representing separation; the poet writes that her life "sinks down to death, oppressed with melancholy" (45, line 8), until the time that the "messengers" return, assuring the poet of the youth's "fair health".

Although Elizabeth uses the images of light and heavy pairs of elements (as understood by Elizabethans) to symbolise her alternating feelings, it is clear that she is writing about an actual exchange of letters, and her joy on receiving news from across the Channel and sadness while awaiting the reply. We should note that there is no evidence that William Shakespeare ever communicated with someone overseas.

Ignoring the obvious, some scholarly commentators have chosen to disregard the biographical and geographical significance of these two sonnets, and interpret them as dealing with abstract notions. For example, Burrow[7] considered the whole discourse on the elements of earth, water, air and fire in sonnets 44 and 45 to be purely figurative. But his notes on sonnet 45 are illuminating – they reveal the residual doubt in the mind of a perceptive but over-cautious scholar. He admits that line 14 suggests that "the poet is actually in control of when fire and air are sent on their embassies", but then, losing courage, he baulks at concluding that if the poet was "in control", then the poet and the young man were actually exchanging real letters. Likewise, Kerrigan, commenting on sonnet 44, noted that "the poet is separated from the young man by the very elements [earth and water] of which he is wrought (the sea and the land)" but, like Burrow, he recoiled from deducing that the poet and the young man were corresponding with each other[8]. Thus a common-sense conclusion is ditched in favour of a convoluted explanation that takes the sonnets out of the realm of everyday experience.

Sonnet 48 describes the beginning of a journey. Before setting off, the poet locks up jewels. We know from numerous portraits that Elizabeth had a large collection of jewels, and we can be sure she locked these away before she travelled. In contrast there is no evidence that Shakespeare had any – none are mentioned in his will. The sonnet describes the youth as both a "comfort" and the poet's "greatest grief" and in danger of being stolen – "the prey of every vulgar thief" – because (unlike the jewels) he is not locked up in a chest. Although the poet feels the youth's presence in her breast, she is worried about losing the youth's affection.

Sonnet 48
How careful was I when I took my way,
Each trifle under truest bars to thrust,
That to my use it might un-used stay
From hands of falsehood, in sure wards of trust?
But thou, to whom my jewels trifles are,
Most worthy comfort, now my greatest grief,
Thou best of dearest, and mine only care,
Art left the prey of every vulgar thief.
Thee have I not locked up in any chest,
Save where thou art not, though I feel thou art,
Within the gentle closure of my breast,
From whence at pleasure thou may'st come and part,

And even thence thou wilt be stol'n I fear,
For truth proves thievish for a prize so dear.

Although the reference to "breast" is not in itself proof of a reference to a female poet, the words "within the gentle closure [cleavage] of my breast" seem to indicate female authorship (as deduced for the similar use of words in sonnet 24). But caution is required, because in Shakespeare's poem *Venus and Adonis* the mythical male figure Adonis resists the bewitching advances of Venus, telling her he doesn't want her disturbing the "quiet closure of my breast" (line 782). However, the invitation to the lover in sonnet 48 to "part" the writer's "gentle closure" "at pleasure" seems to be a clear invitation to a partner to participate in playful lovemaking[9], and implies female authorship. The straightforward explanation is that the female poet has a miniature picture of the young man hanging between her breasts.

Because of Essex's prolonged absence the Queen becomes depressed. The theme that the poet is growing old reasserts itself (49). The poet fears that her body will develop "defects" that will alienate the youth ("When I shall see thee frown on my defects") and that the youth will give "lawful reasons" why he no longer loves her. As previously discussed, the fears expressed in sonnet 49 can be explained by the huge disparity between Elizabeth's and Essex's ages. Sonnet 49 is assigned to August 1591 when Elizabeth was almost fifty-eight years old, and Essex was twenty-six (Appendix 3).

The sentiment of resigned despair is repeated in sonnets 50 and 51, but in the specific context of the sad poet being separated from the youth and journeying on horseback away from him. We read the much-loved lines about the plodding horse.

Sonnet 50
How heavy do I journey on the way,
When what I seek (my weary travels' end)
Doth teach that ease and that repose to say
Thus far the miles are measur'd from thy friend.
The beast that bears me, tired with my woe,
Plods duly on, to bear that weight in me,
As if by some instinct the wretch did know
His rider lov'd not speed being made from thee:
The bloody spur cannot provoke him on,
That some-times anger thrusts into his hide,
Which heavily he answers with a groan,
More sharp to me than spurring to his side,
    For that same groan doth put this in my mind,
    My grief lies onward and my joy behind.

Sonnets 46–49 about separation and travel, and the sad sonnets 50 and 51, referring to the poet's increasing distance from the youth ("my grief lies onward and my joy behind"), can be linked to Elizabeth's 1591 weary journey home to London with a heavy heart, after failing to rendezvous with Essex and Henri IV in Portsmouth at the end of August. (Both Essex and Henri IV remained in France, campaigning.) Once again, the biographical details of the Elizabeth-Essex relationship are a perfect match for what we read in the sonnets.

Her journey home followed her visits to Cowdray, Petworth, Chichester, Titchfield Abbey, and Southampton as well as Portsmouth, all on or near the English south coast[10]. The south coast rip was interrupted for four days by lavish displays arranged by the Earl of Hertford at Elvetham, Hampshire where Elizabeth watched a water pageant and a performance that included actors dressed as gods and fairies of the forest, which may have inspired the writing of *A Midsummer Night's Dream*[11].

As for Shakespeare, we have no idea what he was up to at this time. He is not recorded as being present at Elvetham. We can, however, be pretty sure that he was not travelling on horseback. He probably never owned a horse. How would he have looked after a horse while living in lodgings in London? People of his class walked.

Sonnet 52 is telling. The poet has arrived home and writes about a key and inspecting her "sweet up-locked treasure" that was secured in a chest before she left on her progress (sonnet 48). She compares re-inspection of her valuables to her affection for the youth and concludes that the youth is extra special because she seldom sees him.

> *Sonnet 52*
> So am I as the rich whose blessed key,
> Can bring him to his sweet up-locked treasure,
> The which he will not ev'ry hour survey,
> For blunting the fine point of seldom [infrequent] pleasure.
> Therefore are feasts [religious festivals] so solemn and so rare,
> Since seldom coming in the long year set,
> Like stones of worth they thinly placed are,
> Or captain [prominent] Jewels in the carconet [coronet].
> So is the time that keeps you as my chest,
> Or as the wardrobe which the robe [curtain] doth hide,
> To make some special instant special blest,
> By new unfolding his imprison'd pride [prize possession].
>   Blessed are you whose worthiness gives scope,
>   Being had, to triumph; being lacked, to hope.
>   [If you're present, I'm happy; if you're away, I hope].

As usual, when Essex is away, Elizabeth idealises him, but the real Essex falls short of the ideal. In sonnet 53 she writes that the classical figures of Helen and Adonis and even springtime in all its glory are nothing compared to the beauty, shape and colours of the youth. But this sonnet is not a repeat of sonnet 18 ("Shall I compare thee to a summer's day?"). The praise is qualified: the youth seems to be rather too popular with the common people, for in the sonnet's first two lines the poet asks what qualities the youth possesses that makes the crowds adore him. Ostensibly the sonnet is complimentary, but it is probably meant to be ironic: the youth is being teased for basking in the flattery of admirers, who credit him with attributes which she doubts he really possesses. Elizabeth finds this flattery puzzling. She writes, somewhat wistfully, that he has only one important characteristic (line 3), and that is his constant heart (last line).

> *Sonnet 53*
> What is your substance, whereof are you made,
> That millions of strange shadows on you tend
> [That so many strangers venerate you]?
> Since every one, hath every one, one shade [people have but one character],
> And you but one, can every shadow lend
> [Everyone sees in you something to admire]:
> Describe *Adonis* and the counterfeit [copy],
> Is poorly imitated after you,
> On *Helen's* cheek all art of beauty set,
> And you in *Grecian* tires [raiment] are painted new:
> Speak of the spring, and foison [abundance] of the year,
> The one doth shadow of your beauty show,
> The other as your bounty doth appear,
> And you in every blessed shape we know.
> > In all external grace you have some part,
> > But you like none, none for your constant heart.

The important biographical information we glean from this sonnet is that not only is the youth publicly known, he is popular. Essex took every chance to curry favour with the general population, particularly to promote himself as the military champion of the Protestant cause. However, he failed to realise that popularity did not equate to political power and influence.

Three reflective sonnets follow – Essex must still be absent from court. Sonnet 54 reflects on the transient quality of showiness in contrast to the lasting qualities of truth and virtue. It uses the metaphor of the rose and its sweet odour to illustrate this point: "The Rose looks fair, but fairer we it deem For that sweet odour, which doth in it live".

In the last three lines of sonnet 54 Elizabeth anticipates the time when she herself (characterised as the sweet-smelling eglantine rose) will die, but like the fragrance of the sweet rose that persists after the rose has died, her verses will ensure that, after the "beauteous and lovely" attributes of the youth have faded, Essex's greatest virtue (truth) will live on. But some doubt has crept into Elizabeth's mind, for although in the sonnet's final couplet Elizabeth expresses a positive sentiment, the poem recognises that in some people appearances can deceive and will not survive the test of time because showiness is their only virtue: "their virtue only is their show" (line 9).

Elizabeth has come to realise that Essex's character might not be quite as noble as it seemed when they first met.

> *Sonnet 54*
> Oh how much more doth beauty beauteous seem,
> By that sweet ornament which truth doth give.
> The Rose looks fair, but fairer we it deem
> For that sweet odour, which in it doth live:
> The Canker blooms [common roses] have full as deep a dye,
> As the perfumed tincture of the Roses,
> Hang on such thorns, and play as wantonly,
> When summer's breath their masked buds discloses:
> But for their virtue only is their show,
> They live unwoo'd, and unrespected fade,
> Die to themselves. Sweet Roses[12] do not so,
> Of their sweet deaths, are sweetest odours made:
>> And so of you, beauteous and lovely youth,
>> When that shall fade, by verse distills your truth.

From 1593 to 1595 Essex had a quieter life and was employed in domestic politics. In February 1593 Elizabeth appointed him to the Privy Council. At the time it might have appeared that the maturing youth had put his military ambitions aside in favour of a future role as a royal advisor and administrator. But Essex was his own worst enemy. He lacked three necessary attributes of a statesman: emotional maturity, even temperament and ability to compromise. He was no more successful campaigning at court than campaigning in France. He misunderstood politics, staking everything on his personal power to charm (which at a personal level generally worked well with the Queen and her maids of honour), rather than building on friendships, developing trust, and gaining broad support for his ideas by patient argument, hard work and lobbying. He was then repeatedly surprised when his sincere but naïve simplistic approach resulted in rebuffs. In the winter of 1593 he more than once disappeared from court in a sulk. He irritated the Queen by his persistent lobbying for his friend Francis Bacon to be appointed Attorney General. On one occasion the Queen, tired of Essex's arguments for Bacon's preferment, lost her temper and bid him go to bed if he could talk of nothing else. Trusting her own judgment, she appointed the more experienced Edward Coke instead.

During this time Essex set up his own spy network to rival that of the Cecils. Uncovering what he thought was a plan by foreign agents to poison the Queen, he revealed to her that her doctor, a Portuguese Jew named Dr Lopez, was implicated. Elizabeth told him that he was "a rash and temerarious youth"[13] to accuse the doctor of treachery. Essex, offended because he had not been taken seriously, abruptly left the court.

Essex returned to court in time for the masques, dancing and feasting of the Twelfth Night celebrations of 1594. The old happy familiarity between him and the Queen was restored. Anthony Standen remarked in a letter that at this festive and happy occasion the sixty-year-old Queen was "as beautiful to my old sight, as ever I saw her, and next to her chair the Earl, with whom she often devised [behaved/conversed] in a sweet and favourable manner"[14]. But when the holiday was over the disagreements continued. Not learning from his rebuff over the Attorney General appointment, Essex argued that Francis Bacon should be appointed to the lesser position of Solicitor General. Elizabeth again took an independent line and appointed Sergeant Fleming instead, a decision that sent Essex into a rage.

---

[1] Pinnaces were fast lightweight sailing ships with fore-and-aft sails used for communication and short voyages. They did not carry cargo or heavy guns.

[2] Neale (1961, p. 328).

[3] Hammer (1999, p. 106) details the Queen's wavering support for the Normandy campaign.

[4] Hammer (1999, p. 103).

[5] Hammer (1999, pp. 129 and 196) cites evidence that the mail system used for official correspondence (roughly equivalent to the 'diplomatic bags' used for correspondence between governments and embassies in pre-electronic times) carried both official communications, generally containing few personal details or opinions, and personal communications written in a less guarded manner.

[6] Lacey (1971, p. 85).

[7] Burrow (2002, pp. 468 and 470).

[8] Kerrigan (1986, p. 229).

[9] Burrow (2002) disingenuously explains that "come and part: means "come and go", a most unlikely explanation given that the subject of "come and part" is the closure of the breasts mentioned in the previous line. But Burrow hedges his academic bets: he also admits that closure "can imply physical constriction".

[10] Nichols (1969).

[11] Guy (2016, p. 158). The performance at Elvetham included a Fairy Queen and a Fairy King named Auberon.

[12] The sweet rose or sweet briar is the common name for the eglantine rose (*Rosa rubiginosa*) which has strongly scented flowers and leaves and is common on the chalk downlands of southern England, and a rampant weed in the drier New Zealand high country. The eglantine rose was identified with Elizabeth I (Strong 1987). The "canker blooms" of line 5 must refer to a wild rose species without a strong perfume, but probably not the dog rose (*Rosa canina*) suggested by several non-botanical commentators (Kerrigan 1986; Burrow 2002; and tentatively by Duncan-Jones 2010), as this species is scented. The strange conclusion that "canker blooms" refer to poppies (Duncan-Jones 1995) is clearly fanciful and incorrect as poppies lack the thorns mentioned in line 7.

[13] Hammer (1999, p.138).

[14] Devereux (1853a, p. 289).

15. Roses and Courtly Imagery

From fairest creatures we desire increase,
That thereby beauty's Rose *might never die*

– Sonnet 1

In sonnets 1 and 54 the words Rose and Roses begin with capital letters, as if they refer to a person. This convention is followed every time the image of the rose is mentioned (1, 54, 67, 95, 98, 99, 109 and 130).

Today we associate roses mostly with women, but in 'Shakespearean' texts the rose image is linked to both sexes, but is applied mostly to royalty or rulers. For example, the rejected Ophelia refers to Prince Hamlet as "Th'expectancy and Rose of the fair State" (*Hamlet*, Act 3, scene 1); Hotspur praises King Richard II as "that sweet lovely Rose" in *King Henry IV Part 1* (Act 1, scene 3); and Anthony characterises young Caesar as wearing "the Rose of youth upon him" (*Anthony and Cleopatra*, Act 3, scene 13).

In his book *The Cult of Elizabeth*[1] Roy Strong researched the use of the rose as a royal symbol in Elizabethan England. He pointed out that the Queen represents both the white rose of the House of York and the red rose of the House of Lancaster. And roses are the flowers of love: the Elizabethan scholar George Reynolds wrote in 1947 that "the theme of . . . love-sickness and the symbolism of the roses is redolent of Elizabethan poetry and the atmosphere of court life"[2]. In portraits and decorative art Elizabeth is represented by both white and red roses, but above all by the rose she chose as an emblem – the pink and white eglantine rose or sweet briar, *Rosa rubiginosa*. To celebrate Elizabeth's birthday in 1595 George Peele wrote "Wear eglantine, And wreaths of roses red and white put on In honour of that day"[3].

Building on earlier research by the art historian David Piper, Roy Strong analysed miniatures by the Elizabethan artist Nicholas Hilliard, in particular the famous *Young Man among Roses* portrait that epitomises the love-sick Elizabethan courtier (Figure 2). This portrait, Strong argues, is of Essex, painted during the first flush of his infatuation with Elizabeth, probably in about 1588. The courtier is dressed in black and white, the royal colours favoured by Elizabeth, and is entwined by white[4] eglantine roses.

The symbolism is not hard to understand. Essex is hopelessly in love with the virgin Queen (or at least this is the image Essex wished to project in 1588[5]), but because of their age difference (she is thirty-two years his senior) and the political and social conventions of the time, his love can never be consummated. He is therefore doomed to play the role of the perpetually unhappy courtier (which, one suspects, was a role he rather enjoyed playing). Hence the motto on the miniature: *Dat pœnas laudata fides*[6], which can be loosely translated as 'My praised faithfulness gives me pain'. In modern English we might say (less poetically) 'My loyalty comes at a personal cost'.

Figure 2. The *Young Man among Roses* portrait by Nicholas Hilliard. This is Hilliard's largest miniature portrait (20 x 14 cm). Roy Strong suggested that the portrait represents the second Earl of Essex. It is full of symbolism. The young man has his hand on his heart – he is in love. The oak tree against which he is leaning represents constancy. The briars which entwine him are roses, symbolising the Queen. He is dressed in black and white – the Queen's preferred colours. The caption (over the man's head), not readable in this reproduction, reads *Dat pœnas laudata fides*. © *Victoria and Albert Museum, London.*

The inferred 1588 date of the *Young Man* portrait is consistent with the commencement of the Elizabeth/Essex relationship and the likely date of composition of the early sonnets. Essex himself may have commissioned the portrait in about 1588, in the early heady days of his friendship with Elizabeth. The motto on the portrait is remarkably similar to the line in sonnet 141: ". . . she that makes me sin, awards me pain". It is another indicator of a connection between the sonnets, Essex and Elizabeth I.

The *Young Man among Roses* portrait may be mentioned in sonnet 47. While the youth is away, the poet sleeps with a picture of the youth close at hand: "thy picture in my sight Awakes my heart, to heart's and eyes' delight" (47). The picture gives the poet comfort while the youth is away: "So either by thy picture or my love, Thy self away, are present still with me." (One can imagine a portrait perched on Elizabeth's bedside table.) The sonnet describes how the heart imagines an image of the youth, and the eyes observe a real image, so when the heart and eyes work together the poet feels she is with the youth all the time.

Sonnet 47
Betwixt mine eye and heart a league is took,
And each doth good turns now unto the other,
When that mine eye is famished for a look,
Or heart in love with sighs himself doth smother;
With my love's picture then my eye doth feast,
And to the painted banquet bids my heart:
An other time mine eye is my heart's guest,
And in his thoughts of love doth share a part.
So either by thy picture or my love,
Thy self away, are present still with me,
For thou nor farther than my thoughts can'st move,
And I am still with them, and they with thee.
    Or if they sleep, thy picture in my sight
    Awakes my heart, to heart's and eyes' delight.

That the picture referred to is a miniature portrait can also be inferred from Sir James Melville's accounts of his meetings with the Queen. He noted that Elizabeth kept miniature paintings of her favoured courtiers in a cabinet in her bedroom:

> She took me to her bedchamber and opened a little desk, wherein were divers little pictures wrapped within paper, and their names written with her own hand upon the papers.[7]

In sonnet 67 there may be another reference to the *Young Man* portrait. Apparently criticising both the image of the youth (i.e., Essex) and the portrayal of roses in a painting, the poet asks the youth (lines 5–8) 'why should

I need an image of yourself painted amongst roses, since I'm real, I'm your Rose, I'm here in the flesh, and I love you truly?'[8].

Sonnet 67, lines 5–8
Why should false painting[9] imitate his cheek,
And steal dead seeing [a lifeless image] of his living hue [figure, complexion]?
Why should poor beauty indirectly seek,
Roses of shadow [Pretend or painted roses], since his Rose is true?

It is likely that this sonnet was written during a period when Essex was misbehaving (see chapter 18) and Elizabeth was contemplating the *Young Man among Roses* portrait of her favourite that had been commissioned and painted in better times.

There is another reference to the eglantine rose in sonnet 99. The poet imagines that the flowers she sees have stolen their colour or fragrance from her beloved. As previously mentioned, the eglantine rose (representing the Queen) has both pink and white colours, which she imagines have been acquired from white and red roses.

Sonnet 99, lines 6–13
The Lily I condemned for thy hand,
And buds of marjoram had stol'n thy hair,
The Roses fearfully on thorns did stand,
One blushing shame, an other white despair:
A third nor red, nor white, had stol'n of both,
And to his robb'ry had annexed thy breath,
But for his theft in pride of all his growth [in his prime]
A vengeful canker eat him [her?] up to death.

The poet goes on to say that the eglantine rose has annexed the breath (i.e. fragrance) of the youth (Essex), but is being eaten up by a cancer. Elsewhere in the writings of 'Shakespeare', for example, in Act 1, scene 2 of *The Tempest*, grief is described as beauty's cancer. In this sonnet, written in 1599 when their relationship was 'on the rocks' (chapter 20), is Elizabeth saying that her expression of love (and possibly her lovemaking with Essex), has caused her shame and despair, and broken her heart?

In the much earlier sonnet 24 (chapter 8) there is another reference to a miniature painting. The poet writes that the poet's body is the frame in which the youth's picture is held, and the picture "in my bosom's shop is hanging still". Although in Elizabethan times the word "bosom" could refer to either a man's or a woman's chest, its use with the word "shop" implies something that can be opened and entered, i.e. the cleavage between a woman's breasts.

In the same sonnet playful lovemaking is hinted at in the lines which describe the youth's eyes as "windows to my breast, where-through the Sun [Essex?] Delights to peep, to gaze therein on thee [the picture]".

Figure 3. The Nicholas Hilliard miniature portrait (1588) *Man Clasping a Hand from a Cloud*. The black and white clothes of the young man, the date, the inscription, and the long fingers of the female hand reaching down from the clouds all fit the interpretation that this is a picture of the Earl of Essex painted around the time of the first flowering of his relationship with Queen Elizabeth I. © *Victoria and Albert Museum, London*.

The miniature portrait referred to in sonnet 24 is likely to be another enigmatic painting by Nicholas Hilliard: *Man Clasping a Hand from a Cloud* painted in 1588 (Figure 3) in London's Victoria and Albert Museum. This portrait is small (6 x 5 cm) – much smaller than the *Young Man among Roses* painting (20 x 14 cm) and, unlike the latter miniature, was almost certainly designed to be worn as a pendant. It was donated to the British Museum in 1754 accompanied by the catalogue entry "The picture of the Earl of Essex in whose hand is another coming from the clouds, supposed to be that of Queen Elizabeth".

The portrait depicts a fair-faced young man with light brown curly hair, a short light reddish-brown beard and a long nose. His raised hand holds a woman's, which has exceptionally long and delicate fingers. The hair colour matches that of Essex – later portraits show him with a reddish-brown beard. The image corresponds to the description of the fair youth in *A Lover's Complaint* (published with *Sonnets*): "His browny locks did hang in crooked curls" and the clothes are those of a courtier – black and white were Elizabeth's preferred colours for courtiers at ceremonial court events. The clothes and hair colour in this portrait are also similar to the clothes and hair colour in a miniature portrait of a younger Essex painted by Isaac Oliver[10].

In 1588 Essex could have been sporting his first beard. Perhaps the image depicts his early passionately happy days with his sovereign, whose presence is discreetly suggested by the slender hand reaching down to his – we know that Elizabeth was inordinately proud of her beautiful hands and long fingers.

The word "Attici" in the motto *Attici amoris ergo* in the *Man Clasping a Hand from a Cloud* portrait can be literally translated as 'Athenians' but was used in literature to represent orators, poets, artists and learned people in general. The motto can be loosely translated as 'Poets because of love', reflecting Essex's and Elizabeth's shared love of poetry and literature.

That the courtier in this miniature represents Essex is supported by a second version of this painting, previously held in Castle Howard, Yorkshire. According to the Shakespeare scholar L. Hotson[11], who bought the Castle Howard portrait in 1961, this version has a frame inscribed with the words "Earl of Essex". Perhaps Essex had one portrait painted for the Queen, and another for himself.

Let's now return to the Roses theme. The Queen would have been guarded about inserting any clues to her identity in the sonnets once she had decided that she wished them to be published, under Shakespeare's name. However, such caution might not have applied when she committed to paper the first sonnets to come into her mind. These would have been spontaneous expressions of her private thoughts, written without considering that more than 150 poems and publication would follow. So we might expect the earlier sonnets to reveal more about their author than later more guarded poems.

In the very first lines of sonnet 1 both the word "Rose" and the word "we" are used. It is possible that this is a case of the royal poet is using the 'royal we' but we can't be certain: here the pronoun could represent 'people in general':

From fairest creatures we desire increase,
That thereby beauty's *Rose* might never die

However, in sonnet 53 there is no ambiguity: the 'royal we' substitutes for 'I': "And you in every blessed shape we know". And in sonnet 54 the poet writes:

> The Rose looks fair, but fairer we it deem
> For that sweet odour, which doth in it live:

It seems that royal writing customs were hard to relinquish. We can conclude that when writing the sonnets Elizabeth was generally cautious about using vocabulary that might reveal her identity, but occasionally habit prevailed over caution, or perhaps her editor (if she had one) failed to detect and correct these examples.

It would of course have been very strange and indeed pretentious for a commoner like William Shakespeare to write using the 'royal we'.

---

[1] Strong (1987).
[2] Strong (1987, p. 68).
[3] Strong (1987, p. 70).
[4] The petals of the eglantine rose (*Rosa rubiginosa*), the Queen's emblem, are pink with a white base. The roses portrayed in the miniature are white, so either they do not represent the eglantine rose, or the original pink pigment in the painting has faded over time. As the organic pigments rose madder and red lake are both prone to fading, I have assumed that fading has caused the roses in this portrait to appear white. For further notes on the interpretation of the portrait see the discussion and references in https://collections.vam.ac.uk/item/O17315/young-man-among-roses-portrait-miniature-hilliard-nicholas/.
[5] Hammer (1999, pp. 205–211) discusses Essex's frequent use of portraiture to promote himself.
[6] A quote from the Roman poet Lucan.
[7] Donaldson (1969, p. 37).
[8] Burrow (2002, p. 514) discards the capital R in Rose and suggests that "rose" refers to the real hue of the youth's cheeks, and indicates unfeigned and faithful love. This interpretation is most unlikely to be correct given the original typography and the critical tone of the poem: "wherefore with infection should he live" (line 1) and "wealth she [Nature] had, In days long since, before these last so bad" (lines 13 and 14). The poem is not about the youth's faithful love – quite the opposite.
[9] Kerrigan (1986, p. 258) writes "The old theory that *painting* refers to portraiture is hardly plausible" but gives no reason for coming to this conclusion.
[10] Portrait of Robert Devereux, second Earl of Essex, by Isaac Oliver; in the Beauchamp collection.
[11] Hotson (1977, p. 203).

16. Wasteful war

When wasteful war shall Statues over-turn
— Sonnet 55

Let us now return to where we left off in the sonnet sequence. The reflective sonnet 54 (chapter 14) was probably written while Essex was absent from court. It may date to 1595 when Essex had to ride to the north of England to ensure order was maintained in this volatile region after the death of Lord Huntingdon. (Following the northern rebellion of 1569, Huntingdon served the Queen as president of the Council for the North until his death.)

In contrast to the gentle themes of sonnet 54, sonnet 55 dwells on the melancholy themes of war, destruction, doom, judgment day, the relentless advance of time, and the spirit of the youth living on in the poems after his death – not the usual subjects shared between two young lovers.

> *Sonnet 55*
> Not marble, nor the gilded monuments
> Of Princes shall out-live this powerful rhyme,
> But you shall shine more bright in these contents
> Than unswept stone, besmear'd with sluttish time.
> When wasteful war shall *Statues* over-turn,
> And broils root out the work of masonry,
> Nor *Mars* his sword, nor war's quick fire shall burn:
> The living record of your memory.
> 'Gainst death, and all oblivious enmity
> Shall you pace forth, your praise shall still find room,
> Even in the eyes of all posterity
> That wear this world out to the ending doom.
>   So till the judgement [judgment day] that [when you] your self arise,
>   You live in this, and dwell in lovers' eyes.

At the personal level the message is positive: the youth's characteristics will live on in the sonnets, despite the ruinous consequences of wars, conflicts and time itself. This association of ideas suggests that Essex himself is involved in a dangerous military campaign. In the sonnet's first two lines we have confirmation that what Elizabeth probably first envisaged to be private reflections and a medium for working out her thoughts she now expects to be read by others. She is writing for publication and posterity.

Sonnet 56 provides some further clues as to what is happening to the young man, the sonnet's subject. It mentions "this sad *Interim*" – the youth is absent. The poet likens their separation to a sea between two shores on which two lovers stand. Taking the subject matter of sonnets 55 and 56 together, we can conclude that not only is Essex taking part in a military campaign, but also that he is overseas.

Sonnet 56, lines 9–14
Let this sad *Interim* [period of separation] like the Ocean be
Which parts the shore, where two contracted new [two newly engaged lovers],
Come daily to the banks, that when they see:
Return of love [the beloved], more bless'd may be the view.
    As [Or] call it Winter, which being full of care,
    Makes Summer's welcome, thrice more wish'd, more rare.

Significantly, this mention of separation corresponds with Essex's known activities at the time. After returning to London from the north on 23 December 1595, he left for the south coast to help prepare the English fleet for a raid on Cadiz. The Queen's concern for Essex while he was joint commander of the fleet bound for Cadiz can be linked to sonnet 55 mentioning wasteful war, the sword of Mars and death, and sonnet 56 describing lovers separated by sea.

The spectacular Cadiz raid almost did not happen. English plans, painstakingly prepared by Essex and based on intelligence reports from Essex's agent, Captain Peter Wynn[1], were put into disarray when in March 1596 Spanish troops unexpectedly began a siege of Calais. As a result, the naval force destined for Cadiz was made ready for relieving the French town. But during the first half of April the Queen dithered and to Essex's intense annoyance she twice cancelled the order to cross the Straits of Dover. On 14 April 1596 she finally gave permission for the fleet to sail. But it was too late: while troops were embarking Calais fell, and the relief effort had to be abandoned.

Preparations for the Cadiz raid resumed. On 24 May 1596 the Queen ordered the fleet to depart[2]. Once again, Essex had a chance to prove his military prowess. He seized it. He and a large fleet left Plymouth on 13 June 1596. On 30 June they arrived off Cadiz, taking the inhabitants by surprise.

There followed a brilliant naval and military action – but it was not as financially brilliant as it could have been. The joint commanders Essex, Lord Howard of Effingham and Sir Francis Vere, together with distinguished subordinates Sir Walter Ralegh, Sir Charles Blount and others led a force that seized the city and two other small towns, Faro and Loulé. The spoils were smaller than anticipated. A rich merchant fleet in Cadiz's inner harbour was scuttled by the Spanish while the English effort was directed ashore. As a consolation prize Essex relieved the Bishop of Faro of his library, which he donated to Thomas Bodley, founder of the Bodleian Library in Oxford.

In August 1596 the Cadiz fleet returned. Essex returned as the darling of the London citizenry. His success at Cadiz cemented his position as leader of the martial careerists, a gallant knight in the chivalric tradition. But Elizabeth was less than pleased with her dashing favourite. The cost of the Cadiz venture relative to the meagre spoils she received disappointed her, and the adulation poured on Essex on his return as conquering hero she found annoying. She did not appreciate competitors for public affection. When the Archbishop of Canterbury ordered a thanksgiving throughout the kingdom to celebrate the military success, she restricted celebrations to London. She also banned the publication of Essex's propaganda pamphlet *A True Relation of the Action of Cadiz* written by his public relations agent and Oxford scholar, Henry Cuffe. Essex circulated handwritten copies of *A True Relation* to friends and supporters[3], thus circumventing the censor, but this act of blatant self-glorification risked alienating the Queen and powerful people at court[4]. It was another example of Essex allowing his passionate self-belief to work against his own long-term advantage.

Although initially the Queen received Essex coldly, her attitude changed on learning that, had Essex's advice been followed by the joint commanders at Cadiz, treasure ships making their way towards Lisbon could have been intercepted and seized. (It was Ralegh who had argued against lying in wait for the Spanish ships.)

On his part Essex was miffed by his cool reception at home and infuriated that, while he was away fighting for his country, the bureaucrat Robert Cecil, who had been acting Secretary of State for five years, had been formally appointed to the position. This appointment gave Robert Cecil extraordinary power to influence the Queen and national policy. The upshot was that, while Essex's success at Cadiz increased his popularity at home, it did nothing to further his political career[5]. Popular acclaim was no substitute for carefully cultivated support in high places.

If Essex was upset by the Queen's attitude to what he regarded as an outstanding blow to the King of Spain's pride, the Queen must have been equally upset that Essex's much anticipated return, which she had written would be like "Summer's welcome" (56) after winter, was not the happy homecoming she anticipated. Her coolness towards her favourite is evident in the ironic and regretful lines of sonnets 57 and 58.

At this point we must recall the discontent Elizabeth expressed in sonnet 53, in which she expressed irritation about Essex's popularity after his return from the Normandy campaign. In this earlier sonnet her comments were restrained and simply questioned Essex's qualities and his reception: "What is your substance, whereof are you made, That millions of strange shadows [strangers] on you tend?"

But in sonnet 57, written after Essex's return from Cadiz, the Queen is more outspoken and writes (line 1 and 2) with biting irony about how Essex's overconfidence affects her: "Being your slave what should I do but tend, Upon the hours, and times of your desire?" The sarcastic tone is maintained throughout the sonnet – she pretends that she has nothing better to do than "to watch the clock for you" while Essex organises his schedule.

Sonnet 57
Being your slave what should I do but tend,
Upon the hours, and times of your desire?
I have no precious time at all to spend;
Nor services to do till you require.
Nor dare I chide the world-without-end [endless] hour,
Whilst I (my sovereign) watch the clock for you,
Nor think the bitterness of absence sour,
When you have bid your servant once adieu.
Nor dare I question with my jealous thought,
Where you may be, or your affairs suppose,
But like a sad slave stay and think of nought
Save where you are, how happy you make those.
    So true a fool is love, that in your Will,
    (Though you do any thing) he thinks no ill.

    Clearly Elizabeth isn't getting the attention she expects from her favourite. Notice the little joke about a sovereign in line 6. If "my sovereign" refers to the preceding "I", this is a gentle reminder to Essex about who is really the boss in their relationship. If, on the other hand, "my sovereign" is addressed to Essex, then Elizabeth is writing in the style of someone facetiously replying 'Yes, your lordship!' to the demands of a person putting on airs and pretending they are frightfully important.
    Although sonnet 57 ends with a hopeful couplet expressing the conventional sentiment that she is so much in love that she cannot think ill of Essex, the next shows the Queen's true feelings:

Sonnet 58
That God forbid, that made me first your slave,
I should in thought control your times of pleasure,
Or at your hand th'account of hours to crave
[Or demand how you spend your time],
Being your vassal bound to stay your leisure.
Oh let me suffer (being at your beck)
Th'imprison'd absence of your liberty,
And patience tame, to sufferance bide each check [endure each rebuke],
Without accusing you of injury [Without blaming you].
Be where you list, your charter is so strong,
That you your self may privilege your time
To what you will, to you it doth belong,
Your self to pardon of self-doing crime.
    I am to wait, though waiting so be hell,
    Not blame your pleasure be it ill or well.

    In present-day English the first two lines might be written: 'God forbid that you should think I'm trying to control how you spend your leisure time'. Elizabeth complains that Essex holds himself in such high regard that he makes a point of doing what he, rather than others, want: "your charter is so strong, That you yourself may privilege your time To what you will" (lines 9–11). She complains of neglect: "I am to wait, though waiting so be hell" (line 13). There is no doubt that Essex is emotionally more important to Elizabeth than Elizabeth is to Essex, but Elizabeth will not admit this. Essex of course was playing with fire. His popularity had gone to his head. He had forgotten that his position and his power depended entirely on the Queen's favour.

Following these ironic poems is a sequence of reflective sonnets (59–66) on melancholy subjects. We might infer that Essex was again absent from court, or misbehaving, or both. History tells us that this inference is correct.

First, Essex argued with Elizabeth in February, prompting him to retire to bed with illness. When the Queen visited him, he miraculously recovered. But another disagreement occurred when Lord Cobham, Warden of the Cinque Ports, died on 5 March. Elizabeth and Essex argued over who should succeed to his position. Essex's suggestions fell on deaf ears and he left court, intending to visit his estates in Wales. He only got as far as Somerset House before the Queen's messenger intercepted him, carrying an order for him to return. Essex and the Queen patched up their differences and on 10 March Elizabeth pacified him by making him Master of the Ordnance.

In sonnet 59 Elizabeth longs for the 'good old times'. She compares her problems with Essex to those of going through childbirth for the second time (perhaps imagining that her 'first' child was her ideal Essex, and the 'second' the real Essex). She imagines her ideal Essex as he might have appeared in an antique book written 500 years previously. But the rub is in the last couplet: she is sure that former poets have praised less worthy subjects. Not really a compliment when you think about it.

> *Sonnet 59*
> If there be nothing new, but that which is,
> Hath been before, how are our brains beguiled,
> Which labouring for invention bear amiss
> The second burden [reincarnation] of a former child?
> Oh that [If only the] record could with a back-ward look,
> Even of five hundred courses of the Sun [years],
> Show me your image in some antique book,
> Since mind at first in character was done [thoughts were first written down].
> That I might see what the old world could say,
> To this composed wonder of your frame,
> Whether we are mended [better made], or were better they,
> Or whether revolution [by the passage of time] be the same [we are all similar].
>   Oh I am sure the wits [learned people, poets] of former days,
>   To subjects worse have given admiring praise.

The next sonnet is written from the point of view of an old person. It is all about time and ageing (as its number 60 implies). Like waves breaking on a pebbly beach "our minutes hasten to their end". "Nativity . . . crawls to maturity". Malignant events ("crooked eclipses") contend with success ("glory") in people's lives. In human lives time at first provides opportunity, but later becomes a limitation: "And time that gave, doth now his gift confound". Nothing can stand in the way of time's scythe – even beautiful young people end up with lines on their foreheads. But Elizabeth repeats the familiar refrain that Essex's worth (his good qualities) will be recorded in her verses, regardless of time's impacts. She still finds it possible to view her relationship with Essex through rose-tinted spectacles, at least when he's absent.

> *Sonnet 60*
> Like as the waves make towards the pebbled shore,
> So do our minutes hasten to their end,
> Each changing place with that which goes before,
> In sequent toil all forwards to contend.
> Nativity [The newborn] once in the main [wide world] of light,
> Crawls to maturity, wherewith being crown'd [when success seems assured],
> Crooked eclipses [Malignant events] 'gainst his glory fight,
> And time that gave, doth now his gift confound.
> Time doth transfix the flourish set on youth,
> And delves the parallels in beauty's brow,
> Feeds on the rarities of nature's truth,
> And nothing stands but for his scythe to mow.
>   And yet to times in hope, my verse shall stand
>   Praising thy worth, despite his cruel hand.

Critics might counter that such interpretations are too literal, and that a poet may infuse his or her poems with a world-weary outlook, in order to make a point about their own misfortune or the human tragedy around them. A classic example is A. E. Housman's creation of a mood of *fin-de-siècle* melancholy in his anthology *A Shropshire Lad*, published in 1896. But, as pointed out in chapter 2, in *Sonnets* the references to death, ageing and being past one's best, and also to the age discrepancy between the author and the much younger youth, are too frequent and particular to relate to anything other than real and personal circumstances. They must concern the deeply experienced feelings and moods of the older partner, i.e., the author. The historical analysis presented here supports this interpretation.

    By 1597 the Queen was well aware of the effects of the "cruel hand" of time on her. She had the appearance of an old woman, despite her portrayal in official portraits as eternally young. In December of this year she granted the French ambassador André Hurault-Sieur de Maisse an audience and in his journal he described the sixty-four-year-old Queen:

> Her bosom is somewhat wrinkled as well as one can see for the collar that she wears round her neck, but lower down her flesh is exceeding white and delicate, so far as one could see. As for her face, it is and appears to be very aged. It is long and thin, and her teeth are very yellow and unequal, compared to what they were formerly, so they say, and on the left side less than on the right. Many of them are missing so that one cannot understand her easily when she speaks quickly.[6]

In 1598 the German traveller Paul Hentzner gained permission to enter the Queen's presence chamber at Greenwich Palace. He also made notes on her appearance:

> Her face oblong, fair, but wrinkled; her eyes small, yet black and pleasant; her nose a little hooked; her lips narrow, and her teeth black . . . She wore false hair, and that red . . .[7]

The sonnets' vocabulary of age and imminent death fits the age disparity between Elizabeth and Essex perfectly. Elizabeth was about fifty-five years old and Essex was about twenty when she began to take a serious interest in him. Their relationship lasted until she was sixty-seven years old. That a childless but passionate woman became besotted with a handsome, charming and spirited youth who gave her his attention and paid her compliments is understandable. Essex was at once the husband Elizabeth never had and the son she never bore. As Lytton Strachey voyeuristically wrote in regard to her relationship with Essex: "He satisfied the peculiar cravings of a virgin of sixty-three"[8].

---

[1] Hammer (1999, pp. 127 and 190).

[2] Hammer (1999, pp. 250–251). The official aim was to destroy the Spanish fleet in harbour and to take as much plunder as possible, but Essex had his own ambitious and impractical plan: to establish a base in Spain so that at least part of the Spanish coastline could be patrolled and controlled (blockaded) by an English fleet. That Essex believed he could ignore orders and garrison Cadiz with English troops without prior permission, without official funding and without a provisioning plan shows how out of touch he was with the practical realities of logistics and long-term military campaigning, which required more than enthusiasm and grand gestures. He was severely testing the Queen's patience.

[3] Guy (2016, p. 266).

[4] Hammer (1999, p. 315).

[5] In fact it was probably counter-productive. By appointing Robert Cecil as Secretary Elizabeth had broken a promise that she would take no action while her favourite was away. Her action may have been prompted by Essex's letter to the Privy Council, read out on 13 June (Hammer 1999, p. 368) while he was still at sea, which requested that the Council should persuade the Queen that soldiers on the expedition should be permitted to establish a base on the Spanish mainland,

totally contrary to Elizabeth's intentions. Essex was trying to force the Queen's hand. Cecil's appointment (and particularly its announcement while Essex was away) may have been calculated to take Essex down a peg or two. It did. His influence with those who mattered at home and abroad never recovered.

[6] Harrison and Jones (1931).
[7] Walpole (1797).
[8] Strachey (1971).

17. Adventures at Sea

For thee watch I, whilst thou dost wake elsewhere,
From me far off, with others all too near

– Sonnet 61

The year 1597 was a time of squabbles and reconciliations between Essex and the Queen, reminiscent of those between ill-matched married couples. The words of sonnet 61 confirm the inference, made in the previous chapter, that Essex is absent from court. It describes the youth as being "far from home" and separated from the poet: "thou dost awake elsewhere, From me far off, with others all too near".

Sonnet 61
Is it thy will, thy Image should keep open
My heavy eyelids to the weary night?
Dost thou desire my slumbers should be broken,
While shadows like to thee do mock my sight?
Is it thy spirit that thou send'st from thee
So far from home into my deeds to pry,
To find out shames and idle hours in me,
The scope and tenure of thy Jealousy?
O no, thy love though much, is not so great,
It is my love that keeps mine eye awake,
My own true love that doth my rest defeat,
To play the watch-man ever for thy sake.
    For thee watch I, whilst thou dost wake elsewhere,
    From me far off, with others all too near.

Why Essex was away is no mystery. During 1597 Elizabeth was persuaded to back another raid in Spanish waters. The first objective was to destroy the Spanish naval fleet at Ferrol near Corunna in northwest Spain. Then the English would sail to the Azores to intercept treasure galleons from the Americas. The expedition became known as the Islands Voyage. In May Essex was appointed commander. Between leaving London and sailing from Plymouth on 10 July he and the Queen exchanged impassioned letters, with Essex writing almost daily.

Shortly after setting sail from Plymouth the huge fleet of ninety-eight ships was dispersed by a storm and returned to port. Essex's ship was the last to come in and the Queen expressed anxiety about his survival. But Essex did survive and Elizabeth wept when she heard of his safe return. Even the usually unemotional Cecil wrote warmly to Essex "The Queen is so disposed now to have us all love you, that she and I do every night talk like angels of you"[1]. Clearly the Queen was still infatuated with her favourite. Cecil's love and sincerity is questionable.

Sonnet 61 describing absence, and the reflective sonnets 62–63, were probably written while Essex was away from court, busy preparing for the Islands Voyage. The latter two describe Elizabeth's despondency not only about her own appearance ("Beated and chop'd with tanned antiquity" and "With time's injurious hand crush'd and o'er-worn") but also the inevitable ageing of her beloved Essex: he will develop "lines and wrinkles" and she envisages a time when "all those beauties whereof now he's King Are vanishing, or vanish'd out of sight" and only preserved in the "black lines" of the sonnets.

> *Sonnet 62, lines, lines 9–14*
> But when my glass shows me my self indeed
> Beated and chop'd with tanned antiquity,
> Mine own self love quite contrary I read:
> Self, so self loving were iniquity,
>   T'is thee (my self) that for my self I praise,
>   Painting my age with beauty of thy days.

> *Sonnet 63*
> Against my love shall be as I am now
> With time's injurious hand crush'd and o'er-worn,
> When hours have drained his blood and filled his brow
> With lines and wrinkles, when his youthful morn
> Hath travail'd on to Age's steepie [arduous] night,
> And all those beauties whereof now he's King
> Are vanishing, or vanish'd out of sight,
> Stealing away the treasure of his Spring.
> For such a time do I now fortify [prepare myself]
> Against confounding Age's cruel knife,
> That he shall never cut from memory
> My sweet love's beauty, though my lover's life [my lover's life will end].
>   His beauty shall in these black lines be seen,
>   And they shall live, and he in them still green [young and fresh].

The following sonnets (64 and 65) contain specific references to the sea ("the hungry Ocean", the "wat'ry main" and "the boundless sea") and even coastal erosion ("the hungry Ocean gain Advantage on the Kingdom of the shore" and "rocks impregnable are not so stout . . . but time decays"). The poet also ruminates on separation and loss ("Time will come and take my love away"). This combination of subject matter indicates that these sonnets are likely to concern an ocean voyage. Perhaps they were written after news reached London of the severe storm that struck the English fleet early in its voyage, including reports that Essex had perished.

Essex's ocean voyage (the longest of his career) and the issues of death and inevitable decline were probably troubling the poet. If we accept the chronology (Appendix 3) associated with the Elizabeth-Essex hypothesis, then sonnet 64 was written when the Queen was in her sixty-fourth year and feeling her age. Apprehension made the Queen weep for "that which it fears to lose" (64). But in a statement that should inspire all writers of romances she assures herself (65) that Essex's beauty and her expression of love will live on in her writings: "in black ink my love may still shine bright".

Sonnet 64
When I have seen by time's fell hand defaced
The rich proud cost of outworn buried age,
When sometime lofty towers I see down razed,
And brass eternal slave to mortal rage.
When I have seen the hungry Ocean gain
Advantage on the Kingdom of the shore,
And the firm soil win of the wat'ry main,
Increasing store with loss, and loss with store.
When I have seen such interchange of state,
Or state itself confounded, to decay,
Ruin hath taught me thus to ruminate
That Time will come and take my love away.
    This thought is as a death which cannot choose
    But weep to have, that which it fears to lose.

Sonnet 65
Since brass, nor stone, nor earth, nor boundless sea,
But sad mortality o'er-sways their power,
How with this rage shall beauty hold a plea,
Whose action is no stronger than a flower?
O how shall summer's honey breath hold out,
Against the wrackful siege of batt'ring days,
When rocks impregnable are not so stout,
Nor gates of steel so strong but time decays?
O fearful meditation, where alack,
Shall time's best Jewel from time's chest lie hid?
Or what strong hand can hold his swift foot back,
Or who his spoil of beauty can forbid?
    O none, unless this miracle have might,
    That in black ink my love may still shine bright.

Richard II's famous "hollow crown" speech in *Richard II*, Act 3, scene 2, first published in 1597, uses similar vocabulary ("brass impregnable") to that in sonnet 65 ("rocks impregnable"). Note also the words "brass eternal" in sonnet 64's fourth line. These observations support the proposition that sonnets 64 and 65 were written in 1597.

On 17 August the depleted fleet re-embarked. It avoided an engagement at Ferrol and sailed to the Azores. The voyage was unsuccessful both tactically and financially. Storms continued to hamper the expedition. There were disagreements between Essex and Ralegh leading to lost opportunities for gains ashore, and a poorly organised blockade failed to intercept the Spanish fleet carrying treasure worth about three and a half million pounds sterling in today's money. Whereas the Cadiz raid had dented the pride of King Philip and been a huge morale boost for the English, the Islands Voyage was militarily a shambles and merely a minor annoyance for the enemy.

On 26 October Essex returned from the expedition with nothing to show for all the expense and effort incurred. Arriving in London in early November he was berated by the Queen for not engaging the third armada at Ferrol, for missing the chance to plunder six treasure ships *en route* to the Azores, and for not intercepting Spanish warships near Blavet, Brittany[2].

---

[1] Neale (1961, p. 350).
[2] Guy (2016, p. 281).

18. "The Rank Smell of Weeds"

thou dost common grow
– Sonnet 69

When he returned to England Essex was in a touchy mood. This time he was no hero: there was little to celebrate. On learning that the Queen had given Lord Admiral Howard the title of Earl of Nottingham for his lifetime of military service, but in particular for his part in the Cadiz raid, Essex took umbrage at the supposed slight to his own reputation. In his own mind he was the architect of the successful raid. He retired to sulk at Wanstead House, his home just north of Elizabethan London, feigning sickness. Here, over-confident, jealous and ill-advised by friends and relatives, he resisted the expectation of the Queen that he should attend at court. He failed to appear at the Accession Day tilts held annually in November to honour the Queen. By absenting himself from the court he began a dangerous contest of wills with his sovereign, which he could not win.

Rumours spread that he had had an affair with the Countess of Derby before embarking on the Islands Voyage. The pregnant Countess was forced to leave court during July, and it is recorded that the affair resulted in Essex being "in no great grace" with the Queen[1]. In modern jargon, such a youthful indiscretion (if it actually occurred) was not a good career move. Not only was Essex wholly dependent on Elizabeth's goodwill for favours, but Lady Derby was the granddaughter of William Cecil (Lord Burghley), the Queen's chief advisor and arguably the most powerful member of Elizabeth's court.

The next nine sonnets (66–74) reflect the Queen's anguish concerning Essex's behaviour. In sonnet 66 we read an inventory of worldly injustices. The Queen is depressed and writes with all the despair, tiredness and despondency of old age: "Tir'd with all these for restful death I cry". (We must remind ourselves that William Shakespeare was only in his early thirties when this sonnet was written.)

Clearly the youth's return from overseas was not the happy event anticipated. In her earlier expressions of concern during absences (55, 56, 60–65) Elizabeth wrote about her feelings of longing and tolerance. Sonnets 67–70 record a change of attitude – she is now unequivocally critical. Her words reflect her irritation with Essex's churlish and childish behaviour following his return from the Islands Voyage. She still expresses love for Essex, but her love is tempered by serious reservations. The youth is receiving "outward praise" and is mixing with bad company: "wherefore with infection should he live [why is he associating with the wrong sort?], And with his presence grace impiety [give credibility to rogues]?" (67). She calls to mind her idealised image of Essex from earlier times "In days long since, before these last [recent] so bad".

Sonnet 66
Tir'd with all these for restful death I cry,
As to behold desert a beggar born [a deserving person born into poverty],
And needy Nothing trimm'd in jollity,
And purest faith unhappily forsworn [innocence expediently exploited],
And gilded honour shamefully misplaced,
And maiden virtue rudely strumpeted,
And right perfection wrongfully disgrac'd,
And strength by limping sway disabled,
And art made tongue-tied by authority,
And Folly (Doctor-like) controlling skill,
And simple-Truth miscalled Simplicity,
And captive-good attending Captain ill.
    Tir'd with all these, from these would I be gone,
    Save that to die, I leave my love alone.

Sonnet 67
Ah wherefore with infection [bad influence] should he live,
And with his presence grace impiety [give credibility to rogues],
That sin [So that evil] by him advantage should achieve,
And lace itself [enmesh itself] with his society?
Why should false painting imitate his cheek,
And steal dead seeing [a lifeless image] of his living hue [figure, complexion]?
Why should poor beauty indirectly seek,
Roses of shadow [Pretend roses], since his Rose is true?
Why should he live, now nature bankrupt is [has given him all her gifts],
Beggar'd of blood to blush through lively veins,
For she hath no exchequer now but his,
And proud of many, lives upon his gains?
    O him she stores, to show what wealth she had,
    In days long since, before these last so bad.

The last two lines of sonnet 67 can be read as referring to Essex as nature's store of beauty: 'nature has invested in him, but it's not evident at the moment'. However, the lines can also be read as meaning that Elizabeth herself has stored Essex's better qualities. The latter interpretation would link lines 13 and 14 to lines 7 and 8: "Why should poor beauty indirectly seek, Roses of shadow, since his Rose is true?" Perhaps she is looking at the idealised image of him in the *Young Man among Roses* portrait in her store of pictures and musing nostalgically about better times.

If ever Essex had a chance to peruse the following sonnet (68), he would have read an ominous message. His sovereign has detected in him "bastard signs of fair" and "false Art". She has separated Essex's character into two parts: the present-day (worldly) Essex and the ideal Essex who reminds her of what true unadorned beauty was in the romanticised past ("In him those holy antique hours are seen"). Her disintegration of Essex's character into these two parts is frightening: taken to its logical conclusion it could mean that only the idealised image of the youth (stored by Nature as a "map" or template for beauty) is worth loving – the actual Essex is dispensable.

> *Sonnet 68*
> Thus is his cheek the map of days out-worn,
> When beauty liv'd and died as flowers do now,
> Before these bastard signs of fair were born,
> Or dur'st [dared] inhabit on a living brow:
> Before the golden tresses of the dead,
> The right of sepulchres, were shorn away,
> To live a second life on second head,
> Ere beauty's dead fleece made another gay:
> In him those holy antique hours are seen,
> Without all ornament, it self and true,
> Making no summer of an other's green [not embellished],
> Robbing no old to dress his beauty new,
> > And him as for a map doth Nature store,
> > To show false Art what beauty was of yore.

Essex is receiving superficial outward praise ("bare truth"), presumably because he is still popular with the crowds, but the Queen writes that those who look into his deeds (69, lines 9–12) will find that he's not as perfect as he appears. The criticism continues to be hard-hitting: "thy odour matcheth not thy show", "thou dost common grow" and "To thy fair flower [you allow churls to] add the rank smell of weeds".

> *Sonnet 69*
> Those parts of thee that the world's eye doth view,
> Want nothing that the thought of hearts can mend:
> All tongues (the voice of souls) give thee that due,
> Utt'ring bare truth [superficial praise], even so as foes Commend [as foes do].
> Thy outward thus with outward praise is crown'd,
> But those same tongues that give thee so thine own,
> In other accents do this praise confound
> By seeing farther than the eye hath shown.
> They look into the beauty of thy mind,
> And that in guess they measure [guessingly measure, estimate] by thy deeds,
> Then churls [common people] their thoughts (although their eyes were kind)
> To thy fair flower add the rank smell of weeds [Contaminate your fair self],
> > But why thy odour matcheth not thy show,
> > The soil [solution] is this, that thou dost common grow.

"Thou dost common grow" is the most crushing and direct comment Elizabeth has made about Essex. By mixing with bad company (sonnet 67, line 1 and the churls of sonnet 69), the "fair flower" (Essex) has become vulgar and uncouth.

Then for the first time the sonnets mention slander and gossip about the youth. Sonnet 70 blames the fair youth for some unspecified misdemeanour of a personal nature: "for slander's mark was ever yet the fair"[2]. The youth is getting a bad press and the Queen's attitude is hardening: she no longer excuses his bad behaviour. In the final couplet she remarks that if people didn't suspect the youth of having a character defect, he could win the hearts of whole kingdoms.

> *Sonnet 70*
> That thou are blam'd shall not be thy defect,
> For slander's mark was ever yet the fair,
> The ornament of beauty is suspect,
> A Crow that flies in heaven's sweetest air.
> So [If] thou be good, slander doth but approve [enhance],
> Thy worth the greater being woo'd of time,
> For Canker vice the sweetest buds doth love,
> And thou present'st a pure unstained prime.
> Thou hast pass'd by the ambush of young days,
> Either not assail'd, or victor being charg'd,
> Yet this thy praise cannot be so thy praise,
> To tie up envy, evermore enlarged,
> > If some suspect of ill masked not thy show,
> > Then thou alone kingdoms of hearts should'st owe.
> > [Then you could command respect from multitudes].

The language used in these sonnets – "to thy fair flower add the rank smell of weeds", "thy odour matcheth not thy show" and "Canker vice the sweetest buds doth love" – indicates a misdemeanour of a personal nature. Sonnets 69 and 70 may refer to Essex's rumoured affair with the Countess of Derby. The word slander is used twice in sonnet 70 indicating that Essex was the subject of malicious gossip.

The following sonnets (71–74) are exceptionally gloomy. The subject matter is Elizabeth's own death. We read of the vile world, funeral bells, ruined churches, ashes of youth, being eaten by worms, being compounded [mixed] with clay, twilight years, black night, memorials, and the dregs of life. Perhaps Elizabeth was ill and severely depressed at the end of 1597. Alternatively, was she so disheartened by Essex's behaviour after the Islands Voyage that she longed for death, for without the 'old' Essex by her side life just wasn't worth living?

Sonnet 71 asks Essex to forget her if thinking about her causes him to be unhappy, or makes others laugh at him.

> *Sonnet 71*
> No Longer mourn for me when I am dead,
> Then you shall hear the surly sullen bell
> Give warning to the world that I am fled

From this vile world with vilest worms to dwell:
Nay if you read this line, remember not,
The hand that writ it, for I love you so,
That I in your sweet thoughts would be forgot,
If thinking on me then should make you woe.
Or if (I say) you look upon this verse,
When I (perhaps) compounded am with clay,
Do not so much as my poor name rehearse;
But let your love even with my life decay.
    Lest the wide world should look into your moan,
    And mock you with me after I am gone.

In sonnet 72 the dejected (and rejected) Queen continues in a slightly different vein – she regards herself as being unworthy of Essex's love:

Sonnet 72, lines 3–4 and 11–14
After my death (dear love) forget me quite,
For you in me can nothing worthy prove.
. . .
My name be buried [Let my memory be buried] where my body is,[3]
And live no more to shame nor me, nor you.
    For I am shamed by that which I bring forth,
    And so should you, to love things nothing worth.

In sonnet 73 the emphasis is on the Queen's age (in late 1597 she was sixty-four years old). She pretends that her age enhances Essex's love, because he loves her all the more, realising that she will soon be gone. (It is almost unimaginable that Shakespeare, now in his thirties, with the peak of his career still before him, should write with this degree of conviction about old age and impending death. But this significant issue is studiously ignored in the standard commentaries.)

Sonnet 73
That time of year thou may'st in me behold,
When yellow leaves, or none, or few do hang
Upon those boughs which shake against the cold,
Bare ruin'd quires [ruined churches], where late the sweet birds sang.
In me thou see'st the twi-light of such day,
As after Sun-set fadeth in the West,
Which by and by black night doth take away,
Death's second self that seals up all in rest.
In me thou see'st the glowing of such fire,
That on the ashes of his youth doth lie,
As the death bed, whereon it must expire,
Consum'd with that which it was nourished by.
    This thou perceiv'st, which makes thy love more strong,
    To love that well, which thou must leave [be separated from] ere long.

Finally, sonnet 74 returns to the theme of the spirit of a person living on in literature. This time, though, the Queen is referring to her own spirit (her better part) which she is putting into words as a sonnet ("this line" of line 3 and "this" in line 14) as well as consecrating (donating) to Essex. Her old body, which she describes as "the dregs of life", she envisages being returned to the earth as "the prey of worms", unremembered by Essex: "Too base of thee to be remembered".

Sonnet 74
But be contented when that fell [cruel] arrest [death],
Without all bail shall carry me away,
My life hath in this line some interest,
Which for memorial still with thee shall stay.
When thou reviewest this, thou dost review,
The very part was consecrate to thee,
The earth can have but earth [her body], which is his due,
My spirit is thine the better part of me,
So then thou hast but lost the dregs of life,
The prey of worms, my body being dead,
The coward conquest of a wretch's knife,
Too base of thee to be [Not worthy of being] remembered,
    The worth of that, is that which it contains,
    And that is this, and this [this sonnet] with thee remains.

Reading sonnets 71–74 one might think that Elizabeth was on her deathbed and the relationship with Essex was all over. She wasn't and it wasn't. The poet did not become the prey of worms – the resigned tone of sonnets 71–74 ("After my death (dear love) forget me quite") was put aside as the Queen records thoughts of a more positive nature in sonnets 75–77 ("And you and love are still my argument"). But although these sonnets reflect a softening of attitude of the Queen towards Essex, and sonnet 75 tells us that the poet and the young man began meeting again, it is clear that the meetings were erratic and unsatisfactory: "Some-time all full with feasting on your sight, And by and by clean starved for a look".

Sonnet 75
So you are to my thoughts as food to life,
Of [Or] as sweet season'd showers are to the ground;
And for the peace of you I hold such strife,
As twixt a miser and his wealth is found.
Now proud as an enjoyer, and anon
Doubting the filching age will steal his treasure,
Now counting best to be with you alone,
Then better'd [glad] that the world may see my pleasure,
Some-time all full with feasting on your sight,
And by and by clean starved for a look,

> Possessing or pursuing no delight
> Save what is had, or must from you be took.
> > Thus do I pine and surfeit day by day,
> > Or gluttoning on all, or all away.

Reading this sonnet 75 (and the next, reproduced below) we might conclude that Essex has returned from his self-imposed exile from the court and has re-joined Elizabeth's circle. Is this conclusion supported by the historical record?

Indeed it is. Again, we find that there is an exact correlation between what we read in the sonnets and actual events. History tells us that the Queen and Essex did patch up their differences: in mid-December Essex returned to London. Initially he chose not to involve himself in state affairs. He was effectively 'going slow' in an attempt to force the Queen's hand. In this endeavour he was successful: on 28 December the Queen decided she could no longer tolerate the strained atmosphere. She restored precedence to her favourite by giving him the honorary title of Earl Marshal of England, which technically gave him precedence over the Earl of Nottingham, whose promotion had prompted Essex's withdrawal from court. It was Lord Nottingham's turn to feel aggrieved. But for the Queen Essex's promotion had its desired effect: on 11 January 1598 Essex renewed his attendance in the House of Lords.

He may have felt that he had won a personal victory, but in finding fault with the Queen's judgement in the matter of the Earl Marshall appointment Essex showed himself to be petty-minded and petulant, hardly desirable qualities for a statesman whose primary concern should have been advancing the Queen's and the nation's interests, not his own.

Despite Essex's erratic and self-centred behaviour, in the first half of 1598 he was given a chance to show that he could be a dependable and useful advisor to the Queen as well as her favourite. He temporarily took over Robert Cecil's post of Secretary while Cecil represented the Queen in France. This period was a relatively quiet time in his life, possibly because he felt he had been given responsibility commensurate with his intellectual abilities. He also had the leisure to exercise his less intellectual skills with the court ladies Mary Howard, Elizabeth Brydges and Elizabeth Russell – the Queen boxed the ears of the two Elizabeths for having assignments with Essex in the privy galleries. He also achieved a small personal success: the Queen relented over her ruling barring Leicester's widow and Essex's mother Lettice Knollys from the court and there was a perfunctory reconciliation between the two proud women.

Sonnets 76 and 77 do not mention relationship difficulties and seem to have been written when Elizabeth was in a quiet and happy frame of mind – perhaps because she was seeing Essex quite often. Sonnet 76 appears to be a simple love poem, but its subject matter is not as simple as might first appear. Lines 5 to 8 should make the reader very curious. In these lines the poet asks a very odd question, considering that Thomas Thorpe's prominent title page and running headline promoting SHAKE-SPEARES SONNETS would appear in his 1609 publication. In modern English the poet is saying 'Why do I always write on the same subject, and why is my creativity always expressed in a similar manner, so that every word almost reveals my name, my origins ("birth") and my upbringing ("where they did proceed")?'

> *Sonnet 76*
> Why is my verse so barren of new pride?
> So far from variation or quick change?
> Why with the time do I not glance aside
> To new found methods, and to compounds strange?
> Why write I still all one, ever the same,
> And keep invention [inspiration] in a noted weed [the same clothes],
> That every word doth almost tell my name,
> Showing their birth, and where they did proceed [originate]?
> O know sweet love I always write of you,
> And you and love are still my argument:
> So all my best is dressing old words new,
> Spending again what is already spent:
>> For as the Sun is daily new and old,
>> So is my love still telling what is told.

Those who believe Shakespeare wrote these lines need to explain why he wrote "every word doth almost tell my name", knowing that his name would appear in Thomas Thorpe's title page. Despite his later claims to gentility, his humble origins were well known: he was the son of a Stratford tradesman who could not write, an actor and shareholder in a London theatre, and a landowner at the time of *Sonnets* publication. Shakespeare had no interest in concealing his origins, which were no mystery. They were unlikely to be of particular interest to anyone or worthy of comment in a sonnet.

The answer to the riddle "Why write I still all one, ever the same . . . That every word doth almost tell my name, Showing their birth, and where they did proceed?" is actually quite simply found – in the sonnet itself. Line 5 puns on Elizabeth I's motto *semper eadem* (always the same). Line 5 could in fact be written 'why do I write *semper eadem, semper eadem*?' Between Essex and Elizabeth this line would have been an 'in' joke. It is strange that no commentators have ever noticed her motto in this sonnet[4].

Sonnet 77 reiterates the concerns expressed in sonnet 59 and reminds the youth that he himself is ageing: "Thy glass will show thee how thy beauties were, Thy dial [face] how thy precious minutes waste [pass]". The youth by this time must have developed a few worry lines: "The wrinkles which thy glass will truly show". The poet seems to have given the youth a blank notebook ("waste blanks"), so that he can write down his thoughts before he forgets them, and re-read them in the future, for his own benefit ("profit").

Sonnet 77
Thy glass will show thee how thy beauties were,
Thy dial [face] how thy precious minutes waste [pass],
The vacant leaves thy mind's imprint will bear,
And of this book, this learning may'st thou taste.
The wrinkles which thy glass will truly show,
Of mouthed [open] graves will give thee memory,
Thou by thy dial's shady stealth may'st know,
Time's thievish progress to eternity.
Look what thy memory cannot contain,
Commit to [Write on] these waste blanks[5], and thou shalt find
Those children nursed, deliver'd from thy brain,
To take a new acquaintance [interpretation?] of thy mind.
    These offices, so oft as thou wilt look,
    Shall profit thee, and much enrich thy book.

Perhaps Elizabeth was prompted to write the untroubled sonnets 76 and 77 because the post-Christmas period of 1597 and early 1598 was a happy time for her and Essex – they were companions again. The book with the "vacant leaves" mentioned in sonnet 77 may have been a present to her favourite. But she soon had a problem to tackle. This took the form of competition for Essex's attention, not from attractive women, but from irritating poets who insisted on praising him.

---

[1] Hammer (1999, p. 321). Lady Derby (Elizabeth, William Cecil's granddaughter and Robert Cecil's favourite niece) was unhappily married to William Stanley, the 6th Earl of Derby. Essex's liaison with her may have begun in 1595. Shortly before Christmas 1596 Anne Bacon (Francis Bacon's mother), accused Essex of adultery with Lady Derby. His involvement with Lady Derby is unlikely to have endeared him to Robert Cecil, who after being appointed Secretary of State in 1596 was consolidating his position as the most powerful person in England after the Queen.
[2] Elizabeth also uses the phrase "slander's mark" in her 1598 translation of Erasmus' version of Plutarch's *De Curiositate* (Mueller and Scodel 2009, p. 423).
[3] Alternatively, in this line the poet could be telling the reader 'my true identity will be found in my tomb'.
[4] None of the editors of the standard works on *Sonnets* (Kerrigan 1986; Wyndham 1999; Burrow 2002; Duncan-Jones 2010) have recognised Elizabeth I's motto in this sonnet. Alone among the editors Burrow (2002, p. 532) notes that "birth" (line 8) means "rank, station, position" but he fails to build on this observation, or explain how these terms might apply to Shakespeare, or why Shakespeare should think his lowly rank is worth mentioning.
[5] Thorpe's 1609 edition has "blacks" but this word makes little sense in the context, and is probably a misprint.

19. The Rival Poets

a better spirit doth use your name
– Sonnet 80

Elizabeth was displeased when Essex was idolised by the public (53, 57, 58), but she became particularly annoyed when Essex captured the attention of other writers – Essex was hers, not theirs. She devoted eight or nine sonnets (78–86) to working out her views on this problem. (Sonnet 81, in the middle of the rival poets sequence, does not mention a rival poet).

The intriguing references to rival poets have kept commentators occupied. Even Kerrigan, who argued that the sonnets were "not biographical in a psychological mode" conceded that it was "unlikely that the antagonist was merely invented"[1]. One of the rival poets is referred to as "a better spirit" (80) so he or she was probably a poet with some standing.

Essex was popular, both with the common people and the literary public. He was never dull – he was always 'up to something'. He liked being in the news. He cultivated popularity by accepting dedications to over fifty books, many promoting the Protestant cause[2]. He was also the subject of several laudatory poems. The poet George Chapman compared him to the legendary Achilles. Praise also came from the poets Edmund Spenser, John Mundy, Thomas Watson and George Peele. Of course, much of this praise and flattery derived from self-interest. Essex's name in a dedication helped sales, and if Essex himself liked the publication a gratuity might be forthcoming. For Essex, his name in a book's dedication enhanced his status among the educated public.

1598 was George Chapman's big year, in which he not only published his translation *Seven Books of the Iliad*, but also his book *Achilles' Shield*. In the epistle to the former he addressed Essex as "The most abundant President of true Noblesse" and "most true Achilles whom by sacred prophecy Homer did but prefigure in his admirable object and in whose unmatched virtues shine the dignities of the soul and the whole excellence of royal humanity".

Chapman's tactless mention of Essex's "royal humanity" raised Essex's standing to that of the Queen. It probably inspired her sarcastic response (sonnet 78, line 8) that a rival poet, when praising the youth, has "given grace a double Majesty" (i.e., has equated Essex with royalty), and strongly indicates that Chapman is the rival poet to whom Elizabeth refers.

Sonnet 78
So oft have I invok'd thee for my Muse.
And found such fair assistance in my verse,
As [And it seems as if] every *Alien* pen hath got my use,
And under thee their poesie disperse.
Thine eyes, that taught the dumb on high to sing,

And heavy ignorance aloft to fly,
Have added feathers to the learneds' wing,
And given grace[3] a double Majesty.
Yet be most proud of that which I compile,
Whose influence is thine, and born of thee,
In others' works thou dost but mend the style [you just add embellishment],
And Arts with thy sweet graces graced be.
    But thou art all my art, and dost advance
    As high as learning, my rude ignorance [my amateur creations].

Edmund Spenser, in his poem *Prothalamion*, also lauded Essex. After Essex's return from Cadiz he described him as "great England's glory and the world's wide wonder". He argued that Essex should further the cause of Protestantism in Ireland and wrote "such a one I could name upon whom the eye of all England is fixed and our last hopes now rest" – another slight on Elizabeth, implying that England's last hopes no longer rested on her.

George Peele in his verse[4] called him the "Shepherd of Arcadia" and in 1589 urged Essex to "royalise his fame" – almost an invitation to commit treason. The poets John Mundy and Thomas Watson were similarly effusive.

No other candidates that might qualify as the fair youth of the sonnets were as widely praised by poets as Essex. The documented adulation of Essex by Elizabethan poets, and in particular by George Chapman, when compared to the vocabulary of the rival poet sonnets, all but confirms that the "fair youth" praised by the rival poets of the sonnets is Essex.

In sonnet 80 Elizabeth imagines Essex to be the ocean ("broad main") bearing the Queen's small boat ("saucy bark", representing her amateur poetic efforts) alongside tall ships ("the proudest sail", representing the works of established poets).

Sonnet 80
O how I faint when I of you do write,
Knowing a better spirit doth use your name,
And in the praise thereof spends all his might,
To make me tongue-tied speaking of your fame.
But since your worth (wide as the Ocean is)
The humble as the proudest sail doth bear,
My saucy bark [small boat] (inferior far to his)
On your broad main doth wilfully appear.
Your shallowest help will hold me up afloat,
Whilst he upon your soundless deep doth ride,
Or (being wreck'd) I am a worthless boat,
He of tall building, and of goodly pride.
    Then If he thrive and I be cast away,
    The worst was this, my love was my decay.

The last six lines of the sonnet make the essential point: whether her poetic work survives (stays "afloat") or not ("wreck'd") depends entirely on him (their mutual affection) whereas the big boats of the poetic establishment proudly sail on regardless (implying that their writings are conventional and mechanical and not based on mutual love or reciprocated personal commitment).

Sonnet 81 interrupts the rival poets sequence and returns to a familiar theme: that the poet is old but the youth's qualities will live on in the poet's verse ("Your monument shall be my gentle verse"), which will be read by men [people] far into the future, because of the "virtue" (read 'high quality') of the poet's writings.

Sonnet 81
Or shall I live your Epitaph to make,
Or you survive when I in earth am rotten,
From hence your memory death cannot take,
Although in me each part will be forgotten.
Your name from hence immortal life shall have,
Though I (once gone) to all the world must die,
The earth can yield me but a common grave,
When you entombed in men's eyes shall lie,
Your monument shall be my gentle verse,
Which eyes not yet created shall o'er-read,
And tongues to be, your being shall rehearse,
When all the breathers of this world are dead,
    You still shall live (such virtue hath my Pen)
    Where breath most breathes, even in the mouths of men.

Some editors infer that the term "common grave" in line 7 refers to a communal or undistinguished burial, or charnel house[5]. But in these lines the poet is not contrasting a "common grave" with an elaborate grave, but is contrasting a "common grave" in the sense of 'a grave in the usual style' by which the poet will be remembered with the "monument" *in verse* by which the youth will be remembered, i.e., the sonnets she is busy writing.

Elizabeth must have been familiar with the effusive flattery ("strained ... Rhetoric") addressed to potential sponsors by poets in their dedications: "The dedicated words which writers use Of their fair subject, blessing every book" (82) and argues that their flattery would be better applied to subjects more in need of praise than Essex:

Sonnet 82, lines 13–14
And their gross painting might be better us'd,
Where cheeks need blood, in thee it is abus'd.

In sonnet 83 she comments on her own restraint ("being mute"), which is ironic, since she is writing her 83rd sonnet under Shakespeare's name! But it is unlikely that anyone (with the possible exception of Essex) knew of her poetic reflections – the sonnets were Elizabeth's private diary. Then she continues her criticism of insincere praise written by others – their lifeless words are like a tomb, and Essex's real qualities are vastly preferable to the words of both poets (perhaps meaning Chapman and another poet, or possibly Chapman and herself):

> *Sonnet 83, lines 11–14*
> For I impair not beauty, being mute,
> When others would give life, and [but instead] bring a tomb.
>   There lives more life in one of your fair eyes,
>   Than both your Poets can in praise devise.

We get more insight into the youth's character in sonnet 84 – he is vain and likes to be praised, which only encourages his poetic flatterers: "You . . . add a curse, Being fond on [of] praise, which makes your praises worse". Elizabeth remarks (85) that the "praise richly compil'd" by the rival poets restrains her own creativity. While others publish highly polished adulatory verses, she keeps quiet because she "holds his [her] rank before" i.e., she restrains herself because of her royal status, so as to maintain her self-respect and protect her public image.

> *Sonnet 85*
> My tongue-tied Muse in manners holds her still [is respectfully quiet],
> While comments of your praise richly compil'd,
> Reserve [Add to] their Character [subject] with golden quill,
> And precious phrase by all the Muses fil'd [filled].
> I think good thoughts, whilst other write good words,
> And like unlettered clerk still cry Amen,
> To every Hymn [song of praise] that able spirit [poet] affords,
> In polish'd form of well refined pen [an able writer].
> Hearing you prais'd, I say 'tis so, 'tis true,
> And to the most of praise add some-thing more,
> But that is in my thought, whose love to you
> (Though words come hind-most) holds his rank before
> [I keep quiet because I'm conscious of my image],
>   Then others, for the [?their] breath of words [shallow volubility] respect,
>   Me for my dumb thoughts, speaking in effect.

George Chapman was passionate about Greek literature and Homer in particular. Educated Elizabethans would have been familiar with his introduction to *The Shadow of Night* (1594) in which he wrote that the true poet cannot succeed without receiving inspiration from a "heavenly familiar"[6]. Chapman considered that his celestial help came from Homer, for in his book *The Tears of Peace* (published in 1609) he acknowledged communing by night with the shadow (spirit) of the ancient poet. In sonnet 86, in which Elizabeth writes "was it his spirit, by spirits taught to write . . . that struck me dead?" (lines 5–6), it is likely that she was referring to George Chapman and Homer:

> *Sonnet 86*
> Was it the proud full sail of his great verse,
> Bound for the prize of (all too precious) you,
> That did my ripe thoughts in my brain inhearse [bury],
> Making their tomb the womb wherein they grew?
> Was it his [?Chapman's] spirit, by spirits taught to write,
> Above a mortal pitch, that struck me dead?
> No, neither he, nor his compeers [associates] by night
> Giving him aid, my verse astonished [inhibited].
> He nor that affable familiar ghost [?Homer]
> Which nightly gulls [provides] him with intelligence,
> As victors of my silence cannot boast,
> I was not sick of any fear from thence.
>   But when your countenance [presence] fill'd up his [the rival poet's] line,
>   Then lacked I matter, that enfeebled mine.

---

[1] Kerrigan (1986, p. 272).
[2] Hammer (1999, p. 212).
[3] Kerrigan (1986, p. 272) argues that "grace" refers to the rival poets, but his conclusion results from a misreading of the sonnet. In lines 5 and 6, the poet associates the rival poets with negative qualities: they are "dumb" and possessed by "heavy ignorance", so "double Majesty" and "grace" must refer to the gracious (cultured) youth himself. Note also that in line 12 the "sweet graces" of the youth are mentioned. Paraphrased, lines 5–8 could be rewritten: 'Your eyes have bewitched all sorts of dumb poets, and now these mediocre scribblers are excelling themselves by doubling your good qualities to royal proportions'. In addition, it should be noted that in Elizabethan times the word grace was commonly used to describe aristocrats, but not poets. For example, in sonnet 40 the poet addresses the promiscuous youth as "Lascivious grace".
[4] In Peele's *Eclogue Gratulatorie*, published in 1589 (Hammer 1999, pp. 215–216).
[5] For example, Burrow (2002, p. 542).
[6] Spivack (1967, p. 16).

20. A Relationship on the Rocks

Farewell thou art too dear for my possessing
— Sonnet 87

When Elizabeth first met Essex, she could only praise him. He was the world's ornament. In sonnets 19–86 we noted the gradual change in the relationship between Elizabeth and Essex after their first encounter. These sonnets progress from simple regard, to adoration, to love. Subsequently, beginning with the youth's capacity for "murd'rous hate" (10), the poems become more critical, though interspersed with assurances of the poet's commitment.

As the relationship becomes more complex, Elizabeth recognises more faults in the youth – he is temperamental, argumentative, has affairs, is vain, doesn't pay Elizabeth enough attention, and loves flattery. He travels, but homecomings are not the happy occasions envisioned by the Queen. His popularity, and the praise heaped on him by other poets, she finds annoying. But despite recognising Essex's imperfections she remains positive. Her recurring theme is that she longs for Essex's company and that his beauty will live on in her verse after her death, which she foresees as imminent.

Sonnet 75 describes a reconciliation of sorts, after the coolness between the two following the Islands Voyage. Subsequently the royal poet was distracted by the attention given to Essex by other poets. But sonnet 87 begins a long sequence of poems describing a relationship under great strain. The poet is exasperated and considers breaking off the relationship for ever. Sonnet 87 begins with her goodbye: "Farewell thou art too dear for my possessing". Its relentless simple rhymes close each formal one-line statement like full stops. The vocabulary – "possessing", "estimate", "charter", "releasing", "bonds", "determinate", "granting", "patent", "misprision" and "judgement" – is harsh, legal and uncompromising. The poem conjures up an image of Essex in the dock and an angry Elizabeth pacing around the room and blaming herself for what appears to be a breakdown of their relationship.

Sonnet 87
Farewell thou art too dear for my possessing,
And like enough thou know'st thy estimate,
The Charter of thy worth gives thee releasing:
My bonds in thee [claims on you] are all determinate [cancelled].
For how do I hold thee but by thy granting [your desire],
And for that riches where is my deserving?
The cause of this fair gift in me is wanting [I don't deserve you],
And so my patent [right] back again is swerving [reverts to you].
Thy self thou gav'st, thy own worth then not knowing,
Or me to whom thou gav'st it, else mistaking,

> So thy great gift upon misprision [error or misunderstanding] growing,
> Comes home again [Returns to you], on better judgement making.
>> Thus have I had thee as a dream doth flatter,
>> In sleep a King, but waking no such matter.

Each line is a dispassionate and resigned statement of fact – a list of disappointments. Elizabeth describes how she is returning to Essex his gift of love and affection. Her judgment and immense self-control have overcome any soft emotions she might have had for him. She still finds it hard to criticise Essex. She believes, or makes herself believe, that she is undeserving of his attention. She also takes the blame for the relationship breakdown (lines 7–12). Only in the final couplet, containing a hint of the Queen's sadness that the relationship has been like a dream, is there relief from the legal terminology. Notice also the little joke about her being a King in her dreams. The sonnet does not tell us what has caused the upset.

By the time she writes the next sonnet she is in a quieter frame of mind. Sonnet 88 is the logical sequel to the uncompromising statements of the previous sonnet. The Queen asks Essex to take a look at his situation in the cool light of reason and to see her good points as well as the things he dislikes: "When thou shalt be dispos'd to set me light, And place my merit in the eye of scorn". If Essex does this, she will fight against her own inclinations in order to prove him virtuous, while admitting her own "faults conceal'd" with which she is "attainted". By taking the blame for any difficulties, she argues, she does him a favour: "Such is my love, to thee I so belong, That for thy right, my self will bear all wrong".

> *Sonnet 88*
> When thou shalt be dispos'd to set me light[1],
> And place [substitute] my merit in the eye of scorn,
> Upon thy side, against my self I'll fight,
> And prove thee virtuous, though thou art forsworn:
> With mine own weakness being best acquainted,
> Upon thy part I can set down a story
> Of faults conceal'd, wherein I am attainted:
> That thou in losing me, shall win much glory:
> And I by this will be a gainer too,
> For bending all my loving thoughts on thee,
> The injuries that to myself I do,
> Doing thee vantage, double vantage me.
>> Such is my love, to thee I so belong,
>> That for thy right, my self will bear all wrong.

In the following sonnets (89–96) hatred, falseness, revolt, loss and hurt are the main themes. These sonnets are crucial to our understanding of the whole sonnet sequence. We have here evidence of a very serious breakdown of the relationship between the poet and the youth. What has happened to cause the relationship to disintegrate to the point that the youth has poured scorn on the Queen (88, line 2)? If Elizabeth is the author of the sonnets, and they are about Essex, history should record a major disagreement between Elizabeth and Essex in 1598.

The historical record does not disappoint. On 1 July 1598 an incident occurred that presaged Essex's downfall. The earl, always easily slighted and temperamental, turned his back on the Queen during a heated Privy Council discussion on who should be Lord Deputy of Ireland. The equally fiery Elizabeth boxed his ears. Essex reportedly reacted by instinctively putting his hand on his sword as if to draw it, but was restrained by Privy Councillors present. Neither Essex nor the Queen would apologise for their impulsive and imprudent actions and there was a long stand-off. However, they did correspond, Essex on one occasion referring to "this scandal".

This incident, that appeared to have ended their relationship for all time (remember how it is described in sonnet 87: "Farewell thou art too dear for my possessing"), is surely the event behind the estrangement and exasperation described in sonnets 87–88, and the next eight. The separation was unlike earlier partings following tiffs, because trust had been betrayed and lost.

The estrangement as recorded in the sonnets becomes really serious. There is a long stand-off. The words "hate" and "hatred", "revolt", "inconstant" and "false" creep into the sonnets. In sonnet 89 Elizabeth again offers to take all blame, but by the time she writes sonnets 90 and 91 her thoughts have moved on. She has come to the realisation that, after all, the fault lies with Essex and not with her – he is misbehaving and spinning out the quarrel in order to gain the upper hand: "Give not a windy night a rainy morrow, To linger out a purpos'd over-throw" (90). The long stand-off makes Elizabeth feel "most wretched" (91).

> *Sonnet 90*
> Then hate me when thou wilt, if ever, now,
> Now while the world is bent my deeds to cross [while I have other troubles],
> Join with the spite of fortune, make me bow,
> And do not drop in [crush my spirits] for an after loss:
> Ah do not, when my heart hath 'scaped this sorrow [when I'm recovering],
> Come in the rearward of a conquered woe,
> Give not a windy night a rainy morrow,
> To linger out [prolong] a purpos'd [planned] over-throw [rejection].
> If thou wilt leave me, do not leave me last,
> When other petty griefs have done their spite,
> But in the onset come [be 'upfront' about how you feel], so shall I taste
> At first the very worst of fortune's might [Let's deal with the big issues first].
>> And other strains of woe [disappointments], which now seem woe,
>> Compar'd with loss of thee, will not seem so.

Sonnet 91 is a simple uncontrived poem. It compares the pleasures of the rich to the pleasures of being loved. Notice how aristocratic the recreational pleasures are. The love of the youth is not compared to the rustic diversions of a Warwickshire landowner or the artistic achievements of a London actor; it is compared to the enjoyment afforded by the accoutrements of high birth: wealth, the latest fashions, owning horses, and hunting with hawks and hounds.

Sonnet 91
Some glory in their birth, some in their skill,
Some in their wealth, some in their body's force,
Some in their garments though new-fangled ill:
Some in their Hawks and Hounds, some in their Horse
And every humour hath his adjunct pleasure,
Wherein it finds a joy above the rest,
But these particulars are not my measure,
All these I better² in one general best.
Thy love is better than high birth to me,
Richer than wealth, prouder than garments' cost,
Of more delight than Hawks or Horses be:
And having thee, of all men's pride I boast.
    Wretched in this alone, that thou may'st take,
    All this away, and me most wretched make.

Elizabeth is deeply unhappy. She no longer pretends that she is at fault. But she still doesn't criticise Essex directly. She simply points out that the pleasure she and people of her class usually derive from fine clothes etc. matter little ("these particulars are not my measure") in comparison with the delight of having a loving soul mate. But Essex has the power to destroy their relationship and make her feel wretched.

In sonnet 92 we see that Elizabeth is coming to terms with the fact that Essex does have quite serious character faults which she unequivocally describes in negative terms: for example "inconstant mind" and "revolt". Notice that in the last line Elizabeth writes that she wants to believe that Essex is a better person than he appears. He may be false, but she's not sure. She has left the door open a chink, to allow for a reconciliation.

Sonnet 92
But do thy worst to steal thy self away,
For term of life thou art assured mine,
And life no longer than thy love will stay,
For it depends upon that love of thine.
Then need I not to fear the worst of wrongs,
When in the least of them my life hath end,
I see, a better state to me belongs
Than that, which on thy humour doth depend.

> Thou can'st not vex me with inconstant mind,
> Since that my life on thy revolt doth lie
> [I would be as good as dead without you],
> O what a happy title do I find,
> Happy to have thy love, happy to die!
>> But what's so blessed fair that fears no blot,
>> Thou may'st be false, and yet I know it not.

But the impasse continues, as is evident from the increasingly negative tone of the sonnets. Sonnets 93 and 94 don't reveal an improvement in their relationship: "Thy looks with me, thy heart in other place" (93). In sonnet 94 the first ten lines dwell on the nature of greatness, self-control and magnanimity; the next four on greatness and magnanimity corrupted. The poet reflects on how powerful people who resist temptation "inherit heaven's graces". But if those from whom much is expected get infected by evil they become more despicable than ordinary bad people: "Lilies that fester, smell far worse than weeds".

> *Sonnet 94*
> They that have power to hurt, and will do none,
> That do not do the thing, they most do show,
> Who moving others, are themselves as stone,
> Unmoved, cold, and to temptation slow:
> They rightly do inherit heaven's graces,
> And husband nature's riches from expense,
> They are the Lords and owners of their faces,
> Others, but stewards of their excellence:
> The summer's flower is to the summer sweet,
> Though to it self, it only live and die,
> But if that flower with base infection meet,
> The basest weed out-braves his dignity:
>> For sweetest things turn sourest by their deeds,
>> Lilies that fester, smell far worse than weeds.

There is no doubt that she is referring to Essex. He persisted to act in a most disappointing way. Refusing to apologise to the Queen about his behaviour in the Privy Council meeting, he remained at his home in Wanstead, licking his festering wounds.

Having organised her thoughts on decomposing lilies, Elizabeth then contemplates the paradox that Essex's vices are contained in such a beautiful frame. They are compared to canker in a rose (95). Sonnet 95 is entirely about appearances concealing reality: the fragrant rose is diseased; Essex's sins are concealed by his sweet nature; his vices are concealed in a mansion (probably meaning his attractive body); his veil of beauty conceals every "blot" [imperfection]. As usual the summing-up is in the last two lines, and takes the form of a direct warning: "Take heed (dear heart) . . . The hardest knife ill us'd doth lose his edge", i.e., Essex's outstanding talents and good qualities will become irrelevant if he continues to misbehave. Once again we observe a sonnet that so appropriately sums up the contrast between Essex's appearance and behaviour that there can be no doubt that it was written by someone deeply attached to him, who wishes he was as fair as he appears.

> *Sonnet 95*
> How sweet and lovely dost thou make the shame,
> Which like a canker in the fragrant Rose,
> Doth spot the beauty of thy budding name?
> Oh in what sweets dost thou thy sins enclose!
> That tongue that tells the story of thy days,
> (Making lascivious comments on thy sport)
> Cannot dispraise, but in a kind of praise,
> Naming thy name, blesses an ill report.
> Oh what a mansion have those vices got,
> Which for their habitation chose out thee,
> Where beauty's veil doth cover every blot,
> And all things turns to fair, that eyes can see!
> > Take heed (dear heart) of this large privilege,
> > The hardest knife ill us'd doth lose his edge.

Elizabeth remarks that even the cheapest jewel will look good on the finger of a Queen: "As on the finger of a throned Queen, The basest Jewel will be well esteem'd" (96, lines 5–6). In this pithy couplet the Queen is saying it is she who has raised him from relative obscurity, and he only sparkles in court and in public affairs because he is associated with her. (Had Essex read these lines, they would have sent a shiver down his spine.) But Elizabeth still keeps open the possibility of a reconciliation: she writes "But do not so, I love thee in such sort, As thou being mine, mine is thy good report"[3].

> *Sonnet 96*
> Some say thy fault is youth, some wantoness,
> Some say thy grace is youth and gentle sport,
> Both grace and sport are lov'd of more and less:
> Thou mak'st faults graces, that to thee resort:
> As on the finger of a throned Queen,
> The basest Jewel will be well esteem'd:
> So are those errors that in thee are seen,
> To truths translated, and for true things deem'd.
> How many Lambs might the stern Wolf betray,
> If like a Lamb he could his looks translate.
> How many gazers might'st thou lead away,
> If thou would'st use the strength of all thy state?
> > But do not so, I love thee in such sort,
> > As thou being mine, mine is thy good report.

The sonnet sequence 87–96 began with Elizabeth taking the blame for the relationship difficulties and ended with her admitting that the fault for their relationship breakdown lies not with her but with Essex. Then we note a change of tone – sonnet 97 is more reflective. The youth is described as "the pleasure of the fleeting year". The poet expresses a yearning for the youth's company but also feelings of sadness and apprehension. The reason is clear: the youth is not around, the poet misses him, and consequently is less critical – "And thou away, the very birds are mute" (line 12). Usefully for researchers looking for clues as to when he was absent, the sonnet tells us he was away in summer and autumn (lines 5 and 6).

> *Sonnet 97*
> How like a Winter hath my absence been
> From thee, the pleasure of the fleeting year?
> What freezings have I felt, what dark days seen?
> What old December's bareness every where?
> And yet this time remov'd was summer's time,
> And teeming Autumn big with rich increase,
> Bearing the wanton burden of the prime,
> Like widowed wombs after their Lords' decease:
> Yet this abundant issue seem'd to me,
> But hope of Orphans, and un-fathered fruit,
> For Summer and his pleasures wait on thee,
> And thou away, the very birds are mute.
>   Or if they sing, 'tis with so dull a cheer,
>   That leaves look pale, dreading the Winter's near [imminent Winter].

Those who still doubt the Elizabeth-Essex hypothesis might ask this relevant question: does history tell us that Essex was still absent from court in the autumn of 1598? It does. Essex, still sulking, fell ill in September 1598, and Elizabeth, by way of a peace gesture, offered him her doctor's services. He only returned to court in late September or early October of that year.

---

[1] Seymour-Smith (1963) writes that "set me light" means "to despise me". But it could also mean 'to clarify the situation' as in 'shed light on the subject'.

[2] Seymour-Smith (1963) replaces "bitter" in the 1609 edition by 'better', which makes better sense.

[3] The generally critical sonnet sequences 33–36 and 87–96 both end with the same couplet. The optimistic couplet possibly served as a kind of refrain to lift the poet's spirits.

21. Laughing Saturn and the Irish Campaign

heavy Saturn laughed and leapt
– Sonnet 98

Sonnet 97 tells us that the poet and the youth were separated for much of the summer and autumn of 1598. The next sonnet tells us that they are again separated, this time in spring, and specifically in April: "From you have I been absent in the spring, When proud pied [colourful] April (dressed in all his trim) Hath put a spirit of youth in every thing" (98). In this cheerful spring season even "heavy *Saturn* laughed and leapt".

Sonnet 98
From you have I been absent in the spring,
When proud pied [colourful] April (dressed in all his trim)
Hath put a spirit of youth in every thing:
That heavy *Saturn* laughed and leapt with him.
Yet nor the lays of birds, nor the sweet smell
Of different flowers in odour and in hue,
Could make me any summer's story tell:
Or from their proud lap pluck them where they grew:
Nor did I wonder at the Lily's white,
Nor praise the deep vermilion in the Rose,
They were but sweet, but figures of delight:
Drawn after you, you pattern of all those.
    Yet seem'd it Winter still, and you away,
    As with your shadow I with these did play.

William Lilly, writing in 1647, described a person whose ruling planet is Saturn as "in his Acts severe, in words reserved, in speaking and giving very spare, in labour patient, in arguing or disputing grave, in obtaining the goods of this life studious and solicitous, in all manner of actions austere."[1]. Similar sentiments were expressed in Elizabethan times: the discreet and trusted Treasurer William Cecil (Lord Burghley) was described, somewhat maliciously, as "old Saturnus" by Sir Edward Norris in 1591: "old Saturnus is a melancholy and wayward planet but yet predominant here"[2] – because Norris resented the way Cecil exerted his power and influence. But in sonnet 98 the author writes that the normally austere ("heavy") Saturn was laughing and leaping. What does this line mean?

The Shakespeare scholar George Wyndham was the first to point out that if, in sonnet 98, the poet is referring to Saturn being unusually conspicuous in the night sky (which seems likely), then the reference to April, spring and Saturn may provide enough astronomical detail to date this sonnet[3]. In the late 1880s Wyndham checked with a Mr Heath, an astronomer at the Royal Observatory, Edinburgh, as to when Saturn was particularly bright in the night sky in the years 1592 to 1609. He selected these years because not only do they span the years when the sonnets are likely to have been written, but also because during this time Saturn was periodically in opposition (a technical term meaning the planet was on the opposite side of the Earth to the Sun, with the Sun, Earth and Saturn approximately in line) and therefore especially bright and conspicuous. Mr Heath in turn consulted sixteenth century research by the Czech astronomer Leovitius, and specifically his publication *Ephemeris*. Leovitius calculated that Saturn was at its brightest on 24 March 1599, 4 April 1600, 17 April 1601, 29 April 1602 and 11 May 1603 in the Elizabethan (Julian) calendar.

Figure 4. The night sky as it would be seen by an observer looking south from London on the evening of 24 March 1599 (3 April 1599 in our Gregorian calendar). On this date Saturn was in opposition (on the opposite side of Earth to the Sun) and the brightest it had been for several years. It was also in the constellation Virgo, and formed a pair with Spica, the brightest star of this constellation. (The constellation Leo is shown for reference.) The celestial pairing of Saturn and Spica in Virgo may have inspired the laughing and leaping imagery in sonnet 98, and if this is the case, sonnet 98 was probably written in late March or early April 1599. *The image on which this figure is based was produced using the* Stellarium *program and was kindly supplied by Dr Brad Tucker, Mt Stromlo Observatory, Canberra.*

The Canberra astronomer Bruce Peterson, using the *Ephemeris* program, confirmed these dates and observed that Saturn would have been especially bright for several days either side of 24 March 1599. He also showed that Saturn would have risen in the early evening sky in the constellation Virgo, rising high alongside Spica, the brightest star in this constellation (Figure 4). The planet and Spica would have looked like twins, "but Spica would have appeared blue-white, and Saturn yellow-white"[4].

The next question to ask is: what was going on in Essex's life around 24 March 1599, and does it have any relevance to what we read in sonnet 98, and Bruce Peterson's observations?

The answer is particularly interesting. In late 1598 Essex saw a potential solution to his dispute with the Queen and the impasse over what to do about the Irish rebellion – he would seek military glory by crushing the rebels with an army led by himself (perhaps forgetting that his father lost his fortune, health and his life trying to achieve a similar result). He offered his services to the Queen. The Queen initially dithered but eventually accepted his offer. On 27 March 1599, with Saturn shining brightly in the night sky alongside Spica, Essex left London in style, in charge of a force of twenty thousand infantry and two thousand cavalry – a huge army. In April 1599 he arrived in Dublin to take up his post of Lord Deputy and begin his campaign against Tyrone's rebels. Writing sonnet 98 (probably in early April 1599) Elizabeth must have wondered whether she would ever see him again. So once again, the historical events in Essex's life fit exactly with what we read in *Sonnets*.

But there is more to be gained from this sonnet. As mentioned, in late March Saturn was visible in the constellation Virgo, appearing alongside the bright star Spica. Such a bright celestial pairing in a constellation with special significance for the Virgin Queen is, I suggest, the reason why Elizabeth (who loved dancing) mentioned Saturn laughing and leaping in sonnet 98.

Essex was away for months – the Irish campaign dragged on without a decisive result. Although Essex had departed from London and England with a strong army, with the Queen's blessing, and in the full expectation that he would bring the Irish rebels to heel, his campaign was a big disappointment. Essex was not an effective commander. In the field he was as temperamental and impetuous as at court. He was unsuited to a long morale-draining struggle demanding strategic thinking. His campaign was slow and unfocused. His army was plagued by illness and desertions; by 30 July 1599 Essex was leading only 600 infantry and 500 cavalry[5], a fraction of the original force. He squandered military effort on secondary targets while failing to engage Tyrone's forces in a decisive battle. But there is also evidence that he was set up to fail by his enemy at court, Robert Cecil, who diverted resources intended to facilitate a base at Loch Foyle in Ulster (the harbour for Londonderry) to Dublin, making the original plan for a northern base unworkable[6].

As we have learned to expect, the poet becomes more reflective when the youth is absent. During the extended separation from Essex Elizabeth is true to form. Sonnet 99 (strictly not a sonnet as it has 15 lines) describes the flowers that have acquired ("stolen") Essex's attributes: the violet has stolen his sweet breath and the "purple pride" of his cheeks. The lily has stolen the whiteness of his hands. The golden marjoram has stolen the colour of his hair. Finally, Elizabeth comes to the point: the pink eglantine rose ("nor red, nor white") representing the Queen has stolen [acquired] Essex's breath [his soul or life force] but "A vengeful canker eat him up to death" (i.e. she is dying from grief) because he's absent and she knows that their relationship is fragile.

Sonnets 100–107 are also sonnets of separation and, as noted for sonnets written during Essex's previous absences from court (27–28, 37–39, 43–52, 54–56 and 60—65), are more philosophical and reflective than those written when he is present. This set of eight sonnets portrays a relationship less troubled than the actual. The first four all mention the poet's muse and are full of sad reflections. Elizabeth tells her muse to be active and not to be silent: "Where art thou Muse that thou forget'st so long, To speak of that which gives thee all thy might?" (100). In the same sonnet she urges her muse "Give my love fame faster than time wastes life, So thou prevent'st his scythe, and crooked knife". The message of sonnet 101 is similar: it lies within her muse's power "To make him [Essex] much out-live a gilded tomb: And to be prais'd of ages yet to be"; she demands "Then do thy office Muse", i.e. 'Get working!'.

What is really happening is that Elizabeth's muse is failing her because Essex is failing her. She is finding it increasingly difficult to express regard for Essex: "sweets grown common lose their dear delight" (102); "Alack what poverty my Muse brings forth" (103); and "Oh blame me not if I no more can write" (103). But she still tries hard to be positive, and as usual finds it easier to think positively when Essex is absent and she can idealise her relationship with him. It was summertime when sonnet 102 was written – "Not that the summer is less pleasant now" – which would date this sonnet and sonnet 104 (below) to about July 1599. The latter sonnet recognises that Essex is growing older, and that he is losing his youthful good looks. His beauty is slowly disappearing, like the movement of the hands of a clock, at a barely perceptible but relentless pace (lines 9–10).

> *Sonnet 104*
> To me fair friend you never can be old,
> For as you were when first your eye I eyed,
> Such seems your beauty still: Three Winters cold,
> Have from the forests shook three summers' pride,
> Three beauteous springs to yellow *Autumn* turned,
> In process [As a procession] of the seasons have I seen,
> Three April perfumes in three hot Junes burn'd,
> Since first I saw you fresh which yet are green.
> Ah yet doth beauty like a Dial [clock] hand,
> Steal from his figure, and no pace perceiv'd [imperceptibly],
> So your sweet hue [form, appearance], which me thinks still doth stand
> Hath motion [Is changing], and mine eye may be deceived.
>   For fear of which, hear this thou age unbred [people still to be born],
>   Ere you were born was beauty's summer dead.

The sonnet tells us that the poet has known the youth for nine years[7]: three winters have replaced three summers, three springs have turned to autumn, and three Aprils have turned to June "since first I saw you fresh which yet are green [youthful, full of vigour]". (The word "fresh" in line 8 is open to different interpretations: it could mean 'for the first time', 'again', or 'in all your beauty'. Alternatively, it may have the sexual connotation of naked and impudent, matching the association of green with sexual vigour and virility[8].) By 1599 Elizabeth and Essex had been associated with each other (and possibly intimate) for about nine years – they became close some time after the Earl of Leicester's death in 1588 – which is another indication that the sonnets' chronology matches details of the Elizabeth-Essex relationship.

Although Essex's beauty is fading, Elizabeth insists (at least when he is not present) that he has a beautiful character, described as "fair, kind and true" (105). She deludes herself that he is "constant in a wondrous excellence".

Sonnet 105
Let not my love be call'd Idolatry
Nor my beloved as an Idol show,
Since all alike my songs and praises be
To one, of one, still such, and ever so.
Kind is my love today, to morrow kind,
Still constant in a wondrous excellence,
Therefore my verse to constancy confin'd,
One thing expressing, leaves out difference.
Fair, kind, and true, is all my argument,
Fair, kind and true, varying to other words [to words having the same effect],
And in this change is my invention spent,
Three themes in one, which wondrous scope affords.
    Fair, kind, and true have often liv'd alone.
    Which three till now, never kept seat in one.

The ponderous and stately sonnet 107 is the last of the reflective sonnets in this sequence. The references to "dreaming on things to come", "the wide world" and "this most balmy time" suggest that the poet is thinking about big political or historical events. Commentators have speculated at length on which events the poet had in mind. For example, Kerrigan[9] devoted almost 8 pages of notes to this sonnet. However, scholars cannot agree on what the poet is referring to.

Sonnet 107
Not mine own fears, nor the prophetic soul,
Of the wide world, dreaming on things to come,
Can yet the lease of my true love control,
Suppos'd as forfeit to a confin'd doom.
The mortal Moon hath her eclipse endur'd,
And the sad Augurs mock their own presage [predictions],

> Uncertainties now crown them-selves assur'd,
> And peace proclaims Olives of endless age.
> Now with the drops of this most balmy time,
> My love looks fresh, and death to me subscribes,
> Since spite of him I'll live in this poor rhyme,
> While he [my love] insults [triumphs] o'er dull and speechless tribes.
>   And thou in this shalt find thy monument,
>   When tyrants' crests and tombs of brass are spent.

The line "the mortal Moon hath her eclipse endur'd" is unlikely to refer to an actual eclipse of the moon since lunar eclipses (caused by the moon passing through the Earth's shadow) are common, not something to be endured, and poets are unlikely to have thought them significant. There are other interpretations[10]. For example, some commentators think the line refers to the crescent-shaped Spanish Armada of 1588. But the Armada did not endure, it was defeated, so a reference to the Armada is improbable. In addition, "mortal" is an odd adjective to apply to a fleet.

A similar rebuttal can be directed at those who argue that the line refers to the death of the Queen (sometimes referred to as Cynthia, the moon goddess) in 1603, and the accession of James I: a dead queen has not endured. Those academics who support this argument strike an awkward problem in line 14, for if line 5 refers to the accession of James I, then line 14 presumably refers to the previous regime, which necessitates the interpretation that Elizabeth was a tyrant. K. Duncan-Jones[11] seemed particularly confused on this subject and managed to label both the "present" and the "previous regime" as tyrannies: "the use of the word "tyrant" serves both to hint that the present period, however apparently *balmy*, may be presided over by a "tyrant", and that the previous regime [Elizabeth's] was a tyranny". We can be certain that these interpretations were not intended by the poet and are incorrect, for publishing lines like these in 1609 about monarchical governments past and present would have been considered treasonous. Neither Thomas Thorpe nor William Shakespeare would have taken the risk.

Others believe that line 5 refers to 1595–1596, when Elizabeth I was in her sixty-third year, which in popular superstition was considered a dangerous age. But "eclipse" seems too explicit a word to use to describe an unfounded superstitious fear.

A fourth theory is that the line refers to the rumoured illness of the Queen in 1599. This theory has merit, for two reasons. Firstly, because in line 6 the sonnet refers to rumours later proven to be untrue: "And the sad Augurs mock their own presage", which in modernised language can be written as 'the prophets of doom have been proved wrong'. Secondly, because Elizabeth was extremely sensitive to any suggestion that she was on her last legs. When the Bishop of St David's preached a sermon at court in late March 1596, taking as his text "Teach us to number our days so that we may apply our hearts unto our wisdom" (from Psalm 90), she was so affronted with this reminder of her own mortality that she clapped the bishop in prison[12]. As the earlier mention of "mortal Moon" is probably a reference to the Queen (the moon-goddess Diana, as well as Cynthia, Phoebe or Belphoebe, was represented by a crescent moon and each of these names was applied to Elizabeth) the lines "the mortal Moon hath her eclipse endur'd" can be interpreted to be Elizabeth's rejoinder to those who thought she was on the way out: 'in defiance of all your predictions I'm still here'.

The remainder of the sonnet also supports a reference to the 1599 rumours, for the end of a century is generally both a time to take stock of the past as well as consider what the future may bring. Elizabeth was acutely aware that she had steered her country successfully through a sea of troubles. With the threat of a Spanish invasion now greatly diminished she was entitled to expect peace and stability to continue when she eventually died and passed her crown to a successor, and it would be natural for the royal poet to refer to the prospect of stable government continuing (see lines 8 and 9: "Olives of endless age" and "this most balmy time") in the new century.

Line 8 is also significant because its words "peace proclaims Olives of endless age" are similar to those in *Henry IV Part 2*, Act 4, scene 4: "Peace puts forth her olive everywhere"[13], probably written in late 1598 or early 1599[14]. In both the last line of sonnet 107, and in *Henry IV Part 2*, the writer had rebellions in mind, for the full quote from *Henry IV Part 2* reads:

> There is not now a rebel's sword unsheath'd,
> But Peace puts forth her olive everywhere.

The personal references in this sonnet again indicate that the poet realises that death is imminent: "My love looks fresh, and death to me subscribes" – which fits perfectly with Elizabeth's age and increasingly frail physical condition in early 1599, when she was sixty-five years old[15].

Meanwhile the youth appears to be occupied in some sort of campaign against inferior uneducated people – "while he insults [triumphs] o'er dull and speechless tribes". A book published in 1609 by Barnaby Rich shows that the English at the time had an extremely low regard for the Irish, whom Rich describes as "more uncivil, more unclean, more barbarous and more brutish in their customs and demeanours than in any other part of the world that is known"[16]. It is likely that the phrase "dull and speechless tribes" in sonnet 107 refers to Tyrone's Irish rebels, because no other campaigns against so-called 'primitive' people were being waged at the time.

The sonnet's reference to a military operation also matches Essex's efforts in the Irish campaign of 1599. The fighting put him in danger, hence we read in lines 3 and 4 of "my love . . . forfeit to a confin'd doom". The last lines of the sonnet confirm that tyrants were on the poet's mind. There is no doubt that Elizabeth thought of Tyrone as a tyrant, and at this time still expected Essex's army to defeat him.

1. Lilly, W. 1647. Christian Astrology. Quoted in Wyndham (1999, p. 309). See also University of Warwick (2022).
2. MacCaffrey (1994).
3. Wyndham (1999, p. 245).
4. B. Peterson, Mt Stromlo Observatory, Canberra, Australia (personal communication 29 October 2002).
5. Guy (2106, p. 310).
6. Guy (2016, p. 310).
7. Most editors interpret these lines to mean three years have passed. But the sonnet text does not read 'Three winters have turned to spring, three springs have turned to summer, and three summers have turned to autumn'. Instead it describes three winters replacing three summers, three springs turning to autumn, and three Aprils turning to June. These seasonal changes cannot be accommodated consecutively in a three-year period. Furthermore, in line 1 the poet notes that the youth is showing signs of ageing since their first acquaintance, although the poet likes to think he will never age; in a young man significant signs of ageing would be barely noticeable over a three-year period, but would be clearly apparent over nine.
8. Partridge (1969, pp. 111 and 116).
9. Kerrigan (1986, pp. 313–320).
10. Kerrigan (1986, p. 313) lists the options.
11. Duncan-Jones (2010, pp. 324–325).
12. Hammer (1999, p. 363).
13. The note on line 8 by Duncan-Jones (2010, p. 324) begins by mistakenly referring to *Henry VI Part 2*, not *Henry IV Part 2*.
14. Humphreys (1987).
15. Kerrigan (1986) erroneously explains that "death to me subscribes" means that death "submits to me [the poet], acknowledges that I am his superior". There are two good reasons for rejecting this interpretation: firstly, there is no record of "subscribe" meaning submit in Elizabethan times; subscribe meant 'give one's consent to' and was first recorded in the 1540s (see www.etymonline.com; accessed 18 March 2012); and secondly, in line 10 of the sonnet the poet clearly contrasts the youth's freshness with the poet's advanced age, and in the next line (11) speaks of his living "in this poor rhyme" "in spite of him [death]". There is nothing in these lines to indicate the poet is referring to his/her superiority over death; quite the reverse – the poet realises death is imminent and it is the sonnets, not the poet, which will live on. The phrase "death to me subscribes" should therefore be read as meaning 'death consents to my imminent physical departure from this world'.
16. Akrigg (1968, p. 79). William Cecil (Lord Burghley) was no more complimentary. He referred to Ireland as "Bogland" and to the Irish as the "Boglish" (Hammer 1999, p. 394).

22. Paradise Lost

vulgar scandal stamped upon my brow
— Sonnet 112

Sonnets 98 to 107 are optimistic and reflect the Queen's hope that her favourite will live up to her ideal of being a "fair, kind and true" companion. They must have been written before news of Essex's ineffective (and indeed disastrous) campaign reached London. Learning of the true state of Irish affairs she wrote numerous official letters[1] to him expressing irritation at his lack of progress. No doubt she was also acutely aware of the huge costs incurred by the campaign – she hated spending money for no tangible result.

Essex's forces were outmanoeuvred by Tyrone's rebels, who knew their home terrain intimately and used guerrilla tactics. Rather than withdraw ignominiously, Essex met Tyrone personally at Ballacinch Ford and against orders agreed to a truce, without any witnesses being present. (This was an error of judgement. It allowed his enemies at home to question what had been agreed and insinuate that the settlement reached had not been in the best interest of the Queen.) He then deserted his army and rushed back to England and his Queen, presumably thinking that he could use his charm and influence to explain his actions and neutralise any negative interpretation of the truce he had negotiated.

Having left Dublin on 24 September 1599 he reached London's Whitehall before dawn on the 28th. He then headed south to the royal palace at Nonesuch in Surrey. Arriving shortly after 10 a.m., while still clad in his soiled riding gear, he burst into the Queen's room while she was dressing. (She was a habitual late riser.) The Queen remained calm and greeted him politely.

There is no doubt that Essex had disgraced himself and disobeyed orders. His return presented her with both a political and personal dilemma: how should she deal with a commander who had disregarded instructions and failed militarily, and how could she continue a personal relationship with him?

Sonnet 108 is the last optimistic sonnet. The poet meditates on the unlikelihood of love between youth and age. The first twelve lines of the sonnet reflect on her continued love for the "sweet boy" and argue (in forlorn self-deception) that the fair youth's love is "eternal" and not affected by the poet's aged appearance. She insists that despite the "dust and injury of age" Essex belongs to her and she belongs to Essex: "thou mine, I thine". But the final couplet is ambiguous and allows for two possible interpretations. The first is that love persists between the aged Queen and Essex ("Finding the first conceit of love there bred") despite their great age difference ("time and outward form would show it dead") – an interpretation that seems to follow logically from the musings in the previous twelve lines. But another less personal and more political interpretation is that "outward form" may not refer to the physical appearance of the Queen, but to her public (outward) image. She may be saying that she cannot demonstrate affection for Essex in public because of his reprehensible handling of the Irish campaign. It may have been the poet's intention to allow two equally valid alternative interpretations.

> *Sonnet 108*
> What's in the brain that Ink may character,
> Which hath not figur'd to thee my true spirit,
> What's new to speak, what now to register,
> That may express my love, or thy dear merit?
> Nothing sweet boy, but yet like prayers divine,
> I must each day say o'er the very same,
> Counting no old thing old, thou mine, I thine,
> Even as when first I hallowed thy fair name.
> So that eternal love in love's fresh case [clothing, garb],
> Weighs not the dust and injury of age,
> Nor gives to necessary wrinkles place,
> But makes antiquity for aye his page,
> > Finding the first conceit of love there bred,
> > Where time and outward form would show it dead.

Elizabeth decided to dissociate herself from Essex. On 1 October Essex was detained at York House, the residence of Lord Keeper Egerton. By December his health had deteriorated. He may have had an emotional collapse or nervous breakdown on realising the enormity of the Irish fiasco and the state of his now tenuous relationship with the Queen.

Elizabeth retained some softness towards him for she ordered her own doctors to attend to him. She sent him some broth with the message that "she would, if she might with her honour [without compromising herself], visit him"[2]. However, there is no record that she did visit. Essex recovered in January, but the Queen kept her emotional distance. Pointedly, she refused his New Year's present. He was later arrested and on 5 June 1600 was cross-examined on his conduct.

Sonnets 109 and 110 relate to this period of Essex's disgrace. Their subject matter is undoubtedly a troubled relationship. A repentant traveller addresses his love: "if I have rang'd, Like him that travels I return again" (109) and "I have gone here and there, And made myself a motley to the view [a fool in the eyes of others]" (110). These two sonnets include a catalogue of faults and frailties which seem to relate to the youth's transgressions. They also refer to a "stain'd" character – the biblical prodigal son comes to mind. The writer regrets this wayward behaviour and in the last two lines of sonnet 109 declares that his Rose is his universe.

> *Sonnet 109*
> O never say that I was false of heart,
> Though absence seem'd my flame to qualify [to indicate declining interest],

As easy might I from my self depart,
As from my soul which in thy breast doth lie:
That is my home of love, if I have rang'd,
Like him that travels I return again,
Just to the time [On time], not with the time exchang'd [not altered by time],
So that my self bring water for my stain [I shed tears of regret],
Never believe though in my nature reign'd,
All frailties that besiege all kinds of blood,
That it could so preposterously be stain'd,
To leave for nothing all thy sum of good:
    For nothing this wide Universe I call,
    Save thou my Rose, in it thou art my all [you, my Rose, are my universe].

Sonnet 110
Alas 'tis true, I have gone here and there,
And made my self a motley to the view,
Gor'd mine own thoughts, sold cheap what is most dear,
Made old offences of affections new.
Most true it is, that I have looked on truth
Askance and strangely: But by all above,
These blenches gave my heart an other youth,
And worse assays [unsatisfactory liaisons] prov'd thee my best of love,
Now all is done, have what shall have no end,
Mine appetite I never more will grind
On newer proof [new lovers], to try an older friend,
A God in love, to whom I am confin'd.
    Then give me welcome, next my heaven the best,
    Even to thy pure and most most loving breast.

Both sonnets seem to be written from the youth's point of view. The catalogue of faults matches Essex's faults – we cannot pin them on the Queen. It seems likely that these two self-deprecating, apologetic and defensive sonnets were not written by Elizabeth but by Essex, and perhaps sent to the Queen ("my Rose") to demonstrate contrition. Subsequently Elizabeth included them in her collection.

Essex's travels "here and there" (110) must be a metaphorical reference to Essex's straying affections. This explanation is corroborated by the youth's admission that he has made "worse assays [unsatisfactory liaisons]" with others (110, line 8) and his sexual appetite has made him test new lovers (line 11). He assures his long-suffering "older friend" that he won't seek young lovers again, and he argues (not very convincingly) that his sleeping around has had the effect of proving to himself how much he loves the poet whom he describes as "a God in love". Whether "older" means 'old' (i.e. the poet is old) or whether it means 'longstanding' (i.e. refers to the long friendship between the youth and the poet, in contrast to the "newer proof" lovers mentioned in the same line) we cannot tell.

These two sonnets show that the happy carefree times of the loving couple are well and truly over. They paint a picture of desperation. They were written in desperate times, by a commander who knows he has made huge mistakes, deceived his lover and destroyed his reputation, but who seeks forgiveness and a return to the breast of his long-suffering mistress.

In sonnet 111 we see the picture from the other side – the wronged woman. The sonnet refers to the branding (tarnishing) of Elizabeth's name. The issues of penance, bitterness, harmful deeds and correction dominate. The tone is heavy and serious. Elizabeth writes with the detachment we saw first in sonnet 87, which began with the words "Farewell thou art too dear for my possessing", and which continued with a list of the reasons why she and Essex had to end their friendship. This time there is no list. Instead there is a strong suggestion that Essex has not just ignored Elizabeth, but has committed a serious crime that requires a serious punishment, and that Elizabeth is prepared to mete it out.

> *Sonnet 111*
> O for my sake do you wish fortune chide [blame, chastise],
> The guilty goddess [= goddess of fortune] of my harmful deeds,
> That did not better for my life provide,
> Than public means [common justice] which public manners [demand] breeds.
> Thence comes it that my name receives a brand [my reputation is sullied],
> And almost thence my nature is subdu'd
> To what it works in, like the Dyer's hand,
> Pity me then, and wish I were renew'd,
> Whilst like a willing patient I will drink,
> Potions of Eysell [vinegar] 'gainst my strong infection,
> No bitterness that I will bitter think,
> Nor double penance to correct correction.
> > Pity [Forgive] me then dear friend, and I assure ye,
> > Even that your pity is enough to cure me.

The first five lines show that the poet is a public figure with an image to protect, and the youth is a public figure who has brought his own status into disrepute, and thereby threatened to compromise the poet's reputation – "Thence comes it that my name receives a brand". We must remember that in a major error of judgement it was Elizabeth who had appointed the temperamentally unstable Essex as Lord Deputy of Ireland, and it was she who had put him in charge of army that had to fight an elusive foe in unfamiliar and difficult terrain. There was a risk that blame for the Irish debacle would fall on her, and she needed a scapegoat.

In sonnet 111 Elizabeth is asking for understanding from Essex for being so hard on him in public. She deflects potential criticism from Essex: she urges him to blame Fortune (the "guilty goddess" of line 2) rather than her for her having to use "public means" and "harmful deeds" to correct him, because she has no choice; Fortune made her Queen and a responsible Queen must apply sanctions ("harmful deeds") which may hurt individuals. She explains further that her actions are so much against her true nature that she will do anything, even drink vinegar ("Eysell") to "correct correction", i.e. to avoid having to impose a punishment on Essex, and asks for the youth's forgiveness ("pity").

Clearly a disaster has occurred. Elizabeth has the power to impose a public sanction on Essex to correct his misdemeanours, and has used this power. Just what is going on here?

As usual, the historical record enlightens us, and confirms that the references in sonnet 111 concern Essex. In late 1599 it was common knowledge that Essex had failed militarily and disgraced himself personally. The sonnet can be linked to the turbulent endgame played out between Essex and his queen between September 1599 and February 1601.

Both before his release from detention on 26 August 1600 and afterwards Essex wrote many grovelling letters to the Queen. He several times refers to correction, requests his Queen "to correct, not to ruin" and implores her to allow him to "kiss your Majesty's fair correcting hand"[3]. He had a brief reunion with the Queen but there was no return to the old intimacy. Essex himself documented in a letter that she thrust him from his presence with her own hands[4].

On 8 February 1601, seeing no other option, ill-advised and vastly overestimating his support in the city, he and a small band of followers including the Earl of Southampton attempted to seize power in London. The populace did not rise with him and he was arrested to face treason charges. He was convicted and executed on Tower Hill on 25 February.

Sonnet 111 must relate to Elizabeth's agonising deliberations while coming to the conclusion that Essex had to receive the ultimate judicial sanction for his treasonous activities: the death penalty. It contains words remarkably similar to those used in contemporary documents. The reference to "public means" matches the words used by Elizabeth in October 1599: referring to Essex's professional misconduct in Ireland, she insisted "that such contempt ought to be publicly punished"[5]. The reference to the poet being willing to drink vinegar if such a deed ("penance") could reverse the necessity to correct Essex ("to correct correction") reflects the wording of a letter from the disgraced Essex (August 1600) to the Queen imploring her to allow him to "kiss your Majesty's fair correcting hand". Unfortunately for Essex, the Queen was no longer interested in his kisses. She didn't "correct correction". She corrected.

The first twelve lines of the next sonnet (112) confirm the dark scenario described in sonnet 111. Lines 1 and 2 indicate that the Queen has apparently received the forgiveness requested – presumably Essex acknowledged the "vulgar scandal" of his military failures and insurrection which challenged her reputation and position. (Note that the reference to "vulgar scandal" matches the Queen's own words that the peace conditions agreed to between Essex and

Tyrone were "full of scandal to our realm"[6] and may also reflect her reaction to the wording of broadsheets at the time, which supported Essex and attacked her. The Queen criticised these as "railing speeches and slanderous libels"[7]).

> *Sonnet 112*
> Your love and pity doth th'impression fill,
> Which vulgar scandal stamp'd upon my brow,
> For what care I who calls me well or ill,
> So [If] you o'er-green [cover-up] my bad, my good allow?
> You are my All-the-world [everything to me] and I must strive,
> To know my shames and praises from your tongue,
> None else to me, nor I to none alive,
> That my steel'd sense or changes right or wrong,
> In so profound *Abisme*[8] [Abyss] I throw all care
> Of others' voices, that my Adder's[9] sense,
> To critic and to flatterer stopped are:
> Mark how with my neglect I do dispense
> [Note how, by my inaction, I let events run their course]
>   You are so strongly in my purpose bred [etched in my imagination],
>   That all the world besides me thinks y'are dead.

Lines 7 and 8 ("None else . . . right or wrong") are difficult to interpret and probably written when Elizabeth was highly distressed. Kerrigan's paraphrase[10] of these lines seems likely to be right: "there is no one else who exists for me, or for whom I exist, in such a way that they can change my hardened sensibility (my by now obdurate will) towards either virtue or evil". Elizabeth then writes that she has thrown care into the abyss, has made herself insensitive to critics and to flatterers, and chillingly concludes with the words that will seal Essex's fate – she intends to allow events to run their course without her intervention: "Mark how with my neglect I do dispense".

The sonnet's last line should make readers sit up and take notice – "all the world besides me thinks y'are dead". The poet writes that the world thinks the youth is dead. In modern English we might paraphrase the final couplet: 'your life and mine were always so entwined, that in my mind you are still alive, although everyone else thinks you are dead'. The statement as written in the sonnet is unambiguous: the youth is indeed dead, but in the poet's imagination he still lives. The statement comes at *exactly* the point in the sonnet sequence where we expect a reference to Essex's execution.

But the rather obvious and straightforward reading that the youth is dead has not found favour with traditional Shakespearean editors, presumably dismayed by the thought that the youth is dead, with 42 sonnets still to come. Those who assert that the M^r.W.H. of the Dedication (see chapter 6) is the attractive young man of the sonnets also have a problem: if the youth was already dead in 1609, the year of *Sonnets*' publication, how is it that the Dedication wishes him "all happiness"?

In order to avoid the embarrassment of having to deal with a dead body, traditionally minded editors have taken it upon themselves to conclude that at this point the youth must still be alive and kicking, and that there is some mistake in the text. They have contrived amendments to the offending last line, such as "methinks are dead", "methinks is dead", "you think me dead", or "they're dead"[11]. It seems that many combinations of words are acceptable, other than those that Thomas Thorpe printed.

But the printed words are explicit. What right has an editor to change them? There are no obvious errors in the typesetting, and the words make sense. Editorial liberties that fundamentally change a sonnet's meaning must be considered unacceptable.

The contraction "y'are" is crucial. If the scholarly emendators could demonstrate from elsewhere in 'Shakespeare's' works that "y'are" is *not* a contraction of "you are," they might have a case. But where the contraction "y'are" appears in 'Shakespeare's' plays, the construction invariably represents "you are" and no one has ever suggested otherwise[12]. In addition, the definitive work by A. C. Partridge on contractions in Shakespeare's poetry and drama lists no instances of "they are" being contracted to "y'are"[13]. We must therefore conclude that "y'are" means "you are" and be wary of scholars who rewrite this sonnet to correct imaginary errors or to support pet theories. As the *Sonnets* scholar G. Wyndham so aptly and wisely remarked in another context, "it is risky to tamper with enigmas"[14].

There is no reason to reject the simplest explanation. History tells us that Essex was executed on 25 February 1601. Sonnet 112 tells us that the youth of the sonnet sequence is dead. The world had lost an arrogant, brave, colourful but unstable aristocrat. The sonnet concludes the perfect correlation between sonnets 1–112 and the most important events in the tragic Elizabeth-Essex relationship.

If an epitaph were to be written for Essex, we would be hard pressed to improve on J. E. Neale's penetrating irony: "All the qualities for a brilliant career were his, save judgment, an equable temper, and discretion"[15].

---

[1] Marcus et al. (2002).
[2] Devereux (1853b, p. 91).
[3] Devereux (1853b, pp. 91–127).
[4] Devereux (1853b, pp. 129–130).
[5] Somerset (1991, p. 535).
[6] Somerset (1991, p. 535).
[7] Somerset (1991, p. 536).
[8] This is an old French and Catalan word for a bottomless gulf. It is also used in Act 1, scene 2 of *The Tempest*. Elizabeth uses it in the ninth stanza of her French poem *With the blinding so strange* (Mueller and Marcus 2003, p. 38). It is also a personal name, occurring in the early French story the *Song of Roland*, dating from the late

11th century. Brault (1978, p. 208) describes Abisme as "the most diabolical character in the *Song of Roland*. The blackness of his skin is likened to molten pitch . . . Abisme is a repository for every vice imaginable and he is guilty of countless crimes". That Elizabeth should use a French/Catalan word rather than the English "abyss" is curious. Bearing in mind that her mother's initials were AB and that Anne Boleyn died tragically and Elizabeth had great regard for her, this word, which can be read as the assertion "*AB is me*", may have had special significance for the Queen.

9 The image of the deaf adder is derived from Psalm 58: "They are as venomous as the poison of a serpent: *even like the deaf adder that stoppeth her ears*" (Authorised Version).

10 Kerrigan (1986, p. 327).

11 Kerrigan (1986, p. 328). In attempting to justify the unjustifiable, Kerrigan writes disingenuously and hopefully: "To adopt *they're* is thus, strictly, to modernize, not emend".

12 See for example, *Measure for Measure*, Act 1, scene 1, line 11, in which the Duke addresses Angelo "y'are". There are numerous other examples in the plays.

13 Partridge (1964).

14 Wyndham (1999, p. 275).

15 Neale (1961, p. 309).

23. A Backward Look

Those lines that I before have writ do lie
— Sonnet 115

There are 42 sonnets remaining. Tradition tells us that twenty-eight of these (127–154) are mostly about the so-called Dark Lady, and these I shall examine in Part 4 of this book. Fourteen sonnets (113–126) precede the 'Dark Lady' sonnets. If sonnet 112 tells us that Essex is dead, what are these intervening sonnets all about?

A cursory reading indicates that several have been written retrospectively – they refer to a friend or lover in the past tense: "I did strive to prove The constancy and virtue of your love" (117); "To keep an adjunct [souvenir] to remember thee, Were to import [imply] forgetfulness in me" (122); and "That you were once unkind be-friends me now" (120). A crime is also mentioned: "once I suffered in your crime" (120); "the fools of time, Which die for goodness, who have liv'd for crime" (124).

Some sonnets in this sequence idealise the youth and the concept of love: "Love alters not with his [Time's] brief hours and weeks, But bears it out [persists] even to the edge of doom" (116). Others indicate that the distressed poet is hallucinating and interpreting images of living things and inanimate objects as being images of the youth: in sonnet 113 we read that when the distressed poet sees "The most sweet-favour or deformed'st creature . . . it shapes them to your feature" and "Since I left you, mine eye is in my mind" [Since I abandoned you, my visual world is dominated by my imagination] (113); even monsters "your sweet self resemble" (114).

There can be little argument about the circumstances that led to the writing of these fourteen sonnets – their subject matter must be the intense distress Elizabeth felt about the breakdown of her relationship with Essex. With the death of Leicester in 1588 she lost her emotional anchor – someone to whom she could express love and receive love and kindness in return, and laugh with. She chose Essex as Leicester's successor but she chose badly. The relationship started well, but Essex's later actions had disastrous consequences for him, and heart-breaking consequences for her.

* * *

The sonnets immediately preceding sonnet 113 were concerned with rights and wrongs, scandals and the effects of the young man's actions on the poet and others (111 and 112); with eternalising the image of the young man in the poet's lines (107 and 108); and, in the two sonnets probably written by Essex (109 and 110), with expressions of contrition and undying love. Sonnet 113 marks a dramatic change of subject matter.

Sonnet 113
Since I left [abandoned] you, mine eye is in my mind,
And that which governs me to go about,
Doth part his function, and is partly blind,
Seems seeing, but effectually is out:
For it no form delivers to the heart
Of bird, of flower, or shape which it doth lack,
Of his quick [living] objects hath the mind no part,
Nor his own vision holds what it doth catch:
For if it see the rud'st or gentlest sight,
The most sweet-favour or deformed'st creature,
The mountain, or the sea, the day, or night:
The Crow, or Dove, it shapes them to your feature.
 Incapable of more, replete with you,
 My most true mind thus maketh mine untrue.

In this sonnet the youth's qualities and his actual relationship with the poet are not mentioned. There has been a final parting (line 1). Since the parting the youth has become an abstract concept, a memory and a mere idea (although a dominant idea) in the poet's imagination. There is no longer any word of meeting him, seeing him, forgiving him, loving him, or constructing monuments of verse about him. Instead the poet describes how she sees the young man's image in everything she observes: in crows and doves, in birds and flowers, in inanimate objects, even in the very divisions of time (day or night). She knows her mind is still sharp – in line 14 she writes "my most true mind thus maketh mine untrue" – but also realises it is playing tricks on her.

One doesn't need to be a psychologist to identify such thoughts as those of a person in emotional distress and suffering from grief and shock after trauma. For Elizabeth, deeply attached to Essex despite his faults, it is clear that the memory of her experiences with Essex provoked the mind tricks recounted in this sonnet.

In true fashion the next sonnet is more analytical. Having begun (in sonnet 113) with *what* she is feeling and observing, Elizabeth then pulls herself together and, in her first step towards restoring her mental equilibrium, analyses *why* her mind is working as it does:

Sonnet 114
Or whether [So why] doth my mind being crown'd with [dominated by] you
Drink up the monarch's plague this flattery?
Or whether shall I say [Or should I say] mine eye saith true,
And that your love taught it this *Alchemy* [transformation of thoughts]?
To make of monsters, and things indigest [unpleasant],
Such cherubins as your sweet self resemble,
Creating every bad a perfect best [Making ugly things look good]
As fast as objects to his beams assemble [objects are seen by my eyes]:
Oh 'tis the first, 'tis flattery in my seeing,

And my great mind most kingly drinks it up,
Mine eye well knows what with his gust is 'greeing [is agreeing with its taste],
And to his palate doth prepare the cup [creates the image it wants to see].
    If it be poison'd, 'tis the lesser sin,
    That mine eye loves it and doth first begin.

This sonnet is Elizabeth's first attempt to rationalise her distress. She first asks (lines 1 and 2) whether the images she sees are a result of her being deceived by the youth's flattery, or whether they result from the youth altering the working of her mind so much that even ugly things look good ("Creating every bad a perfect best"). She concludes (line 9) that the first explanation is correct.

We can speculate that for a person with an ego as big as Elizabeth's this was the psychologically least-damaging explanation. It was more convenient to diagnose her misreading of Essex's character as an occupational hazard of monarchs (a susceptibility to flattery) than to admit that her commitment to Essex had deranged her mind. We note in passing that the sonnet is dominated by regal images: "being crown'd with you", "the monarch's plague" and "most kingly", as if Elizabeth is retrospectively stamping her sovereign authority on an unfortunate chapter of her life. We also note that, along with references to authority, the sonnet mentions the poet's "great mind" (line 10) which indicates a return of Elizabeth's natural confidence. Also interesting is the reference to a poisoned cup (lines 12 and 13). Bearing in mind that sonnet 114 was probably written shortly after Essex' execution in late February 1601, readers will recall that a poisoned cup also features in *Hamlet* which was written at about the same time, and definitely before July 1602, when it was listed in the *Stationers' Register*.

Elizabeth continues to rationalise her tragic love for Essex in sonnets 115 and 116 in which she assures herself that love can exist and grow despite the accidents of time which can even change the decrees of kings (115). Love is "an ever fixed mark That looks on tempests and is never shaken" and doesn't alter with time's "brief hours and weeks, But bears it out even to the edge of doom" (116). In the perceptive words of one editor: "The sonnet [116] celebrates Love as an absolute, but it is burdened with a sense that Love's 'Perfection' is divorced from the 'lips and cheeks' of the imperfect flesh"[2].

Sonnet 115, lines 1–8
Those lines that I before have writ do lie,
Even those that said I could not love you dearer,
Yet then my judgment knew no reason why,
My most full flame should afterwards burn clearer.
But reckoning time, whose millioned accidents
Creep in twixt [between] vows, and change decrees of Kings,
Tan sacred beauty, blunt the sharp'st intents,
Divert strong minds to th'course of altering things:

Sonnet 116
Let me not to the marriage of true minds
Admit impediments, love is not love
Which alters when it alteration finds,
Or bends with the remover to remove.
O no, it is an ever fixed mark
That looks on tempests and is never shaken;
It is the star to every wandering bark [small ship],
Whose worth's unknown, although his height [angle, location] be taken.
Love's not Time's fool, though rosy lips and cheeks
Within his bending sickle's compass come,
Love alters not with his brief hours and weeks,
But bears it out even to the edge of doom:
    If this be error and upon me proved,
    I never writ, nor no man ever loved.

In isolation these two sonnets seem idealistic: love is an "ever fixed mark" that is not shaken by outside influences. However, in the context of Elizabeth's connivance with Essex's execution they are disquieting. She expresses greater love for the image of Essex after his execution than she did while he was still living: "my judgment knew no reason why, My most full flame should afterwards burn clearer".

The next two sonnets have quite different subject matter. The first reads like a legal deposition and an appeal by the accused. The second records the judge's summing-up. Let's consider sonnet 117 first.

Sonnet 117
Accuse me thus, that I have scanted all,
Wherein I should your great deserts repay,
Forgot upon your dearest love to call,
Whereto all bonds do tie me day by day
That I have frequent been with unknown [lesser] minds,
And given to time [wasted on others] your own dear purchas'd right,
That I have hoisted sail to all the winds
Which should transport me farthest from your sight.
Book [Record] both my wilfulness and errors down,
And on just proof surmise, accumulate,
Bring me within the level of your frown [Aim your frown at me],
But shoot not at me in your wakened [newly aroused] hate:
    Since my appeal says I did strive to prove
    The constancy and virtue of your love.

This sonnet repeats some of the personal failings listed in sonnet 110 (chapter 22), which I concluded was written by Essex in August 1600 or shortly afterwards, during his period of disgrace. The subject matter suggests that sonnet 117 was also written by Essex. The writer admits he has been neglectful ("scanted all"), hasn't paid attention to his dearest love, has wasted time with "unknown minds" (i.e., nonentities, possibly in the sense of shady characters) instead of paying attention to his loved one, and has "hoisted sail to all the winds". Compare these lines with lines 1 and 2 of sonnet 110: "I have gone here and there, And made myself a motley to the view".

The sonnet is essentially a list of faults admitted and an appeal for forgiveness. The writer asks the person he is addressing to record all his character defects and misdemeanours ("Book both my wilfulness and errors down") and come to a valid conclusion based on the accumulated evidence ("on just proof surmise, accumulate"). Like a prisoner in the dock he makes an appeal for mercy: frown at me but don't destroy me with your newly aroused hatred (lines 11 and 12). Finally, in a desperately weak defence (lines 13 and 14) that recalls lines 10 and 11 of sonnet 110, he makes the assertion that he only went astray "to prove The constancy and virtue of your love".

In late August 1600 Essex had only one weapon left in his arsenal, and that was to use his charm (now distinctly tarnished) to ingratiate himself with the Queen. If the interpretation that sonnet 117 was written by Essex is correct, sonnet 118 is the Queen's response.

Sonnet 118
Like as to make our appetites more keen
With eager compounds we our palate urge,
As to prevent our maladies unseen,
We sicken to shun sickness when we purge.
Even so being full of your near cloying sweetness[3],
To bitter sauces did I frame my feeding [my response was to withdraw];
And sick of wel-fare [rich food] found a kind of meetness,
To be diseas'd [negative] ere [before] that there was true needing.
Thus policy in love t'anticipate
The ills that were not, grew to faults assured,
[Those faults I had not recognised in you became clear]
And brought to medicine a healthful state
[Withdrawing from you was good for my mental health]
Which rank [surfeiting] of goodness would by ill [critical thinking?] be cured.
    But thence I learn and find the lesson true,
    Drugs poison him [me] that so fell sick of you.

In these complex lines dealing with illness and medicinal remedies Elizabeth is saying that to make "our appetites" (i.e. her love for Essex) "more keen" and to prevent future illness (i.e. deterioration in their relationship) it was useful to take a purge. His "near cloying sweetness" was overwhelming, which she countered by feeding on "bitter sauces". Surprisingly, she found that taking this medicine (probably consisting of outwardly maintaining a cool and detached attitude towards Essex and inwardly being critical of him, which personally she found to be a harsh course of action to take) suited her because it allowed her time to understand her emotions, although initially she thought that she didn't really need to take this course of action (she "found a kind of meetness, To be diseas'd ere there was true needing"). Unexpectedly she then found that "The ills that were not, grew to faults assured" (i.e., Essex's faults and bad characteristics became more apparent when she kept her distance) and taking the medicine proved to be useful after all (line 11).

The final couplet is sadly ironic and sums up the whole. It puns on the word sick as in love-sick and sick meaning unwell: Elizabeth found that the "bitter sauces" that she had taken as a temporary measure had not only poisoned her (the "him" in line 14) but also her relationship with Essex. In modern English a lover might say 'Things were getting too intense and complicated, so I had to cool the friendship and distance myself from my lover to understand myself, clarify my thoughts, and keep myself sane. But when I did this I found that it didn't improve things at all; instead our differences became plain and our previous rapport collapsed'.

In the light of this interpretation, a poem by Essex, which R. Strong describes as "pastoral with a tinge of melancholy bursting into frustration"[4] is significant because it contains the same imagery as the *Young Man among Roses* portrait and, significantly, uses the words "cloyed with sweetness" which are intriguingly similar to the words "near cloying sweetness" in sonnet 118, line 5:

Essex's poem
While all the swarm [other courtiers] in sunshine taste the rose;
On black fern's root I seek and suck my bane:
    Whilst on eglantine the rest repose
    To light on wormwood leaves they me constrain;
    Having too much they still repine for more
    And cloyed with sweetness forfeit on their store.

This is a poem probably written in one of Essex's periods of self-imposed exile from court. In his best self-pitying style, it describes how his privileged court rivals still surround the Queen (represented as "the rose" and the "eglantine"), while he has to be content (or discontent) with only the basics of life (which in Essex's case were probably rather more than wormwood and the bitter juices of fern roots – Essex was not renowned for understatement). When responding (118) to Essex's sonnet (117) Elizabeth may have recalled this earlier poem of his.

The reference to "ruin'd love" in sonnet 119 indicates that Elizabeth has finally crossed a psychological boundary. The sonnet represents another step in Elizabeth's return to a healthy state of mind.

Sonnet 119
What potions have I drunk of *Siren* tears [evil apparitions]
Distill'd from Lymbecks[5] foul as hell within [from eyes concealing evil],
Applying fears to hopes, and hopes to fears,
Still losing when I saw myself to win?

[Still failing when I thought we would love each other again?]
What wretched errors hath my heart committed,
Whilst it hath thought it self so blessed never [never before so favoured]?
How have mine eyes out of their Spheres been fitted
[How have I been so deceived]
In the distraction of this madding fever?
O benefit of ill, now I find true
That better is, by evil still made better [evil has improved things].
And ruin'd love when it is built anew
Grows fairer than at first, more strong, far greater.
    So I return rebuked to my content,
    And gain by ills thrice more than I have spent.

Elizabeth at last realises that she has been led on by evil, because her eyes have played tricks on her (lines 1–4). Her heart was committed to loving Essex, and she thought she had never been so blessed, but she realises that her perceptions were incorrect (her eyes were operating "out of their Spheres") and her infatuation with Essex has been like a "madding fever" (lines 5–8). But (she argues) the evil she has experienced has benefits: now that she has recovered she is mentally stronger than before and (surprisingly) she feels the new abstract love more strongly than the real (but now ruined) love she previously experienced (lines 9–14).

In the next sonnet (120) she tries to come to terms with her failure to avoid mutual recriminations (probably a slanging match) in a "night of woe".

Sonnet 120
That you were once unkind be-friends me now,
And for that sorrow, which I then did feel,
Needs must I under my transgression bow
[I should have grovelled and apologised],
Unless my Nerves were brass or hammered steel [Had I not been inflexible].
For if you were by my unkindness shaken
As I by yours, y'have passed a hell of Time,
And I a tyrant have no leisure taken
To weigh how once I suffered in your crime.
O that our night of woe might have remem'bred
My deepest sense [fundamental awareness], how hard true sorrow hits,
And soon to you [I should have tendered to you], as you to me then tend'red
The humble salve [balm], which wounded bosoms fits! [to comfort us both!]
    But that [However] your trespass now becomes a fee,
    Mine ransoms yours, and yours must ransom me.

The poet recognises the sorrow she has caused ("Needs must I under my transgression bow") during a serious argument, which probably occurred on the "night of woe" (line 9) and regrets not apologising (lines 10–12). This may be a reference to the actual meeting mentioned by Essex in a letter to his Queen written in November 1600, when she thrust him out of her presence:

> I sometimes think of running [in the tiltyard], and then remember what it will be to come in armour triumphing into that presence, out of which both by your own voice I was commanded, and then by your hands thrust out.[6]

Colin Burrow supported a similar interpretation. He wrote that lines 11–12 mean "if only it [our mutual distress] had prompted me quickly to offer you, as you had offered to me in our night of woe, the healing balm of a humble apology, the best cure for a wounded heart". However, being an orthodox Shakespeare scholar, he did not apply his interpretation to an altercation between the Queen and Essex[7].

But the Queen did not apologise. Balm was not applied to wounded hearts. The sonnet's last couplet describes the ominous bargain Elizabeth has devised: Essex must pay a fee for his crime – he must give her something and in return she will give him something. Unluckily for Essex, in this game of mutual exchange the Queen not only held all the aces but also made the rules.

The last six sonnets (121–126) in the sequence are less complex than those considered above and may have been written after Elizabeth had decided that Essex had to pay the ultimate price for his crimes and her mental anguish had subsided. The sonnets tidy up the wreckage of their relationship.

Sonnet 121 uses questionable logic to present an argument that could be construed as self-serving – if other people judge me to be bad or abusive, this doesn't mean that I am actually bad, because it is impossible for people whose reason is distorted or diseased ("bevel") to judge people of sound mind, and I'm not going to change anyway: "I am that I am" – words reminiscent of Elizabeth's motto *Semper eadem* (Always the same).

> *Sonnet 121, lines 9–12:*
> No, I am that I am, and they that level [take aim]
> At my abuses, reckon up their own [should look at their own faults],
> I may be straight though they them-selves be bevel [crooked, angled];
> By their rank [diseased] thoughts, my deeds must not be shown [judged]

We cannot be sure of the circumstances that prompted the Queen to pen this defensive argument, but it is noteworthy that in October 1600 an angry Essex, on being told about "the Queen's conditions", is reported to have said that the Queen was "as crooked in her disposition as in her carcass"[8] and the line "I may be straight though they themselves be bevel" may be Elizabeth's reply to Essex's ill-chosen words. These were so personally insulting to a Queen super-sensitive about her appearance that they probably destroyed any vestige of sympathy she had for her erstwhile favourite.

It seems that when these sonnets were written Elizabeth was not only getting her thoughts into order, but also her personal possessions. We can speculate that sonnet 122 was written after she had disposed of Essex's papers and gifts.

Sonnet 122
Thy gift, thy tables [notebooks], are within my brain
Full character'd with lasting memory,
Which shall above that idle rank remain
Beyond all date even to eternity.
Or at the least, so long as brain and heart
Have faculty by nature to subsist,
Till each to raz'd oblivion yield his part
Of thee, thy record never can be missed:
That poor retention could not so much hold,
Nor need I tallies [souvenirs] thy dear love to score,
Therefore to give them from me was I bold,
To trust those tables [the sonnets?] that receive thee more,
    To keep an adjunct [memento] to remember thee,
    Were to import [imply] forgetfulness in me.

In this sonnet the Queen writes that she doesn't need to keep a formal tally of the good times and hasn't kept mementos, and that his gift, his tables (notebooks) are written out in full ("full character'd") within her brain. It is noteworthy that line 12 refers to "tables that receive thee more". These may have been the leaves of Elizabeth's own book of sonnets. She may be saying that she has recorded all the important points about Essex in her collection of sonnets, so she doesn't need physical items to remind herself of him.

Having given away mementos, while keeping a record in some other form, the poet returns to an old and favourite theme – the ravages of time (123 and 124). But in these sonnets, in contrast to the dominant subject matter of sonnets 1–112, it is not the survival of the youth's beauty in the sonnets' immortal lines that concern the poet, it is the survival of her *own* character (123) and the record of her love (124). Sonnet 123 begins and ends with emphatic statements again recalling the Queen's motto *Semper eadem* which also figured in slightly different words in sonnets 76 and 121.

Sonnet 123
No! Time, thou shalt not boast that I do change,
Thy pyramids built up with newer might
To me are nothing novel, nothing strange,
They are but dressings of a former sight:
Our dates are brief, and therefore we admire,
What thou dost foist upon us that is old,
And rather make them born to our desire,
Than think that we before have heard them told:
Thy registers and thee [Time] I both defy,
Not wond'ring at the present, nor the past,
For thy records, and what we see doth lie,
Made more or less by thy continual haste:
    This I do vow and this shall ever be,
    I will be true despite thy [Time's] scythe and thee.

Elizabeth defies history's "registers" and presents her view that the historical record and "what we see" is a lie. (Henry Ford expressed the same sentiment more forcefully but less eloquently.) These are big claims. Is Elizabeth questioning the historical record in general, or is she indicating that something more specific was misrepresented by history?

Not content with raising these universal issues, in the next sonnet Elizabeth, with supreme confidence, raises another by redefining the concept of love. She disengages love from everyday life (we might say from life itself) – from changes of fortune, time, accidents, pomp, discontent, policy (meaning self-interested scheming), or short-term advantage. Writing metaphorically, she states that love doesn't grow with heat (i.e., in good times) or decline in showers (bad times). To drive home the point she's making she contrasts her ideal of abstract and unchangeable love with the love of "fools" (read 'Essex') whose feelings are diverted by these worldly buffetings: "the fools of time, Which die for goodness [i.e., while pretending to be fighting for good], who have liv'd for crime". Although Essex has lost his head, both figuratively and historically speaking, her love will last forever.

> *Sonnet 124*
> If my dear love were but the child of state [product of circumstance, a whim],
> It might for fortune's bastard be unfathered [subject to Fortune's changes],
> As subject to time's love, or to time's hate,
> Weeds among weeds, or flowers with flowers gather'd.
> No it was builded far from accident,
> It suffers not in smiling pomp, nor falls
> Under the blow of thralled discontent [popular criticism],
> Whereto th'inviting time our fashion calls [Which is fashionable at present]:
> It fears not policy [scheming] that *Heretic*,
> Which works on leases of short number'd hours [for short-term advantage],
> But all alone stands hugely politic [stoutly independent],
> That it nor grows with heat, nor drowns with showers.
>   To this I witness call the fools of time,
>   [I call the fools of time to stand witness],
>   Which die for goodness who have liv'd for crime.
>   [Who, consider themselves martyrs but are actually evil].

We know that Elizabeth was fooling herself. To say that her love had been ideal and constant, while Essex had behaved less nobly, was oversimplifying the cause of their differences. If she had been more perceptive and exercised reason and sound judgement, she would never have become besotted with her attractive but unstable courtier in the first place. But she couldn't admit to being a "fool of time". The grotesque idea that her love could now persist in glorious isolation, separated from everyday events, fortune and misfortune, and even from the real person (now dead) that was once the object of her affection may have comforted her in her loneliness.

The bargain alluded to in sonnet 120 (lines 13 and 14) reappears in sonnet 125. The poet begins by reflecting on the worth of pomp and ceremony and suggests that ostentatious display is pointless if any positive effects are short-lived. She then considers the show put on by others and the fawning and flattery ("form and favour") practised to gain advantage – hasn't she seen favourites playing high stakes for "compound sweet" only to "lose all," while forgetting simple honest pleasures ("simple savour")? The phrase "dwellers on form and favour" is probably a general comment on courtiers seeking personal advantage. But the words "compound sweet" must surely refer to the 'sweet wines' monopoly, which was Essex's chief source of income and the subject of the desperate letters sent by Essex to Elizabeth in late 1600 – he knew he would be impoverished if she withdrew his exclusive right to claim the sweet wine excise.

Elizabeth was unyielding. In October 1600 she noted that Essex's supplications were merely attempts to regain her favour so that she would renew his monopoly. She withdrew the privilege and Essex was financially ruined.[9] (Sonnet 125 may have been written before Essex's execution.)

Sonnet 125
Wer't ought to me I bore the canopy
[Was it worth my setting great store on display?],
With my extern the outward honouring,
Or laid great bases for eternity,
Which proves more short than waste or ruining?
Have I not seen dwellers on form and favour
Lose all, and more by paying too much rent
For compound sweet; Forgoing simple savour,
Pitiful thrivors in their gazing spent.
[Pitiful survivors, who have lost everything by yearning for too much].
No, let me be obsequious in thy heart,
And take thou my oblation, poor but free [simple and unsophisticated],
Which is not mixed with seconds [is pure], knows no art,
But mutual render [surrender], only me for thee.
    Hence thou suborn'd *Informer*, a true soul
    When most impeached, stands least in thy control.

Notice that in lines 9–12 she feigns simplicity and suggests to her disgraced lover that they should relate without artfulness or hidden agendas ("not mixed with seconds, knows no art"). But she is not proposing reconciliation, she is proposing a bargain of mutual surrender "only me for thee." The terms of the bargain are not explicitly stated, but Elizabeth seems to be saying "I'll relate simply and honestly to you, if you relate simply and honestly to me". These terms required Essex to admit guilt. In the final couplet she delivers her crushing conclusion, which in modern English we might paraphrase: 'You aligned yourself with the forces of evil, so you no longer have any control over me [the "true soul"] or yourself [the "most impeached"]'.

In the final sonnet of this sequence (possibly the last sonnet Elizabeth ever wrote) the poet reflects on the triumph of Nature and Time over the life of her "lovely Boy". Like sand simultaneously accumulating and depleting in an hourglass he grew while Elizabeth withered. (Shakespeare wasn't withering, he was happily buying real estate.) The sonnet lacks its final couplet, which may have been discreetly deleted by a careful editor. The sonnet confirms that Nature's final action will be to surrender her "lovely Boy" to Time. Nature's audit required him to pay his debt in full. He did.

> *Sonnet 126*
> O thou my lovely Boy who in thy power,
> Dost hold time's fickle glass, his sickle, hour:
> Who hast by waning grown, and therein show'st [thereby emphasising],
> Thy lover's withering, as thy sweet self grow'st.
> If Nature (sovereign mistress over wrack [disaster])
> As thou goest onwards still will pluck thee back,
> She keeps thee to this purpose, that her skill
> May time disgrace, and wretched minutes kill.
> Yet fear her O thou minion of her pleasure,
> She may detain, but not still keep her treasure!
> Her *Audit* (though delay'd) answer'd must be,
> And her *Quietus* [final action] is to render [surrender] thee [to Time].

---

[1] The entry for "A booke called the Revenge of Hamlett Prince Denmarke" on 26 July 1602 describes it as being "latelie acted" by the Lord Chamberlain's Men, Shakespeare's company.

[2] Kerrigan (1986, p. 54).

[3] The 1609 edition prints "nere" which, according to Burrow (2002, p. 616) is the standard abbreviation for 'never'. However, Burrow's conclusion is unlikely to apply to sonnet 118. Although "nere" certainly stands for 'never' in sonnet 17 in which line 8 (retaining 1609 spelling) reads "Such heavenly touches nere toucht earthly faces" and also has the meaning of 'never' in sonnets 89 and 144, 'never cloying' makes no sense in the context of sonnet 118, in which the poet writes that she is so full of the youth's cloying sweetness that she prefers to feed on "bitter sauces". Which is to say that she is fed up with Essex's attempts to charm her and prefers her own realistic assessment. As "neere" in other sonnets (61 and 136) undoubtedly means 'near', not 'never', and as Elizabethan spelling is inconsistent, we are justified in concluding that "nere cloying" in sonnet 118 should be read as 'near cloying' ('almost cloying'). This interpretation matches the sonnet's critical tone.

[4] Strong (1987, p. 81).

[5] A lymbeck (alembic) is an old-fashioned distillation apparatus. In Elizabethan poetry the word is used for eyes which, like a still, produce drops of fluid (tears).

[6] Devereux (1853b, pp. 129–130).

[7] Burrow (2002, p. 620).

8 The anecdote was apparently recorded by Sir Walter Ralegh (Oldys and Birch 1829, p. 329) who related Essex's remark to the Queen's refusal to renew his farm (monopoly) on the sale of sweet wines. Some authors, notably Guy (2016, p. 284), relate the outburst to the testy behaviour of Essex at the Privy Council meeting of 30 June or 1 July 1598. The actual words Essex used vary according to the source. Interestingly the old woman who complains of being deceived by a fair youth in *A Lover's Complaint* is described as "The carcass of a beauty spent and done" – this may be Elizabeth's wry acknowledgement that there was some truth in Essex's observation concerning her physical condition.

9 Francis Bacon recorded that Elizabeth remarked that "My Lord of Essex had written her some very dutiful letters, and that she had been moved by them; but when she took it to be the abundance of his heart, she found it to be but a preparation to a suit for the renewing of his farm [monopoly] of sweet wines" (Devereux 1853b, p. 125).

PART THREE. THE PLAYS

24. Dating the Plays

The play's the thing
— *Hamlet*, Act 2, scene 2

In Parts 1 and 2 of this book I show that the subject matter of the first 126 sonnets corresponds exactly with the history of the Elizabeth-Essex relationship. In addition, most of these sonnets are written from Queen Elizabeth's point of view. Together, these observations mean it is highly likely that the Queen wrote *Sonnets*.

Before turning the reader's attention to the intriguing issue of the 'Dark Lady' sonnets, I would like to raise an important question: if Elizabeth wrote the *Sonnets* attributed to Shakespeare, did she also write the plays? When considering this question the issue of when each play was written is of paramount importance, since if it can be shown that any play by 'Shakespeare' was definitely written after 1603, serious doubt must be cast on the 'Elizabeth-equals-Shakespeare' hypothesis.

Many books on the plays publish a list of their likely dates of composition, approximating to that shown in Table 2, derived from E. K. Chambers' chronology published in 1930[1]. This chronology, or something very similar, has remained largely unchallenged.

At first glance the list in Table 2 looks reasonable: in a brilliant twenty-three-year stint beginning about 1590 'Shakespeare' systematically wrote one to three plays a year. If we accept a chronology like this then about thirteen plays were written after 1603, so either the hypothesis proposed in this book is incorrect, or Elizabeth did indeed write *Sonnets*, but another great author, perhaps William Shakespeare the actor, wrote the plays, or at least the later plays, sometimes with a little help from his friends[2].

However, the verbal links between the sonnets and plays suggest that *Sonnets* and most of the plays are written by the same person. Consequently, we have a stark choice: we must either discard the Elizabeth-Essex hypothesis completely (despite the evidence presented in Parts 1 and 2 of this book) or we must question the traditionally accepted chronology of the plays.

Table 2. The traditional chronology of Shakespeare's plays, after Chambers (1930).

Play	Approximate date
Henry VI Part 2	1590–1591
Henry VI Part 3	1590–1591
Henry VI Part 1	1591–1592
Richard III	1592–1593
The Comedy of Errors	1592–1593
Titus Andronicus	1593–1594
The Taming of the Shrew	1593–1594
The Two Gentlemen of Verona	1594–1595
Love's Labours Lost	1594–1595
Romeo and Juliet	1594–1595
Richard II	1595–1596
A Midsummer Night's Dream	1595–1596
King John	1596–1597
The Merchant of Venice	1596–1597
Henry IV Part 1	1597–1598
Henry IV Part 2	1597–1598
Much Ado About Nothing	1598–1599
Henry V	1598–1599
Julius Caesar	1599–1600
As You Like It	1599–1600
Twelfth Night	1599–1600
Hamlet	1600–1601
The Merry Wives of Windsor	1600–1601
Troilus and Cressida	1601–1602
All's Well That Ends Well	1602–1603
Measure for Measure	1604–1605
Othello	1604–1605
King Lear	1605–1606
Macbeth	1605–1606
Anthony and Cleopatra	1606–1607
Coriolanus	1607–1608
Timon of Athens	1607–1608
Pericles, Prince of Tyre	1608–1609
Cymbeline	1609–1610
The Winter's Tale	1610–1611
The Tempest	1611–1612
Henry VIII	1612–1613
The Two Noble Kinsmen	1612–1613

The latter looks like a daunting task – almost all scholars assume that the chronology presented in Table 2 is about right. But consensus isn't proof. We need to approach the date of composition issue with an open mind, and for each play apparently written in late 1603 or subsequently examine external evidence (e.g. publication date) and internal evidence (e.g. contemporary references within the play) to decide whether the commonly accepted date of its composition is soundly based.

Let's summarise the methods employed to evaluate external and internal evidence. Because no dated authorial manuscripts (technically defined as 'holographs') have survived, researchers have estimated when the plays were written using evidence from a variety of sources, for example, first publication date; mention in the *Stationers' Register*, the official record of new works submitted to the Stationers' Company of London[3]; mention of a play by a contemporary; borrowing of words, phrases or plots within a 'Shakespearean' play by other authors; borrowings by 'Shakespeare' from the published works of others; and allusions in the plays to topical events. All these ways of estimating when a play was written have their limitations.

Publication may follow an unrecorded public performance, or the gap between composition and printing may be several years as is evident for those plays published only in the First Folio, seven years after Shakespeare's death, And not all plays were entered in the *Stationers' Register*, and in some entries the author's name is not given.

Substantial amounts of text in common between two authors, or shared details of plots or narratives, or shared use of uncommon words or phrases indicate that one author borrowed from another. But dating a play by this means can be difficult because it may not be apparent who borrowed from whom – who was first?

References to topical events have the potential to provide the earliest possible date of composition. But this method of dating has a serious weakness: allusions may be inserted into a play after a play's completion in order to improve its topicality and public appeal. For example, present-day producers of Gilbert and Sullivan light operas, originally written and composed in Queen Victoria's reign, often replace Gilbert's satirical lines on Victorian society and politics with up-to-date comments on today's society and recent political events, in order to engage the audience.

Bearing in mind the above limitations, it is still useful to discuss the more dependable ways of dating the plays. Those indicating the *latest* possible date of composition are: listing of a play in the *Stationers' Register*; date of first printing; and recorded mention of a play (performance or publication) by a contemporary Elizabethan or Jacobean. In contrast the *earliest* possible date of composition is indicated by the publication date or date of circulation of a source used in the plays, with the date of the most recent source being the most useful.

In Table 3 I list when the plays attributed to Shakespeare are first mentioned in the *Stationers' Register*, their dates of first publication, and the first year in which the plays are mentioned by a contemporary. I have divided the plays into the traditional "Early" and "Late" sequences[4], with the latter sequence beginning after the appearance of *Hamlet*. For interest I have included the poems in this list. Also included are relevant instances of borrowing from other texts and apparently contemporary allusions. Tabulating the historical evidence in this way shows up some interesting patterns which, I believe, have not been given the attention they deserve.

Firstly, if we take the latest possible date of composition (Table 3) of a play as a crude estimate of when it was written, the period 1591 to 1603 (13 years) was a time of frenetic creativity: 25 plays and three volumes of poems were written – on average a major work every six months. Creativity after 1603 was apparently less: only 13 plays were written, as well as *Sonnets* and *A Lover's Complaint*, so if we assume William Shakespeare to be their author his production rate slowed to about one major work per year after 1603. (But remember that the post-1603 dates determined by this method are *latest* possible dates of composition – some works may have been written earlier.)

Secondly, we see that there is a gap of 4 years and 9 months (between 7 February 1603 and 26 November 1607), when no 'Shakespeare' plays were recorded in the *Stationers' Register*. There is also a 5-year gap in publication between 1603, when *Hamlet* was first published, and 1608, when Nicholas Okes published *King Lear*. How can these gaps be explained?

Thirdly, eighteen plays had to wait for the publication of the First Folio before they became available in print to the public[5]. Although ten of these are recorded as being performed publicly before 1623, two were performed only at the court[6] and for the remaining six plays there is no evidence that they were known to the public before 1623.

These observations are intriguing if we believe that the plays were written by a Warwickshire playwright who went to court to claim a debt of a few shillings and was supposedly making his living by either having his plays performed or selling printed copies. Why wouldn't William Shakespeare have ensured that all plays, potentially big earners for him and his company, were staged in a public venue? And why were 16 plays published between 1594 and 1603, but only three more before he died in 1616?

Evolution of style has the potential to be a useful dating tool if an author's style has evolved over time and (importantly) some firm dates of composition are known, to enable calibration points to be established. Analyses of style commonly look at use of unusual words, changes of rhyme types or changes of emphasis within lines. But dating by style analysis has its drawbacks: results can be inconclusive or misleading if a composition has been revised, written over a long period, edited after being written or co-authored, or if an author has chosen to adopt a particular writing style to produce a desired dramatic effect.

Table 3. List of plays and poems attributed to Shakespeare. In bold type in column 5 are the earliest dates that a play was brought to the attention of the public, derived from the evidence listed in column 2, 3 or 4.

Play or Poem	First record in the *Stationers' Register*	First known dated publication	Date derived from evidence of borrowing, or contemporary allusions, or mention in a contemporary text	Latest possible date of composition based on evidence in columns 2, 3 and 4
EARLY PLAYS				
Titus Andronicus	6 February **1594**	1594 John Danter for Edward White and Thomas Millington	Meres 1598; the name Alarbus may come from Puttenham's *The Arte of English Poesie* (**1589**)	**1589**
Two Gentlemen of Verona	8 November 1623	1623 First Folio	Meres **1598**; borrows from John Lyly's *Midas* 1589	**1589**
Romeo and Juliet	22 January 1607 (rights transferred)	1597 John Danter	**1591** – internal reference to 11 years since the 1580 earthquake; Meres 1598	**1591 for Act 1?** (see discussion in chapter 38)
The Taming of The Shrew (*Love's Labours Won?*)	The related play *The Taming of A Shrew* was entered in the *Stationers' Register* on 2 May 1594	1623 First Folio	Meres 1598, if *The Taming of The Shrew* = *Love's Labours Won*; written before June 1593 on the basis of borrowing in play *Beauty Dishonoured*, and in or before 1592 based on borrowings in *A Knack to Know a Knave*	**1592?**
Henry VI Part 2	12 March **1594**	1594 by Thomas Creed for Thomas Millington	*Henry VI Part 3* is a sequel, so *Henry VI Part 2* likely to have been written in 1591 or 1592	**1592**
Henry VI Part 3	8 November 1623	1595 P. S. for Thomas Millington	Greene parodied a line in *Groatsworth* (**September 1592**)	**1592**
Richard III	20 October **1597**	1597 Valentine Sims for Andrew Wise	Marlowe's *Edward II* (**1592**) possibly influenced by *Richard III*; Meres 1598	**1592?**
Venus and Adonis	18 April **1593**	1593 Richard Field	Meres 1598	**1593**
The Rape of Lucrece	9 May **1594**	1594 Richard Field	Meres 1598	**1594**
The Comedy of Errors	8 November 1623	1623 First Folio	Revels 28 December **1594**	**1594**

Richard II	20 June **1597**	1597 Valentine Simmes for Andrew Wise	Private performance at Edward Hoby's house, **1595**; Meres 1598	**1595**
A Midsummer Night's Dream	8 October 1600	1600 for Thomas Fisher	Meres 1598	**1598**
Love's Labours Lost	22 January 1607 (rights transferred)	1598 W. W. for Cuthbert Burby	Quarto mentions performance for the Queen "last Christmas" (**1597**); Meres 1598	**1597**
Henry IV Part 1	25 February **1598**	1598 P. S. for Andrew Wise	Meres 1598	**1598**
King John		1623 First Folio	Meres **1598**	**1598**
The Merchant of Venice	22 July **1598**	1600 I. R. for Thomas Heyes	Reference to ship the *St Andrew* captured 1597; Meres 1598	**1598**
Julius Caesar	8 November 1623	1623 First Folio	Thomas Platter **1599**	**1599**
Henry V	4 August 1600 (blocking entry)	1600 Thomas Creede for Thomas Millington and John Busby	Chorus contains a probable reference to Essex's campaign in Ireland, **1599**	**1599**
As You Like It	4 August **1600** (blocking entry)	1623 First Folio		**1600**
Much Ado About Nothing	4 August **1600** (blocking entry)	1600 V. S. for Andrew Wise and William Aspley		**1600**
Henry IV Part 2	23 August **1600**	1600 V. S. for Andrew Wise and William Aspley		**1600**
The Phoenix and the Turtle		1601 Richard Field		**1601**
Twelfth Night	8 November 1623	1623 First Folio	Virginio Orsini, Duke of Bracciano, visited London in winter of 1601/1602; Manningham's diary 2 February **1602**	**1602**
The Merry Wives of Windsor	18 January **1602**	1602 T. C. for Arthur Johnson		**1602**
Henry VI Part 1	19 April **1602**	1623 First Folio		**1602**
*Hamlet****	26 July **1602**	1603 for N. L. and John Trundell		**1602**

LATE PLAYS

5-year gap in printed publications, between *Hamlet* in 1603 and *King Lear* in 1608

Troilus and Cressida	7 February **1603**	1609 George Eld for R. Boniam and H. Walley		**1603**

4-year gap in *Stationers' Register*, between *Troilus and Cressida* in 1603 and *King Lear* in 1607

Measure for Measure	8 November 1623	1623 First Folio	At court 26 November **1604**	**1604**
Othello	6 October 1621	1622 N. O. for Thomas Walkley	Revels 1 November **1604**	**1604**
King Lear	26 November 1607	1608 for Nathaniel Butter	*Stationers' Register* mentions performance at court on 26 December **1606**	**1606**
Pericles	20 May **1608**	1609 for Henry Gosson		**1608**
Anthony and Cleopatra	20 May **1608**	1623 First Folio		**1608**
Shakespeare's Sonnets and *A Lover's Complaint*	20 May **1609**	1609 George Eld for Thomas Thorpe		**1609**
Macbeth	8 November 1623	1623 First Folio	**1610** or **1611** Simon Forman's diary	**1610**[7]
Cymbeline	8 November 1623	1623 First Folio	Forman (undated; **1611** or earlier)	**1611**
The Winter's Tale	8 November 1623	1623 First Folio	Forman 15 May **1611**	**1611**
The Tempest	8 November 1623	1623 First Folio	Revels: performance at Whitehall 1 November **1611**	**1611**
All's Well That Ends Well	8 November **1623**	1623 First Folio		**1623**
Henry VIII	8 November 1623	1623 First Folio	29 June **1613**	**1613**
Coriolanus	8 November **1623**	1623 First Folio		**1623**
Timon of Athens	8 November **1623**	1623 First Folio		**1623**

Table 4. Jackson's (1994) analysis of the stress positions in 'Shakespeare's' blank verse, expressed as "Index A".

Group*	Play, in order of date of composition proposed by Chambers (1930)	'Index A'
A	Henry VI Part 2	34
A	Henry VI Part 3	36
A	Henry VI Part 1	37
A	Richard III	32
A	The Comedy of Errors	33
A	Titus Andronicus	39
A	The Taming of The Shrew	36
A	The Two Gentlemen of Verona	29
A	Love's Labours Lost	26
A	Romeo and Juliet	32
A	Richard II	26
A	A Midsummer Night's Dream	29
A	King John	29
B	The Merchant of Venice	22
B	Henry IV Part 1	23
B	Henry IV Part 2	21
A	Much Ado About Nothing	25
B	Henry V	20
A	Julius Caesar	26
B	As You Like It	21
B	Twelfth Night	19
B	Hamlet	17
Not assigned	The Merry Wives of Windsor	(−7)**
B	Troilus and Cressida	20
C	All's Well That Ends Well	7
B	Measure for Measure	17
B	Othello	18
C	King Lear	7
C	Macbeth	9
C	Anthony and Cleopatra	5
D	Coriolanus	4
C	Timon of Athens	6
C	Pericles, Prince of Tyre, Acts 3-5	11
D	Cymbeline	1
D	The Winter's Tale	−0.4
D	The Tempest	−6
D	Henry VIII	0.3
	The Two Noble Kinsmen	Not studied

*Groups are separated according to the value of Index A: Group A 34–25; Group B 24–15; Group C 14–5; Group D <5.
**Jackson (1994) considered this value to be anomalous because it is based on a small sample of blank verse; most of *The Merry Wives of Windsor* is written in prose.

A leading analyst of style is MacDonald P. Jackson of Auckland University, New Zealand. Using the earlier work of Marina Tarlinskaja[8] as his raw material, he analysed which of the ten syllables in a standard blank verse line (iambic pentameter) in 'Shakespeare's' plays is stressed or emphasised. In theory, in a ten-syllable line every other syllable (syllables 2, 4, 6, 8 and 10) should be stressed, as we can hear in these lines of Berowne's from *Love's Labours Lost*:

> This <u>fel</u>low <u>pecks</u> up <u>wit</u> as <u>pi</u>geon's <u>peas</u>
> And <u>ut</u>ters <u>it</u> a<u>gain</u> when <u>God</u> doth <u>please</u>.

In practice authors vary this rule because repeated steady beats create a sing-song rhythm which can become boring to listen to, so they stress syllables which, in theory, should not be stressed. When Jackson examined the stresses in blank verse in the plays[9] he found that stresses in syllables one and four were less common, and stresses in positions three, six and nine were more common, in plays considered to be written by Shakespeare later in his career. Jackson expressed this trend numerically as 'Index A' (Table 4). The order of plays established using his stress analysis corresponds approximately to the order of their composition proposed by E. K. Chambers (Table 2).

Jackson's 'Index A' as applied to the plays appears to indicate an evolution of 'Shakespeare's' style from more formal (Group A) to less formal (Group D) blank verse (Table 4). We could conclude that his analysis supports Chambers' chronology. However, we must remember that Index A is not actually a dating method, and that the style of writing in a play, as expressed by Index A, may be determined partly by its subject matter. For example, Jackson himself pointed out that the Index A value for *Julius Caesar* (26) is higher than expected for its known date of composition (1599) and remarked that this is not surprising as the play "is stylistically restrained" and that in some respects it is "metrically less advanced than other plays written at about the same time". In other words, the formal classical theme of the play demanded a conventional blank verse style. Conversely, it could be argued that a play like *The Tempest*, which is essentially a fairy tale about castaways on an island and unrelated to a classical text, demanded an informal style. Hence it has a low Index A value of −6.

Index A should therefore be interpreted cautiously. The fact that it correlates well with the traditional dates assigned to the plays doesn't prove that these dates are correct. What it does indicate is that 'Shakespeare' wrote in different styles suited to the subject matter of the various plays. When the plays were written has to be independently verified by rigorous historical and literary research.

In the following chapters I therefore look into the literary history of the 'late' plays that were released publicly in some form after 1603. (I have included in this discussion *Hamlet* (first published in 1603), *Romeo and Juliet* (published in 1597) and *The Taming of the Shrew* (the date of first release is unknown) for reasons that will become apparent.) I begin with *The Tempest*, supposed by most commentators to be Shakespeare's farewell to the stage. It requires special attention as a succession of researchers have linked its storyline to events that occurred in 1609.

---

[1] Chambers (1930); an updated summary of Chambers' chronology can be found at https://en.wikipedia.org/wiki/Chronology_of_Shakespeare%27s_plays
[2] Vickers (2002).
[3] Listing in the *Stationers' Register* gave publishers the legal right to publish a printed work and provided the author with some protection against pirating of a play and unauthorised publication. It was an early form of copyright.
[4] Hieatt et al. (1991, p. 76).
[5] This total assumes that *The Taming of The Shrew* was also known as *Love's Labours Won*.
[6] *The Tempest* was performed at Whitehall in 1611 but there is no record of a public performance. *Measure for Measure* was produced at court in 1604.
[7] Paul (1950) suggested that *Macbeth* was written for a royal performance in 1606 but no historical evidence supports this proposition.
[8] Tarlinskaja (1987).
[9] Jackson (1994).

25. *The Tempest* – Shakespeare's last play?

A very ancient and fish-like smell
— *The Tempest*, Act 2, scene 2

The Tempest is the first play in the First Folio. Apparently, the regular playgoer Simon Forman did not attend a performance in 1611 when he saw *The Winter's Tale* and *Cymbeline*, since he does not mention *The Tempest* in his diary for this year[1]. However, the play was certainly on the stage in 1611: its first recorded performance was by the King's Men before James I and the court at Whitehall Palace on 1 November. It was also performed before the Princess Elizabeth (daughter of James I) and Frederick V (Count Palatine of the Rhine) in the winter of 1612–13. No public performance of the play is recorded before its publication in 1623 in the First Folio.

The play is regarded by most scholars as Shakespeare's farewell to the stage – his "last solo play"[2]. This tradition began in 1808 when the eminent researcher Edmond Malone proposed that the account of the storm in the play was based on Jacobean accounts of a shipwreck in the Bermuda Islands in July 1609[3]. A piece of evidence suggesting a date of composition in 1603 or later is the apparent borrowing by *The Tempest*'s author from John Florio's 1603 English translation of an essay written by Michel de Montaigne.

* * *

I will consider the author's apparent debt to John Florio first. John Florio was the son of Michelangelo Florio who settled in England during the reign of Edward VI, after fleeing Italy and the Inquisition. Michelangelo was a tutor to Lady Jane Grey and associated with William Herbert, first Earl of Pembroke, and his son Henry Herbert. His son John followed in his footsteps. John's interests were essentially academic and educational – for all his adult life he worked on dictionaries, treatises on grammar, books of sayings and proverbs, and translations. In the 1580s he was a tutor of French and Italian at Oxford University. When James I came to the throne Florio was appointed as Italian tutor to young Prince Henry. Florio also instructed the Queen Consort (Anne of Denmark) in languages. He was friends with William Herbert, third Earl of Pembroke and Ben Jonson but had no known association with Shakespeare or the Elizabethan theatre.

Florio's possible connection to *The Tempest* is evident in Act 2. In this act the old Counsellor Gonzalo ruminates on the attributes of an ideal commonwealth:

> I' th' commonwealth I would by contraries
> Execute all things; for no kind of traffic
> Would I admit; no name of magistrate;

Letters should not be known; riches, poverty,
And use of service, none; contract, succession,
Bourn, bound of land, tilth, vineyard, none;
No use of metal, corn, or wine, or oil;
No occupation; all men idle, all;
And women too, but innocent and pure:
No sovereignty . . .

There is no doubt that this passage is based in part either on John Florio's translation, published in 1603, of Montaigne's essay "*Of the Caniballes*"[4] or the original French version published in 1580. Describing a nation in a mythical "golden age", Montaigne (in Florio's translation) writes:

> It is a nation . . . that hath no kinde of traffike, no knowledge of Letters, no intelligence of numbers, no name of magistrate, nor of politike superioritie; no use of service, or riches or of povertie; no contracts, no successions, no partitions, no occupation but idle; no respect of kindred, but common, no apparell but naturall, no manuring of lands, no use of wine, corne or mettle.

The similarity of the two texts is clear: an air of utopian plenty and rural simplicity pervades them both. Importantly, several individual words in *The Tempest* are directly borrowed from Florio's translation of Montaigne's essay: traffic, magistrate, riches, poverty, contract(s), succession(s), occupation, idle, wine, corn and metal. The fact that the two short texts have eleven words in common establishes the author's debt to Montaigne and/or Florio beyond doubt. One might conclude that the obvious dependence of *The Tempest* to Florio's translation is proof that the play was composed after 1603, when the translation was published. But such a conclusion would be simplistic – it does not take into account the gestation of Florio's work, his social connections, and an unexplained publishing delay.

We know from the *Stationers' Register* that Florio had finished his translations of Montaigne's essays by 1600, for on 4 June 1600 "The *Essais* of Michell lord of Montaigne, translated into English by John Florio" were licensed for publication by Edward Blount[5], a London publisher and bookseller. Three years later Blount had the essays printed by Valentine Sims. What delayed publication is not known.

Florio actually began his translations of Montaigne's essays in the late 1590s, after his friend Sir Edward Wotton[6] encouraged him to translate one of the essays into English. Florio obliged and Wotton shared the translation with Lucy, Countess of Bedford[7]. (Which essay Florio translated is not known.) Subsequently the countess asked Florio to translate all Montaigne's 107 essays, which he eventually did.

Lucy was no distant acquaintance of Florio's. She was a patron of the arts and Florio moved in her circle of literary aristocratic friends. He dedicated his translation to Lucy and his other female admirers: Lucy's mother Anne

Harington[8]; Penelope Devereux Rich (Essex's sister and the "Stella" idolised in Sir Philip Sidney's sonnet sequence *Astrophel and Stella*); Elizabeth, Countess of Rutland; Mary Neville, daughter of Sir Thomas Sackville; and Elizabeth Grey, daughter of the Earl of Shrewsbury. Sir Edward Wotton received a mention as his "not-to-be-denied benefactor" and he thanked John Harington (Elizabeth I's godson and a relative of Sir John Harington of Exton, Lucy's father) for his help with the difficult French text. John Harington (or Harrington) the godson was well known at court and among the reading public for his 1591 translation of Ariosto's *Orlando Furioso*, as well as for his invention of the flush toilet.

As Florio received encouragement and support from such a range of influential people his translations of Montaigne's essays are unlikely to have been a secret endeavour. His literary friends included some in regular contact with both Essex and the Queen. We know he shared his first translation with Lucy, Countess of Bedford, and he is also likely to have shared this and his later translations with his wider circle of literary friends and benefactors. William Shakespeare is not known to have been a member of this social group, but Elizabeth I would have had ample opportunity to view Florio's manuscript translations through her contact with Essex, John Harington, the Countess of Bedford or others. Consequently the 1603 publication date for Florio's published work becomes irrelevant for determining a date of composition of *The Tempest*.

* * *

Let's now turn to the claim almost universally made by scholars who have studied *The Tempest*: that the storm scene in the play and the castaways' experiences on a strange island are based in part on accounts of a 1609 shipwreck in the Bermuda Islands[9].

As previously mentioned, this theory was first put forward by the Shakespeare scholar Edmond Malone in 1808. If the play really is based on accounts of this shipwreck, then the entire 'Elizabeth equals Shakespeare' hypothesis collapses, since Elizabeth I died in 1603. Malone's argument therefore requires close scrutiny.

Malone has great standing as a highly respected Shakespeare scholar, but this doesn't mean that we have to accept every word he wrote as gospel. More than two hundred years have elapsed since he published his ideas, so it is pertinent to ask whether any new evidence has come to light. Answers to the following questions will help us decide whether Malone's conclusions are valid[10]. Do we know for certain when *The Tempest* was first performed – was it performed before 1611? Were the relevant accounts of the Bermuda shipwreck written before 1 November 1611, the date of the first recorded performance of the play, and did they reach London in time for them to circulate and influence the writing of *The Tempest*? Are there alternative sources for *The Tempest* that better match the play's text?

Regarding the question of when *The Tempest* was first performed there is scant information. The Revels accounts[11] record a performance at court on "Hallomas nyght" (1 November) in 1611 but as the scholar Frank Kermode[12] pointed out "there is little reason to suppose that it was the first". This is all we know about the first performance.

There are several accounts of the Bermuda shipwreck. Which account was used by the writer of *The Tempest* has to be established before we investigate whether it reached London in time for 'Shakespeare' to use it. Malone suggested that Sylvester Jourdain's *Discovery of the Barmudas* (1610)[13] was a source for *The Tempest*. But later researchers[14] considered that *The Tempest* had more in common with two other narratives: William Strachey's *A True Reportory of the Wreck*[15], apparently written in Virginia by Strachey in 1610 after the Bermuda castaways (including Strachey) eventually arrived there; and the Council of Virginia's *True declaration of the estate of the colonie in Virginia: with a confutation of such scandalous reports as have tended to the disgrace of so worthy an enterprise* (1610)[16].

Strachey was an adventurer and minor writer. His *True Reportory* purports to be a letter to an unnamed lady friend, but whether it really was a private letter or whether the letter device was a literary ruse intended to make his account sound more immediate and personal is not known.

Some researchers have doubted that Strachey's account was actually penned in Jamestown, Virginia. The account was not available in print in 1611; in fact, it did not appear in print until it was published in a book called *Purchas his Pilgrimes* in 1625[17], fourteen years after *The Tempest*'s 1611 stage production, nine years after William Shakespeare's death in 1616, and two years after the publication of the First Folio in 1623.

Commentators dispense with the problem of the late publication (and potentially late availability) of Strachey's account by assuming (1) that the Hallomas performance in 1611 was indeed the first performance of *The Tempest*[18]; (2) that Strachey's account was completed in Virginia, not after his return to London; (3) that Strachey sent his letter on the ship taking Sir Thomas Gates back to England in July 1610[19] and not later; and (4) that Shakespeare either read Strachey's manuscript (or a copy of it) or had contact with Strachey after his return from the colony (possibly in late 1610 or early 1611). These are a lot of assumptions, and despite the assertions of scholars, not all are supported by historical evidence.

Some arguments supporting the Strachey source for *The Tempest* are blatantly circular. For example, while speculating on possible connections between Shakespeare and members of the Virginia Company[20], Frank Kermode (later a Cambridge and Harvard professor) noted that "there seems to have been opportunity for Shakespeare to see the unpublished [Strachey] report, or even to have met Strachey"[21]. Warming to his theory of a Shakespeare-Strachey connection, he remarked that "Shakespeare's knowledge of this unpublished work makes it probable that he was deeply interested in the [Bermuda] story"[22]. Finally, convincing himself that Shakespeare was intimately acquainted with Strachey or Strachey's colleagues, he completed his circular argument by referring to the inferred literary contacts as "these facts"[23]. Thus a scholar of the highest standing transformed possibilities into probabilities and then proceeded to convert these supposed probabilities into certainties. As noted by Stritmatter and Kositsky, "*Tempest* studies are still dominated by a series of propositions, inflated into 'facts' by a previous generation of scholars"[24].

The *Tempest* scholar Alden Vaughan[25] was equally uncritical. Accepting as fact Kermode's view that the Strachey report was circulating in London in the autumn of 1610, he wrote confidently: "With the publication in London of Silvester Jourdain's brief "Discovery of the Barmudas" in the fall of 1610 and the *simultaneous circulation* [my italics] of William Strachey's *True Reportory*..." without providing any historical evidence that Strachey's report was, in fact, circulating in 1610. He also expanded on Kermode's circular argument, referring to "the overwhelming probability that at least two copies [of Strachey's manuscript] circulated widely among [Virginia] Company officials"[26]. Strangely, he even commented on the reading habits of those lucky people who possessed one of the two circulating copies: "'True Reportory' must have been widely read, *often aloud*"[27] [my italics].

In a further descent into circular argument Alden and Virginia Vaughan conjectured that Stephano's discovery of a "monster of the isle, with four legs" in the play (Act 2, scene 2) was somehow related to a 1609 murder on Bermuda (of an individual who happened to have two legs). Recalling that the murder was only reported in print in 1614, they argued that the story must have reached Shakespeare by word of mouth: "that intriguing ingredient of the Bermuda experience... had to be heard rather than read"[28]. In case you haven't followed the argument, it goes something like this: 'In 1609 a murder was committed by one of the castaways on Bermuda. News of the murder was published in London in 1614. *The Tempest* includes a reference to the murder [actually it doesn't]. Therefore the story must have been circulating in London before 1614 and Shakespeare must have heard it.'

Unfortunately this sort of absurd speculation passes as academic scholarship. The facts are these: there is no parallel between the murder and what appears in Act 2 of *The Tempest*; there was no printed record of the murder before *The Tempest*'s first recorded performance in 1611; and there is no independent evidence that the gruesome murder story was circulating in London before 1614.

The Shakespeare scholar David Kathman[29] also treats speculation as fact, and then builds on the doubtful 'facts' to construct an argument. The italics in the Kathman quote below are mine. (None of the italicised statements are supported by evidence, and it would be prudent to consider the possibility that the "Excellent Lady" is an invention of Strachey's.)

Strachey's account is dated July 15, 1610, and *circulated among those in the know*; it is addressed to an unidentifed "Excellent Lady," *who was obviously familiar with the doings of the Virginia Company. As I will show, William Shakspeare had multiple connections to both the Virginia Company and William Strachey, and it is not surprising that he would have had access to Strachey's letter.*[30]

It is worthwhile reminding ourselves (and Kathman, and Alden and Virginia Vaughan) of the wise words of the Elizabethan historian Sir J. E. Neale: "if we set out to credit all that we cannot disprove, we shall write strange history"[31].

* * *

While it is entertaining to point out weaknesses in propositions made by respected academics, we should return to the shipwreck saga itself, and judge for ourselves whether it did in fact influence the writing of *The Tempest*. The real-life story of the Bermudan castaways is an exciting adventure, but equally interesting is the subsequent manipulation or suppression of facts by those in powerful positions in Jacobean society.

In the summer of 1609, William Strachey, Sir Thomas Gates (Governor of the Virginia colony) and Sir George Somers were all on the leading boat, the *Sea Venture*, in a fleet carrying colonists and supplies from England to the fledgling colony in Virginia.

On 25 July *Sea Venture* was separated from the other eight ships by a ferocious storm. The ship developed a severe leak but fortuitously was driven ashore onto the Bermuda Islands in daylight. No lives were lost and much equipment was saved. Pigs, turtles and birds on the islands provided the colonists with ample food and some of the castaways found the islands so pleasant that they planned a mutiny, intending to stay on the islands rather than risk starting new and uncertain lives in Virginia. However, the plot was discovered and the leading dissident was executed. On 10 May 1610, in two newly built pinnaces, the colonial castaways set sail for the North American mainland.

Arriving at Jamestown, Virginia on 23 May they found the colony to be in a desperate state – only 60 of the original 500 settlers were still alive. Gates and the castaways had insufficient stores to feed the settlers as well as themselves, so Gates decided that there was no option but to abandon the colony. The entire community, including the surviving original colonists, the new arrivals from Bermuda, and the new colonists from the remainder of the 1609 fleet (which had limped to Jamestown after the storm) were sailing down the James River on 6 June with the intent of abandoning the colony and returning to England when they met Lord Delawarr and a relief party who had set sail from England in three ships loaded with provisions. Lord Delawarr was optimistic and determined. The colony was re-established and on 12 June he appointed officials to maintain order. Strachey was appointed secretary. Significantly, in his new role as a company official, he was sworn to secrecy.

On 7 July 1610 Lord Delawarr wrote a letter to the Virginia Company in London, signed by himself, Strachey, Thomas Gates and two others, reporting on his success in re-establishing the colony. It mentioned the survival of the Bermuda castaways and their arrival in Jamestown but gave no detailed account of their adventures and did not mention Strachey's report[32] on the same subject. Lord Delawarr's letter emphasising the positives (particularly his successful restoration of order in the colony) and downplaying the negatives (mutinies and poor management) was essentially a piece of self-promotion. It was presumably sent to England with Sir Thomas Gates, who sailed home on 15 July 1610 or soon afterwards.

Eight months later Lord Delawarr became sick and on 28 March 1611 he also sailed for England. It is not known whether Strachey accompanied him, but he was certainly in London in 1612 (and possibly in late 1611) for in 1612 he published his *Address to His Majesties Councell for the Colonie of Virginia Britannia* (prefixed to his *Laws for Virginia*). Significantly, in this 1612 *Address* he admitted that he had *not* been able to bring the full story of his Bermuda and Virginia experiences to the attention of the Council of Virginia:

> I have, both in the Bermudas, and since, in Virginia, beene a sufferer and an eie-witnesse, and the full story of both in due time shall consecrate unto your views, as unto whome by right it apperteineth . . . Howbeit, since many impediments as yet must detaine such my observations in the shadow of darknesse, untill I shall be able to deliver them perfect unto your judgements, I do, in the meantime, present a transcript [of the Laws of Virginia] . . . [33]

Strachey's words "many impediments as yet must detaine such my observations in the shadow of darknesse" could mean that he had either not written his Bermuda report by 1612, or if he had written it, had not been allowed to circulate it. However, in a research paper Tom Reedy has established beyond doubt that Strachey's account *was* composed in 1610 and must have been read by whoever wrote the Council of Virginia's *True Declaration*, published in that year[34]. We can therefore be fairly certain that the sequence of events involving Strachey's report is as follows:

- Strachey's report was written by 15 July 1610;
- It travelled to London with Thomas Gates on 15 July;
- It was seen by the Council of Virginia and edited extracts were included in their *True Declaration*, which also included observations and extracts from Lord Delawarr's report dated 7 July 1610.

It is likely that Strachey's full report concerning the shipwreck and adventures on the Bermuda islands was not received favourably by the worthies making up the Council of Virginia. In 1610 they were fighting a public relations battle. Although accounts of dissent, starvation, deaths, fighting with the native Americans, shipwrecks and bad management undoubtedly reached London through sailors and returning settlers, the Council had no interest in publishing candid eye-witness accounts, such as Strachey's *True Reportory*, that reflected badly on the colony and its organisation. We should note that the company also declined to publish Strachey's *Historie of Travaile into Virginia Britannia* when he completed it in 1612, probably because it too laid bare episodes of poor leadership, factionalism, general disorder and bad decision-making. However, the Council were happy to include inoffensive extracts of Strachey's Bermuda account in their own sanitised version of events in the *True Declaration*.

It is highly probable that because Strachey had been sworn to secrecy when appointed as a company official in 1610, he was not free to circulate his full report on his own initiative. Hence his cryptic 1612 comment that his observations were detained "in the shadow of darknesse".

Despite many claims to the contrary, there is absolutely no historical evidence that Strachey's Bermuda account circulated in printed or manuscript form before its publication in 1625, despite its manifest appeal as a true adventure story – a ripping yarn that would have been a bestseller if published. William Shakespeare may have heard the Bermuda stories from Strachey himself, or from others, in late 1610 or afterwards, or he may not – we have no way of telling. In 1621 Strachey died and by 1625 the Virginia Company had been disbanded (its charter was revoked in 1624). It can be assumed that by 1625, fourteen years after the events described, enthusiasm for assigning blame for the disasters that had plagued the Virginian colony had waned and Samuel Purchas, judging that the Bermuda survival story would be eminently saleable, went ahead with publication[35].

* * *

The idea that the Bermuda accounts were used by Shakespeare when writing *The Tempest* has not been unopposed. The Reverend Joseph Hunter published a pamphlet controverting Malone's hypothesis in 1839[36] and almost 100 years ago Stoll[37] wrote: "There is not a word in *The Tempest* about America". 'Oxfordians' (those who believe that the Earl of Oxford wrote the works attributed to Shakespeare), among them Roger Stritmatter, Lynne Kositsky and Nina Green[38], have published arguments refuting recent claims by scholars (chiefly Alden and Virginia Vaughan, David Kathman, and the late Frank Kermode[39]) that the Bermuda accounts were a major source for *The Tempest*. Although A. and V. Vaughan are staunch supporters of the Strachey connection, they too have expressed reservations: "the bulk of the information in the Bermuda and early Virginian tracts is not directly relevant to *The Tempest*"[40]. A. Vaughan was similarly cautious in his 2008 paper: "a thorough rummaging through English and continental literature might uncover earlier possible sources for many, if not most, of *The Tempest*'s similarities to 'True Reportory' "[41].

The obsession of scholars with the Bermuda accounts and a possible North American connection has meant that other narratives which may have served as sources or part sources for the storm and island descriptions in *The Tempest* have not received the attention they deserve. Storms are common at sea and shipwrecks occurred regularly in the golden age of European exploration that followed Columbus' first voyage to the West Indies. Rudimentary maps, uncharted coasts, and no methods to determine longitude accurately added to the risks of sea voyages. Disasters were common. Inevitably stories of wrecks and castaways strongly resemble each other: there is a storm; the ship is damaged to the extent that it is no longer under the full control of the crew; desperate attempts are made to keep the ship afloat by bailing, pumping and discarding unnecessary cargo (and sometimes masts and rigging) overboard; orders are given in a futile attempt to avoid a lee shore; there is panic among the crew and passengers; the ship runs aground; it commonly breaks up; useful debris is retrieved; there is tragedy for some, dry land for others; survivors search for food and shelter in unfamiliar terrain; a craft may be built to take survivors back to civilisation and safety; and finally, if some of the party are literary minded, someone writes an account of hostile shores, privation, amazing adventures, and deliverance.

* * *

Before we investigate alternative sources for the play, we should document what is actually described in *The Tempest*'s storm scene.

During the storm (Act 1, scene 1) the sailors are ordered to take in the topsail. The aristocratic passengers argue with the boatswain and generally make a nuisance of themselves by getting in the way of the sailors. The boatswain orders the topmast to be lowered[42] (not a straightforward task in the middle of a storm). There is howling within the boat while the aristocrats continue arguing with the boatswain, who, in an attempt to clear the lee shore, orders two large sails to be set (two "courses"). However, the sailors admit failure and imminent disaster: "All lost, to prayers . . .". An aristocratic passenger exclaims "we split" and bids farewell to wife and children.

The passengers and crew survive and are cast ashore on an island inhabited by Prospero, Miranda (his daughter), and Caliban (son of Sycorax the witch). The spirit Ariel describes the apparently wrecked ship as being "safely in harbour . . . in the deep nook, where once Thou call'dst me up at midnight to fetch dew From the still-vex'd Bermoothes". Under instruction from Prospero, Ariel ensures that the crew are kept out of the way under the hatches of their stranded boat while the other castaways continue their adventures. Wolves and bears live on the island; the trees on the island are pines and oaks[43]. Although the "island seems to be desert, uninhabitable, and almost inaccessible", in fact it has "everything advantageous to life" and green lush grass; Caliban describes how Prospero gave him "water with berries in it"; he also refers to crabs, jays, marmosets (South American monkeys), scamels[44], filberts (hazel nuts) and pig-nuts.

The witch Sycorax is described as believing in the god Setebos. The aristocratic villains arriving with the castaways are Antonio, Sebastian and Alonso (but Alonso's qualities improve by the end of the play). A trusted councillor has the name Gonzalo and the good prince is named Ferdinand. Antonio and Sebastian plan to kill Alonso and Gonzalo and claim to have heard lions, but when they draw their swords to put their murderous plan into action they are discovered by the waking Gonzalo.

In Strachey's Bermuda account the relevant events can be summarised as follows. In the storm women and passengers are heard to shriek. The ship springs a serious leak, resulting in water five-foot deep in the hull, above the ballast. Strachey writes that the Bermuda Islands are considered by most to have "no habitation for men, but rather [they are] given over to devils and wicked spirits" but notes that the shipwrecked mariners find them to be "as habitable and commodious as most countries of the same climate and situation". The Spanish author Gonzalus Ferdinandus Oviedus[45] is mentioned. Cedars, oaks and palms grow in the forests and the castaways eat palm and cedar berries; they also describe fruits (nuts?) like almonds, and find that certain berries "made a kind of pleasant drink" when allowed to stand for three or four days. The birds on the island are sparrows, robins, swans and sea-meawes (gulls) and the animals are pigs and turtles (also called tortoises). Strachey lists twelve types of fish that the castaways catch, as well as lobsters, crabs, oysters and whelks.

If 'Shakespeare' drew on Strachey's Bermuda account in order to describe the storm it should be possible to prove precise verbal parallels where similar scenes are described. The comparison[46] is less than convincing. In *The Tempest* the topsail is taken in, the topmast is ordered lowered and two large sails are set in an effort to clear the lee shore; no such desperate attempt to gain sea room is mentioned by Strachey, who says the sails were kept "wound up" (furled) and at most a storm sail ("hollocke") was used to guide the ship. There is a general but inexact correspondence of 'Shakespeare's' "howling" within the boat and Strachey's "strikes" [shrieks?] of the women and passengers. Prayers are mentioned by 'Shakespeare' and by Strachey, but again the correspondence of the texts is not close: 'Shakespeare's' characters utter religious platitudes ("Mercy on us" etc.) but Strachey writes that prayers were on the lips of unspecified people (probably the passengers) but could not be heard above the shouting of the officers. In *The Tempest* story Ariel "flam'd amazement" on the prow, deck, poop, topmast (was it still standing?), yards and bowsprit, and in the cabins, and his fire, "cracks" and thunderclaps were accompanied by sulphurous roaring. Miranda describes the lightning as being like burning pitch being poured down from the sky. In Strachey's account wind, rain and tumultuous seas are described but not lightning; thunder is only mentioned in passing. Instead Strachey reports that a "little round light" or a "sparkling blaze" is seen on the main mast, jumping between the shrouds and travelling along the length of the main yard and then returning. The prow, deck, poop, topmast, bowsprit and cabins are not mentioned. Ariel's fire terrified both passengers and crew; Strachey's "little round light" was innocuous and the subject of wonder.

Miranda describes the ship as "dash'd all to pieces" but Ariel, after Prospero has worked his spell, assures him that the same ship is "safely in harbour . . . in the deep nook [inlet]". Neither description has a parallel in Strachey's report or in the reports of the Council of Virginia or Jourdain – in these the leaking ship is deliberately run aground, where it wedges between rocks.

'Shakespeare's' island is inhabited by Prospero, Miranda and Caliban; Strachey's Bermuda was uninhabited. 'Shakespeare's' island has a temperate fauna and flora (wolves and bears, pines and oaks) and freshwater springs. On Strachey's Bermuda island water could only be found by digging; wolves, bears and pines are not mentioned – the shipwrecked sailors instead remark on the palms, cedars and oaks, a prickly pear, a wide variety of birds and fish, and pigs and tortoises (turtles).

Prospero's "water with berries in it", which he gave to Caliban, could possibly be derived from Strachey's account of making a drink out of berries but the verbal parallel is inexact: the Bermudan castaways let their berries stand for days, implying fermentation was occurring, whereas Prospero's beverage appears to have been berry-flavoured water. Both 'Shakespeare' and Strachey list unusual food items but of those listed by Caliban (crabs, jays, marmosets, scamels, filberts and pig-nuts) only crabs appear in Strachey's list.

Out of context, the reference in *The Tempest* to the Bermuda Islands (or Bermoothes, as the islands are named in the play) seems to indicate a definite link between the play and the Bermuda accounts. However, a close reading of *The Tempest* and Strachey's account reveals the contrary. In the Strachey account there is no doubt that the Bermuda Islands are the islands reached by the castaways after the storm. In contrast, in *The Tempest* the Bermoothes are somewhere else, far away: Prospero instructs Ariel to fetch dew "from the still-vex'd Bermoothes". If one lives (say) on Easter Island one does not ask one's helper to fetch something *from* Easter Island. It follows that Prospero's instruction to Ariel must refer to a place that is *not* the island inhabited by Prospero and Miranda.

The phrase "the still-vex'd Bermoothes" may be relevant for determining the date of composition of *The Tempest*. It implies that *The Tempest*'s author considered the islands to be unfavourable for habitation, and that *The Tempest* was written *before* the Bermuda castaways' reports of the pleasant and benign nature of the islands were circulated.

However, the reference to the Bermoothes may not be a reference to the Bermuda Islands at all, since in Jacobean times the Bermoothes suburb was known as a London brothel district[47] as were other areas on London's South Bank[48]. If this interpretation of "Bermoothes" is intended, Prospero is not only asking Ariel to obtain something from somewhere far away, but he is also asking Ariel to achieve a task impossible for mortals: to find dew (signifying purity) in a place where it is least likely to be found. The wry humour would not be lost on playgoers who had come to hear a comedy.

The textual comparisons summarised above show that there is only general agreement between the detail in the Bermuda accounts and that in the fictional *Tempest* account. But David Kathman[49], in an article published in 2005, listed fifty parallels which he insisted are "evidence that in writing *The Tempest*, Shakespeare made extensive use of narratives describing the wreck and redemption of the ship the *Sea-Venture* in Bermuda in 1609, and the events which ensued when the crew made it safely ashore".

In his eagerness to discredit Oxfordians who have led the argument that *The Tempest* was written before the Earl of Oxford died in 1604, Kathman overstates his case. He writes "Strachey's account . . . circulated among those in the know" but this is speculation, not evidence. He fails to appreciate that we actually know nothing about the manuscript's circulation, or whether it was circulated outside the confines of the Virginia Company. He writes that Strachey's account is addressed to an unidentified Excellent Lady "who was obviously familiar with the doings of the Virginia Company" but he allows neither for the possibility that the Excellent Lady mentioned is Strachey's literary device to make his account appear to be a private letter (thus allowing him to deflect accusations of breaking his oath of secrecy) nor does he present evidence that any candidates for the Excellent Lady addressee were "obviously familiar" with the doings of the company. Finally, he states that "William Shakespeare had multiple connections to both the Virginia Company and William Strachey, and it is not at all surprising that he would have had access to Strachey's letter". Perhaps 'Shakespeare' did have "multiple connections" and perhaps he didn't. The statement is too dogmatic and the argument is circular. Hard evidence is needed.

Like the Oxfordians whom he is intent on discrediting, Kathman oversimplifies his argument. The questions that should be asked are broader than the simple one 'Did the Bermuda accounts serve as sources for *The Tempest*?' Kathman has not considered two possibilities. Firstly, that the text of *The Tempest* printed in the 1623 First Folio may not have matched that used by the actors for the stage production of 1611 or the author's original – it may have been edited by other hands, as happened with several plays published after 1603[50]. Secondly, that Strachey himself may have edited the manuscript of his *True Reportory* before he died in 1621, and could have done this *after* seeing a performance of *The Tempest* or reading the play in manuscript. We must remember that Strachey was not a historian in the modern sense. He was a minor writer, an investor in the theatre and a friend of writers and playwrights. While his *True Reportory* undoubtedly is based largely on eye-witness records, the more subjective parts like the description of the storm may have been embellished to heighten the contrast between the near-death experience of those on board the ship and their subsequent miraculous deliverance.

It is not sufficient for Kathman to show that the play and Strachey's *True Reportory* have words and happenings in common; Kathman needs to show that there is *more* in common between the play and *True Reportory* than between the play and other accounts of storms and landfalls in strange lands. In addition, his list of about fifty detailed parallels is faulty. They have been refuted (in a rather formal pedantic fashion) by Nina Green[51]. This chapter is not the place to consider them all in detail, but the example of Kathman's writing given below is typical of the weakness of his style of argument. He is writing about the similarity between the mention of 'hatches' in *The Tempest* and in Jourdain's and Strachey's accounts of the Bermuda storm:

> Jourdain writes "all our men, being utterly spent, tired, and disabled for longer labour, were resolved, without any hope of their lives, to shut up the hatches". Strachey also mentions a general determination to "shut up hatches" once it became obvious that the exhausted crew could not pump or bucket out the water entering the boat fast enough to save it.

Hatches are indeed mentioned in the play. Ariel describes "The mariners all under hatches stow'd" in the miraculously preserved ship (Act 1, scene 2, line 230). In Act 5, scene 1, lines 98–99 Prospero informs Ariel that he [Ariel] will find "the mariners asleep Under the hatches" (apparently forgetting that this knowledge was given to him earlier by Ariel). In Act 5, scene 1, lines 230–231 the boatswain tells Alonso "We were dead of sleep And – how we know not – all clapp'd under hatches".

There is no parallel between the description of Bermudan events involving hatches and the text of the play, apart from the use of the single word "hatches". Neither Strachey nor Jourdain says that the sailors retired to their bunks or hammocks under the hatches (which would have been a suicidal course of action in a sinking boat with a serious leak). What they apparently did resolve to do was to close the hatches, i.e., abandon their exhausting work of pumping and bailing, for it was all to no avail.

Interestingly the researcher Barry Clarke[52] has noted a close parallel between the boatswain's comment above and a report on Thomas Cavendish's 1591 voyage to South America and the Magellan Strait in which it is written "the next day the storm ceased, and most of our young sailors . . . being weary with their night's work that was past, were under hatches asleep". (Note that the sailors on Cavendish's voyage were not on a sinking ship; they only retired under the hatches after their exhausting night-time exertions and after a storm.) Another example of stowing people under hatches is found in a description of Francis Drake's circumnavigation: after taking Spanish prisoners at Valparaiso, Drake "stowed them under hatches"[53], words very similar to those in *The Tempest*: "the mariners all under hatches stowed."

With these earlier reports in mind, we can be sure that in the play 'Shakespeare' did not need to read the Bermuda accounts to be reminded of this convenient means of getting unwanted personnel out of the way so that the aristocrats could go about their important business of arguing with each other and falling in love on a small island. In addition, we should remember that Drake reported directly to the Queen after his circumnavigation and gave her his written account of the voyage – she may have picked up the idea of clapping potentially troublesome sailors under hatches from Drake himself.

* * *

In summary, the parallels between 'Shakespeare's' storm scene and that described in the Bermuda accounts are not strong: there are general similarities of the type expected in descriptions of a storm involving wooden ships, but there is little detailed correlation, and the words common to the Bermuda accounts and the play are those that any author might use, given the similar overall context of the historic (Bermuda) or fictional (*Tempest*) accounts. As the Shakespeare scholar J. D. Rea remarked in 1919: "none of the [Bermuda] accounts contain any striking points of similarity to Shakespeare's storm, except such as are natural in any description of a shipwreck . . . Mr. Malone has given the [his] argument all the advantage it could derive from the artful aid of capitals and italics, but he seems to me to fail to show coincidence in anything, except what has been common to all storms and all disastrous shipwrecks from the beginning of the world"[54].

Importantly, those proposing links between Strachey's *True Reportory* and the play seem to be unaware of several relevant issues: the uncertainty concerning the date of composition of *The Tempest*; the fact that Strachey was sworn to secrecy about Council of Virginia matters; that Strachey's *True Reportory* was, in all likelihood, suppressed by the Virginia Company; the absence of any evidence that *True Reportory* was in circulation in 1611, or indeed at any time before its 1625 publication; and the possibility that *True Reportory* may have been edited or embellished between being written in 1610 and being published in 1625.

Confident statements such as "that Shakespeare knew these narratives is now generally agreed"; "he was deeply interested in the [Bermuda] story"; "Shakespeare was interested in the Gates expedition and in the New World generally"; "he was certainly acquainted with members of the Virginia Company"[55]; or "Shakespeare's almost certain familiarity with some of the [Virginia Company's] councilors"[56] are pure speculation unsupported by evidence. Stoll's 1927 conclusion that "This proof rests upon a few slight verbal parallels, most precariously. There is not a word in *The Tempest* about

America..." is correct: the play contains no certain direct reference to Virginia or the shipwreck of the *Sea Venture* as described by Strachey.

Although modern commentators mostly agree with Malone (1808) and Luce (1901) that the plot of *The Tempest* is partly sourced from the Bermuda accounts, this conclusion does not withstand critical examination. Are there alternative accounts that may have served as sources for *The Tempest*?

---

[1] Simon Forman's *The Bocke of Plaies and Notes* is an account by the astrologer Simon Forman of the plays he saw; it is catalogued as MS 208 in The Ashmolean Museum in Oxford.

[2] For example, see Vaughan and Vaughan (2003, p. 1).

[3] Malone (1808).

[4] Florio (1603).

[5] Hadfield (2013, p. 81).

[6] Sir Edward Wotton was the older brother of Sir Henry Wotton (1568–1639), who served as secretary and informant for Robert Devereux, Earl of Essex.

[7] Lucy was a patron of writers. She was the daughter of Sir John Harington of Exton, first cousin of Mary, Countess of Pembroke and a friend of Essex's sister Penelope Devereux Rich.

[8] Before her marriage Anne was at one time a maid of honour to Queen Elizabeth I.

[9] The following text in this chapter and that in chapter 26 is based in part on the journal article by McIntosh (2012) and I thank the publishers Taylor and Francis for permission to use the earlier text in an edited and extended form.

[10] McIntosh (2012) examined Malone's hypothesis, and the ideas of researchers who support his conclusions.

[11] Stamp (1930).

[12] Kermode (1964, p. xxii).

[13] Kermode (1964, 141) provides an accessible version of the relevant passages of Jourdain's account.

[14] Luce (1901); Kermode (1964, p. xxviii); Vaughan (2008); Vaughan and Vaughan (2003, 2011).

[15] The most relevant parts of Strachey's report, first published by Purchas in 1625, are reproduced by Kermode (1964, pp. 135–140) and Vaughan and Vaughan (2003, pp. 288–302).

[16] Force (1844) includes the Council of Virginia report.

[17] Purchas (1905) is a relatively modern edition of the original 1625 text.

[18] For example, in their Introduction to the 1999 Arden edition Vaughan and Vaughan (2003, p. 1) wrote "First performed in 1611" without commentary or supporting evidence.

[19] The earliest date that Strachey's account could have left Virginia is 15 July 1610, when (according to Strachey's account) Sir Thomas Gates planned to set sail for England. Gates may have actually sailed a few days later.

[20] In April 1606 King James, by means of a charter, granted private investors in a joint-stock company (The Virginia Company of London) permission to establish a colony in North America. By this means the King encouraged colonisation at little cost to the Crown.
[21] Kermode (1964, p. xxviii).
[22] Kermode (1964, p. xxvii).
[23] Kermode (1964, p. xxviii).
[24] Stritmatter and Kositsky (2009, p. 8).
[25] Vaughan (2013).
[26] Vaughan (2008, p. 273).
[27] Vaughan (2008, p. 271).
[28] Vaughan and Vaughan (2011, pp. 141–142).
[29] Kathman (undated); https://shakespeareauthorship.com/tempest.html (accessed June 2018).
[30] Kathman (undated); https://shakespeareauthorship.com/tempest.html (accessed June 2018).
[31] Neale (1958, p. 99).
[32] Major (1849) prints the contents of this letter in his introduction to Strachey's book *The Historie of Travaile into Virginia Britannia*.
[33] Major (1849, p. xxi); the manuscript of *The Historie of Travaile into Virginia Britannia* exists in two states in which this quote varies slightly.
[34] Reedy (2010). Tom Reedy also demolished the arguments presented by Stritmatter and Kositsky (2009) in support of Strachey writing his report after 1610 and his supposed borrowing from *A True Relation*.
[35] Purchas (1905).
[36] Major (1849).
[37] Stoll (1927).
[38] Stritmatter and Kositsky (2007, 2009); Green (2005).
[39] Kermode (1964), Vaughan and Vaughan (2003), Vaughan (2008) and Vaughan (2013).
[40] Vaughan and Vaughan (2003, p. 43).
[41] Vaughan (2008); A. Vaughan added that Strachey's packaging of the descriptions of the storm, landfall and survival in one document lent support to the proposal that Strachey's *True Reportory* was Shakespeare's source.
[42] The reason for taking down the topmast is to lessen the leeway the ship makes as a result of the force of the wind on the mast and rigging, and to lessen the rolling motion of the ship by reducing the weight aloft. Reducing leeway is especially important when attempting to clear a lee shore. Lowering of the topmast would normally be carried out when stormy weather was anticipated; it would be a difficult and dangerous procedure to attempt in the middle of a storm.
[43] Cedars are mentioned by Prospero in his speech rejecting magic in Act 5, scene 1, but not in the context of a description of the island's attributes.
[44] According to the Chambers Dictionary (10th edition; Anonymous 2006) a scamel is "alleged to be a Norfolk name for the bar-tailed godwit"; Vaughan and Vaughan (2003, p. 217) suggested scamels were shellfish and perhaps mussels. As Caliban promises Stephano "young scamels from the rock" the shellfish meaning is considered most likely to be correct.

45 Strachey uses the latinised form of the name of the Spanish author Gonzalo Fernández de Oviedo y Valdéz. Oviedo published a novel *Claribalte* (1519) and two other books: *Historia General Y Natural de Las Indias* (in many volumes) and *Las Quinquagenas de la Noblesse de España*. The first part of the *Historia General de las Indias* was printed in Seville in 1535 and later appeared in French and English translations, by Poleur in 1555 and Eden in 1556 respectively.

46 Kathman (undated); https://shakespeareauthorship.com/tempest.html (accessed June 2018) listed parallels.

47 Vaughan and Vaughan (2003, p. 165). However, some researchers believe that the London district referred to only acquired the name 'Bermoothes' sometime after Bermuda was settled in 1612.

48 Karras (1996, p. 38). Vaughan (2008), quoting a source from the 1620s, points out that the name "Bermudoes" applied to a residence in Millford Lane, London (present-day Milford Lane, near the Strand) used by the ex-Governor of Bermuda after his return in 1615. This may be so, but the use of this name for a house in Millford Lane does not exclude the use of the name Bermoothes for a district elsewhere.

49 Kathman (undated). See endnote 46 above.

50 Vickers (2002).

51 Green (2005).

52 Clarke (2016).

53 Purchas (1905, volume 2, chapter 3, p. 130). First published 1625.

54 Rea (1919). The second part of this quote is Rea's reproduction of Hunter's reply to Malone, as quoted by Furness (1892), who did not provide references.

55 All four quotes are from Kermode (1964, pp. xxvi and xxvii).

56 Vaughan (2008, p. 261).

26. *The Tempest* – the Spanish-American connection

What see'st thou else In the dark-backward and Abisme of Time?
– The Tempest, Act 1, scene 2

We know for certain that *The Tempest* includes European knowledge of South America: the play mentions marmosets (South American monkeys) and the demon Setebos (god of Sycorax the witch) who was invoked for help by the hapless Patagonian captured and shackled by Magellan's crew, as described in Antonio Pigafetta's (1525) account of the first circumnavigation of the globe[1]. Pigafetta also described St Elmo's fire, tempests and assorted giants and cannibals, making it likely that Pigafetta's Italian account (or the 1577 English translation and summary by Richard Eden) was a source used by the author of *The Tempest*. An additional source may be Francis Fletcher's account of Francis Drake's 1577–1580 circumnavigation of the world, in which Setebos is again mentioned, as is a deadly tempest and a native addicted to wine[2].

But what prompted 'Shakespeare' to search in accounts of South American voyages for a suitable name for a pagan god associated with witches, when he or she could have easily chosen a character from the more familiar rich classical mythology of Europe? After all, Prospero's fictional island is located in the Mediterranean Sea in Greece's backyard, not in some distant ocean, and the main characters have Italian or Spanish names.

The South American link to *The Tempest* is well established and irrefutable. It is therefore a little surprising that most researchers have insisted on the primacy of the Bermuda accounts as sources for *The Tempest* and not explored possible South American links (many of which concern Spanish seafarers) more thoroughly. Could it be that these researchers, mostly working in British or North American universities, unconsciously favour the supposed North Atlantic and Virginia connections?

Stritmatter and Kositsky[3] have investigated alternative sources. They have shown that Peter Martyr's first three books of *De Orbo Novo* [*From the New World*][4], as translated by Richard Eden, are full of images and descriptions that also occur in *The Tempest*: apparently uninhabitable landscapes found to be fair and fruitful, spirits imprisoned in trees, food such as pignuts, and animals including jays, tortoises and marmosets. Of the personal names mentioned by Eden, those of Alonso the Duke of Milan, Antonio, Stephano, Sebastian, Ceres and Francisco are also found in *The Tempest* but, significantly, not in Strachey's *True Reportory*. Eden also describes conspiracies and mutinies.

Stritmatter and Kositsky argue that the author of *The Tempest* also drew on descriptions and stories in several other works. These include Ludovico

Ariosto's *Orlando Furioso* [*The Frenzy of Orlando*] first published in Italian in 1532 and translated into English by Sir John Harington on the instruction of Queen Elizabeth I and published in 1591. They also suggest as a source the account of the storm in Desiderius Erasmus' *Naufragium* [*The Shipwreck*] published in Latin in 1523. John Rea[5] considered *Naufragium* to be much closer to *The Tempest* than the Bermuda accounts, both in events described (for instance, rich passengers arguing with the crew), and in the description of St Elmo's fire first appearing on the mast and then descending to the lower parts of the ship, and in the tone and the treatment of events. For example, in *Naufragium*, as in *The Tempest*, we are introduced to the storm at its height. We are not told where the storm-tossed ship has come from or where it is going.

Another possible source for *The Tempest* is Gonzalo Fernández de Oviedo y Valdés's fifty-volume work *Historia General y Natural de las Indias* [*General and Natural History of the Indies*], of which part 1 (the first nineteen books) was published in 1535. Although Oviedo completed a manuscript of the other 31 books by 1549 the full work was not published before his death in 1557. Book 50 by Oviedo, entitled (in translation) *Misfortunes and Shipwrecks in the Seas of the Indies, Islands, and Mainland of the Ocean Sea*[6], describes numerous storms and shipwrecks and miraculous accounts of survival under harrowing circumstances.

It is noteworthy that one account in book 50 describes "The marvelous case of a Portuguese ship that left the port of Santo Domingo to return to Portugal and was blown to the Island of Bermuda" where the ship foundered on shoals. The crew saved the cargo and survived by eating palm shoots, turtles and fish and drank water from shallow holes they dug in order to collect water from seepages. They then built a new boat from cedars growing on the island and sailed back to Santo Domingo. It is tempting to suggest that this historical event, as well as others described by Oviedo in book 50, might have influenced the writer of *The Tempest*. However, book 50 was only published in the 1850s[7]. Although the historian Glen Dille reports that Oviedo's sixteenth century writings were available to scholars who "were able to consult and copy the manuscripts"[8] and remarked that that multiple copies of the manuscripts exist[9], none of these copies is known to have reached England in Elizabethan or Jacobean times.

Clearly there are many possible sources for the story of *The Tempest*. It is probable that more than one source was used, for the sixteenth century was the golden era of Spanish exploration, and thanks to Richard Eden, many accounts of adventures in new lands were available to the educated English. But literary historians seem to have missed the accounts of another South American explorer and writer who, I believe, could have influenced the writer we call Shakespeare. Let me introduce him.

* * *

Fifty years after the Portuguese explorer Magellan, sailing under the Spanish flag, passed through the strait now bearing his name the Spaniards had consolidated their hold on South America. But Francis Drake's attacks on Spanish ships and towns along the western seaboard of South America in 1578 and 1579 prompted another seafarer and adventurer, Pedro Sarmiento de Gamboa, to suggest to King Philip II of Spain that he should finance a venture to colonise and fortify Magellan Strait, which at the time was considered by the Spanish to be the only access to the Pacific Ocean from the east. (Drake's discovery of Drake's Passage, the open ocean between South America and Antarctica, was kept secret by the English.) It probably all sounded very logical to the King – to protect the Pacific coast you must fortify the narrow passage connecting the South Atlantic and South Pacific, and in this way close the door to English pirates. He funded Sarmiento's expedition.

In 1579 Sarmiento set out from Peru on a reconnaissance of Magellan Strait, making notes in his journals on the topography, climate, vegetation, animals and people encountered on the voyage[10]. At one location Sarmiento noted that the forest trees were cypress, fir, holly, myrtle, evergreen and oak[11] – "trees like those of Spain" – and on an island in the western part of Magellan Strait he noted "there are plenty of small fruits, like black grapes"[12]. The sailors supplemented their diet with shellfish: "of fish we saw red prawns – a good fish – cockle shells and an immense quantity of other shells"[13]. On 1 February 1580 he had to put down a mutiny[14]. On 7 February he described lights in the sky, which were probably a display of *aurora australis*: "During this night, at one o'clock, to the SSE we saw a circular, red, meteor-like flame, in the shape of a dagger, which ascended in the heavens. Over a high mountain it became prolonged and appeared like a lance, turning to a crescent shape between red and white"[15]. Sailing eastwards, on 13 February, near Santa Ana Point he noted that "the footmarks of tigers and lions were seen". (These may have been puma tracks.)

Like a real estate agent, he had his eye on enticing people to settle. He remarked that the "air [was] healthful . . . there seemed to be land here with good climate suitable for a settlement . . . this region is warmer and has a better climate than those we had passed [in the western part of the Strait]. Moreover it is pleasant to look upon, is capable of sustaining a large population, and wild and tame flocks, and would yield grain" and "there were large glades and spaces of very good pasture".

During this voyage Sarmiento saw enough to enable him to convince the King that a second voyage to establish a Spanish settlement on land adjacent to the Strait was worthwhile. He embarked on his second voyage with sixteen ships on 9 December 1581. Storms reduced his fleet to ten. These left the southern coast of Brazil on 13 January 1582. At the River Plate there was a mutiny: the Captain General of Chile, Don Alonso de Sotomayer, abandoned the expedition and landed his troops. On 1 February 1584, with his remaining five vessels, Sarmiento arrived at the eastern end of Magellan Strait. With extraordinary determination he established two Spanish settlements (doomed to failure) in the extremely remote environment. The first settlement (in the east) he named City of Jesus and the second (about 50 km southwest of present-day Punta Arenas) he named Don Felipe. Gonzalo de Reyna and Fernando de Requeña were two of the witnesses in a ceremony that took possession of the land for King Philip. The Spanish party found "black berries of a thorn tree, well flavoured and nourishing"[16]. An attempt to beach a ship so that she could be unloaded was mismanaged: low tide found the ship stranded in an "arm of the sea" and the boat started to break up while settlers and soldiers were still in the ship: "There were still soldiers and settlers in the ship . . . who were hurled about at every lurch"[17].

While marching with his men to establish the western settlement Sarmiento de Gamboa noted creeping herbs which produced a "sweet and wholesome" small fruit, and another fruit resembling cherries. He remarked "This land is pleasant and fertile, producing much fruit, as well the red cherries as [sic] the berries growing on thorn trees, and there are many wholesome and sustaining shell-fish"[18].

At the western settlement of Don Felipe (later more appropriately renamed Port Famine by English sailors) Sarmiento forestalled a mutiny organised by an ex-soldier named Alonso Sanchez and others named Antonio Rodriguez, Juan Alonso and Francisco de Gody. When apprehended the mutineers "had weapons in their hands with the intent of mutiny"[19]. Sarmiento had Antonio Rodriguez executed. He also mentioned that he helped establish the settlement by chopping wood[20].

While preparing to load stores at the City of Jesus on 26 May 1584 Sarmiento's last remaining ship was blown into the South Atlantic by a furious storm lasting 20 days (at least this is what his journal records). He worked his way up the coast to Bahia harbour where another great storm dashed his ship to pieces. He and a Negro slave survived and reached shore by holding onto planks. All was lost from the ship except two or three barrels of wine and a small piece of artillery.

After this brush with death, which might have defeated a less determined man, he obtained another ship and new provisions and on 13 January 1585 he finally departed from Rio de Janeiro intending to relieve the settlements in the Strait. His journal notes that on reaching latitude 33°S[21] "we encountered a gale from the west and south-west, which was so furious that it was judged to be the worst and most terrible we had seen". As his description of this storm appears to have links to the storm described in *The Tempest*, I quote it in full below:

> . . . todos los elementos andaban hechos un ovillo, y comenzó con un trueno y rayo que quebró sobre nuestras cabezas, tan bajo y horrible, que pareció haberse abierto el mar en un abismo de fuego, quedando todos atronados y fuera de sentido, y mirándonos unos a otros no nos conocíamos, y cada ola

nos comía . . . y comenzamos a correr [a] árbol seco donde el viento quería, y fueron tan terribles los golpes de mar que reventó los barraganetes del navío y lo abrió, de suerte que jugaba la cubierta de popa; y viéndonos sin remedio humano, confiado en Dios . . .

. . . all the elements seemed to be entangled together. The thunder and lightning broke over our heads, so low and horrible, that it seemed as if the sea had opened an abyss of flame. We were all amazed[22] and without feeling. Looking at each other we could not recognise those nearest to us. Every sea threatened to overwhelm us, and one struck the port quarter of the poop, sending the starboard side under the sea. Then we all thought we must be drowned, and we called to God for help . . . The blows from the sea were so terrible that they tore open the bulwarks and washed over the deck of the poop. Seeing no human remedy, we again commended ourselves to God . . .

There are numerous parallels between descriptions in Sarmiento de Gamboa's journals and those in *The Tempest*. Although accounts of storms and strange experiences at sea necessarily have common themes, the vocabulary used by Sarmiento is closer to that used in *The Tempest* than Strachey's. Both accounts mention thunder and lightning and calls to God for help, but note how in both Sarmiento's account and in *The Tempest* the word "flame" (*fuego*) is used. (In contrast Strachey's vocabulary is different: he describes a "little round light" or "sparkling blaze".) The similarities continue: in *The Tempest* the ship is first wrecked then miraculously preserved in a "deep nook" (secluded harbour) and in Sarmiento's writings a ship is stranded in an arm of the sea, then wrecked. In *The Tempest* mariners remain in the stranded ship; in Sarmiento's account of a ship stranded on the beach "There were still soldiers and settlers in the ship . . . who were hurled about at every lurch".

In Sarmiento's journals we read of islands, lights in the sky, short-statured natives and features having parallels to 'Shakespeare's' description of Prospero's island: berries and shellfish, land which is pleasant and fertile with pastures suitable for supporting animals, and freshwater springs. Sarmiento mentions evergreens and oaks and the writer of *The Tempest* writes of pines and oaks. Significantly there is no mention in *The Tempest* of the prickly pear and palms of Bermuda — surely these exotic plants would have stuck in the mind of any writer reading Strachey's account. Sarmiento mentions shellfish (identified as mussels), as does Fletcher in his account of Drake's voyage, and so does the writer of *The Tempest*. Sarmiento, Fletcher and Caliban find springs of water but Strachey specifically notes their absence. Sarmiento himself "set to work to cut wood" and in *The Tempest* Prospero sets Ferdinand to work carrying logs.

The mutineers who challenged Sarmiento's authority have the names Alonso or Antonio; these are the names used for villains in *The Tempest*. Sarmiento's party includes officials named Gonzalo and Fernando (a name equivalent to Ferdinand); these names correspond to the names of the trusted councillor and the good prince in *The Tempest*. Sarmiento describes wine casks being washed ashore after a shipwreck; a wine cask is washed ashore in *The Tempest*.

In both *The Tempest* and in Sarmiento's account mutineers are apprehended with weapons in their hands. In *The Tempest* the mutineers excuse their drawing of swords by saying they had heard the bellowing of bulls or lions; Sarmiento mentions seeing the tracks of tigers and lions. Sarmiento notes strange lights in the sky in the Strait of Magellan and voices of devils are heard in the Azores; both observations have parallels in *The Tempest*.

Considered in isolation, some of these parallels could be expected to occur by chance, but in total they establish the likelihood of a connection between Sarmiento's account and *The Tempest*, especially as Sarmiento's parallels are more specific than the supposed parallels between the Bermuda accounts and *The Tempest*.

Sarmiento's journals, in combination with Antonio Pigafetta's (1525) account of the first circumnavigation of the globe, the 1577 English translation and summary of the same by Richard Eden, Francis Fletcher's account of Francis Drake's 1577–1580 circumnavigation[23] and Desiderius Erasmus' *Naufragium* contain all the necessary information to explain the details of the shipwreck, geography, superstition and natural history mentioned in *The Tempest*. But how, one might ask, did an author living in London in a nation at war with Spain become aware of Sarmiento's unpublished Spanish journal?

Sarmiento himself provides the answer. Significantly it fits perfectly with the hypothesis that Elizabeth I was *The Tempest*'s author. Let's resume the story of this larger-than-life adventurer.

After the storm of January 1585, Sarmiento was stranded on the South American mainland. Incredibly, he built another ship and he sailed from Bahia on 22 June 1586. This time his aim was to cross the Atlantic and seek help for his isolated colonists by directly appealing to the King of Spain. On 11 August he was near the Azores when misfortune struck again – his vessel was attacked by English ships commanded by Jacob Whiddon, in the service of Sir Walter Ralegh[24]:

> La estadía de Sarmiento de Gamboa en Inglaterra se prolongó durante solo dos meses: desde el 31 de agosto de 1586 hasta el 30 de octubre del mismo año. Sarmiento había sido capturado por Jacob Whiddon, un marino al servicio de sir Walter Raleigh, escritor y político de gran influencia en la corte de Isabel Tudor. Sarmiento, que llegó a Inglaterra con la fama de ser el mejor marinero de España, pronto se ganó la confianza de Raleigh y recibió un trato de huésped. Aunque las actividades del gallego durante este tiempo no son del todo conocidas, resulta evidente que se reunió con exploradores y cosmógrafos, y que proveyó a los ingleses de ciertas informaciones geográficas concernientes a la Mar del Sur.

Sarmiento de Gamboa's stay in England lasted for only two months: from 31 August 1586 to 30 October of the same year. Sarmiento had been captured by Jacob Whiddon, a sailor in the service of Sir Walter Ralegh, a writer and statesman of great influence in Elizabeth I's court. Sarmiento, who arrived in England with the reputation of being Spain's foremost seafarer, promptly gained Ralegh's confidence and received guest treatment. Although the activities of the Galician [Sarmiento] during this time are not fully known, it is evident that he met with explorers and cosmographers and provided the English with certain information about the geography of the Southern Ocean.

Sarmiento was captured and taken to Plymouth where he was held until 11 September. He didn't languish in grim confinement – he was too important a catch for this treatment. Instead, on 14 September he was taken to Hampton Court and the next day to Windsor. Here he met Sir Walter Ralegh. The two conversed in Latin and exchanged seafaring stories.[25] Dom Antonio the Portuguese Pretender, at that time resident in London, took issue with the friendliness offered to Sarmiento and, according to the latter, plotted to kill him – an example of another villain called Antonio and another possible link to the plot of *The Tempest*.

Queen Elizabeth also met with Sarmiento and the two conversed in Latin for more than two and a half hours. No meeting with William Shakespeare is recorded. Sarmiento also met Admiral Lord Howard and William Cecil during his six weeks at court. These senior Elizabethans were already familiar with his journals, which were seized when he was captured. They no doubt avidly read these for their geographical descriptions and the information they provided on Spanish intentions in South America. Elizabeth is also likely to have been informed of the existence of the journals and knowing Spanish may have read them herself. Alternatively, she may have quizzed Sarmiento during his audience with her.

Finally, on 30 October 1586 Sarmiento left London for France and Spain. He never made it back to South America. King Philip at this time had other things to think about – the Armada and the invasion of England. His isolated settlers in an ill-conceived and extremely isolated colony had to fend for themselves. Only one is known to have survived.

As mentioned above, there are close verbal parallels between Sarmiento's accounts and *The Tempest*'s text. There is also documentary evidence that Sarmiento's account of his voyage circulated among court officials in London. In contrast, despite claims to the contrary by scholars who should know better, there is no evidence for the circulation of the most detailed of the Bermuda accounts (Strachey's) before 1611, and Strachey's own writings in 1612 indicate that his account of the Bermuda affair was not circulating by this date.

From Sarmiento's account and Sir Walter Ralegh's record of his conversation with him it is apparent that Sarmiento was an affable man of great energy self-confidence and considerable charm. His stories about faraway places, strange peoples, colonisation of remote lands, storms and shipwrecks, survival and hardship, intrigues and mutinies are likely to have circulated widely in court circles in the weeks he spent in Windsor and London, under mild house arrest.

* * *

There is another historical fact that supports the idea that Elizabeth had more than a passing interest in South American geography. On 24 August 1578, Francis Drake was in the Magellan Strait. He named an island in the eastern part of the strait Elizabeth Island after his sovereign. On exiting the western part of the strait unfavourable winds swept his ship southwards to the Tierra del Fuego archipelago. Here he named the southernmost island he encountered Elizabeth Island[26] after the Queen. He took possession of both Elizabeth Islands for the Crown. Francis Fletcher drew a sketch map of the southern island (Figure 5) which appears in a copy of the first part of his journal (the copy was made by John Conyers of London), catalogued as Sloane MS 61 in the British Library.

The island was highly significant for Drake and future navigators. On landing on it and reaching its southernmost extremity[27] he established that, as far as the eye could see, there was open water to the south, separating South America from the putative southern continent, thus disproving the Spanish assumption that Magellan Strait was the only passage around South America to the Pacific[28]. The researcher Helen Wallis identified this second Elizabeth Island with Henderson Island west of Cape Horn[29]. An inspection of Google Earth shows that the sketch by Fletcher, when inverted so that north is at the top, does indeed have points in common with the southern part of the southernmost island of the Henderson Group (Figure 6): a small lake approximately 75 metres wide near the south coast has a roughly rectangular shape and is drained by a stream flowing south to the sea. This could be the "pool" sketched by Fletcher.

We must remember that Drake was not intent on accurately charting the islands of the archipelago or their topographical features (he was actually trying to reach Peru) and it was quite possible that he and Fletcher could not see the northern extent of the island on which they landed because of low cloud or rain or the high ground north of the lake, with the result that Fletcher's sketch displays an island much smaller than the actual.

But let us return to the 'first' (northern) Elizabeth Island. This featured in banter between Sir Walter Ralegh and Sarmiento. Ralegh, in his book *The History of the World*, recounts the conversation:

> I remember a pretty jest of Don Pedro de Sarmiento, a worthy Spanish gentleman, who had been employed by his king in planting a colony upon the Straits of Magellan: for when I asked him being then my prisoner, some questions about an island in these straits, which me thought might have done

benefit or displeasure to his enterprise, he told me merrily, that it was to be called the Painter's Wife's Island, saying, that while the fellow drew that map, his wife sitting by desired him to put in one country for her; *that she, in imagination, might have an island of her own* [30] [my italics].

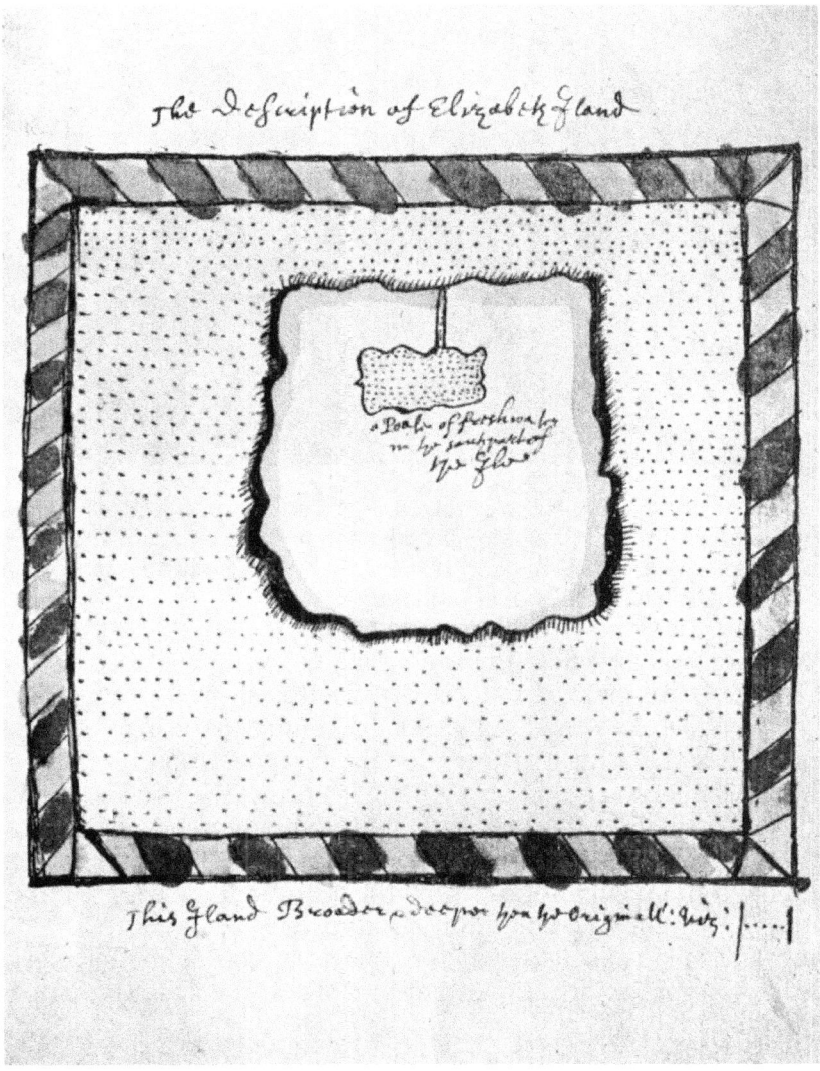

Figure 5. Fletcher's map of the second (southern) Elizabeth Island that Drake named on his circumnavigation. South is at the top. The text written within the island's outline reads "A pool of fresh water in the southern part of the island".

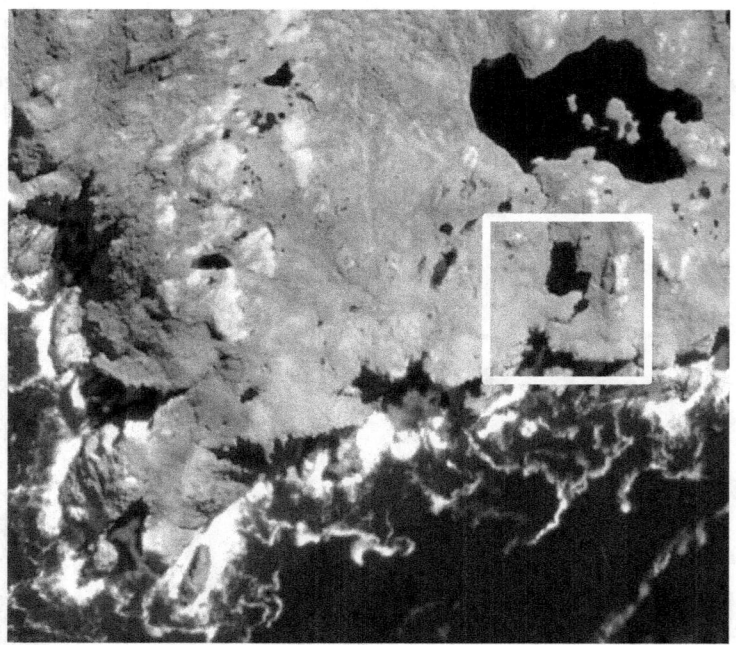

Figure 6. The southernmost island of the Henderson Group, south of Magellan Strait, has a small and roughly rectangular lake about 75 metres wide draining directly into the sea (see box). This may be the "pool" sketched by Fletcher as being located in "Elizabeth Island". *Google Earth image.*

If we take this anecdote at face value, as being the record of banter between two adventurers, the painter Sarmiento referred to must be Drake himself, for when Drake was at sea he spent evenings painting sketches of the coastlines he passed, for future navigational reference. Drake's wife was called Elizabeth so Sarmiento could simply have been making a joke about Drake being influenced by his wife. But, as Helen Wallis pointed out, Sarmiento's comment was probably an attempt to belittle England's claim to the northern Elizabeth Island in Magellan Strait, which had been annexed by Drake in the name of the Queen, the royal investor in his voyage.

A comment made in 1652 by Peter Heylen, a geographer and clergyman, confirms this interpretation: "I fear that the Painter's wife hath many islands and some countries too"[31].

We can be certain that Drake's annexation of the two Elizabeth Islands and his naming of them in honour of the Queen was reported to his sovereign, after his circumnavigation and triumphant return, probably in person by Drake himself during his six-hour conversation with her. The Queen, "in imagination", did have an island of her own (actually two). Francis Drake's act of annexation provided Elizabeth with a ready-made remote territory which she, in her imagination, could inhabit with her own creations: a bookish ruler, sailors and aristocrats; a chess-playing maiden looking for love; and uncooperative or hostile natives.

On this island goodness and intellect eventually triumph over people with sinister intentions, just as they did in the year of the Armada. For Elizabeth it appeared that, like Miranda, she had found a soul mate and true love. *The Tempest* was probably written soon after the momentous events of 1588.

---

[1] Paige (1969).
[2] Vaughan and Vaughan (2003, p. 41).
[3] Stritmatter and Kositsky (2009).
[4] Peter Martyr was an Italian whose accounts (in Latin) of the history of Spanish exploration in Central and South America were first published as an eight-volume collection in 1530. The first three volumes were translated from Latin into English by Richard Eden in 1555. In 1577 Richard Willes republished these volumes, with supplementary notes.
[5] Rea (1919) includes an English translation of the original in his research note.
[6] Dille (2011).
[7] The four-volume edition was edited by J. Amador de los Rios and printed in Madrid in 1851–1855 (Dille 2011, p. 175, note 15).
[8] Dille (2011, p. xxvi).
[9] Dille (2011, p.175, note 13).
[10] For printed versions see documents of the Colección Muñoz (1866) and Rosenblat (1950); quotes in English are from the translation by Markham (1895).
[11] The larger broadleaved trees are likely to have been southern beeches, classified in the *Nothofagus* genus (split into 4 subgenera in 2013), most of which are evergreen. The cypress and fir were probably podocarps of the *Libocedrus* genus.
[12] Markham (1895, p. 118).
[13] Markham (1895, 319) noted that the large bivalve, the Magellan mussel, is the staple food of the Fuegians for most of the year.
[14] Markham (1895, p. 104).
[15] Markham (1895, p. 115).
[16] Markham (1895, p. 305).
[17] Markham (1895, p. 310).
[18] Markham (1895, p. 319).
[19] Markham (1895, p. 325).
[20] Markham (1895, p. 326).
[21] Rosenblat (1950) gives the latitude as 39°.
[22] In Rosenblat (1950) the original Spanish word used by Sarmiento is '*atronados*' which translates as 'deafened', 'bewildered' or 'stunned'. Markham may be using the word 'amazed' in the 'bewildered' or 'stunned' sense.
[23] Published in edited form by Drake's nephew as *The World Encompassed*. Part of Fletcher's diary has survived as a copy, now held in the British Library.
[24] Oerhli and Carrandi (2016).

25 Sir Walter Ralegh, in his *History of the World*, records a seafaring anecdote exchanged with Sarmiento on this occasion. See the quote later in this chapter.
26 Doran (2003, p. 148) reproduces John Conyers' map, copied from the original 1578 sketched by Francis Fletcher, of southern South America. The map includes the southernmost island in Tierra del Fuego, which is labelled Elizabeth Island. Beyond it is open sea (Drake's Passage).
27 According to an anecdote written by Richard Hawkins, and reproduced by Wallis (1984), Drake, on "going ashore, carried a compass with him, and seeking out the southernmost part of the island, cast himself down upon the uttermost point, groveling, and so reached out his body over it. Presently he imbarked, and then recounted to his people, that he had been on the southernmost known land in the world, and more further southwards upon it, than any of them, or any man yet known". It is possible that Drake walked to the southwest promontory shown in Figure 6. This is about 800 m west-southwest of the putative site of Fletcher's "pool of freshwater".
28 Ortelius' map of 1570 showed the imagined southern continent extending to the southern shore of Magellan Strait. The Spanish belief that the Strait was the only access from the South Atlantic to the Pacific justified Sarmiento's proposal that fortification of Magellan Strait would effectively control incursions into the Pacific by state-sponsored pirates like Drake.
29 Wallis (1984).
30 Wallis (1984, pp. 152–153).
31 Wallis (1984, p. 153).

27. The 'late' Roman plays: *Anthony and Cleopatra* and *Coriolanus*

In Nature's infinite book of secrecy A little I can read
  – Anthony and Cleopatra, Act 1, scene 2

Both these 'late' Roman plays explore the role played by individuals during conflicts between great powers. Neither play is known to have appeared in print before 1623. *Coriolanus* is not mentioned in any record before it was printed in the First Folio of 1623, but there is some evidence that *Anthony and Cleopatra* existed by 1608. I will consider the history of this play first.

Although "a booke Called. ANTHONY. & CLEOPATRA" was entered in the *Stationers' Register* in 1608 in the name of the publisher Edward Blount, no publication is known to have followed. The *Stationers' Register* record may have been a 'blocking' entry to assert copyright and prevent publication of a pirated version of the play. Although we cannot be absolutely sure that the "booke" referred to in the *Stationers' Register* was a play, the "booke of PERICLES" was entered on the same day, so it seems likely that both refer to original manuscripts or copies of the plays we now refer to as written by Shakespeare.

Neill[1] argues that plays by other authors on the Anthony and Cleopatra story, published in 1606 and 1607, seem to make use of a Shakespearean text, so presumably the author's manuscript or a copy was circulating early in the first decade of the 1600s, which may account for Blount's blocking entry. But if a manuscript or copy of the play was circulating, it is unlikely that it was in the hands of a company or actors, because there is no record that the play was staged before the First Folio was published. Indeed, the evidence is to the contrary: the stage directions in *Anthony and Cleopatra* introduce several ghost characters who play no part in the action; some stage directions are incorrect, as are some speech prefixes; and several directions are so vague that they are useless for guiding the action on the stage. Noting these deficiencies of the Folio text as "disquieting", Neill[2] concluded:

> "the absence of contemporary production records, when combined with the unsuitability of the Folio text for use in a Jacobean playhouse, makes it possible that the play was never actually performed in Shakespeare's lifetime . . . it seems difficult to credit that the King's Men [Shakespeare's company] would have passed up the opportunity of staging so magnificently theatrical a work . . ."

It certainly *is* surprising that such a powerful play was never staged. But this is indeed the only conclusion that can be drawn from the text available to us. If it had been staged, then surely the First Folio editors Heminges and

Condell, both surviving members of Shakespeare's own company, would have used an edited version of the play when assembling the First Folio material, but they didn't: the First Folio text is not suitable for staging. The only evidence that a stage version might have existed is indirect: when writing his anti-Catholic melodrama *The Devil's Charter* (first performed at King James I's court in February 1607) the playwright Barnabe Barnes described Cleopatra dying by snake bites on her breast rather than on her arm (as in Plutarch, the play's main source), and in 'Shakespeare's' play the same mode of dying is described. But, as Michael Neill has pointed out[3], the idea that Cleopatra applied the snakes to her breast was "widespread" in Elizabethan England and the story appears in both Thomas Nashe's *Christ's Tears over Jerusalem* (1596) and George Peele's *Edward I* (1593). Consequently, the proposition that in 1606 or 1607 Barnes noted this detail about Cleopatra's suicide during a stage performance of 'Shakespeare's' *Anthony and Cleopatra* or by inspecting the author's manuscript is irrelevant. Neill's conclusion is likely to be correct: no stage version had appeared when Blount first registered the play in the *Stationers' Register* in 1607 or indeed before the play's publication in 1623.

This is all very curious: if the play was written by William Shakespeare why, after spending long hours writing the masterpiece, didn't he or a colleague ready it for production by including appropriate stage directions and arranging for it to be performed, so that he and his company could profit from his endeavours?

But what if the play was written by Elizabeth? Let us pause for thought … it describes a tragic love affair between a strong-willed Queen and a military man who is past his prime, who has glorious campaigns behind him but who loses a crucial engagement (which turns out to be his last) with his enemies. He commits suicide and she suicides soon afterwards.

The parallels with Elizabeth's passion for Essex are obvious and have been remarked on by scholars[4]. Although Essex was not a professional soldier like Sir John Norris or Charles Blount, or a state-sponsored pirate like Sir Francis Drake, he did have a spectacular success to his credit: the Cadiz raid (although it wasn't his success alone). He staked his future on being militarily successful in Ireland, but here he failed disastrously. He died on the block. Elizabeth did not commit suicide but her spirit died with him. Two years later she was also dead. We can hypothesise that Elizabeth wrote *Anthony and Cleopatra* in 1601 or 1602 but did not release it to the playhouse as its subject matter was painful to her and a tragic love story concerning a queen and her general was so obviously paralleled by her relationship with Essex that releasing the play publicly in the early 1600s might have generated unpredictable and unwanted comments from the public. As the play appears in the *Stationers' Register* of 1608, it seems probable that in 1607 or 1608 either a manuscript or copy of it had escaped into Edward Blount's hands, or was intentionally released by whoever had charge of Elizabeth's papers.

To test the plausibility of the hypothesis that the play was written in 1601 or 1602 we need to check the source material for the play – can any source be dated with certainty to 1603 or later? I have listed the sources below, with their publication dates:

> *Lives of the Noble Grecians and Romans* (North's translation of Plutarch's work; 1579).
> *Cleopatra* by Giraldi Cinthio (1542)
> *Cleopatra* by Cesare De Cesari (1552)
> *Cléopatra Captive* by Estienne Jodelle (1552)
> *Marc Antoine* by Robert Garnier (1578)
> *The Tragedy of Antony* (the Countess of Pembroke's translation of Garnier's work; 1590)
> *Antonius* by the Countess of Pembroke (1592)
> *A Geographical History of Africa* (John Pory's 1600 translation of Leo Africanus' 1592 work)

As all the sources of the play date to 1600 or earlier, the play could have been written by 1600, or indeed by 1592 if Leo Africanus' work was read in the original 1550 Italian version, or in the French and Latin translations published in 1556. Although, in theory, the play could have been written as late as 1608, when it was recorded in the *Stationers' Register*, nothing in it indicates composition after 1600, and there are no references to contemporary events in the play that support its composition after this date. Therefore, the widely-held view that the play was written in the years 1606–1607[5] has no firm foundation. The reason scholars support a late date of composition may be their unconscious desire to sprinkle a few masterpieces into William Shakespeare's rather lean last thirteen years.

* * *

Now let us turn our attention to *Coriolanus*. The 1623 First Folio contains the earliest known text. No quarto editions[6] of *Coriolanus* have survived and there is no evidence that any were printed. The play is not mentioned in the *Stationers' Register*, or by any playgoer, or in any formal document before being printed in 1623. It is not mentioned by Francis Meres in *Palladis Tamia* (1598). If we assume that Meres listed all the 'Shakespeare' plays with which he was acquainted, then *Coriolanus* had neither been performed nor published before 1598.

As with the plays previously considered, analysis of sources used when writing the play are useful for determining the earliest date of composition. The scholars Malone[7] and Bullough[8] pointed out that the unusual phrase "you have lurch'd your friends of the better half of the garland" (meaning 'you have deprived your friends of the better half of the honours') in the closing scene of Ben Jonson's *Epicœne* (staged 1609 or 1610) is similar to the phrase, spoken by Cominius in *Coriolanus* in Act 2, scene 2, "he lurch'd all swords of the garland" (meaning 'he deprived all other fighters of honours') and suggested that Jonson borrowed the unusual combination of "lurch'd" and "garland" from *Coriolanus*. If the Malone/Bullough argument is accepted, *Coriolanus* must have been written by late 1609 or 1610 and must have either been staged or circulated in some form accessible to Jonson by these approximate dates. But this conclusion, if correct, does not tell us when *Coriolanus* was written.

Muir[9] and Bullough[10] demonstrated the play's dependence on Thomas North's *The Lives of the Noble Grecians and Romans,* a translation of Jacques Amyot's 1559 French translation of Plutarch's *Parallel Lives of the Greeks and Romans*. *Coriolanus* depends on North's translation not only for plot details but also for many words and phrases, showing that North's book was undoubtedly a primary source. The play uses the word *conduits* found in North's 1595 edition, not *conducts* as in the 1579 edition of the same work, so composition in or after 1595 is indicated, unless we assume that *The Tempest*'s author independently corrected 'conducts' to 'conduits'.

An important inclusion in *Coriolanus* is an ancient story that scholars refer to as 'the fable of the belly'. This fable compares the functioning of the state to the inter-dependence of the organs of the human body, which all work together for a common benefit. The fable was used in medieval times to justify the powers of the state or those of the church. It appears in John of Salisbury's *Policraticus*, book VI (1159). In this account, translated into English by J. Dickenson[11], the fable is presented as an apology by Pope Adrian IV for the oppression and avarice of the Church of Rome. In Camden's revised account the fable is also attributed to Adrian IV but is given an Elizabethan context and presented as a justification of taxation and the rule of monarchs.

The fable appears in a speech by Menenius in *Coriolanus* Act 1, scene 1, lines 95–153[12]:

> There was a time, when all the body's members
> Rebell'd against the belly; thus accus'd it:
> That only like gulf it did remain
> I'th'midst o'th'body, idle and inactive,
> Still cupboarding the viand [food], never bearing
> Like labour with the rest, where th'other instruments
> Did see, and hear, devise, instruct, walk, feel,
> And, mutually participate, did minister
> Unto the appetite and affection common
> Of the whole body. The belly answer'd:
> 'True is it, my incorporate friends,' quoth he,
> 'That I receive the general food at first
> Which you do live upon; and fit it is,
> Because I am the store-house and the shop
> Of the whole body. But if you do remember,
> I send it through the rivers of our blood
> Even to the court, the heart, to th'seat o'th'brain;
> And through the cranks and offices [constrictions and parts] of man,

> The strongest nerves and small inferior veins
> From me receive that natural competency
> Whereby they live. And though all at once cannot
> See what I deliver out to each,
> Yet I can make my audit up [account for everything], that all
> From me do back receive the flour of all,
> And leave me but the bran [residue].

Menenius then explains that "The senators of Rome are this good belly, And you [the protesting citizens] the mutinous members".

Philip Brockbank[13], summarising arguments presented by earlier researchers concerning the source of Menenius' fable of the belly in *Coriolanus*, argued for the author's indebtedness to Philemon Holland's 1601 translation of Livy's *Ab Urbe Condita*, William Averell's *A Mervailous Combat of Contrarieties* (1588) and William Camden's *Remaines of a Greater Worke Concerning Britaine* (1605). All these sources contain a version of the fable. A short version of the fable was presented by Sir Philip Sidney in his *An Apology for Poetry* (1595).

Brockbank argued that verbal parallels between Menenius' fable of the belly and the version attributed to Pope Adrian IV by Camden in *Remaines* show that the author of *Coriolanus* had either read the published version of *Remaines* (in or after 1605) or seen a manuscript version, which was probably in existence in 1603, the date of Camden's dedicatory epistle in the printed version. The scholar Bullough[14] was categorical: "The play was certainly written after the publication of Camden's *Remaines*" (i.e. in or after 1605).

Muir[15] was more circumspect: "The actual vocabulary of Menenius' fable owes more to Averell's [1588] version than to any other". In the retelling of the fable in *Coriolanus* Averell's words *cormorant*, *instrument*, *mutually*, *participate*, *rivers*, *sink* and *viand* are all used, and elsewhere in Averell's pamphlet all the significant words employed by Menenius appear, e.g., *contrariety*, *crammed*, *dissentious* and *superfluity*, though not *smile* and *gulf*. The word *smile* is too common to be a source indicator, and Muir noted that the unusual word *gulf* was previously used in *Richard III*, so was already in 'Shakespeare's' vocabulary. Consequently, the absence of these two words is immaterial to the argument, because the other words in common between Averell's pamphlet and *Coriolanus* demonstrate that a debt to Averell is indisputable.

In contrast, the debt to Holland's 1601 translation of Livy is uncertain. Although Brockbank wrote that "To Holland's Livy he [Shakespeare] owes the suggestion that the belly distributes blood through the veins into all parts of the body", an alternative and reasonable explanation is that the original Latin passage in Livy (in the same book II of *Ab Urbe Condita* that contains the biography of Coriolanus), rather than the passage in Holland's translation, was the source for Menenius' description of food being circulated to the body via the bloodstream. A relatively recent translation of the Livy passage reads "the belly . . . did not receive more nourishment than it supplied, sending, as it did, to all parts of the body that blood from which we derive life and vigour, distributed equally through the veins when perfected by the digestion of the food"[16]. Clearly the concept of the blood distributing nourishment through the body was neither Holland's invention nor the result of idiosyncratic translation, but comes from Livy himself, which means that it is not necessary to assume that Holland's translation must be a source. The phrase "rivers of blood" is too common a classical metaphor to be used to deduce a source text. A debt to Holland's version of Livy is therefore doubtful.

To help determine which version of the fable (out of those mentioned above) was the source for Menenius' speech in *Coriolanus* it is useful to list the significant words that each substantial account has in common with the fable as it appears in *Coriolanus* (Table 5). I have included John of Salisbury's version, as translated by Dickenson (1963), in this analysis.

A third of the significant words appearing in the *Coriolanus* version of the fable (43 out of a total of 127) are found in one or more of the other accounts. The *Coriolanus* version has more words in common with the account of John of Salisbury (31) than with that of Camden (18), Livy in a relatively modern translation (16), Livy in Holland's translation (19), or Sidney's version (6). Significantly, of the 18 words common to the accounts in *Coriolanus* and Camden's *Remaines*, only the words *good* and *gulf* are not used by John of Salisbury, and on their own these two words are not sufficient to prove a dependence of the *Coriolanus* account on *Remaines*.

We can conclude that there are greater parallels of vocabulary between Menenius' speech and John of Salisbury's text than to William Camden's *Remaines*. In regard to use of Holland's Livy, it is surprising and possibly significant that 'Shakespeare' did *not* borrow Holland's unusual words *concocting* and *delightsome*, which we might expect to have caught the eye of the great collector of new vocabulary.

In summary, we can be certain that the author of *Coriolanus* borrowed from Averell's 1588 book *A Mervailous Combat of Contrarieties*, but it is unlikely that Menenius' speech is based on either Holland's translation of Livy or Sidney's short account of the fable of the belly. Although there are similarities between Menenius' speech in *Coriolanus* and Camden's account of the fable of the belly, those between Menenius' speech and John of Salisbury's much earlier account (in *Policraticus*, dating to 1159) are greater. For these reasons the argument that Menenius' fable of the belly in *Coriolanus* is sourced from Camden's *Remaines* cannot be sustained.

Table 5. Comparison between the vocabulary of the belly fable in *Coriolanus*, *Policraticus* (John of Salisbury; translated version by Dickenson (1963)); *Remaines of a Greater Worke Concerning Britaine* (Camden); *Ab Urbe Condita* (Livy, translated by Freese et al. (1904) and Holland); and *An Apology for Poetry* (Sidney). In column 1 words or their close derivatives occurring both in the *Coriolanus* version and in any other version are printed in bold type. In columns 2, 3, 4, 5 and 6 words or their derivatives common to that column and column 1 are also printed in bold.

In *Coriolanus*	John of Salisbury	Camden	Livy (Freese et al. 1904)	Livy (Holland)	Sidney
Accused	Abstain	Accord	Accordingly	Agreed	
Accusers	Accumulate	Advice	Afforded	Altogether	
Affection	Acquitted	Agreed	Agree		
All	Action	Allow	Anything		
Agents	Advantage	Allowances	Apparent		
Answer(ed)	Advantageously	**Arms**			
Appetite	**All**				
Apply	Alternates				
Arm	**Arms**				
Audit	Attend				
Back	Belong	Beheld	**Belly**	Befell	**Belly**
Bearing	**Beneficial**	Better	**Blood**	**Belly**	**Body**
Belly	Blame	**Body**(ies)	**Body**	**Blood**	
Benefit	**Body**			**Body**	
Blood	Bold				
Body	**Brain**				
Brain	Brother(s)				
Bran					
Cares	Callous	Cause	Calmly	Came	Concluded
Comes	**Care**	Comforted	Chew	Carefulness	Conspiracy
Common	Cast	**Common**	Conspiracy	Chew	
Cormorant	Cause	**Common-weales**	Convey	Commons	
Competency	Claim	Conspired	**Counsel**	Concocting	
Complain	Cleaving	Consumed		Conspired	
Counsellor	Closely	**Counsel**		Consumption	
Counsels	Commenced	Course		Convey	
Court	**Common**				
Cranks	**Common-wealth**				
Crowned	Conspired				
Cupboarding	Consumes				
	Contend				
	Contrariwise				
	Counsel				
Deliberate	Day	Day	Degree	Delightsome	Devoured
Deliver	**Deliberation**	Desired	Derive	**Digesteth**	
Devise	Denounced	Dim	Desiring	Distributeth	
Digest	Depends		**Digestion**		
Discontented	Devoured		Distributed		
	Devours				
	Dim				
	Distribute(d)				
	Due				

Envied	Ear	Ears	Emaciation	Enjoy	End
Examine	Empty	Enemy	Enjoy	Enough	
Eye	Enemy	Estate	Entered	Extreme	
	Enfeebled	**Eyes**	Entire		
	Eye(s)		Equally		
Fabric	Failed	Faint	**Food**	Famish	Fruits
Feel	Faint	Faltered		Fed	
Find	Fatal	Far		Fell or feel	
First	Feeble	Fareth		**Fit**	
Fit	Feet	Feet		**Food**	
Fitly	Filled	Followed		Fresh	
Flour	Followed	Forbear		Full	
Food	Foot	Functions			
Foremost	Forthcoming				
Former	Fruits				
Friends					
General	Gathered	**Good**	Gratification	Gotten	
Good	Grasping	Grievous		Grind	
Grave	Greediness	**Gulf**			
Gulf	Greedy				
Head	Hands	Hands	Hands		
Hear	Harm	**Heard**	Human		
Heart	**Hearing**	**Heart**			
Helps	**Heart**	Hunger			
	Hungry				
Idle	**Idle**	**Idle**	**Idle**	Intent	
Incorporate	Ills		Indignant	Intestine	
Inferior	Irksome		Indignation	Inward	
Instruct			Individual		
Instruments			Influence		
		Jointly			
Kingly	**King**				
Labour	Labouring	Laboured	**Labour**	**Labour**	**Labour**
Leg	**Labours**	**Labours**	Last	Lands	
Little		Laid open	Language	Like	
Live		Lay open	Life	Limbs	
Lungs		Lazy		**Little**	
		Limbs		**Live**	
Malign	Magistrates	Matter	**Members**	**Man's**	**Mutinous**
Man	Manifold	**Members**	Midst	Meaning	
Members	**Members**	Misery	Mouth	Meat	
Midst	**Midst**			**Member**	
Minister	Military			**Midst**	
Muniments				Minded	
Mutinous				**Ministry**	
Mutually				Mood	
				Mouth	
				Mutinied	
Natural	Necessity	Necessity	Nothing		Notorious
Nerves	Nought		Nourishment		
	Nourished				
	Numb				
Once	Observe	Others	**Office**		
Offices	**Office**				
	Oppressiveness				
	Others				

Patience	Paid	**Parts**	**Parts**	**Parts**	**Part**
Participate	**Part**	Passed over	Perfected	Perfect	Plagued
Parts	Palate	Peace	Pleasures	Fined	Punishing
Petty	Passage	Performed	Presented	Pleasures	
Proceeds	Passed	Persuasion	Provided	Poor	
Public	Pay out	Pine away			
	Peace	Princes			
	Perform	Proclaimed			
	Persuaded	**Public**			
	Pervert				
	Plain				
	Present				
	Pressure				
	Prince(s)				
	Provide				
	Public				
Rascal	Rationer	Reason	**Receive**	Reach	
Rash	Reason	**Receiving**	Reduced	**Receive(d)**	
Rebelled	**Received**	Re-established	**Resting**	Repined	
Receipt	Refuge	Repine			
Receive	**Remains**	Respect			
Remain	**Rest**				
Remember	**Restored**				
Replied	Revived				
Rest					
Restored					
Restrained					
Rightly					
Rivers					
Rome					
Seat	Said	Served	Sending	Same	Short
See	Sated	**Spake**	Service	Sedition	Spender
Senators	**Seeing**	Steward	Several	**Seen**	**Starve**
Send	Seeks	Stomach	**Starve**	Self	
Shop	Senses	Supply	Supplied	Serve	
Sink	Service	Support		Service	
Small	Sick	Swallowing		Several	
Smile	Silence			Small	
Soldier	**Soldier**			Speech	
Speak	Somewhat			Still	
Starvation	Soundness			Stomach	
Steed	Speech			**Strength**	
Storehouse	**Starvation**				
Strongest	Starve(d)				
	State				
	Stomach				
	Strength				
	Supplied				
	Sustain				
	Sustenance				
	Swore				

Tauntingly	Take(n)	Tedious	Teeth	Teeth	Tale
Things	Temporal	Themselves	Time	Thoroughly	Time
Tongue	Themselves	**Tongue**		Thought	Themselves
Touching	Toil	Travelled			Thought
Trumpeter	**Tongue**				
	Took				
	Tribute				
	Truth				
Unactive	Utility				Unprofitable
	Utterly				
Veins	Voracious		**Veins**	**Veins**	
Viand			Vigour		
Vigilant					
Walk	Wages	Want		Wasted	
Way	**Walking**	Wars		Wise	
Weal o'th' common (Commonweale or Commonwealth)	Watchfully	Waxed		Working	
	Weak	Withdrawn			
	Weight	Withdrew			
	Welfare				
	Well-known				
	Whole				
	Withdrew				
	Work				
Yourselves					

Ignoring the above conclusion for a moment, it must be pointed out that those who have insisted that *Remaines of a Greater Worke Concerning Britaine* is a significant source for *Coriolanus* (notably Bullough) have not taken into account the genesis of *Remaines* and Camden's place in London society. If the title is taken at face value, and *Remaines* is in fact a collection of Camden's notes 'left over' from his greater work *Britannia* (published in 1586), Camden is likely to have collected the belly fable before 1603 (when he penned the dedicatory epistle in *Remaines*) or by 1605 at the latest (when *Remaines* was published). Camden was a noted teacher and historian in London in the 1590s and counted Ben Jonson among his acquaintances. His notes for this book could well have been circulated among his friends, colleagues and pupils, or been used as teaching material, long before their publication in 1605, so it is reasonable to assume that his pupils and literary colleagues may have known of his writings well before they were published.

* * *

Allusions to contemporary events in *Coriolanus* have potential for dating the play, and four deserve careful assessment. The first is contained in the statement by Caius Martius (who after his victory at Corioles adopted the name Coriolanus) asserting that the rebellious citizens cannot be trusted (Act 1, scene 1, lines 169–173):

> ... He that trusts to you,
> Where he should find you lions, finds you hares;
> Where foxes, geese: you are no surer, no,
> Than is the coal of fire upon the ice,
> Or hailstone in the sun.

The Shakespeare scholar Bullough argued that line 172 related to a specific event described by Thomas Dekker: the great frost of 1607/8, when "pans of coals to warm your fingers" were available to citizens walking over the frozen Thames[17]. However, Bullough's idea is far-fetched; for his argument to be credible Caius Martius' speech should describe a similar event to the Thames freezing over. But Caius Martius does not mention hard frosts, frozen rivers, pans of coals or cold fingers. He is speaking metaphorically: 'You citizens are no more consistent than cinders on ice: first hot then cold; or hailstones in the sun, first hard then melting away'. We should also note that the Thames froze over at other times, notably around Christmas 1589[18]. As any Elizabethan or Jacobean householder would have been familiar with the throwing out of hot cinders onto winter ice, I suggest that there is no more justification for relating the phrase "coal of fire upon the ice" to an historic hard frost than for relating the phrase "hailstone in the sun" to an historic hailstorm followed by sunshine. Furness was forthright, dismissing this and other supposedly topical allusions with the comment "these evidences are all of slight import"[19].

The second possible allusion to a contemporary event concerns the phrase (Act 2, scene 2, pp. 95–96) "he'll turn your current in a ditch And make your channel his" which Harrison[20] suggested related to a 1609 plan to build a canal from Hertfordshire to London. If Coriolanus had been speaking about engineering works Harrison's argument might have some merit, but Coriolanus is again speaking metaphorically: 'he'll divert the powers of the patricians and senators to advantage himself', and for the ditch metaphor to spring to mind it is doubtful that a writer would need the stimulus of a Hertfordshire canal proposal. For those who insist on an engineering origin for the words one might also point to the 1593 quarrel between the Earl of Shrewsbury and Sir Thomas Stanhope over a weir Stanhope had constructed on the River Trent[21] for diverting water for *his* own advantage. However, it is unnecessary to search further than North's translation of Plutarch for lines concerning diversion of water supplies: North's *Lives* tells how Coriolanus compelled the plebeians to yield to him by cutting off "the pipes and conduits by which the water ran into the Capitol".

Attempts to relate the mention of scarcity of grain in *Coriolanus* to the food riots in the Midlands in 1607/08 can be dismissed with a similar argument: an account of scarcity of grain in Rome occurs in North's *Lives* so it is not necessary to suppose that the author of *Coriolanus* drew from contemporary experiences in rural England. Even if local food shortages did prompt the reference in *Coriolanus*, there were shortages of food and consequent unrest at other times in late sixteenth and early seventeenth century England[22].

Bullough[23] argued that Shakespeare's "reduction of the grievances [of the citizens] almost to the one about dearth was surely topical", but overstated his case, for Rome's unruly citizens do not in fact complain only about dearth. On the contrary they list several grievances (Act 1, scene 1, lines 80–84): they are going hungry while the rich (the patricians) are hoarding grain; the laws support usurers; laws limiting the power of the rich are being repealed; and laws restraining the powers of the poor are being enacted. Bullough's argument also overlooked the fact that in order to achieve dramatic effect 'Shakespeare' undoubtedly simplified, selected, and compressed aspects of the Coriolanus story as told in the source documents. The combining of Plutarch's usury and famine riots into one disturbance need not imply an intent by the author to comment on a recent event in England – the conflation of several events may well have been determined by the demands of the stage.

Muir[24] devoted several pages to comparing the "political theory" contained in *Coriolanus* to that in four books published in the early 1600s, each of which referred to the Coriolanus story. Dudley Digges discussed the use of war for curing internal dissension in *Four paradoxes or Politique Discourse* (1604). Richard Knolles' 1606 translation of Bodin's *Six Bookes of a Commonweale* (1606) warned of the danger of banishing a great man from the state. Edward Forset, in his *A Comparative Discourse of the Bodies Natural and Politique* (1606), promoted the idea that "maladies of the bodie politique" require the firm action of a sovereign physician, and to support his argument he included in his book a brief version of the belly fable. William Fulbecke noted the evils of democracy in his book *The Pandectes of the Law of Nations* (1602).

Muir's analysis demonstrated that issues of privilege, leadership style, state malfunction and the perceived threat of democratic principles were matters of intense discussion among the intellectuals at the time. However, such democratic stirrings within a corrupted parliamentary system, were characteristic of late Elizabethan and early Jacobean writings concerning political theory[25]. The sharing of ideas between authors is not surprising and cannot be taken as proof of borrowing. Evidence of borrowing has to be more specific and Muir fails to provide it. Consequently, Muir's placing of *Coriolanus* in the political and social context of the early 1600s does not indicate a date of composition of the play. Furness' cautionary comment applies: "there is nothing in the political situation of *Coriolanus* which may not come out of Plutarch"[26].

Malone's idea that the mention of the ripe mulberry fruit being too soft to handle (Act 3, scene 2) related to a royal proclamation of 1606 encouraging mulberry propagation was described as "bizarre" by Brockbank[27] and as having "the very accent of folly" by Furness[28] and needs no further consideration.

* * *

If we assume that in his 1598 publication Francis Meres mentioned all the plays of 'Shakespeare' with which he was acquainted, in stage or print versions, then *Coriolanus* must have been written in late 1598 or after this date, as Meres did not mention the play. We can speculate that 1601 is a likely date of composition, because there are parallels between the life of Coriolanus and the life of the second Earl of Essex. Both achieved military victories (at Corioles and Cadiz respectively), both were arrogant and headstrong, both negotiated unwise personal bargains with enemies of the state, and it can be argued that both died as a result of their excessive self-belief and lack of political acumen or sensitivity. *Coriolanus* may have been written by the Queen soon after Essex's fall from grace.

---

[1] Neill (1994, pp. 20–22).
[2] Neill (1994, pp. 22–23).
[3] Neill (1994, p. 321).
[4] For example, Bullough (1964, vol. 5, pp. 215–216).
[5] For example, Hunter (1986), Neill (1994), Wilders (1995), Bloom (1998), Kermode (2000).
[6] Early editions of 'Shakespeare's' plays were printed in the Quarto size, i.e., on folded paper having final dimensions slightly larger than a present-day A4 sheet. The first collected edition of Shakespeare's plays, published in 1623, was printed in the much larger Folio size (12 x 19 inches, or approximately 34 x 48 cm).
[7] Malone (1790, pp. 372–376).
[8] Bullough (1964, pp. 453–454).
[9] Muir (1957, pp. 219–214).
[10] Bullough (1964).
[11] Dickinson (1963), Book VI, chapter 24.
[12] Brockbank (1994). Note that the 1994 Arden Shakespeare reprint states that the editorial matter is that of the 1976 Methuen edition (Brockbank 1976), but the 1994 'reprint' contains an introduction differing in many important details from that published in 1976.
[13] Brockbank (1994, pp. 29–30).
[14] Bullough (1964, pp. 453–454).
[15] Muir (1978, pp. 238–251).
[16] Freese, Church and Brodribb (1904).
[17] Bullough (1964, p. 562).
[18] Guy (2016, p. 135).
[19] Furness (1928, p. viii).
[20] Harrison (1948, pp. 239–240).
[21] Neale (1949, p. 53).

[22] Bullough (1964, pp. 456 and 553–534). For example, there was a severe shortage of grain in 1596, prompting disturbances in Oxfordshire and a sermon by George Abbott (later Archbishop of Canterbury) about poor summers and bad harvests (Hammer 1999, p. 374).
[23] Bullough (1964).
[24] Muir (1978, pp. 238–251).
[25] Neale (1949, pp. 244–245; 398–401).
[26] Furness (1928, p. 61).
[27] Brockbank (1994, p. 25).
[28] Furness (1928, p. 610).

28. *Troilus and Cressida*

A never writer, to an ever reader. News.
— Preface to *Troilus and Cressida*

Troilus and Cressida has a similar history of publication to *Anthony and Cleopatra*. The first mention of the play is an entry, on behalf of the publisher Mr Robertes, in the *Stationers' Register* of 7 February 1603:

> Mr Robertes. Entred for his copie in Full Court holden this day. to print when he hath gotten sufficient aucthority for yt. The booke of Troilus and Cresseda as yt is acted by my lo: Chamberlens Men

No public performance of the play in Elizabethan or Jacobean times is recorded, but the phrase "as yt is acted" in the above entry implies that it was being performed in February 1603 or earlier, possibly in private[1]. The 1603 entry hints that Roberts either possessed a copy of the play, or had been promised the right to print the play, but had not received permission to go ahead with its printing. The entry may represent his attempt to secure rights to publication of the play after he or others had seen it at a private performance. That publication did not follow immediately suggests that before he was able to gain permission to publish Roberts' plans were overtaken by events beyond his control.

We can assume that permission was delayed for six years because in 1609 the play was re-entered in the *Stationers' Register*, this time followed by publication. The preface in the printed version described it as "a new play, neuer stal'd with the Stage". The printer was George Eld, who printed *Sonnets* in the same year. How Mr Eld got hold of the play is as much of a mystery as how *Sonnets* arrived at Mr Thorpe's publishing house. The theory that court officials held back the play for six years is supported by the clever and amusing preface. Like the Dedication to *Sonnets* and Ben Johnson's verses introducing the First Folio, the preface is a literary curiosity that invites the reader to read between its lines. For this reason I have reproduced it in full below, in its original spelling.

A neuer writer, to an euer reader. Newes.
Eternall reader, you haue heere a new play, neuer stal'd with the Stage, neuer clapper-clawd with the palmes of the vulger, and yet passing full of the palme comicall; for it is a birth of your braine, that neuer vnder-tooke any thing commicall, vainely: And were but the vaine names of commedies changde for the titles of Commodities, or of Playes for Pleas; you should see all those grand censors, that now stile them such vanities, flock to them for the maine grace of their grauities: especially this authors Commedies, that are so fram'd to the life, that they serue for the most common Commentaries, of all the actions of

our liues, shewing such a dexteritie, and power of witte, that the most displeased with Playes, are pleasd with his Commedies. And all such dull and heauy-witted wordlings, as were neuer capable of the witte of a Commedie, coming by report of them to his representations, haue found that witte there, that they neuer found in themselues, and haue parted better wittied then they came: feeling an edge of witte set vpon them, more than euer they dreamd they had braine to grinde it on. So much and such sauored salt of witte is in his Commedies, that they seeme (for their height of pleasure) to be borne in that sea that brought forth *Venus*. Amongst all there is none more witty then this: And had I time I would comment vpon it, though I know it needs not, (for so much as will make you thinke your testerne [entrance fee; one shilling] well bestowd) but for so much worth, as euen poore I know to be stuft in it. It deserues such a labour, as well as the best Commedy in *Terence* or *Plautus*. And beleeue this, that when hee is gone, and his Commedies out of sale, you will scramble for them, and set vp a new English Inquisition. Take this for a warning, and at the perrill of your pleasures losse, and Iudgements, refuse not, nor like this the lesse, for not being sullied, with the smoaky breath of the multitude; but thank fortune for the scape it hath made amongst you. Since by the grand possessors wills I beleeue you should haue prayd for them rather then beene prayd. And so I leaue all such to be prayd for (for the states of their wits healths) that will not praise it. *Vale*.

This preface has no parallel in publications of the time. The author packs into it as many puns and allusions as can be accommodated on one page. It is headed by the words: "A neuer writer, to an euer reader. Newes." which can be paraphrased: 'From someone who never wrote, to a reader who will always read – news'. Like Robert Greene's provocative comments in 1592 (chapter 3), the heading implies the 'writer' is a fraud. But does 'writer' refer to the writer of the preface or the writer of the play? We cannot be sure, but the second interpretation is more likely, given the implication of fraud – why would the writer of the preface wish to label himself an impostor?

While Elizabeth I still reigned the words "A neuer writer, to an euer reader", implying that William Shakespeare never wrote anything, would have elicited an instant response from an offended establishment, as did Robert Greene's "upstart crow" comment in 1592. However, seventeen years later, in 1609, Elizabeth had been dead for six years and there was far less chance of the court taking exception to the insinuations of the preface, or even noticing a slight on 'Shakespeare's' reputation.

Another odd feature of the 1609 preface is its claim that the play is "a new play, neuer stal'd with the Stage" when we know from the *Stationers' Register* entry of February 1603 that it was being acted early in that year, or possibly in late 1602. We must conclude that these early performances were private. If this conclusion is correct it is almost certain that the performances were at court since only members of the aristocracy had the wherewithal to stage plays for small audiences[2]. The play's exceptionally learned vocabulary, and comments by the critic Bullough support this supposition: "[with its] mingling of noble ideas and cynicism about human conduct, its mockery of the heroic and the romantic, it was probably written for a cultured audience".

The third odd feature in the preface is its repeated reference to *Troilus and Cressida* as a comedy. In the First Folio it is grouped with the Tragedies.

The fourth odd feature is the reference to "this author" and "his comedies" without mentioning the author by name. It does, however, warn that "when hee is gone, and his Commedies out of sale, you will scramble for them, and set vp a new English Inquisition". It is strange to anticipate the death of a living author, especially one who is only forty-four years old and might be expected to live at least another 10 years. And what is the reference to setting up an Inquisition (a panel of enquiry concerning beliefs) when the comedies are "out of sale" supposed to mean? Publishers in the late sixteenth and early seventeenth centuries frequently reprinted books that were out of print. *Venus and Adonis* (1593) was so popular that it was reprinted 15 times before 1640.

We should also ask why the writer of the preface suggests to readers that the author's comedies "seeme . . . to be borne in that sea that brought forth *Venus*". In classical legends Venus is born from sea foam. The writer seems to be suggesting that the same life force that gave us the goddess Venus gave us the plays. The royal implications are obvious.

Finally, readers are told to be thankful "for the [e]scape it [the play] hath made amongst you. Since by the grand possessors wills I beleeue you should haue prayd for them . . .". These words imply that the manuscript of the play has escaped from safe keeping by courtiers or court officials ("grand possessors"). Just what might have prompted the 1609 escape of the manuscript has never been established – did some high-ranking aristocrat or court official give instructions for the release of the play (and perhaps *Sonnets* too) in this year or in late 1608?[2]

Let's now look at the play's content. As I noted above, although the play is described as a comedy in the preface, it was printed together with the tragedies in the 1623 First Folio. But a comedy it is, written in a sardonic and cynical style. In Act 1, scene 2 Cressida surveys and passes comment on the Greek and Trojan warriors returning from the battlefield as nonchalantly as a sports journalist might comment on members of the Australian and English cricket teams walking off the pitch at Lords at teatime.

Later in the play warriors and generals make great speeches or declarations of principle and then either do nothing or the opposite to what they have declared to be the noble course of action. Ulysses makes a resounding speech about the importance of respect for privilege and the ruling class, but no one takes any notice Instead, the legendary Greek warriors Achilles and Ajax lie sullenly in their tents until shamed or psychologically manipulated to fight. (Essex was compared to Achilles by Elizabethan authors and the description of Achilles' behaviour may be a comment on Essex's tendency to sulk at home when he imagined he had been wronged.) Troilus and Cressida swear eternal love to each other but when Cressida is exchanged for a Greek prisoner and leaves Troy, she all too readily succumbs to the advances of the Greek commander Diomedes and subsequently allows herself to be kissed by four Greek fighters. (We can assume that the kissing scene is meant to imply that more intimate sexual favours were granted.)

Troilus is apparently a distinguished fighter, but in name only – he does nothing to distinguish himself on the battlefield. Hector the noble Trojan is killed by Achilles, not in glorious one-to-one combat but in a cowardly fashion after he is discovered disarmed by Achilles, before the Greek retreat has been sounded to end hostilities for the day. The heroes are so flawed that Thersites the foul-mouthed Greek ends up having most of our sympathy because he is at least consistent and speaks the truth as he perceives it – he calls the great Nestor (the ancient Greek commander mentioned on Shakespeare's Stratford monument) "a stale old mouse-eaten dry cheese" and dismisses the legendary Ulysses as "not proved worth a blackberry".

The play is a comedy of the bleakest sort. The lascivious Cressida gets her men. The weak Troilus loses his loose woman (lucky for him!). Achilles unheroically kills the defenceless Hector and receives no honour for doing so. Troilus meets Diomedes (who seduced his love Cressida) but declines the opportunity to challenge him to a fight for his (and Cressida's) honour's sake. Instead, he (apparently) has more mundane things on his mind: "pay the life thou ow'st me for my horse" (but "horse" is likely to have sexual connotations relating to Cressida – something you ride on). One can almost hear the raucous laughter of the audience.

The play ends with a speech by Pandarus the pimp, which must rank as one of the most melancholy closing scenes in any 'Shakespeare' play: he tells the audience (whom he abuses and calls "Good traders in the flesh") that he will make his will in two months' time and "Till then I'll sweat and seek about for eases, And at that time bequeath you my diseases". And with these cheerful words the dark comedy concludes.

Apart from being a cynical critique of the inconstancy of those who profess high principles and eternal love, the play is a wry commentary on the shallowness of virtues professed by the aristocratic and military class, an exposure of the posturing of those who think highly of themselves, and a reflection on the incessant jostling of unprincipled courtiers seeking patronage and advantage, while purporting to have high moral values. The play's purpose seems to be twofold – to point out that true love is a delusion, and to demonstrate that grandees have the same human weaknesses as 'ordinary' people, although, unlike the great unwashed, they are able to mask their failings with fine words. Lesser mortals lack the airs and graces of the privileged but at least some of them (like Thersites) have refreshing honesty and tell life as it really is. Edward Dowden commented in 1939 that the play was "full of pain [and] bitterness and loss of faith in man" and asked the question "Did Shakespeare write *Troilus and Cressida* to unburden his heart of some bitterness by an indictment of *the illusions of romance, which had misled him*?"[4] (my italics). To which we can reply: No, Shakespeare didn't, but Elizabeth did[5].

Elizabeth's death in 1603 could explain why publication of *Troilus and Cressida* was delayed for six years. If the Queen was in the habit of indirectly authorising publication of her works, then her illness and death in early 1603 would be the obvious cause of the delay. After her death court officials had more important issues to worry about.

Troilus and Cressida is a late play, as shown by its parallels to *Hamlet*, for example in the exchange between Pandarus and Troilus: "What says she there?" "Words, words, mere words, no matter from the heart"[6]. The play can be interpreted as the aged playwright's sad farewell to the court she once dominated, loved and manipulated and her final commentary on all the intrigues, flattery and insincerities she has observed, experienced, and survived.

---

[1] Partridge (1964, p. 102) suggested that it was written shortly after *Hamlet*, as early as 1601, for performance at the Inns of Court.
[2] Bullough (1966, p. 86).
[3] Richard Bancroft, Archbishop of Canterbury, who was present at Elizabeth's death, and died in November 1610, is a suspect for the person entrusted to release the manuscripts. We can speculate that he may have acted in accordance with Elizabeth's deathbed instructions.
[4] In Bullough (1966) pp. 85–86.
[5] The critic Middleton Murry thought that *Troilus and Cressida* was "the product of a wounded spirit" and Tucker Brooke imagined that Shakespeare was "anatomizing the England of the dying Elizabeth" (Bullough 1996, pp. 85–86).
[6] Compare with Hamlet's response to Polonius (*Hamlet*, Act 2, scene 2): "words, words, words". See also endnote 1 (above).

29. *Measure for Measure*

O, it is excellent to have a giant's strength,
But it is tyrannous to use it like a giant.
    – Measure for Measure, Act 2, scene 2

As far as we know *Measure for Measure* was first published in the First Folio of 1623. It appears as one of the comedies, but it does not fit easily in this category. At the personal level it is a play about the double standards of those who wield power. At the philosophical level it is about alternative ways of maintaining moral values – natural 'common-sense' humanist justice versus the rigorous enforcement of inflexible laws.

While the Duke of Vienna is absent from the city the temporary governor Angelo imposes strict rules concerning immoral behaviour. Angelo has Claudio arrested and imprisoned for having pre-marital sex with Juliet, who is bearing his child. For his crime Claudio is due to be beheaded. Claudio's sister Isabel pleads with Angelo for Claudio's freedom. Angelo lusts for Isabel and offers her a villainous choice: if you have sex with me I will spare your brother. The issue is resolved by a swapping of bedmates (thereby preserving Isabel's virginity) followed by the return of the Duke who dispenses justice with the wisdom of Solomon. The low-life characters – the brothel madam Mistress Overdone and her sidekick Pompey – offer some comic relief but are not important to the plot, except to show "that the lower ranks have a better grasp of common justice and humanity . . . than the educated Angelo"[1]. The go-between Lucio who has sordid thoughts and equally sordid habits is paradoxically the most attractive and entertaining character in the play because, like Thersites in *Troilus and Cressida*, he is so honest about his weaknesses and so human. In contrast Isabel is too good, Claudio is too weak, the Duke is too wise, and Mistress Overdone is too grubby.

The first recorded performance of *Measure for Measure* is the one recorded in the Revels Accounts in which the play is listed as having been acted in the banqueting hall of Whitehall (i.e. at court) on St Stephen's Night (26 December) of 1604. However, the sources of the play were all available much earlier[2, 3]. Among the many sources are Cinthio's *Hecatommithi* (1565) and his posthumous drama *Epitia* (1583), Whetstone's play *The Right Excellent and famous History of Promos and Cassandra* (1578), and the same author's story in *Heptameron of Civil Discourses* (1582).

Despite these strong indications of interest by 'Shakespeare' in works published in the late 1570s and early 1580s (and significantly, no interest in works published later), the play is generally considered to have been written in late 1603 or early 1604. This is because it contains an apparent reference to James I's proclamation of 16 September 1603 that houses in the London suburbs should be pulled down as a precaution against "dissolute and idle persons" spreading the plague. (The play is actually set in Vienna, but London playgoers in 1603 or 1604 would have immediately understood the demolition allusion.)

There are other supposed contemporary references in the play. These have been discussed by J. W. Lever[4]. None of the references are particularly convincing. In Act 1, scene 2 a gentleman identified as "1. Gent" holds forth against a peace agreement with the King of Hungary:

Heaven grant us its peace, but not the King of Hungary's!

This statement has been linked with a peace agreement between the Turks and the Holy Roman Emperor in 1606 or alternatively with the peace agreement between England and Spain signed in 1604. Reference to either of these is unlikely as it is doubtful that a London audience would make a connection between the King of Hungary and either treaty. In addition, no playwright would risk criticising James I's peace initiative with Spain in front of the king himself at Whitehall. Furthermore, in the same act and scene the brothel keeper Mistress Overdone complains about a shortage of clients as a result of a war, not the arrival of peace:

Thus, what with the war, what with the sweat, what with the gallows, and what with poverty, I am custom-shrunk. (Act 1, scene 2, lines 35–37)

Lever suggested[5] that this list of complaints can be related to circumstances in London in the winter of 1603–4: the war with Spain was dragging on, plague had arrived in the city again, there were executions, and of course there was always poverty. But *Measure for Measure* is not an historical play, and these troubles were not unique to 1603–4. The list of troubles may not have any historical significance. It may simply have been inserted by the playwright to explain the brothel keeper's discontent.

Let us now return to the apparent reference to the 1603 proclamation that houses in the London suburbs should be pulled down as a precaution against "dissolute and idle persons" spreading the plague. Such an unmistakable allusion to contemporary social politics (see lines 45–55 in Table 6) is highly unusual in a 'Shakespeare' play, but this particular allusion cannot easily be dismissed or disregarded. On first reading it appears to prove a late 1603 or 1604 date of composition. But we need to be cautious, because some commentators have detected extensive reworking in *Measure for Measure* by an author other than 'Shakespeare'. Thomas Middleton is the favoured culprit[6]. It has been suggested that he altered *Measure for Measure*'s text to pander to the tastes of Jacobean audiences[7] and that Middleton's rewritings make up about five percent of the play's text[8].

Table 6. Extract from *Measure for Measure* beginning with the second part of Act 1, scene 2 and including scene 3; as printed in the First Folio, with modern spelling.

Line	Scena Secunda Enter Bawd	Notes
1	*Luc.* Behold, behold, where Madam *Mitigation* comes.	
2	I have purchas'd as many diseases under her Roof,	
3	As come to	
4	2.*Gent.* To what, I pray?	
5	*Luc.* Judge.	
6	2.*Gent.* To three thousand Dollours a year.	
7	1.*Gent.* I, and more.	
8	*Luc.* A French crown more.	
9	1.*Gent.* Thou art always figuring diseases in me; but	
10	thou art full of error; I am sound.	
11	*Luc.* Nay, not (as one would say) healthy: but so	
12	sound, as things that are hollow; thy bones are hollow;	
13	Impiety has made a feast of thee.	
14	1.*Gent.* How now, which of your hips has the most	
15	profound Sciatica?	
16	*Bawd.* Well, well: there's one yonder arrested, and	
17	carried to prison, was worth five thousand of you all.	
18	2.*Gent.* Who's that, I pray thee?	
19	*Bawd.* Marry Sir, that's *Claudio*; Signior *Claudio*.	19–27. In this exchange Mistress Overdone informs Lucio that the prisoner is Claudio, and his "crime" is getting Juliet with child.
20	1.*Gent. Claudio* to prison? 'tis not so.	
21	*Bawd.* Nay, but I know 'tis so. I saw him arrested:	
22	saw him carried away: and which is more, within these	
23	three days his head to be chop'd off.	
24	*Luc.* But, after all this fooling, I would not have it so:	
25	Art thou sure of this?	
26	*Bawd.* I am too sure of it: and it is for getting Madam	
27	*Julietta* with child.	
28	*Luc.* Believe me, this may be: he promis'd to meet	28–30. Lucio's reply is appropriate in response to lines 21–23: as a result of his arrest Claudio missed his meeting with Lucio.
29	me two hours since, and he was ever precise in promise	
30	keeping.	
31	2.*Gent.* Besides you know, it draws something near	31–33. These three lines don't follow on from Lucio's comment in lines 28–30; this is the first mention of the proclamation.
32	to the speech we had to such a purpose.	
33	1.*Gent.* But most of all agreeing with the proclamation.	

34	*Luc.* Away: let's go learn the truth of it. *Exit*	*Another non-sequitur – are they departing to find the truth about the proclamation, or about Claudio?*
35 36 37 38	*Bawd.* Thus, what with the war; what with the sweat, what with the gallows, and what with poverty, I am Custom-shrunk. How now? what's the news with you. *Enter Clown.*	*35–38. These lines could have originally introduced a scene in which Mistress Overdone first appears.*
39 40 41 42 43 44	*Clo.* Yonder man is carried to prison. *Baw.* Well: what has he done? *Clo.* A Woman. *Baw.* But what's his offence? *Clo.* Groping for Trouts, in a peculiar River. *Baw.* What? is there maid with child by him?	*40–44. But Mistress Overdone already knows what Claudio's "crime" is – she gave Lucio this information in lines 26–27.*
45 46 47 48 49	*Clo.* No: but there's a woman with maid by him: you have not heard of the proclamation, have you? *Baw.* What proclamation, man? *Clow.* All houses in the Suburbs of *Vienna* must be pluck'd down.	*45–49. The abrupt change of subject by the Clown appears to be a contrivance to introduce the proclamation.*
50 51 52 53 54 55 56 57 58 59 60 61 62 63	*Bawd.* And what shall become of those in the City? *Clow.* They shall stand for seed: they had gone down too, but that a wise burgher put in for them. *Bawd.* But shall all our houses of resort in the Suburbs be pulled down? *Clow.* To the ground, Mistress. *Bawd.* Why, here's a change indeed in the Commonwealth: what shall become of me? *Clow.* Come: fear not you: good Counsellors lack no Clients: though you change your place, you need not change your Trade: I'll be your Tapster still; courage, there will be pity taken on you; you that have worn your eyes out in the service, you will be considered.	
64 65 66	*Bawd.* What's to do here, *Thomas* Tapster? let's withdraw? *Clo.* Here comes Signior *Claudio*, led by the Provost to prison: and there's Madam *Juliet*. *Exeunt*	*64–66. It is surprising that the bawd and Pompey leave at this point.*

		Scena Tertia	
	67	*Enter Provost, Claudio, Juliet, officers; Lucio, & 2. Gent.*	
	68	*Cla.* Fellow, why do'st thou show me thus to th'world?	
	69	Bear me to prison, where I am committed.	
	70	*Pro.* I do it not in evil disposition,	
	71	But from Lord *Angelo* by special charge.	
	72	*Clau.* Thus can the demi-god (Authority)	
	73	Make us pay down, for our offence, by weight:	
	74	The words of heaven; on whom it will, it will,	
	75	On whom it will not (so); yet still 'tis just. (straint	
	76	*Luc.* Why how now, Claudio? Whence comes this re-	
	77	*Cla.* From too much liberty, (my *Lucio*) Liberty	
	78	As surfeit is the father of much fast,	
	79	So every Scope by the immoderate use	
	80	Turns to restraint. Our Natures do pursue,	
	81	Like Rats that rain down their proper Bane,	
	82	A thirsty evil, and when we drink, we die.	
	83	*Luc.* If I could speak so wisely under an arrest, I	
	84	would send for certain of my Creditors: and yet, to say	
	85	the truth, I had as lief the foppery of freedom, as	
	86	the morality of imprisonment: What's thy offence,	86–87. From his
	87	*Claudio*?	conversation with the Bawd (26–27) *Lucio* already knows why *Claudio* was arrested.
	88	*Cla.* What (but to speak of) would offend again.	
	89	*Luc.* What, is't murder?	
	90	*Cla.* No.	
	91	*Luc.* Lechery?	
	92	*Cla.* Call it so.	
	93	*Pro.* Away, Sir; you must go.	
	94	*Cla.* One word, good friend	
	95	*Lucio*, a word with you.	
	96	*Luc.* A hundred:	
	97	If they'll do you any good: Is *Lechery* so look'd after?	
	98	*Cla.* Thus stands it with me: upon a true contract	
	99	I got possession of *Julietta's* bed,	
	100	You know the Lady; she is fast my wife,	
	101	Save that we the denunciation lack	
	102	Of outward Order. This we came not to,	
	103	Only for propagation of a Dowry	
	104	Remaining in the Coffer of her friends,	
	105	From whom we thought it meet to hide our Love	
	106	Till Time had made them for us. But it chances	
	107	The stealth of our most mutual entertainment	
	108	With Character too gross, is writ on *Juliet*.	

109	Luc. With child, perhaps?	Lucio was told the answer to this question in lines 26–27.
110	Cla. Unhappily, even so.	
111	And the new Deputy, now for the Duke,	
112	Whether it be the fault and glimpse of newness,	
113	Of whether that the body public, be	
114	A horse whereon the Governor doth ride,	
115	Who newly in his seat, that it may know	
116	He can command; let it straight feel the spur:	
117	Whether the Tyranny be in his place.	
118	Or in his Eminence that fills it up	
119	I stagger in: But this new Governor	
120	Awakes me all the enrolled penalties	
121	Which have (like unscour'd Armour), hung by th'wall	
122	So long, that nineteen zodiacs have gone round,	
123	And none of them been worn; and for a name	
124	Now puts the drowsy and neglected Act	
125	Freshly on me: 'tis surely for a name.	
126	Luc. I warrant it is: And thy head stands so tickle on	
127	thy shoulders, that a milkmaid, if she be in love, may	
128	sigh it off: Send after the Duke, and appeal to him.	
129	Cla. I have done so, but he's not to be found.	
130	I prithee (*Lucio*) do me this kind service:	
131	This day my sister should the Cloister enter,	
132	And there receive her approbation.	
133	Acquaint her with the danger of my state:	
134	Implore her, in my voice, that she make friends	
135	To the strict deputy: bid her self assay him,	
136	I have great hope in that; for in her youth	
137	There is a prone and speechless dialect,	
138	Such as move men: besides, she hath prosperous Art	
139	When she will play with reason, and discourse,	
140	And well she can persuade.	
141	Luc. I pray she may; as well for the encouragement	
142	of the like, which else would stand under grievous im-	
143	position: as for the enjoying of thy life, who I would be	
144	sorry should be thus foolishly lost, at a game of tick-	
145	tack: I'll to her.	
146	Cla. I thank you, good friend *Lucio*.	
147	Luc. Within two hours.	
148	Cla. Come, Officer, away. *Exeunt.*	

The detailed stylistic evidence supporting the Middleton hypothesis need not concern us here. But if we look closely at the scene (Act 1, scene 2) in which the reference to the 1603 royal proclamation about demolishing houses in the suburbs occurs, we find that it contains evidence of serious interference (should we say meddling?) with its text.

In Table 6 I have highlighted where unnatural breaks occur in Act 1, scene 2. The first thirty lines of the extract, which precede the reference to the pulling down of houses in the suburbs, appear to make sense. Lucio is having a lewd exchange with his smart-arse gentlemen acquaintances. Mistress Overdone, the bawd or brothel Madam, joins in. She informs Lucio that Claudio (visible "yonder", i.e. off-stage) has been arrested and is on his way to prison for "getting Madam Julietta with child" (lines 26–27). Lucio, in character, makes a smart answer (lines 28–30). But in the following three lines (31–33) the gentlemen change the subject to a matter (a proclamation) unrelated to Claudio's misdemeanour:

> *Lines 31–33*
> 2.*Gent.* Besides, you know, it draws something near
> to the speech we had to such a purpose.
> 1.*Gent.* But most of all agreeing with the proclamation.

But no one in the play has previously mentioned the proclamation referred to, nor have Lucio and the two gentlemen had an earlier conversation ("the speech we had to such purpose") about getting Juliet with child. The conversation of the gentlemen seems to be completely out of place, and if these three lines are deleted some logical coherence is restored to the conversation.

In lines 35–38 the subject of the conversation again changes abruptly. These lines look very much like an introduction to a scene:

> *Bawd.* Thus, what with the war; what with the sweat, what with the gallows, and what with poverty, I am Custom-shrunk. How now? what's the news with you.

'Shakespeare' often opens scenes in the middle of a conversation, to create the illusion that the members of the audience are privileged listeners to a private and intimate exchange. (The first scene of *All's Well that Ends Well* is a good example.) In this case the audience hears Mistress Overdone summarising her complaints about bad times in the brothel business.

But line 35 does not mark the beginning of a scene – Mistress Overdone is already on stage. And her complaint about low numbers of clients does not follow on from anything she or anyone else has said previously. Lines 40–44 are even more perplexing. In this conversation, apparently occurring within sight of Claudio (still on his way to prison), Mistress Overdone (the Bawd) asks Pompey (the Clown) what Claudio's offence is:

> *Clo.* Yonder man is carried to prison.
> *Baw.* Well: what has he done?
> *Clo.* A Woman.
> *Baw.* But what's his offence?

But Mistress Overdone already knows why Claudio is being sent to prison – it was she herself who informed Lucio fifteen lines earlier that Claudio's offence is "getting Madam Julietta with child", i.e., pre-marital sex. So, either the playwright had second thoughts about who knew what about Claudio's predicament and forgot to delete lines 26–27, or the text has been tampered with.

Pompey's reply to Mistress Overdone's question about Claudio's offence must be the funniest description of illicit sex in the English language: "Groping for Trouts, in a peculiar River". Then we read another *non-sequitur*. Pompey changes the subject to inform Mistress Overdone of the proclamation to pull down houses in the suburbs (lines 45–49):

> *Clo.* No: but there's a woman with maid by him: you have not heard of the proclamation, have you?
> *Baw.* What proclamation, man?
> *Clow.* All houses in the Suburbs of *Vienna* must be pluck'd down.

We should note that Mistress Overdone has already heard about the proclamation during the speech of the first gentleman (line 33). Her question "What proclamation, man?" is therefore decidedly odd. Even odder is that at the point when she and Pompey have a chance of meeting Claudio on stage and learning more about his troubles, they make themselves scarce (lines 64–66), which is out-of-character behaviour for a couple of fervent gossips.

Finally, in scene 3 Lucio and his gentlemen acquaintances intercept the arrested Claudio (who apparently is still being escorted to prison – it must have been a long street). For the third time the audience hears an actor ask what offence Claudio has committed – this time it is Lucio who asks (lines 86–87, and line 109). But this question is also out of place – in lines 19–27 Mistress Overdone has already informed Lucio of Claudio's offence.

If the garbled scene 2 (as we read it in the First Folio) is cropped from the play little is lost except a few gags. Scene 3 tells the audience all they need to know in order to follow the play's action: the unfortunate Claudio and the street-smart man-about-town Lucio are introduced, Claudio's offence is briefly explained, and the stage is set for the later scene in which Claudio's sister Isabel meets the despicable magistrate Angelo, with Lucio's help.

What scene 2 originally looked like we shall never know, but we can guess it was an amusing conversation between Lucio, the two town gentlemen, Mistress Overdone and Pompey about the pleasures and pitfalls of low-life London, and included plenty of sexual innuendo, and probably some of the exchanges we read in scene 2 as it appears today. But we can be sure that neither 'Shakespeare' nor a later meddling author meant scene 2 to be played on the stage "as is" – it doesn't work as a conversation and it doesn't make sense dramatically.

What we read in the First Folio is a mangled revision of scene 2, possibly including deletions, marginal insertions and inserted sheets of text, which the typesetters had to make the best of. Perhaps a couple of pages of text including a reference to King James' proclamation about pulling down houses in the suburbs were hurriedly inserted into the author's original manuscript, so that the acting company (The King's Men) could produce a stage version likely to please King James in the Whitehall performance of 1604.

Thomas Middleton may have been employed to introduce the topical reference of the 1603 proclamation into the existing play. He must have realised that the obvious place for the proclamation reference was in the conversation between the two characters most affected by it – a brothel madam and her pimp – and drafted a new version of scene 2.

The doctored play may have once made sense on the stage, but it certainly did not survive in a playable form in the years between the performance and typesetting for the First Folio. Perhaps the playbook got torn or amendments on loose bits of paper got misplaced – we shall never know. Reconstruction of the original text is impossible[9]. Whatever actually happened, we can be sure that the First Folio version was not the version actually acted on the stage.

Because the evidence for a botched and late modification of Act 1, scene 2 is overwhelming, the case for a late 1603 or 1604 date for the composition of the primary text of *Measure for Measure* collapses. This conclusion also applies to the other supposed contemporary references (those to the peace agreement with the King of Hungary and the shortage of clients in brothels) because these are also found in the badly rehashed scene 2. Consequently, there is no convincing argument that *Measure for Measure* was written any later than the late 1580s or the 1590s, although the sombre moralising in the play does suggest a late date sometime after the composition of the carefree comedies.

Measure for Measure, like *The Merchant of Venice, Cymbeline, The Winter's Tale* and *All's Well that Ends Well*, features a fearless heroine who controls the action, either overtly or from behind the scenes. Justice favouring the heroine is finally achieved, but only after she has endured trials and misfortunes, brought about in many instances by the foolishness or lack of moral fibre of the leading male figures. The writer's emotional sympathy in all these plays primarily resides with the female heroines, which leads one to suspect the hand of a female author in these plays rather than the hand of a man.

---

[1] Gibbons (1991, p. 25).
[2] Lever (1965).
[3] Gibbons (1991),

4 Lever (1965, pp. xxxi–xxxv).
5 Lever (1965, p. xxxii).
6 Jowett and Taylor (1993).
7 Jowett and Taylor (1993); Bourus and Taylor (2014).
8 Bourus and Taylor (2014).
9 Jowett and Taylor (1993) tried to reconstruct an 'original' text, but any such effort inevitably descends into subjective assessment of what constitutes good (i.e. 'Shakespearean') writing and writing of a lower standard (i.e. the work of others).

30. More Fantasies: *Cymbeline* and *The Winter's Tale*

Well then, here's the point: You must forget to be a woman
– Cymbeline, Act 3, scene 4

Literary critics and academics occasionally insist that *Cymbeline* has noteworthy dramatic merit, but when judged by the simplest measure of dramatic appeal – the popularity of the play on the stage – *Cymbeline* fails miserably: it is hardly ever produced. If we use memorable quotations as a rough measure of literary merit *Cymbeline* again fails: the *Penguin Dictionary of Quotations*[1] prints only 16 quotes from *Cymbeline* compared to 205 from *Hamlet*.

The reason for *Cymbeline*'s failure on both counts is not hard to find. It has a hotch-potch plot made up of several elements: a wager between renaissance-style merchants about female constancy; a villain concealing himself in a chest to gain access to a princess' bedroom; kidnapped princes living the life of noble cavemen and hunters in ancient Britain; an international dispute resulting in a Roman invasion and a battle; a king (Cymbeline) who appears seldom and does little – "a puppet who never comes to life"[2]; and an evil witch of a Queen acquainted with poisons who tries to marry off her evil son Cloten (a Caliban-like figure) to the paragon of virtue Imogen (King Cymbeline's daughter by his first wife).

In his diary the quack doctor and play-goer Simon Forman recorded his undated attendance at a performance of *Cymbeline*. This was sometime before 12 September 1611, when he died. This is the earliest record of a stage performance. It does not help us ascertain when the play was written.

Traditionally the play has been linked with *The Tempest* and *The Winter's Tale*. The three plays have been collectively portrayed as 'Romances' written late in Shakespeare's career[3]. On the basis of a verse 'stress test' (which measures which syllables are stressed in blank verse lines) MacDonald P. Jackson[4] not only linked *Cymbeline* with *The Winter's Tale* and *The Tempest*, but also with *Anthony and Cleopatra* and *Coriolanus*. But it is important to recognise that this stress test does not, in itself, prove late composition; it simply groups plays of similar linguistic character. And as I show in this chapter and chapters 25–27, a post-1603 date of composition for these plays is by no means certain.

The early twentieth century scholar E. M. W. Tillyard[5], like Nosworthy (1969) and Warren (1998), considered that the 'Romances' were late plays and commented that Shakespeare "fumbled in *Cymbeline*, did better in *The Winter's Tale* and only in his last attempt [*The Tempest*] achieved full success". But the idea that 'Shakespeare' struggled with both plot and characterisation in *Cymbeline* so soon after displaying supreme mastery of both plot and character in tragedies such as *Hamlet, King Lear* and *Othello*, and earlier in the delightful comedies *Twelfth Night* and *As You Like It*, seems most improbable. So it is worth investigating the actual evidence for the long-accepted notion that *Cymbeline* is a late work.

If scholarship did not insist that the play, along with *The Winter's Tale* and *The Tempest*, belongs to Shakespeare's late (Jacobean) period, we might conclude that it was written by an apprentice author experimenting with a new genre (fantasy) and more interested in the intricacies of convoluted plotting (and making a difficult plot work) than character development. The play reminds one of an Agatha Christie detective novel – complexity seems to be deliberately introduced to ensure that readers or play-goers are astonished that the disparate strands of the tangled plot eventually make sense in the unifying last act.

Firstly, let's consider the sources of the stories embedded in *Cymbeline*. In this regard Nosworthy's summary is very useful[6]. Some historical detail comes from Holinshed's chronicles, but the key component of *Cymbeline* is an ancient popular tale with a plot taking the form of wager between two men about womanly constancy. The details in *Cymbeline* closely follow Boccaccio's version that appears in his book *Decameron*, written in Florentine Italian in the fourteenth century and published as an illustrated edition in Venice in 1492. However, some details of the wager story in *Cymbeline* are closer to those in a tale modelled on Boccaccio's: *Frederyke of Jennen* [Genoa], first published (in English) in 1518 and reprinted in 1520 and 1560.

Interestingly, no English version of the *Decameron* was published before 1620, so 'Shakespeare' must have read it in the Italian original, which is embarrassing for traditional 'Stratfordians', because there is no evidence that William Shakespeare knew Italian. However, Elizabeth I both read and wrote the language. Other details in *Cymbeline* were sourced from two plays on stage in the 1580s and 1590s[7]: *The Rare Triumphs of Love and Fortune* (performed before Elizabeth I at Windsor castle on 30 December 1582 and printed in 1589) and Robert Greene's *Mucedorus* written in about 1590.

The sources mentioned above and Forman's 1611 diary entry establish that *Cymbeline* must have been written at some time between 1590 (give or take a year or two) and 1611. As no sources of *Cymbeline*'s plot post-date 1590, an earlier date of writing within this 21-year time range seems likely.

An early date is also supported by internal linguistic evidence showing that *Cymbeline* was written in the sixteenth century, not the seventeenth: the First Folio edition of the play uses the old-style verb "hath" 33 times and the form "has" (more popular with playwrights after 1600[8]) only four times. Since no seventeenth-century editor or typesetter is likely to have substituted the old-fashioned "hath" for "has", the occurrence of "hath" in the text is almost certainly authorial, and therefore indicates early (pre-1600) composition. In places the poetry in the play is written in a style popular in the 1590s[9].

Cymbeline contains abundant links to other 'Shakespearean' works written around the turn of the century or earlier. I have listed those I have detected:

- In Act 1, scene 6 Giacomo describes Imogen with the words: "She is alone th'Arabian bird" (i.e., the phoenix). This imagery is similar to that used in *The Phoenix and the Turtle* (published in 1601) (see chapter 46): "Let the bird of loudest lay, On the sole *Arabian* tree".
- The legend of Philomel is mentioned in Act 2, scene 2 and also in sonnet 102, dated to 1599 (Appendix 3).
- In Act 2, scene 3 the musician sings the famous ditty opening with the line "Hark, hark the Lark at Heaven's gate sings" which matches the wording of lines 11 and 12 of sonnet 29, dated to 1590 (Appendix 3): "(Like to the lark at break of day arising) From sullen earth sings hymns at Heaven's gate".
- In Act 3, scene 2 Pisanio refers to black ink: "O damn'd paper, Black as the Ink that's on thee!" Sonnet 65 uses the words "black ink" and was probably written in 1597 (Appendix 3).
- Imogen's argument against suicide ("self-slaughter") in Act 3, scene 4 is the same as that used by Prince Hamlet *(Hamlet,* Act 1, scene 2) written by 1602.
- Guiderus' democratic statement in Act 4, scene 2, that in death "Thersites' body is as good as Ajax's" links the play to the satirical treatment of both these characters in *Troilus and Cressida* (written by 1603 or earlier) in which the foul-mouthed lower-class Thersites gains our sympathy and Ajax is presented as arrogant and ineffective.
- The legal language in Posthumus' speech in Act 5, scene 3: "render", "clement" and "audit" is reminiscent of that in sonnet 126, dated to 1601 (Appendix 3) in which the words "audit" and "render" are also used.
- Characters named Innogen [*sic*] and Leonato occur in the 1600 quarto edition of *Much Ado about Nothing*.
- Nosworthy notes that the imagery and vocabulary of the poem *Venus and Adonis*, published in 1593, "was very much in Shakespeare's thoughts when he was writing *Cymbeline*" and "both play and poem exhibit the same Arcadian features" and "both move within the same range of imagery"[10]. The similarities noted by Nosworthy need not be repeated here; suffice to say that there are too many to be coincidental and they make it highly likely that the play and the poem were written at about the same time.
- Likewise, A. Kent Hieatt and co-authors[11] link the bird/choir/autumn leaves vocabulary in Act 3, scene 3 of *Cymbeline* to that in sonnet 73, dated to 1597 (Appendix 3) and to similar vocabulary in *Henry VI Part 2* (1594) and *Richard II* (1597).

Cymbeline, *Act 3, scene 3, lines 43–44 and 60–64:*
We make a **choir**, as doth the prison'd **bird**,
And **sing** our bondage freely...
                      ... then was I as a tree
Whose **boughs** did bend with fruit. But in one night,
A storm, or robbery (call it what you will)
Shook down my **mellow** hangings, nay, my **leaves**,
And left me **bare** to weather.

Sonnet 73, lines 1–4:
That time of year thou may'st in me behold
When **yellow leaves**, or none, or few, do hang
Upon those **boughs** which **shake** against the cold,
Bare, ruin'd **choirs**, where late the sweet **birds sang**.

- In Act 1, scene 5 Imogen tells how the entry of her father is like the north wind that "Shakes all our buds from growing", a simile similar to that in sonnet 18, probably written in 1587 (Appendix 3), in which the poet writes "rough winds do shake the darling buds of May".
- Finally, the phrase "the chance of war" spoken by Caius Lucius in Act 5, scene 5 is also used in *Henry IV Part 1* (Act 1, scene 4) (published 1598) and in the prologue to *Troilus and Cressida* (written by 1603 or earlier).

To summarise: the above allusions or phrases in *Cymbeline* are all linked to 'Shakespearean' works known or deduced to have been written between 1587 and 1603; the sources of *Cymbeline* provide no evidence for a date of composition after 1603; and linguistic criteria indicate sixteenth century rather than seventeenth century composition.

* * *

If *Cymbeline* is 'Shakespeare's' attempt at writing fantasy, where do we place the third 'Romance', *The Winter's Tale*?

The Winter's Tale has strong similarities to *Cymbeline*. Both are tales of reconciliation. The leading characters in both plays have similar names: Leontes in *The Winter's Tale* and Posthumus Leonatus in *Cymbeline*. Both Leontes and Leonatus are basically good, but foolish and gullible. Jealousy makes them despise the women most dear to them. Despite their husbands' foolishness the women remain steadfast optimists, even though the men at certain points in time wish their wives dead. After trials and tribulations, experienced chiefly by the strong-minded women, misunderstandings are explained and the apparently unworthy Leontes and Leonatus are reunited with their long-suffering and uncritical wives in happy endings. (In contrast, although in *Othello* jealousy and misunderstandings are also a crucial part of the plot, in this play the outcome is not reconciliation but murder.)

The first documented account of *The Winter's Tale* appearing in any form is Forman's diary in which he notes seeing the play on Wednesday 15 May 1611[12]. But as remarked previously for *Cymbeline*, this diary entry is not evidence that the play is a seventeenth century invention. To establish when the play was written we need to investigate sources and any other indications of date of composition.

The primary source of *The Winter's Tale*'s fable of a lost child of noble birth being brought up by simple country folk is undoubtedly Greene's *Pandosto*, published in 1588. Greene's popular tale ran to many editions, but the phrase "The king shall live without an heir" (reproduced in Act 3, scene 2 of *The Winter's Tale*) is only found in the 1588, 1592 and 1595 editions so one of these was almost certainly the source for *The Winter's Tale*. Minor sources were Ovid's *Metamorphoses* (Arthur Golding's English translation was published in 1567) and other works by Greene.

The reference to Alexander the Great in Act 5, scene 1 "The Crown will find an heir. Great Alexander left his to th'worthiest" comes from the tenth book of Quintus Curtius' *The Acts of Alexander the Great, King of Macedon* translated from the Latin by John Brende in 1553, which uses the words "They demanded to whom he would leave his kingdom. He said: to the worthiest".

Many names of characters in the play were taken from Plutarch's *Parallel Lives*, translated into English by Thomas North and first published in 1579 as *The Lives of the Noble Grecians and Romans*[13]. There are also a few parallels with phraseology contained in works of Francis Sabie published in 1595[14] but it is unclear who was the borrower: Sabie could have borrowed from the play, or 'Shakespeare' from Sabie. A similar caution must be applied to other possible minor sources discussed by Pafford[15].

As all major and minor sources of *The Winter's Tale* were available around 1588 to 1595, and there is no specific evidence for a post-1595 source, *The Winter's Tale* was probably written at some time around 1590. The fact that Sir George Buck apparently licensed the play for stage production[16] sometime between 1606 and 1610 has no bearing on the date of *writing* of the play, except to show that it was written by 1610.

Support for a 1590s date comes from the play's use of 1590s slang in the light-hearted Act 5, scene 2 in which the Clown, in turn, dubs the Shepherd then Autolycus "a tall fellow" (meaning a 'smart guy' in today's idiom) which was an address in vogue at this time[17]. This phrase is unlikely to have been written into any play ten to twenty years later – in the early 1600s the phrase would have appeared as dated and out-of-place as addressing someone as a 'cool dude' in a play today. Another indication of a 1590s date of composition comes from the phrase "Nor brass, or stone . . ." in Act 1, scene 2; the words are similar to the words "Since brass, nor stone . . ." used in sonnet 65, dated to 1597 (Appendix 3).

While generalisations like "*The Winter's Tale* is beyond doubt one of the group which also includes *Pericles*, *Cymbeline*, *The Tempest* and *Henry*

VIII"[18] are supported by linguistic analysis[19], such analysis is not, in itself, a dating method – it simply groups plays with linguistic similarities. Vaguely worded appeals to unreferenced scholarship like "practically all authorities now consider that these are very late plays"[20] are irrelevant.

* * *

Cymbeline and *The Winter's Tale* appear to be experimental. Although they both have admirable scenes, their infrequent appearance on the stage suggests that most people find them inferior to other 'Shakespearean' plays. I agree with Nosworthy who wrote of *Cymbeline*: "it is the creation of a man [sic] perpetually fascinated by his dramatic experiment, surprised and exhilarated by the new sensations and discoveries which the elaboration of his unfamiliar material has yielded"[21]. But we should remember that writers generally experiment early in their careers while they are searching for modes of expression that best represent their evolving and sometimes immature thoughts, their developing views of the world around them, and their new experiences.

As all sources for *Cymbeline* and *The Winter's Tale* predate 1603 and most predate the mid-1590s, we can conclude that these plays are not late works. They are almost certainly experimental works written in the 1590s. *The Tempest*, which (almost all commentators would agree) is a more mature work, was probably written soon after *Cymbeline* and *The Winter's Tale*.

Nosworthy commented that "*Cymbeline* ... has the appearance of being the outcome of some peculiar, and perhaps decisive turning point in Shakespeare's private or professional life"[22]. Like Nosworthy, we know nothing about Shakespeare's life that might correspond to this possible "turning point", but we do know that in the 1590s Elizabeth and Essex frequently had tiffs and arguments resulting in brief separations followed by reconciliations. As established for the sonnets (Appendix 3), the biographies of Elizabeth and Essex provide the relevant context for the writing of *Cymbeline* and *The Winter's Tale*, which Shakespeare's biography does not. Both plays have positive endings. Misunderstandings and differences are resolved and true love prevails, largely through the persistence and bravery of the heroines. The plays belong to Elizabeth's optimistic period, which came to an abrupt end as a result of the confrontation with Essex at the Privy Council meeting of 1 July 1598.

---

[1] Cohen and Cohen (1960).
[2] Nosworthy (1969, p. li).
[3] Nosworthy (1969, pp. xl–lxi); Warren (1998).
[4] Jackson (1994). The stress test (Table 3) shows that there is an apparent progression from more regular stress distribution to less regular stress

distribution when the plays are put in the traditional order of composition suggested by Chambers (1930). But because the stress test is not an independent dating method this correspondence is not proof that Chambers' order of composition is correct. It is quite possible that the author of the plays experimented with a different (and arguably more conversational) style when writing the fantasies, and then reverted to an earlier more formal style. Which is to say that the author's stylistic development may not have been linear.

5 Tillyard (1938, p. 1).
6 Nosworthy (1969).
7 Nosworthy (1969, pp xx–xxviii).
8 Vickers (2002, p.89) and Partridge (1964, p. 64).
9 Nosworthy (1969, p. xxxvi) points out that the poetry of the vision (Act 5, scene 4) is written in 'fourteeners' (lines with 14 beats) which were popular in the 1590s.
10 Nosworthy (1969, pp. xvii–lxx).
11 Hieatt, Hieatt and Prescott (2001, p. 71).
12 Pafford (1963, p. xxi) provides a transcript of Forman's notes, which are held by The Ashmolean Museum, Oxford.
13 Pafford (1963, p. 163).
14 Pafford (1963, p. xxxiii).
15 Pafford (1963).
16 Pafford (1963, pp. xvi and xxiii).
17 Pafford (1963, p. 153).
18 Pafford (1963, p. xxii).
19 Jackson (1994).
20 Pafford (1963, p. xxii).
21 Nosworthy (1969, p. xlii).
22 Nosworthy (1969, p. xi).

31. *All's Well that Ends Well*

Your old virginity is like one of our French withered pears:
it looks ill, it eats drily
  – *All's Well that Ends Well*, Act 1, scene 1

All's Well that Ends Well belongs to that group of plays for which there is no record of any production before the publication of the First Folio in 1623. Researchers agree that what was printed in the First Folio was an advanced draft lacking the editing necessary for a stage production, which supports the inference that it was never performed (and incidentally, supports the inference that the play was not written by a professional actor).

The deficiencies in the text indicating it was never staged include inconsistent speech prefixes, plot notes apparently inserted by the author, vague stage directions, and entrances for 'ghost' characters who say nothing and are superfluous to the plot. For example, the old countess has the speech prefixes *Mo.* (for Mother), *Cou.* (for Countess), *Old Cou.* (for Old Countess) and *La.* (for Lady). The two lords are given the speech prefixes *E* and *G* but are also indicated by numbers *1* and *2*. To add to the confusion Lord *E* is not invariably Lord *1* and Lord *G* is not invariably Lord *2*. To add further confusion, in the stage directions which define entrances and exits by actors, they are also named either "*two Gentlemen*" or "*the Frenchmen*". Such vagueness would have created havoc both on stage and backstage. Any Elizabethan or Jacobean director or stage manager would have found it necessary to regularise the text so that he, the actors and the prompter knew precisely who was required for the next entry.

If the play was never staged before it was published in 1623 we are justified in asking the same question that we asked about the great tragedy *Anthony and Cleopatra*: why would William Shakespeare who, most people believe, authored the works attributed to him, and who apparently depended on writing plays for earning his living, put aside a competently written work that had taken him weeks if not months to write, without tidying up his advanced draft in order to gain a financial return for his efforts? This important question has never been considered seriously by Shakespeare scholars.

Let's consider the subject matter of the play. *All's Well that Ends Well* is not often produced on stage. It is seen as a 'difficult' play. It is a dark comedy, but it is also a romance to the extent that the poor (but well brought-up) orphan Helen has fallen in love with the aristocrat Bertram. But Helen has a problem: Bertram hasn't fallen in love with her. Helen has acquired useful knowledge about herbal remedies from her father, and this gives her access to the King, for he has an apparently incurable illness. Helen is able to cure the King. The King rewards her by allowing her free choice of husband from among his subjects. Helen chooses Bertram and the King marries the two. But Bertram refuses to consummate the marriage and runs away to fight in a war, together with his sidekick Parolles, who (arguably) is the funniest character in the play – especially when reflecting on the 'pros and cons' of virginity:

> 'Tis a commodity [that] will lose the gloss with lying; the longer kept, the less worth. Off with't while 'tis vendible; answer the time of request . . . virginity, like an old courtier, wears her cap out of fashion, richly suited [clad], but unsuitable . . . your old virginity is like one of our French wither'd pears: it looks ill, it eats drily; marry, 'tis a wither'd pear; it was formerly better; marry, yet 'tis a wither'd pear.

Helen pursues Bertram and buys the cooperation of an Italian widow and her virgin daughter with whom Bertram happens to be besotted. By swapping places with the daughter in a night-time assignment she manages to get herself bedded with and pregnant by Bertram. (In *Measure for Measure* Isabel uses a similar bed-trick to avoid having to lie with Angelo.) Eventually, after the evasive Bertram has told numerous lies and demonstrated what a worthless adventurer he is, he and Helen have a reconciliation of sorts – although the audience must wonder whether he is truly committed to matrimony. The play ends at this point. In the penultimate line of the play the King remarks "All yet seems well" – he doesn't appear to be convinced. The very title of the play may be ironic – does everything really end well?

Critics have difficulty with the play. There are no heroes or heroines for the audience to identify with. Bertram is a lying good-for-nothing. There is no doubt that Helen is clever but she is also manipulative and opportunistic and has appalling judgement – why on earth is she so keen to marry the shallow Bertram whose prime aims in life seem to be to evade responsibilities, play soldiers and chase skirts? The scholar G. K. Hunter presented the critical consensus: he complained of the play's "harsh discord which seeks resolution, but achieves less than is sought" and wrote that Bertram's failure to achieve a change of heart "is the major thematic failure of the play"[1]. Elsewhere he generalised that there is "too much complication leading to too little resolution" and suggested that in this play "Shakespeare was not primarily interested in personal reconciliation"[2].

What G. K. Hunter and other scholars really seem to be saying is that the play does not fit any accepted genre. It is not a light-hearted comedy like *Twelfth Night* or *As You Like It*. It is not a tragedy like *Hamlet* or *King Lear*. It is not a fantasy like *Cymbeline* or *The Winter's Tale*. It is not a history play like *Richard III* or *Julius Caesar*. In mood it is closest to *Troilus and Cressida* – neither play has a happy ending. Both are anti-romantic. Loose ends remain loose ends and in both plays the author seems happy to leave sombre issues concerning love and commitment unresolved. But surely this is precisely what the author intended. The play was not meant to be the equivalent of a modern 'feel-good movie'. It is intended to be disquieting and intended to demonstrate that in true life tricky personal issues may never be resolved. As the unidentified writer of the preface to *Troilus and Cressida* wrote so perceptively: "this author's comedies . . . are so framed to the life that they serve for the most common commentaries of all the actions of our lives".

We would be able to appreciate the play better if we knew more about its historical context: when was it written, why was it written, and why was an advanced draft put aside by the author and not released for performance?

Firstly, let's ascertain the date of writing. The ultimate source of the play's plot is the ninth story told on day three in Boccaccio's *Decameron* (published in Italian in the middle of the 14th century). The author of *All's Well that Ends Well* may have read the Italian edition, or an English translation by William Painter (published in 1566, 1569 and 1575), or a French translation by Antoine Le Maçon (completed to meet a request of Margaret of Navarre) published in Paris in 1569, or all three.

G. K. Hunter considered that the part of the clown in the play was designed for Robert Armin, who probably joined Shakespeare's company in 1599, so the play is likely to have been written in 1599 or later[3] (unless the clown's text was later inserted into an almost complete play).

The only other evidence we can use to estimate a date of writing is the rather subjective method of comparing the play's subject matter and style with these attributes in other plays. It is an obvious twin of *Measure for Measure* which is also about how a low-born but virtuous heroine succeeds in marrying an aristocrat. For those who prefer tidy endings *Measure for Measure* is the more satisfying play – everybody who matters gets paired off in the last scene. For those who don't need to escape to a happily-ever-after world *All's Well that Ends Well* may appeal. We might suspect that the more cynical *All's Well that Ends Well* represents the world-view of an older author, just as *King Lear*, with its vivid depiction of an aged monarch's descent into madness is probably a later creation than *Hamlet*. But these comparisons between plays do not help to date the *All's Well that Ends Well*, except that we might conclude that the similar cynical approaches to matters of the heart in *All's Well that Ends Well* and *Troilus and Cressida* could date the play to around 1601 to 1602.

Why the play was written is a question almost impossible to answer for those who believe William Shakespeare was the author. What events would lead a middle-aged man to write such a bleak comedy about an enforced marriage between an ill-matched couple? Stratfordians might reply that the play was written because William Shakespeare was unhappily married to Anne Hathwey and he wrote the play to express his bottled-up negative feelings concerning Anne, but this would be no more than speculation. We know nothing about Shakespeare's love life other than the fact that he was married in 1582 when he was eighteen and Anne was twenty-six years old and that they had three children. Even if we convince ourselves that Shakespeare wrote the play because of his unsatisfactory relationship with Anne, why, as a professional playwright and actor dependent for his income on success in the theatre, did he not stage it?

If we accept that the historical context of the play is the Elizabeth-Essex relationship all difficulties disappear. As the tragic events of 1601 unfolded Elizabeth must have at last realised that her infatuation with Essex had been a disastrous error of judgement. This enigmatic and charming young man was all show and no substance. Like Bertram, Essex was an adventurer who liked going off to war and chasing women. Like Helena, Elizabeth had power, and therefore had some control over people and events. In her dreams she might have fantasised being married to Essex, but like the uneasy marriage in the play, her relationship to Essex was a 'marriage' that did not signify a meeting of minds and was without an emotional commitment on the part of Essex, although he was clever enough to fool the love-starved Elizabeth most of the time. His betrayal in 1601 hit hard – and she wrote a play about it.

---

[1] Hunter (2009, pp. xxix and xxxvii–xxxviii).
[2] Hunter (2009, p. xxiv and liv).
[3] Hunter (2009, p. xxi).

32. *Macbeth*

Fair is foul, and foul is fair
— *Macbeth*, Act 1, scene 1

We can be certain that a version of *Macbeth* was written by 1610 or 1611 because in his diary entry dated Saturday 20 April 1610 the quack doctor, astrologer and serial seducer Simon Forman made notes on the play, which he reported seeing at the Globe theatre:

> In Mackbeth at the Glob. 1610, the 20 of Aprill [symbol for Saturday], ther was to be observed, first, how Mackbeth and Bankco, 2 noble men of Scotland, Riding throwe a wod, the[r] strode before them 3 women feiries or Nimphes, And saluted Mackbeth, saying 3 tyms unto him, haille Mackbeth, King of Codon . . .

However, 20 April falls on a Friday not a Saturday in the Julian calendar. Forman either misremembered the day he saw the play or he mistakenly wrote 1610 instead of 1611: in the latter year 20 April does fall on a Saturday. That he incorrectly recorded the date or day is not surprising as his remarks on the plot seem to have been written after a significant interval – his notes on the Lady Macbeth sleepwalking scene, which in the play precedes the battle at Dunsinane where Macbeth is killed, were added as an afterthought after his notes on the play's action. Ascertaining the play's date of composition is also complicated by the likelihood that, in common with the 'late' plays researched by Brian Vickers[1] it contains additions which may not be 'Shakespeare's'.

Macbeth is loosely based on Holinshed's Scottish chronicle[2], but in Holinshed the women Macbeth and Banquo meet are not hideous witches but "women in strange and wild apparel" considered to be "either the weird sisters, that is (as ye would say) the goddesses of destinie, or else some nymphs or feiries, indued with knowledge of prophesie"[3]. Holinshed's description "nymphs or feiries" matches the "feiries or Nimphes" that Forman noted, which suggests that either Forman's memory of the play was augmented by his reading of Holinshed (as suggested by Nicholas Brooke[4]) or that what Forman saw on the stage was not the version printed in the First Folio of 1623, but an earlier version with closer parallels to Holinshed's text.

Traditionally the composition of Macbeth has been dated to the mid-1600s. Clark and Mason (2015, p. 134) wrote that "There seems no good reason to doubt the generally accepted view that Macbeth was written in 1606"[5]. But this date is far from certain, and the "generally accepted view" requires support of firm evidence before it can be regarded as correct. Brooke was more cautious: "There is no evidence to contradict 1606 [as the date of composition of the play] but there is also very little to support it"[6].

Clarke and Mason recognised that revision of the play was an issue but failed to address it: "Many editors consider that there are problems with the integrity of the play as a whole, and although there is no intention here to discuss these in any detail, the position needs briefly to be reviewed". However, their brief review of the evidence for editorial meddling (pp. 321–336) is unsatisfactory: it contains no new analysis but instead summarises the various arguments made by other researchers for and against late interpolations and changes, without resolution. Although they acknowledge that "The Folio text of Macbeth is probably not the original version that Shakespeare wrote in 1606" (p. 336), they are apparently reluctant to admit that, if the text has indeed been modified, then the "generally accepted" 1606 date for *Macbeth*'s composition must be doubted, and two significant dates need to be established: the date of composition of the primary text and the date (or dates) of its modification. The question of who executed the modifications also needs attention. This chapter addresses these issues.

The playwright Thomas Middleton probably collaborated in writing the play, or added to it, or edited it without consulting 'Shakespeare', since the witches' songs referred to in Act 3, scene 5 and Act 4, scene 1 (but not printed in the First Folio text), are those that also appear in Middleton's play *The Witch*, probably written in 1615 or thereabouts[7]. (Witches were a topical subject in Jacobean England, probably because King James had an interest in them. His book entitled *Daemonology* was published in 1597 and another entitled *Basilikon Doran* [*The King's Gift*] was published in 1599.) Brooke suggested that Middleton added the songs to *Macbeth* in about 1609 or 1610[8], i.e. *before* he wrote his own play, but failed to provide evidence to support his suggestion.

These dates for Middleton's additions seem improbable for two reasons. Firstly, if Middleton did write the songs[9], he would have been more likely to have used them in a work of his own before using them to embellish the work of a competing author of 'Shakespeare's' stature, thereby risking losing the credit due to himself. It follows that the songs were probably added to *Macbeth* between about 1615 and 1623, *after* Middleton had finished his own play *The Witch* and tested it on the stage (where it wasn't well received). Secondly, why would an author capable of writing masterpieces such as *Hamlet* and *Anthony and Cleopatra* bother to collaborate with a lesser writer for the purpose of adding witches' songs (and possibly the doggerel incantations too) into his tragedy?

If Middleton did add the witches' songs to *Macbeth*, we are justified in asking how much other material he added or modified. And if Middleton added to the play, or embellished what 'Shakespeare' had written, was he also the person responsible for transforming the nymphs and fairies (as portrayed by Holinshed and noted by Simon Forman) into the evil creatures casting charms while dancing around a cauldron in the First Folio version of *Macbeth* (the only version of the play that we know today) in order to pander to James

I's interest in witches? In relation to the latter question, it is relevant that Simon Forman's 1610 diary account not only fails to mention witches, but also makes no mention of the scene in which they utter prophesies (Act 4, scene 1). These omissions are surprising and significant because Forman was an astrologer, and one might expect that prophesies made by semi-supernatural beings would have been especially interesting to him.

These apparent omissions support the proposition that what Forman saw in 1610 was a version of the play pre-dating the Middleton additions – a play in which spirits, weird sisters, nymphs or fairies (but not witches) predict the future. If this proposition is accepted, then it is likely that after the 1610 performance Middleton not only added the witches' songs previously referred to, but also much of Act 4, scene 1 in which the powerfully portrayed but stereotypical witches chant their sinister verses.

Another piece of text that is almost certainly a topical reference and therefore potentially useful for dating the play is the mention of an equivocator in the drunken porter scene (Act 2, scene 3). When the drunken porter hears knocking at the castle gates, he imagines he is unlocking the gates of hell for new entrants, and we are treated to three 'knock, knock' jokes, similar to the 'knock, knock' jokes that have entertained school children for centuries. (The spelling and punctuation in the quotation below follow the First Folio text; stage directions are in italics):

> *Knock.* Knock, Knock, Knock. Who's there, i'th'name of Belzebub? Here's a Farmer, that hang'd himself on th'expectation of Plentie. Come in time, have napkins enow [enough] about you, here you'le sweat for't. *Knock.* Knock, knock. Who's there in th'other Devil's name? Faith, here's an Equivocator, that could sweare in both the Scales against either Scale, who committed Treason enough for Gods sake, yet could not equivocate to Heaven: oh come in, Equivocator. *Knock.* Knock, Knock, Knock. Who's there? Faith here's an English Taylor come hither, for stealing out of a French Hose: Come in Taylor, here you may rost your Goose. *Knock.* Knock, Knock. Never at quiet: What are you? But this place is too cold for Hell. Ile Devill-Porter it no further: I had thought to have let in some of all Professions, that go the Primrose way to th'everlasting Bonfire.

The first entrant to the gates of hell is a farmer. The second entrant is an equivocator. Equivocators were topical in 1606. After a trial in which "he fell into a large discourse of defending equivocations" a certain Father Garnet was convicted of conspiring in the Gunpowder Plot and hanged on 3 May 1606. Equivocating seems to have been the buzz word of the times[10], and it has been plausibly suggested that the Porter's comments are a reference to Garnet, because Garnet equivocated at his trial, and, as he was a priest, the description of the equivocator committing treason "for God's sake' but not equivocating convincingly enough to go to heaven is appropriate[11]. In which case we could conclude (as most traditional scholars do) that in 1606 William Shakespeare was still busy writing for the stage. But there is evidence to support another explanation: that the reference to Garnet's equivocation is a late addition, added to give the play Jacobean topicality.

The other two men welcomed to enter the imaginary gates of hell have the professions of farmer and tailor, and the Porter himself declares in lines 19–20 that he "had thought to have let in some of all *professions* [my italics], that go the primrose way to th'everlasting bonfire". But equivocating is not a profession – which suggests that the reference to Garnet's trial is a late and opportunistic insertion into the play, substituted for the Porter's damning remarks about a third profession.

Another topical reference is the mention of a ship called the *Tiger* by the first witch, in Act 1, scene 3. The reference (reproduced below using the spelling and punctuation in the First Folio and line numbers of the Arden edition[12]) is specific:

7	Her Husband's to Aleppo gone, master o'th' *Tiger*:
...	
19	Sleepe shall neyther Night or Day
20	Hang upon his [the master's] Pent-house Lid [eyelid]:
21	He shall live a man forbid [cursed]:
22	Wearie Sev'nights [weeks], nine times nine,
23	Shall he dwindle, peake and pine;
24	Though his Barke [ship] cannot be lost,
25	Yet it shall be Tempest-tost.

Tiger was a popular name for a ship in Elizabethan times. In 1564 John Hawkins sailed a 50-ton ship of this name on a slaving trip between Africa and Spanish South America[13]. In 1585 the Queen donated her own ship of this name to Ralegh to assist his colonisation of Virginia[14]. In September 1585 a 200-ton *Tiger* sailed from Plymouth as part of Sir Francis Drake's fleet that raided Spanish central America[15]. The writer, geographer and historian Richard Hakluyt describes the adventures of the crew of yet another ship of that name that set out in 1583 carrying merchants to trade with the inhabitants of Syria and Mesopotamia. The crew sent letters home from Aleppo before returning to England on another vessel in 1588[16]. Another ship called *Tiger* (170 tons), owned by the Duke of Cumberland, took part in the Battle of Flores (1592) in which the ship's crew helped seize the huge Portuguese carrack *Madre de Deus* and its rich cargo[17].

The ship of 1583 is the only *Tiger* having an association with Aleppo and surely must be the *Tiger* referred to by the witches (who in the original 'Shakespearean' version were probably characterised as the 'weird sisters'). If so, it tells us that at least this part of *Macbeth* was probably composed sometime in the late 1580s or early 1590s, when the story of the *Tiger* voyage and the crew's adventures in Aleppo and elsewhere were still in the minds of the author and playgoers. However, the researcher E. A. Loomis[18] had other ideas. He proposed that the *Tiger* voyage referred to was that of a ship called *Tiger* which sailed on the 5 December 1604 from Cowes in the Isle of Wight to Japan and returned to Milford Haven in southwest Wales on 27 June 1606. His proposal was based on the calculation that this *Tiger* was away for 567 days, which, he argued, equals the number of days at sea mentioned in the witch's statement "Weary se'nnights [weeks] nine times nine" (Loomis' spelling and punctuation), i.e. 7 x 9 x 9 = 567 days.

Loomis' calculations and conclusions looked convincing enough for Brooke to write: "The coincidence is surprising, and hard to ignore. If it is significant, then this passage cannot have been written before the beginning of July 1606 . . . Shakespeare cannot have begun the play much sooner"[19].

But Loomis' argument is less convincing than it appeared to be to Brooke. The argument's most significant shortcoming is the obvious one: the voyage to Japan of 1604 had no connection at all to Aleppo.

The second shortcoming is that Shakespeare never shows off mathematical prowess in his plays. In fact, he generally shows scant regard for dates, historical accuracy or real time. To expect an audience to calculate seven times nine times nine in their heads, and then relate the derived number of days to the duration in days of a 1604 voyage to Japan that lasted just over 18 months, and then link this voyage to an excursion to Aleppo twenty-one years earlier by the crew of another ship of the same name is an extreme case of special pleading.

The third shortcoming is that the assumption behind Loomis' mathematics is faulty. The *Tiger* was away from 5 December 1604 to 27 June 1606. Let's assume that it left at noon on the 5 December and returned at noon on the 27 June. On this basis it was away for 26 days in December 1604, 365 days in 1605, and 178 days in 1606, which comes to 569 days, i.e. a total of 569 full 24-hour periods. In his calculation Loomis had to omit the date of leaving and the date of arrival (which he described disingenuously as the "two days the *Tiger* was in port") to obtain his 567-day result, but there is absolutely no justification for this time adjustment. (If, say, my yacht crosses the starting line for the Sydney–Hobart yacht race at 1 p.m. on a Sunday, and happens to arrive in Hobart at 1 p.m. on the following Sunday, everyone would agree that I had completed the race in seven days. The race committee would find laughable any assertion that I had completed the race in five days on account of being "in port" on both Sundays.) Consequently, contrary to Loomis' assertion, there is no coincidence between the total days away calculated from the text of the play (567) and the actual duration of the *Tiger*'s 1604–1606 voyage (569 days).

Furthermore, another point ignored by Loomis is that the voyage of the *Tiger* finished at Portsmouth (close to Cowes, its port of departure) on 9 July 1606[20], not at Milford Haven. If this additional leg of the journey is admitted, the voyage took 581 days.

Loomis' so-called evidence for *Macbeth*'s authorship after July 1606 can be firmly rejected for the above reasons. We can conclude that the *Tiger* reference is indeed to the voyage of 1583, which lasted many weary weeks, and that the phrase "nine times nine" is not meant to be taken literally as a multiplication factor but was included by 'Shakespeare' in the incantation to indicate in a general way that the ship was away for a long time.

It has been suggested that *Macbeth* was written for performance before King James on the occasion of a visit by his father-in-law King Christian of Denmark in 1606[21]. However, Brooke comprehensively debunked the theory, describing it as a "fantasy" based on "no evidence whatsoever"[22].

Finally, there are two other references in the play which have been presented as evidence of its composition in Jacobean times. These are the references to the two-fold balls and sceptres of Banquo's descendants in Act 4, scene 1 and to the King's power to cure maladies in Act 4, scene 3. The context of the first reference is Macbeth's meeting with the witches. Macbeth asks the witches:

> ... Tell me, if your Art
> Can tell so much: Shall Banquo's issue ever
> Reigne in this kingdom?

By way of reply, the witches conjure up a vision of future kings (Banquo's issue) that greatly troubles the usurper. The quote below is reproduced as it appeared in the First Folio, and the line numbers are those of the Arden edition[23]:

> *A show of eight Kings, and Banquo last, with a glasse in his hand.*
> *Macb.* Thou art too like the Spirit of *Banquo*: Down: Line 112
> Thy crowne do's seare mine Eye-bals: and thy haire
> Thou other Gold-bound-brow, is like the first:
> A third, is like the former. Filthy Hagges,   Line 115
> Why do you shew me this? – A fourth? Start eyes!
> What will the Line stretch out to'th'cracke of Doome[24]?
> Another yet? A seaventh? Ile see no more:
> And yet the eight appeares, who bears a glasse[25],
> Which shewes me many more: and some I see,
> That two-fold Balles, and trebble Scepters carry.   Line 120
> Horrible sight: Now, I see 'tis true[26],
> For the Blood-bolter'd *Banquo* smiles upon me,
> And points at them for his.   Line 124

In this vision Banquo's ghost unsettles Macbeth by showing him a line of Scottish Kings descended from Banquo, not Macbeth. Banquo's ghost then shows him "many more" in a "glasse". Some of these carry "two-fold Balles, and trebble Scepters" and these words have been interpreted to represent, respectively, the uniting of the two kingdoms of England and Scotland as

Britain[27] and the rule of the Stuarts over Britain, Ireland and France[28] (the last in theory only). One could assume that this speech by the troubled Macbeth was designed to flatter King James. The question is, is it 'Shakespearean' or has it been added by another hand?

The structure of the speech suggests interference. In the play Banquo is not a king. He doesn't become a king, but the witches predict that his offspring will become kings. Therefore, the stage direction introducing the vision must be read as meaning that eight kings appear on stage, with Banquo (not a king) following as the ninth person, holding a "glasse". But here we strike a problem: in line 119 Macbeth describes the *eighth king*[29] as holding a "glasse". We can only conclude that either the author of *Macbeth* forgot the structure of the scene (and Banquo's place in it) in a moment of distraction after writing the seven lines that follow the stage direction introducing the vision and the eight kings, which seems unlikely; or that a person who has misunderstood the original stage direction (and didn't write it) has tampered with the text. Assuming the latter conclusion is correct, we can postulate that the original text read something like this (starting at line 118):

> Another yet? A seaventh? Ile see no more:
> And yet the eight appeares. Now, I see 'tis true,
> For the Blood-bolter'd *Banquo* smiles upon me,
> And points at them for his.

... and the tampering editor has considered the pause after "appeares" in line 119 to be an appropriate place within the play to add lines flattering King James with the observation that under his rule England and Scotland have been united within a greater entity:

> ... who bears a glasse,
> Which shewes me many more: and some I see,
> That two-fold Balles, and trebble Scepters carry.
> Horrible sight:

But this rather clumsy editor has bungled the task by his oversight of equating the eighth king with the glass-carrying Banquo.

Later, in the same Act 4, Macduff and the future King Malcolm, in exile in England, appear in a long scene (scene 3) of 139 lines. To test Macduff, Malcolm makes himself out to be completely unsuitable to the task of governing Scotland. Once Macduff finds himself persuaded that Malcolm is indeed unsuitable (thereby revealing his own his high principles) Malcolm reveals his true character. Having passed the character test, Macduff commits himself to Malcolm's cause and they agree to work as brothers to oppose Macbeth's tyrannical rule.

The scene is interrupted by the entry of a doctor, which is surprising as neither of them are ill and a doctor is not mentioned in Holinshed's account, on which scene 3 is based. Malcolm, unprompted, asks the doctor "Comes the King forth, I pray you?" (line 140) which is also surprising, as up to this this point in the scene there has been no suggestion that Macduff and Malcolm are expecting a royal visit or a doctor. And why should Malcolm assume that the arrival of a doctor presages the arrival of the English King?

The doctor responds in five lines. He says that the King (King Edward the Confessor) is indeed expected, as well as a crowd wishing to be cured of illness through the King's touch. In the following fourteen lines Malcolm expands on the doctor's remarks by extolling the curing powers and other virtues of Edward the Confessor, and includes the observation that Edward will pass on his miraculous powers to his successors:

> ... and 'tis spoken
> To the succeeding royalty he leaves
> The healing benediction. With this strange virtue,
> He hath a heavenly gift of prophecy;
> And sundry blessings hang about his throne.
> That speak him full of grace.

These lines (note the reference to "succeeding royalty"), also seem to be intended to flatter King James[30], this time by linking him to supernatural royal healing powers and a former saintly king. They do not advance the plot.

There are three indications that the twenty lines in the doctor sub-scene are an interpolation: the doctor's abrupt entrance, without explanation or introduction, into a private conversation between two exiles; the contrived insertion of text mentioning the power of the English King to cure his subjects' maladies, which bears no relation at all to the preceding conversation; and Malcolm's reference to Edward the Confessor's powers being passed on to future kings (which can be interpreted to be a fawning comment designed to flatter the reigning monarch, James). None of these topics is relevant to the subject matter of the scene, which is the agreement between two exiles to overthrow Macbeth.

If further evidence for interpolation is needed, we can examine the lines immediately preceding the doctor's entry. In the play as we know it Macduff, having listened to Malcolm's description of his feigned character, and then his real one, and having learnt of his noble intent to defeat Macbeth, utters the lines:

> Such welcome and unwelcome things at once
> 'Tis hard to reconcile.

and then the doctor enters, interrupting the conversation. But if the doctor sub-scene is omitted, Macduff's lines read as follows:

> Such welcome and unwelcome things at once
> 'Tis hard to reconcile. See, who comes here.

. . . and then we read the sub-scene in which an agitated Ross arrives and presents Macduff with the heart-rending news that Macduff's wife and children have been massacred by Macbeth's forces, which immediately prompts the two exiles to resolve to return to Scotland immediately to seek revenge.

If the doctor sub-scene is omitted the tension in Act 4, scene 3 builds incrementally: a wary and unhurried Malcolm first tests Macduff's character; he finds him high principled; the two resolve to work together against Macbeth, but at this point in the conversation have devised no specific plan. Finally, hearing from Ross the devastating news from Scotland about Macbeth's latest murderous outrage, they are spurred into action to avenge the deaths of Macduff's wife and children. The doctor sub-scene destroys this carefully crafted dramatic slow crescendo.

* * *

In conclusion, the textual evidence suggesting a late date of composition for Macbeth – the allusion to Garnet's 1606 trial in the porter scene, the reference to two orbs and three sceptres in the vison of eight kings, and the apparent reference to King James having similar curative powers to those of King Edward the Confessor – is almost certainly a result of clumsy late (Jacobean) editing and additions designed to please King James. The play does not contain a reference to the *Tiger* voyage of 1604–1606; the *Tiger* mentioned is much more likely to be a ship of this name that sailed in 1583 with a crew that visited Aleppo. Probable additions to the witches scene and the evidence for clumsy splicing of interpolations into pre-existing text (in the drunken porter scene, the conversation between Malcolm and MacDuff, and Macbeth's vision of Banquo's royal descendants), indicate late modification of *Macbeth* by a hand other than 'Shakespeare's'. Thomas Middleton is the most likely candidate for the meddling author.

Finally, it must be emphasised that the fact that the play has Scottish subject matter does not constitute evidence that the play is a Jacobean creation.

---

[1] Vickers (2002) presented the evidence for the co-authorship of *Timon of Athens*, *Pericles*, *Henry VIII* and *The Two Noble Kinsmen*.
[2] Muir (1984, Appendix A).
[3] Muir (1984, Appendix A).
[4] Brooke (1998, Appendix C).
[5] Clark and Mason (2015, p. 134).

6 Brooke (1998, p. 59).
7 Logan and Smith (1975) considered that *The Witch* was written between 1613 and 1616. It was acted by the King's Men at the Blackfriars Theatre.
8 Brooke (1998, pp. 64–66).
9 It is possible that the songs were not written by Middleton but were popular ditties circulating in Jacobean England, which would account for only their titles being given in *Macbeth*. But if they were popular and well known, making their printing within the play unnecessary, why did Middleton print them in his own play? It seems more likely that the songs, original or not, first appeared in Middleton's play *The Witch*, in which they were written out in full, so that they could be sung on stage. Their earlier documentation in *The Witch* made it unnecessary to include the songs in the manuscript of *Macbeth* because when this later play was staged by the King's Men, who had also staged *The Witch*, the songs were well known to the actors.
10 Muir (1984, pp. xx–xxii).
11 Stunz (1942, pp. 95–105).
12 Muir (1984).
13 Bicheno (2013, p. 81).
14 Bicheno (2013, pp. 179–180); Guy (2016).
15 Bicheno (2013, p. 183).
16 An account of the voyage carrying English merchants John Newberie and Ralph Fitch appears in the second edition of Richard Hakluyt's *Principal Navigations* (1599, volume 2, part 1, pp. 245–271) but the account was probably circulating earlier: on 28 May 1583 John Newberie wrote Richard Hakluyt a letter from Aleppo. After adventures in Mesopotamia, India and present-day Burma and Thailand, Ralph Fitch returned to London on 29 April 1591.
17 Bicheno (2013, p. 304).
18 Loomis (1956, p. 457).
19 Brooke (1998, p. 62).
20 Markham (2017).
21 Paul (1950). Loomis (1956) considered Paul's evidence to be "rather convincing".
22 Brooke (1998, p. 72).
23 Muir (1984).
24 Sonnet 116 uses the phrase "edge of doom" and was probably written by Elizabeth shortly after Essex's execution in 1601.
25 Shakespeare always uses the word "glass" to mean a mirror (except that in sonnet 126 "glass" refers to an hourglass). Muir (1984) suggested that Banquo's glass is a magic glass that can see into the future.
26 The vision created by the witches confirms that Banquo's issue will reign in "this Kingdome".
27 In Elizabethan and Jacobean times Wales was considered to be part of England.
28 Lyle (1977).
29 The Stuart dynasty began with Robert II in 1371. Unless Mary Queen of Scots is counted as a king, the eighth king must be James VI of Scotland (James I of England).
30 Clark and Mason (2015) cite several references.

33. *Timon of Athens* and *Pericles*

Hate all, curse all, show charity to none
— *Timon of Athens*, Act 4, scene 3

These two plays, as well as *Macbeth*, show numerous signs that 'Shakespeare' either collaborated with another author, or that another author modified 'Shakespeare's' original work[1]. Both collaboration and modification complicate the issue of determining when the texts were written, and raise the important issue of why a dramatist as able and eminent as 'Shakespeare' would bother to cooperate with a less gifted author.

* * *

There is no record that either printed or staged versions of *Timon of Athens* appeared before publication of the First Folio in 1623. The play is short and unsuitable for staging without editing. It has been suggested, on the basis of many criteria, that Thomas Middleton wrote some of the play[2]. But if Thomas Middleton worked on the play, did he work with 'Shakespeare', or was he contracted to finish what, for some reason, was left unfinished by the primary author? If the former scenario is correct, we would expect the First Folio text to be ready for the stage, but this is not the case. If the latter scenario is correct, it is odd that an editing playwright, presumably working on the author's rough draft, spent time adding speeches to a play without also paying attention to the play's manifest deficiencies: vague stage directions, ghost characters who appear on stage but have no part to play, characters who speak on stage but are not given stage entries, inconsistencies about the value of money (talents), and confusing speech headings.

What appears to have happened is that Thomas Middleton didn't complete his editing task but abandoned the play after adding substantially to it. Perhaps Middleton found the task too difficult, or realised that the play did not have commercial potential, or considered that he was not being paid enough for his labours. For whatever reason, the play remained unfinished, and the compilers of the First Folio had to 'make do' with the material available to them. Consequently, the First Folio text was typeset from the primary author's text and Thomas Middleton's supplementary material, with the state of both contributions indicating that they were rough drafts apparently prepared independently from each other.

The Timon legend is mentioned by many classical authors but the major source of the story in the play, including most of the important characters' names, is Plutarch's *Lives of the Noble Grecians and Romans*. The Timon legend is mentioned in the biographies of Marcus Antonius and Alcibiades. Plutarch's *Lives* was translated into English from Amyot's French version by Thomas North and first published in 1579. A second edition of North's translation appeared in 1595. As no topical allusions have been identified that might help to date the text, we can only reach the rather unsatisfactory conclusion that the play was written after 1579 – any other conclusion is speculative. (Lacking documentary evidence, commentators have turned to the more subjective evidence of stylistic and linguistic characteristics to determine a date of composition relative to other 'Shakespeare' plays[3]. However, such methods essentially group plays having similar stylistic or linguistic character; they are not in themselves dating methods.)

The play has a relatively simple focus: it is about money and ingratitude[4]. Timon is a rich Athenian. He is generous to colleagues whom he mistakenly regards as friends, not realising that they are abusing his naïve goodwill. When loans to him are called in his finances collapse. He becomes a pauper, and heads for the woods. As an outcast he rails against society's values – a change neatly described by Klein as an "abrupt turn-about from philanthropy to misanthropy"[5]. The parallels between Timon's actions and outbursts and those of King Lear, who divides his kingdom between two calculating daughters only to be rejected by them, has been noted by many researchers.

Commentators have also noted that Act 1, scene 1 in *Timon* has structural and verbal parallels with Act 2, scene 2 in *King Lear*, suggesting that both were written at about the same time[6]. The fact that *Timon of Athens* is a personal story in a short and probably draft form unsuitable for staging without careful editing, and that the subject matter in *King Lear* covers a much larger canvas, suggests that *Timon* preceded *King Lear*[7]. This conclusion is supported by a rigorous statistical comparison of vocabulary conducted by Eliot Slater (1978) in which he found highly significant vocabulary links between the two plays[8]. Furthermore, *Timon* is also closely linked[9] to *Coriolanus* and *Hamlet*, and *Lear* is closely linked to *Hamlet* and *Macbeth*, which suggests that the plays *Coriolanus*, *Timon*, *Hamlet*, *Macbeth* and *Lear* were all written around the same time.

We can speculate that the unfinished *Timon of Athens* was abandoned by the author in favour of *King Lear* when bigger themes demanded attention, and that Thomas Middleton, somehow obtaining a manuscript version, attempted to finish it and make it into a stageable play, only to abandon it. I discuss in chapter 37 that a date of around 1600 is likely for the completion of *King Lear* rather than the generally accepted 1603–1604. (The later date range is based on the erroneous conclusion that the writing of *King Lear* must have post-dated publication of Samuel Harsnett's *Egregious Popish Impostures*.) Consequently, the most likely date of composition of the 'Shakespearean' part of *Timon of Athens* is the late 1590s or 1600, rather than the period 1607–1608[10].

The earlier period is precisely when Elizabeth must have been most conscious of Essex's ingratitude – his high standing at court was entirely of her own making, but her generosity did not make him humble, it made him arrogant and over-confident. After the Privy Council argument of July 1598 he behaved appallingly towards his benefactor. We should also note that 1600 was the year in which Essex was financially ruined when the Queen did not renew his lucrative monopoly on the sale of sweet wines. At a stroke she reversed the deal that had supported Essex's special status as royal favourite. (We should note that there is no evidence to suggest that there were events in Shakespeare's life that would have led him to write a play about ingratitude,)

After Essex's execution in 1601, we can assume that analysing her experiences and feelings regarding Essex's ingratitude by retelling the *Timon of Athens* story seemed less important to Elizabeth than the more pressing personal issues of her own mental and physical decline, which shaped *King Lear*. Hence *Timon* was set aside, never to be completed.

* * *

Pericles is an adult romance in the traditional format: a hero finds true love and happiness after enduring and surmounting enormous and lengthy trials and tribulations. It begins with a visit by Prince Pericles to the court of Antiochus, King of Antioch. Here he is introduced to the King's beautiful daughter. The King presents him with a riddle. Pericles deduces that the riddle's message is that the King has committed incest with his daughter but avoids giving the King a direct answer and returns to his home city of Tyre. Realising that Pericles knows his shocking secret (why did he present Pericles with the riddle in the first place?), and fearful that Pericles will reveal it to others, Antiochus seeks to kill Pericles in his native Tyre. So Pericles sails away, arriving in Tarsus, where he distributes grain from his ship, relieving the famine in the city. (He must have had a large ship.) He sails on, but his ship is wrecked and washes onto the shore of Pentapolis, just in time for Pericles to learn about a tournament the local king is planning, the prize being the hand of his beautiful daughter Thaisa in marriage. Fortunately, Pericles' rusty armour has washed ashore too (unique floating armour!), so he participates in the tournament. Predictably, he wins the hand of Thaisa, who, as luck would have it, is as attracted to the unkempt castaway as he is to her.

Later the duly wedded and pregnant Thaisa and Pericles sail back to Tyre. But during another storm Thaisa gives birth to a daughter, appropriately named Marina. Thaisa appears to die during childbirth, and the superstitious sailors demand that she is buried at sea in order to calm the storm. She is cast overboard in a caulked waterproof chest. (It's always handy to have one of these around.) The ship diverts to Tarsus where Pericles is sure he will be received sympathetically, having saved the population from starvation on his previous visit. Meanwhile, Thaisa's coffin washes ashore at Ephesus. She is found to be alive (was the watertight coffin fitted with a snorkel?) and, believing that her husband has perished in the storm, finds employment as a priestess in the temple of Diana. (What else could a well brought-up lady do?)

Pericles departs from Tarsus to take up the Kingship of Tyre, leaving his daughter Marina in the care of the governor of Tarsus and his wife. As Marina reaches womanhood she is considered to be more beautiful than the governor's daughter. Resenting that their own daughter is only second in the beauty competition, the governor and his wife plot to kill Marina. Marina is 'saved' by pirates who kidnap her, but things get tricky when the pirates sell her to a brothel owner in Mytilene. Marina maintains her virginity by her ability to persuade her clients to be virtuous (a useful attribute in a brothel). One of her clients is the governor Lysimachus, who remains virtuous (at least with Marina). Seeing her income threatened, the brothel madam cuts her losses by renting out Marina as a tutor of the arts. Pericles returns to Tarsus to reclaim his daughter but the governor tells him she has died.

The grieving Pericles takes to the sea yet again, and his next destination happens to be Mytilene. Here he is introduced to Marina by the governor Lysimachus, and Pericles and Marina realise they are father and daughter. Pericles then visits the temple of Diana where he is reunited with his long-lost wife Thaisa. In the last act we learn that the brothel-frequenting Lysimachus plans to marry Marina (how tolerant of her!). And this happy ending completes what Ben Jonson called a "mouldy tale"[11].

The outline above shows that the story of *Pericles* is the medieval equivalent of a B-grade movie or romantic novel of the 'New York best seller' type you can pick up at an airport bookstall. It has minimal character development but numerous improbable action-packed scenes and coincidences in which evil people and great dangers are encountered and overcome, sometimes in the nick of time. It includes the standard requirement for beautiful women to appear alongside the hero and to take charge at critical moments, and a sprinkling of titillating allusions to illicit sex and sexual temptation. Finally, there is the Mills and Boon happy ending: the triumph of true love over adversity.

We are justified in asking why 'Shakespeare' chose this "mouldy tale" for the plot of a new play. The answer is not simply found, for ever since Nicholas Rowe's first observations three hundred years ago, commentators have suspected that the play was written by two authors – so we need to ask why both found such an uninspiring tale worth dramatising. The prime evidence supporting dual authorship is the variable quality of the play's verse, which in the first half of the play is markedly inferior to that in the second. Analysis was largely qualitative and anecdotal before 1876, but in this year F. G. Fleay published a landmark study[12] in which he conducted a number of verse tests on Acts 1–2 (835 lines) and Acts 3–5 (827 lines).

The most striking difference between verses in these two parts is the number of rhyming lines: in Acts 1–2 23% of the lines rhyme whereas in Acts 3–5 only 2% of the lines rhyme[13]. In theory this difference might have resulted from a single author changing his or her style over time, but Fleay countered this potential criticism by pursuing another line of enquiry: he compared the use of rhyme in hundreds of contemporary plays and found that a play by George Wilkins entitled *The Miseries of Enforced Marriage* and the first two acts of *Pericles* had "a marvellously close agreement in percentage" of rhyming lines and other linguistic characteristics. Fleay concluded that Acts 1 and 2 were written by Wilkins.

Later researchers have applied statistical analyses to the text of *Pericles* text and have come to the same conclusion: Acts 1–2 were written by George Wilkins and Acts 3–5 by 'Shakespeare'[14]. With the exception of the editors of a 1998 edition of the play[15], almost all recent scholars support dual authorship of the play by these two dramatists, although the division of the text between the two authors may not be quite as tidy as first thought: linguistic analysis[16] suggests that the brothel scenes in Act 4, scenes 2, 5 and 6[17] (which are scenes 16 and 19 in the original 1609 edition) have greater affinities with Wilkins' style than with 'Shakespeare's'.

The dual authorship of *Pericles* presents new questions: did 'Shakespeare' and Wilkins work together, or did one author complete a play that the other had begun? If the authors worked independently, did the authors work at different times, and if they did, when?

The fact that the two authors' contributions are so distinct strongly suggests that they did not work together around a table, so to speak, but that one author added to the work of the other. In 1876 Fleay commented on the authors' working relationship, making the perceptive observation that Acts 3–5 stand on their own as a complete unit – i.e., as a short play. It is worthwhile quoting his comments[18] in full:

> The theory which I propose as certain, is this: – Shakespeare wrote the story of Marina, in the last three acts, minus the prose scenes and the Gower[19]. This gives a perfect and organic whole: and, in my opinion, ought to be printed as such in every edition of Shakespeare: the whole play, as it stands [i.e. Acts 1–5], might be printed in collections for the curious, and there only. But this story [i.e. Acts 3–5 alone] was not enough for filling the necessary five acts from which Shakespeare never deviated; he therefore left it unfinished.

If we disregard the first two acts and start reading *Pericles* at the beginning of Act 3 we can see that 'Shakespeare' was less interested in writing a play about the adventures of the legendary Pericles than he was in writing a play about the strength of character of Pericles' daughter Marina. As Fleay remarked in 1876, the last three acts create "a perfect and organic whole" and our understanding and appreciation of these acts is not lessened by our being unaware of what has transpired in Acts 1 and 2. (Fleay's comment that the play (Acts 3–5) is "unfinished" is odd, following as it does his comment that the last three acts are "a perfect and organic whole".) Others have also recognised that the second half of the play can stand alone as a drama. For example, in 1738 George Lillo adapted Acts 4 and 5 to create his play *Marina*.

There is no internal evidence that in Acts 3–5 'Shakespeare' followed up on points made in the first two acts[20]. Therefore, like Fleay, we must conclude that 'Shakespeare's' contribution was written first, as a short and complete play, and on obtaining 'Shakespeare's' manuscript or a copy of it, Wilkins extended the action back to earlier times in the well-known story to produce a full-length play suitable for production.

But we still need to establish when the two authors wrote their respective portions. Unfortunately, discussion about date of composition of *Pericles*[21] has paid little attention to actual evidence. Standard commentaries not only fail to separate the issue of the date of the play's first performance from the date of its writing, but also fail to consider the timing of each author's contribution as a distinct issue. For example, F. D. Hoeniger[22], in his discussion concerning evidence for the date of the first performance of *Pericles*, concludes "What can be stated with some conviction is that *Pericles*, as we know it, was *written* [my italics] and staged sometime between 1606 and 1608[23]. This is now the general view of scholars . . .". Such an appeal to "some conviction" and "the general view of scholars", without documentary proof, is, I suggest, an unfortunate case of scholarly wishful thinking: of giving primacy to a desired conclusion rather than the evidence.

A more rigorous approach is required. Examination of original sources does not help: the source of the *Pericles* legend is likely to have been Book 8 of John Gower's *Confessio Amantis*, first published in the 1390s. (A character "John Gower" presents the choruses and commentary in the play.) However, according to Hoeniger[24] there are about a hundred Latin versions of the Pericles legend in medieval literature, so we can't be certain which text was actually used. Secondary sources indicate a date of composition in the last quarter of the sixteenth century. One of these sources is Laurence Twine's *The Pattern of Painful Adventures*, first published in 1576, on which the brothel scenes in Pericles are based. In the older versions of the story the legendary hero is called Apollonius. The name Pericles may have been suggested by the character named Pyrocles in Sidney's *Arcadia* (published in 1590 but circulating in manuscript in 1588[25]) or the Pericles in North's 1595 translation of Plutarch's *Lives*. As the plot in *Pericles* draws on shipwreck details found in Sidney's *Arcadia* this source was probably the one used[26]. The above deductions do not help us date 'Shakespeare's' contribution with certainty.

There is one historical allusion which may be relevant: in Act 4, scene 1 the pirates save Marina from death, and the would-be murderer Leonine complains that "These roguing thieves serve the great pirate Valdes". The scholar Malone suggested that the Valdes name came to the author's mind because Don Pedro de Valdés was an admiral in the defeated Armada of 1588[27]. Don Pedro's ship was the great galleon *Nuestra Señora del Rosario*, which was disabled after it collided with another Spanish ship in the English Channel. Francis Drake took Don Pedro de Valdés into custody on 22 July 1588 and, on a visit to the court in St James' Park in London, introduced his distinguished captive to Queen Elizabeth. In contrast to her friendly treatment of Sarmiento in 1586, the Queen refused to converse with the prisoner. Drake was more tolerant: he lodged Valdés (under benign house arrest) with his relatives. Music and dancing were provided to entertain the prisoner and other guests. In quieter times Valdés occupied himself by revising the first Spanish-English dictionary. (The revision was published in 1591.) He was eventually ransomed for £1500 in 1593[28].

Given the Queen's disdain for Valdés as the hated enemy's representative, a deliberately derogatory reference to the admiral is not surprising, which in turn suggests a date of composition in or soon after 1588, when the reference would still be topical. There are no other historical allusions in Acts 3–5 to help date 'Shakespeare's' half of the play, although there are passages which can be linked to other plays normally considered to be late 'Shakespeare'. For example, the conversation between Dionyza and Cleon in Act 4, scene 3, in which Dionyza berates her husband for being weak and cowardly is similar to that between the murderous Lady Macbeth and her husband in *Macbeth* and that between Goneril and Albany in *King Lear*, Act 4, scene 2.

Hoeniger[29] pointed out that in the *Pericles* sentence "yet thou dost look Like Patience gazing on kings' graves" (Act 5, scene 1) there may be an allusion to an illustration of a smiling Patience in Cesare Ripa's widely circulated book *Iconologia*. Hoeniger suggested a link to an illustration of Patience in the 1603 edition of Cesare Ripa's book, but he overlooked the fact that the earlier (1593) edition also includes an illustration of a smiling Patience. In summary we can conclude that 'Shakespeare's' contribution was written in or after 1588, and possibly around 1593 if an allusion to the *Iconologia* illustration is admitted.

As for George Wilkins' contribution (the first two acts[30]), all Wilkin's works seem to have been written between 1606 and 1608[31], which would explain the 20 May 1608 entry of the play in the *Stationers' Register*.

As concluded by Fleay, it seems likely that Acts 3–5 were written by 'Shakespeare' as a short play, which Wilkins expanded. There is no evidence for the alternative view that Acts 3–5 were written to complete a play begun by Wilkins. Wilkins was a man of many abilities. Included in his various occupations were hack writer, plagiarist, innkeeper, minor criminal, and brothel keeper[32], so he may have considered himself well qualified to write and insert the brothel scenes in the second ('Shakespearean') part of the play.

Those who favour a theory of a period of collaboration around 1606 between William Shakespeare (semi-retired in Stratford) and George Wilkins (innkeeper in London) have a problem, which no scholars have addressed: why should a master dramatist who had recently written *Hamlet* and *King Lear*, and was clearly far from senile or incapable when he wrote Acts 3 to 5 of Pericles, have needed to cooperate with an unsavoury writer like Wilkins to complete a play? Hoeniger was so concerned about this issue that in 1982[33] he recanted his initial (1963) conclusion that 'Shakespeare' finished and polished a play by Wilkins, believing that it was impossible to believe that the two would have cooperated. But Hoeniger was throwing out the baby with the bathwater: he failed to appreciate that joint authorship did not necessarily imply sharing a desk. He was rejecting his own theory for the wrong reason. All the evidence suggests that 'Shakespeare's' portion was written first.

There is also another issue to consider, relating to 'Shakespeare's' professionalism and pride in his work. The problem is the state of the 1609 first edition of the play on which all other early texts were based (the play sold well and was republished in 1609, 1611 and 1619). The 1609 first edition text is not playable on the stage – prose and verse are commonly mislineated (verse is set as prose, and prose as verse), entrances and exits of the players are frequently vague or absent, and in places the text reads as nonsense[34].

These errors are of a kind that can neither be authorial nor attributable to errors during printing. They almost certainly result from a text being based on a deficient manuscript or prepared from the imperfect memories of actors. Are we to assume that William Shakespeare was so uninterested in his work and reputation that, having taken the trouble to cooperate with another author to write a popular play, he allowed his fellow actors to write down their poorly recollected parts and to present their imperfect version text to the printer as the authentic play, to be printed not once but three times during his lifetime? It all seems most improbable.

We can, if we stretch credibility, imagine that Shakespeare's fellow-actors in the King's Men company surreptitiously wrote down their parts without consulting the stage copy or Shakespeare, and stole away to the printer to make some money 'on the side'. But surely Shakespeare, once he found out that his work was being pirated by his own colleagues, in a version that did not reflect well on him (or Wilkins), and for others' profit, would have objected strongly. There is no doubt that Shakespeare would have been justifiably aggrieved by the printed version of 1609, because in this text it is the 'Shakespearean' parts (Acts 3–5) that are the most faulty[35].

These problems disappear completely if we assume Elizabeth I was the author of Acts 3–5. There is no evidence that the 'Shakespearean' parts of the play were written later than 1595, so we can postulate that Elizabeth wrote these acts of *Pericles*, which are chiefly about the strong-minded heroine Marina, in the early-1590s. These acts were possibly written at the same time as *The Tempest*[36] when ships and storms were uppermost in Elizabeth's literary mind. In fact, the beginning of Act 3 bears a remarkable similarity to *The Tempest*'s first act: there is a storm with thunder and lightning (sulphurous flashes), the danger of the ship splitting, and a desperate attempt to regain sea room on a lee shore.

We can speculate that Elizabeth put the manuscript aside, possibly because it was too short for stage production, or she felt it wasn't up to her usual standard. In the mid-1600s, after her death, someone in charge of her papers released the manuscript to the King's Men, William Shakespeare's company. It caught the eye of the second-rate writer George Wilkins who saw his chance to make some money by arranging to share authorship with William Shakespeare, who probably also profited by the arrangement. Shakespeare had no particular interest in the quality of the result – after all, it wasn't his work, and he was essentially retired and living comfortably in Stratford.

---

[1] Vickers (2002) presents the evidence of co-authorship for these two plays and three others: *Titus Andronicus, Henry VIII* and *The Two Noble Kinsmen*.

[2] The most comprehensive review is that of Vickers (2002, p. 244–290) which details the evidence of co-authorship presented by a range of researchers whose results have been published over a period of about 150 years since Charles Knight's ground-breaking study in 1849. The criteria supporting co-authorship include linguistic forms, grammatical preferences, characteristic oaths and exclamations, rare vocabulary, characteristic stage directions, verbal parallels, spellings, use of rhyme, and verse tests. The research summarised by Vickers established beyond doubt that Thomas Middleton was 'Shakespeare's' co-author, and responsible for about one third of the play.

[3] Table 3, from Jackson (1994, table 1).

[4] An essay by Klein (2001, pp. 5–17) considers the bigger issue in *Timon*: how money and usury infect and pervert values in a society.

[5] Klein (2001, p. 34).

[6] Klein (2001, p. 80).

[7] Maxwell (1968, pp. xii–xiii) and Klein (2001) summarise the relationship between the two plays.

[8] With a probability of $p<0.0025$, i.e., the similarity of vocabulary has a less than a 1 in 400 chance of occurring by chance.

[9] With the same probability as noted in note 8 above.

[10] Oliver (1959, p. xl) favoured the 1607–1608 date range. He accepted dates of 1607–1608 for the composition of *Coriolanus* and *Anthony and Cleopatra* and for unexplained reasons believed that while 'Shakespeare' was searching in North's translation of Plutarch for material for *Coriolanus* and *Anthony and Cleopatra* he was also writing *Timon of Athens*. However, basing the date of composition of a play on an author's unknown reading habits is unsound.

[11] Sometime in 1630 Ben Jonson wrote the bitter *Ode to Himself* which included the disparaging lines concerning the popularity of *Pericles*, after the failure of his own play *The New Inn* in 1629.

[12] Fleay (1876).

[13] Vickers (2002, table 5.1, p. 296) reproduces Fleay's analysis.

[14] Vickers (2002) summarises the relevant research.

[15] Del Vecchio and Hammond (1998). This edition was published by Cambridge University Press in the New Cambridge Shakespeare series. The editors were lambasted by Vickers (2002, p. 327). He wrote that the Cambridge edition "wilfully ignores the whole weight of scholarship proving that Shakespeare was

[16] By Jackson (2003); Warren (2003) summarises Jackson's observations and conclusions.
[17] This is the division adopted in the Arden edition (Hoeniger 1963).
[18] Fleay (1876, p. 211)
[19] Fleay is referring to the successive choruses 'spoken' by the medieval poet John Gower, which summarise the action in the play.
[20] Warren (2003, pp. 56–57) suggests (like others before him) that in Act 5, scene 1, Pericles' meeting with his unrecognised daughter, in whom he sees resemblances to his wife Thaisa (believed by him to be dead), has overtones of incest, and that this 'Shakespearean' scene is therefore linked to Act 1, scene 1, written by Wilkins, in which the King of Antioch's incest with his daughter is revealed, which would bring the play's plot full circle. But Pericles remarks only on the physical resemblance of Marina and Thaisa, and their similar way of speaking or singing in "silver voic'd" tones. There is absolutely no suggestion of sexual interest in Pericles' speech. Nor do Pericles' words "thou that beget'st him that did thee beget" (Act 5, scene 1, line 195), spoken when he realises that Marina is his long-lost daughter, have any incestuous implications: Pericles (grieving for his lost wife and daughter, and unkempt and withdrawn), is saying 'you, the daughter begotten by me, have brought me back to life'. Accordingly, the supposed allusion to incest is spurious and not proof that 'Shakespeare' wrote the second half of the play after Wilkins had completed his portion.
[21] Hoeniger (1963, pp. lxiii–lxvi).
[22] Hoeniger (1963, pp. lxiii–lxv).
[23] The play was entered in the *Stationers' Register* on 20 May 1608, so it must have been finished by this date, but may have been written, completed and possibly performed earlier.
[24] Hoeniger (1963, p. xiii).
[25] Wilkes (2006).
[26] Warren (2003, p. 18).
[27] As recounted in Hoeniger (1963, p. 207).
[28] These details of Don Pedro's captivity are from Martin and Palmer (1999, pp. 226–227).
[29] Hoeniger (1963, p. 147).
[30] In the original 1609 edition the play was not divided into acts, only scenes.
[31] Prior (1972).
[32] Warren (2003, p. 6) summarises the evidence for Wilkins' shady and violent activities.
[33] Hoeniger (1982, p. 463).
[34] Hoeniger (1963, pp. xxviii–xxxi) summarises the deficiencies in his section entitled "The condition of the Text".
[35] Hoeniger (1963, p. xxxiv) notes that in Acts 3–5 about 70% of the verse is misaligned, compared to 10% in Acts 1–2.
[36] See chapters 25 and 26.

one of the play's two co-authors" and that Del Vecchio and Hammond "denied their readers the fruits of two centuries' editorial labours".

34. *The Two Noble Kinsmen*

This world's a city full of straying streets
– The Two Noble Kinsmen, Act 1, scene 5

The Two Noble Kinsmen was first published in 1634, eleven years after the publication of the First Folio. The 1634 title page states that it was "Written by the memorable Worthies of their time: Mr John Fletcher [and] Mr William Shakspeare [sic]." The plot is relatively simple: two close friends fall in love with the same woman; they become estranged, and fight for her hand in marriage; the winner dies in an accident; the loser gets his girl. In the middle of the play there are country scenes involving a schoolmaster.

The chief source of the play is Geoffrey Chaucer's *The Knight's Tale*, which in turn is based on Boccaccio's *Teseida*[1]. Chaucer's story had been previously adapted for the stage by Richard Edwards in the play *Palaemon and Arcyte*, which was acted before Queen Elizabeth in Oxford in 1566[2]. Another play on the same topic was commissioned by Philip Henslowe and performed by the Admiral's Men in September 1594.

There are three other possible sources for parts of the story. The first is *The Lady of May* by Sir Philip Sidney, performed for a visit of the Queen to the Earl of Leicester at Wanstead in 1578[3], and probably written shortly beforehand. This one-act pastoral play contains a scene in which a woman has to choose between two suitors. It includes a country schoolmaster who quarrels with the Lady of May. The second is *A Midsummer Night's Dream*, published in 1600 but mentioned by Francis Meres in 1598, which contains scenes of rustic entertainment and a wedding similar to those in *The Two Noble Kinsmen*. The third is *The Masque of the Inner Temple and Gray's Inn* (1613) by Francis Beaumont which also contains a scene involving a schoolmaster and simple country folk.

Whether *A Midsummer Night's Dream* and *The Masque of the Inner Temple and Gray's Inn* are sources or whether they and *The Two Noble Kinsmen* are derived collectively from the earlier works by Boccaccio, Chaucer or Sidney cannot be ascertained.

As with *Pericles*, determining the date of composition of the play is complicated because, as the title page states (and scholarship has confirmed[4]), it was written by two authors. Joint authorship could have been achieved either by the two authors working cooperatively or by one author adding to a draft laid aside by the other. If the latter occurred another question arises: did 'Shakespeare' finish a draft, sketch or unfinished play written by Fletcher, or did Fletcher complete 'Shakespeare's' unfinished text?

To answer these questions, it is useful to list those scenes that research has attributed to Shakespeare or Fletcher. Hallet Smith[5] used the play's imagery and linguistic characteristics such as vocabulary to match acts and scenes to putative authors. Earlier Littledale[6] made a similar attribution of acts and scenes to Shakespeare or Fletcher, through his examination of the frequency of 'light' and 'weak' endings in the blank verse of the play[7]. The review by Brian Vickers[8] supports the division of authorship established by these researchers (Table 7).

Acts 1 and 5, written by the author 'Shakespeare', are almost entirely concerned with the story of Palamon and Arcite's rivalry. This story establishes the structure of the play. In fact, with a little editing (Palamon and Arcite need to fall in love with Emilia at the end of Act 1) all of 'Shakespeare's' contribution would constitute a stageable two-act play (Acts 1 and 5) without the need for any of Fletcher's text. Fletcher contributed the scenes about the jailor's daughter, the schoolmaster, the forest, and the Duke. Fletcher's contribution cannot stand alone – it depends entirely on the structure provided by 'Shakespeare'. This means that we can be confident that Fletcher revised and expanded a draft or a short play by 'Shakespeare', not the reverse.

Table 7. Attribution of scenes in *The Two Noble Kinsmen* to Shakespeare and Fletcher.

Act and scene	Subject matter	Smith (1974)	Littledale (1885) as tabulated by Vickers (2002)
		S = by Shakespeare; F = by Fletcher; U = authorship uncertain; n. d. = authorship not determined	
1.1	Three dowager Theban queens meet Duke Theseus	S	S
1.2	Palamon and Arcite introduced	S	S
1.3	Emilia introduced	S	S
1.4	Theseus enters as victor with battle-scarred Palamon and Arcite as prisoners	U	S
1.5	Funeral procession of Theban queens for their dead knights	U	F
2.1 (prose)	Jailer and his Daughter introduced	S	n. d.
2.2	Palamon and Arcite (in prison) both fall in love with Emilia	F	F
2.3	Banished Arcite meets peasants	F	F
2.4	Jailer's Daughter plans to free Palamon	F	F
2.5	Arcite meets Emilia at country games	F	F
2.6	Jailer's Daughter frees Palamon	F	F

3.1	Palamon and Arcite vow to fight for Emilia's hand	S		S		
3.2	Jailer's Daughter can't find Palamon			F	S	
3.3	Arcite brings Palamon food in the forest			F		F
3.4	Distraught Jailer's Daughter shows first signs of madness			F		F
3.5	Emilia, schoolmaster and Duke Theseus in the forest			F		F
3.6	Palamon and Arcite fight; met by angry Duke Theseus with Emilia			F		F
4.1	Mad Jailer's Daughter in conversation with her father and a friend			F		F
4.2	Palamon and Arcite are to fight for Emilia's hand; she can't decide which of the two she loves the best		U			F
4.3 (prose)	Doctor proposes that a wooer of the Jailer's daughter should pretend he is Palamon, to cure her madness			F		n. d.
5.1 to line 34	Palamon and Arcite exchange pre-contest pleasantries			F	S	
5.1 line 34 to end	Palamon, Arcite and Emilia make pre-contest speeches		S		S	
5.2	Jailer's Daughter accepts that wooer is Palamon			F		F
5.3	Arcite wins the contest		S		S	
5.4	Palamon awaits execution; is reprieved when Arcite falls off his horse and dies; he wins Emilia		S		S	

Fletcher was born in 1579 but did not start his playwright career until about 1606, so this year is probably the earliest that he could have written his contribution. The latest source for 'Shakespeare's' contribution is 1578 (when Sidney wrote *The Lady of May*) so it is likely that 'Shakespeare's' part of *Two Noble Kinsmen* was written several years before Fletcher's part, perhaps more than 20 years earlier. No evidence supports a late date of composition of 'Shakespeare's' part of the play. We can assume that *A Midsummers Dream* gave Fletcher the ideas for the forest scenes, and Ophelia's madness gave him the idea for the Jailor's daughter's similar affliction.

A possible scenario is that Elizabeth started to write a play about suitor rivalry sometime after seeing the 1566 production of *Palaemon and Arcyte* or the later production of 1594[9]. She completed a two-act drama. Following her death in 1603 it was released by a friend of the late Queen or a member of the court, perhaps in 1608 or 1609, along with other works in manuscript such as *Sonnets*, *Pericles* and *Troilus and Cressida*. The short text came into Fletcher's hands, and seeing the commercial potential of a full-length play, he added acts and scenes.

---

[1] In English the full title is *The Theseid, concerning the Nuptials of Emilia*. It was written before 1341, probably in the late 1330s. That the author of *The Two Noble Kinsmen* was familiar with Boccaccio's story as well as Chaucer's is indicated by the fact that in both *The Two Noble Kinsmen* and in *Teseida* Arcite's horse falls backwards on him, rather than pitching him forwards as in *The Knight's Tale* by Chaucer (Dobson and Wells 2001).

[2] Dobson and Wells (2001, p. 500).

[3] Kimborough (1983),

[4] Vickers (2002, pp. 402–432).

[5] Smith (1974).

[6] Littledale (1885) as tabulated by Vickers (2006, table 6.28, p. 414).

[7] Smith (1966, pp. 36 and 37), following Ingram (1874), defines "light" endings as those in which the emphasis in the ten-beat line (iambic pentameter) is not, as expected, on the tenth syllable but on the ninth. Words forcing light endings are "am, are, art, be, been, but (= only), can, could, did, do, does, doth, ere, had, has, hath, have, he, how, I, into, is, like, may, might, shall, shalt, she, should, since, so, such, they, thou, though, through, till, unto, upon, was, we, were, what, when, where, which, whilst, who, whom, why, will, would, yet (= nevertheless), you". In contrast words producing "weak" endings are those which can be understood only by linking them to the next line: "and, as, at, but (= however and except), by, for (prep. and conj.), from, if, in, of, one, nor, or, than, that (rel. and conj.), to, with". 'Shakespeare' used light and weak endings prolifically, Fletcher sparingly (Vickers 2002, table 6.27).

[8] Vickers (2002, pp. 402–432).

[9] We can speculate that Elizabeth's distress concerning the marriage of Essex to Frances Walsingham in 1590 could have prompted her to turn to *Palaemon and Arcyte* for the structure of a play of her own.

35. *Henry VIII*

If I chance to talk a little wild, forgive me; I had it from my father
– Henry VIII, Act I, scene 4

In 1550 the minor French Protestant writer Charles de Sainte Marthe published a one-hundred-page funeral oration[1] commemorating the life of the Catholic humanist Margaret of Navarre (1492–1547). Margaret was a religious progressive who tried to find a middle path between Catholicism and Protestantism. She actively supported poor people, initiated public works and financed needy students. She was a patron of the arts and befriended Leonardo da Vinci and the French authors Rabelais and Marot. Rather surprisingly, she also wrote racy novels about young people in love. Among her friends, acquaintances and correspondents she counted Anne Boleyn, John Calvin and Erasmus.

In his oration Charles de Sainte Marthe recounted a dream that Margaret is purported to have had shortly before her death, in which a beautiful woman presented her with a coronet or garland:

> . . . une très-belle femme tenante en sa main une couronne qu'elle luy monstroit et luy disoit que bien tost [bientôt] elle en seroit couronée . . .

> . . . a very beautiful woman holding in her hand a coronet which she showed her [Margaret] and told her that soon she would be crowned[2] . . .

In Act 4, scene 2 of *King Henry VIII* the dying dowager Queen Katherine, spurned by the King in favour of Anne Boleyn who has just been crowned[3], also dreams that spirits dressed in white mime a similar ceremony. (The text below includes the capitalisation and punctuation of the First Folio edition, but spelling has been updated.)

> Enter solemnly tripping one after another, six Personages, clad in white Robes, wearing on their heads Garlands of Bays, and golden Vizards on their faces, Branches of Bays or Palm in their hands. They first Congee [curtsy] unto her, then Dance: at certain Changes, the first two hold a spare Garland over her Head, at which the other four make reverend Curtsies. Then the two that held the Garland, deliver the same to the other next two, who observe the same order in their Changes, and holding the Garland over her head. Which done, they deliver the same Garland to the last two: who likewise observe the same Order. At which (as it were by inspiration) she makes (in her sleep) signs of rejoicing, and holdeth up her hands to heaven. And so, in their Dancing vanish, carrying the Garland with them. The Music continues.

Despite the greater detail and length of the *King Henry VIII* scene, the imagery of both texts in which spirits crown a queen with either a garland or a coronet is similar and in both the central figure is a dying queen. For these reasons researchers believe that when writing about the dream (or vision as it is called in the play) 'Shakespeare' had in mind the writings of Charles de Sainte Marthe[4].

The question then arises, how did William Shakespeare come across this 1550 Parisian publication by a minor French author? As Shakespeare was lodging at Christopher Mountjoy's house in Silver Street[5], London between 1598 and 1612, and Christopher was a Huguenot who had fled France in 1572, it has been suggested that he obtained a copy of Charles de Sainte Marthe's *Oration* from his landlord[6]. There is no evidence for or against this proposition, but it seems unlikely to be true, given that Mountjoy was a wig- and hat-maker, not known in London either as an intellectual or a friend of continental writers.

The same question can be asked of Elizabeth – how would she have obtained de Sainte Marthe's book about Margaret of Navarre? There is no definite answer, but there are several intriguing links to consider. Firstly, Elizabeth was acquainted with Margaret of Navarre's writings at an early age. When she was only eleven years old she translated a religious and highly personal devotional poem of Margaret's – *Le miroir de l'âme pécheresse* [*The Mirror of the Sinful Soul*] – from French into English prose as a New Year's present for her stepmother Katherine Parr. Secondly, Anne Boleyn, when she was at the French court before her marriage to Henry VIII, may have met Margaret of Navarre; she certainly corresponded with her and Elizabeth may have acquired copies of Margaret's early books from her mother's collection. Thirdly, Francis Walsingham was ambassador to Paris from 1570 to 1573 and may have obtained copies of Charles de Sainte Marthe's writings while in France.

Another source may have been one of the many Elizabethan literature-loving courtiers who visited France or the low countries, among them Robert Dudley, Earl of Leicester; Robert Devereux, Earl of Essex; and Philip Sidney. Finally, the French teacher, writer and painter Nicholas Denisot may have been a source: he became tutor to the Seymour sisters Anne, Margaret and Jane, daughters of the first Duke of Somerset. These sisters published a Latin tribute (in the form of 104 couplets) to Margaret of Navarre in 1550 and sent it to Nicholas Denisot, who republished their work in Paris in 1551[7]. As they were followers of Margaret's ideas it seems likely that they knew of Charles de Sainte Marthe's *Oration* and were inspired to show their own appreciation of Margaret of Navarre's example of pious but practical living. Margaret and Jane Seymour, nieces of Henry VIII's third wife, corresponded with the young Edward VI. Jane later became a Lady of the Bedchamber at the court of Queen Elizabeth.

In short, history tells us that there were numerous channels by which Queen Elizabeth could have become acquainted with Charles de Sainte Marthe's *Oration*.

The next question to ask is "When was the play written?" The answer is complicated by the fact that, although some commentators disagree[8], *Henry VIII* was penned by two authors: 'Shakespeare' and John Fletcher. This conclusion is based on two lines of evidence: (1) analyses of style independently published by J. Spedding and S. Hickson in 1850[9]; and (2) linguistic research by A. C. Partridge, first published in 1949[10] and amended in 1964[11]; and by C. Hoy in 1960[12].

Partridge and Hoy compared the number of instances of common words favoured by Shakespeare (such as "hath", "them" and "you") and words with the same meaning but different spelling favoured by Fletcher (such as "has", "'em" and "ye") in various sections of the play. On the basis of this comparison they were able to attribute scenes or parts of scenes to one of the two authors. Hoy's analysis was more conservative than Partridge's – he attributed more of the play to Shakespeare. The comprehensive 70-page review by Brian Vickers[13] summarises the conclusions of these researchers and other studies, including those undertaken using sophisticated statistical analysis (Table 8). (For good measure, in his review Vickers presents a withering and entertaining demolition of the ideas of literary theorists who argue that the question of authorship is immaterial and that the very concept of authorship is a modern invention[14].)

Table 8. Scenes in *Henry VIII* written by Shakespeare (S) and Fletcher (F).[15]

S		Act 1, scenes 1 and 2
	F	Act 1, scenes 3 and 4
	F	Act 2, scenes 1 and 2
S		Act 2, scenes 3 and 4
	F	Act 3, scene 1
S		Act 3, scene 2a
	F	Act 3, scene 2b
	F	Act 4, scenes 1 and 2
S		Act 5, scene 1
	F	Act 5, scenes 2, 3, 4 and 5
	F	Epilogue

It is remarkable that almost all recent research of any substance supports the conclusion reached by Spedding and Hickson over 100 years ago (Table 8), which is that Fletcher is likely to have written 11 scenes of the play and half of Act 3, scene 2, whereas Shakespeare is likely to have written 5 scenes and the other half of Act 3, scene 2[16].

The main published source used in *Henry VIII* is Holinshed's *Chronicles* (1587) and the scenes written by 'Shakespeare' derive only from this source[17]. Scenes written by Fletcher are also derived chiefly from Holinshed's *Chronicles*, but Cranmer's speech in Act 5 is based largely on Foxe's *Acts and Monuments* (1597) and some lines in Wolsey's parting speech flowing his downfall are based on John Speed's *The History of Great Britain* (1611)[18]. The sources used by the writers of the two parts of the play, and the dates of publication of these sources, are consistent with the proposition that Queen Elizabeth wrote the early 'Shakespearean' parts and Fletcher the rest.

We cannot rule out the possibility that William Shakespeare did write the 'Shakespearean' parts of the play and then, for some unknown reason, passed the unfinished text to Fletcher to complete. However, the treatment of the subject matter is another indication of Elizabeth's authorship. For *Henry VIII* is a play that skilfully avoids any controversial analysis of Henry VIII's character, actions and motives. Even now, five hundred years later, historians and the public find it hard to reconcile the magnificent figure who skilfully unshackled the English church from Rome and disestablished the monasteries with the cruel monster who fabricated a divorce from his faithful and much-loved Spanish Queen in order to marry the already pregnant Anne Boleyn, whom he executed 3 years later. Not to mention his destruction of the scholars Sir Thomas More and William Tyndale (and others) who dared to question or oppose his views. Ideal subject matter for a gripping tale of intrigue, love, betrayal and cruelty one would think.

But instead of a true history we have in *Henry VIII* a revisionist play. Elizabeth's half-sister, the Roman Catholic Princess Mary, is mentioned only in passing. Henry is not presented as a bully and a monster, but as an irascible, short tempered, and ill-advised monarch – a man with tolerable rather than despicable shortcomings. This down-playing of Henry's odious character allows the play's author(s) to blame others (but chiefly Wolsey) for Henry's cruel decisions. Anne is presented as a naïve innocent young woman – not as an active player seducing the King with her feminine charms. This is a distortion of history – she almost certainly was playing a game of 'hard to get' with the aim of securing the ultimate prizes of the King's bed and his Queen's crown.

The background to the annulment of King Henry's marriage with Katherine is presented in a manner that favours Elizabeth. In Act 2, scene 4 (written by 'Shakespeare') the spurious but apparently logical and intellectual reason for Henry seeking an annulment of his marriage is given prominence: the King argues that the legality of his marriage to his brother's wife is worrying his conscience. (In fact, he had tired of post-menopausal Katherine and was obsessed with marrying Anne Boleyn and having a boy child by her.)

A commentator has observed that in the play Queen Katherine "is much more powerfully drawn than in Holinshed"[19]. Henry describes his queen (Katherine) as a "paragon o'th'world". By portraying Katherine as a strong and virtuous woman admired by the King, and minimising Henry's lust for Anne Boleyn, and ignoring the fact that Henry has lost interest in his wife, the author emphasises that the prime reason for Henry's seeking an annulment is his marriage's doubtful legality. The scene is expertly self-serving for Elizabeth. Matters worrying the King's conscience on the matter of legitimacy must prevail. History is not driven by human passion. How convenient!

In the play Katherine conveniently dies soon after Anne's coronation and before the birth of Elizabeth, not afterwards[20]. This creative condensing and rearranging of history in the play avoids the issue of Elizabeth's legitimacy and allows the play to concentrate on less embarrassing topics.

The final two scenes concern the christening of Elizabeth. First we have a 'low-life' exchange between a porter at court and his assistant, who are trying to control the crowd. Then we have the christening ceremony and Cranmer's prediction of the golden age to come, first under Elizabeth and then under James. If we could prove that the scenes about Elizabeth and James were written by William Shakespeare after James I's accession to the throne of England in 1603, the Elizabeth I authorship theory would collapse. But we can't – almost all authorship scholars, from Spedding and Hickson in 1850 to Vickers in 1960, agree that the last scene of Act 5 containing Cranmer's rosy predictions was written by Fletcher, not Shakespeare.

The likely transmission to England of Charles de Sainte Marthe's writing via court sources, the date of publication of the source (Holinshed) used for other 'Shakespearean' parts of the play, and the way in which historical facts and chronology are distorted to favour Elizabeth all suggest that the Queen was indeed the author of the 'Shakespearean' parts of the play. If we accept this argument, then in the 'Shakespearean' parts Elizabeth's chief interest was to gloss over her father's most objectionable character traits and to emphasise the power plays in the Tudor court

The Vision masque in Act 4, scene 2 based on Charles de Marthe's writings has no dialogue. If the conclusion that the masque was written by Elizabeth, who a had strong interest in the works of Margaret of Navarre, is correct then this part of scene 2 may originally have been part of the unfinished 'Shakespearean' play. (It possibly followed Act 2, scene 4 in which Queen Katherine learns of Henry's intention to annul their marriage, and her consequent understandable distress.) While restructuring and adding to the play it seems likely that Fletcher found the Vision masque to be an appropriate insertion into the scene he wrote about the dying queen where, to give him credit, it certainly makes good dramatic sense.

It is evident that the 'Shakespearean' parts of *Henry VIII* provide the play's essential framework, but it seems that the 'Shakespearean' draft was set aside in an unfinished state. Authorship by Elizabeth explains why: as she worked on the play she would have found it impossible to reconcile what she knew about her father with her determination to present him in a good light. Although she was able, with a convenient distortion of facts, to present her mother's usurpation of Queen Katherine as legally justified, she must have realised that, were she to attempt to complete the play, there would be no escaping the inevitable conclusion that her father was not simply a strong-willed cantankerous ruler but a murderous tyrant. So she abandoned her unfinished work.

Fletcher found a straightforward answer to Elizabeth's dilemma. He simply skipped all the uncomfortable facts concerning Henry's execution of Anne Boleyn and his succession of marriages and gave the play a happy but banal ending.

---

[1] Charles de Sainte Marthe published the *Oraison funèbre de la mort de l'incomparable Marguerite Royne de Navarre et duchesse d'Alençon* in French and Latin editions in Paris in 1550.
[2] Duncan-Jones (1961).
[3] The chronology is condensed in the play: Dowager Queen Katherine lived for more than two years after the coronation of Anne Boleyn on 29 May 1533. She died on 7 January 1536.
[4] Duncan-Jones (1961). Other commentators have noted that Anne Boleyn is reported in *Holinshed's Chronicles* as having a dream forewarning her of her death. Holinshed's chronicles may well have provided the idea for the dream in the play, but the imagery of spirits and garlands was furnished from another source.
[5] In the Barbican area of London.
[6] Duncan-Jones (1961).
[7] Hosington (2000).
[8] Foakes (1957).
[9] The original papers that Spedding and Hickson published separately in *Gentleman's Magazine* (August 1850 and October 1850) and in *Notes and Queries* (August 1850 and subsequent issues) respectively were republished in 1874. See Spedding and Hickson (1874).
[10] Partridge (1949).
[11] Partridge (1964).
[12] Hoy (1960).
[13] Vickers (2002).
[14] Vickers (2002, pp. 396–402).
[15] Partridge (1964, p. 152); Vickers (2002, chapter 6) summarises the research leading to the attribution of scenes to the two authors.
[16] I have followed the conclusions tabulated by Partridge (1964, p. 152); see also note 15 above.
[17] Foakes (1957, p. xxxv).
[18] Foakes (1957, p. xxxv).
[19] Foakes (1957, p. xxxviii).
[20] See endnote 3 above.

36. The Royal Hand in *Hamlet*

Though this be madness, yet there is method in't
— *Hamlet*, Act 2, scene 2

Hamlet is an Elizabethan play. It was entered in the *Stationers' Register* on 26 July 1602 and first printed in 1603. A relatively recent review of *Hamlet*'s printing history by A. Thompson and N. Taylor[1] tells us that the first (1603) edition of the play, containing almost 16000 words and referred to as the first quarto (Q1), was probably assembled from actors' recollections of a stage performance. These researchers deduced that Q1 is a shortened version of a much longer play which was too unwieldy to be performed on the stage.

There is agreement among researchers that the version closest to the author's manuscript[2] is the second quarto (Q2) published in 1604[3], which has 27630 words. Interestingly, the scholar Giorgio Melchiori[4] concluded that Q2 was "a play for the closet, not for the stage", i.e., the play was not written for public performance. Similarly, L. Erne concluded that the play was meant to be read, not performed, a conclusion supported by the observation that stage directions in Q2 are so vague and casual that it is sometimes not clear who is supposed to be on the stage[5]. He also suggested that a version for performance (possibly a play similar to Q1) was derived from the "reading" version[6].

The conclusions reached by the above researchers are astonishing. Why would an actor/playwright dependent on the stage for his living write such a long play, surely with full appreciation of its immense dramatic quality and power to draw crowds, if he had no intention of performing it with his acting colleagues, and making a profit for his company and himself?

Once again, the Elizabeth-Essex hypothesis allows everything to fall into place. When the charismatic but unstable Essex disgraced himself in Ireland and then staged an abortive coup against the government, Elizabeth had to work out why she had so misjudged his capabilities and misread his true character. She wasn't starting from scratch: for years she had been analysing her complex relationship with Essex in her sonnets, most of which had probably been written by the time she turned her attention to *Hamlet*. But writing poetry was not enough: she needed to analyse and communicate in a medium allowing the expression of action as well as introspection.

In *Hamlet* she had this opportunity. She was able to work on a large canvas, demonstrating how a brilliant young man having all the advantages bestowed by upbringing, education and a privileged position at court could ruin his own prospects, destroy valuable relationships, and generally create havoc, while professing the noblest thoughts and best of intentions. As the author, she was more interested in mulling over the issues of her relationship with Essex than in paying attention to issues of staging — hence the casual stage directions. She no doubt anticipated that the play would one day be staged, but in the urgency of getting her thoughts and the all-too-real drama onto paper she neglected the tedious job of marking up the manuscript for the stage – there were plenty of play-makers capable of completing this routine task, including William Shakespeare the theatre shareholder and actor.

So Melchiori's description of *Hamlet* as "a play for the closet" is apt. The play was not constructed with the primary purpose of pleasing an audience. It was written as an act of private reflection and private edification. Ironically, this is why the play is so powerful.

It would be missing the point to try to match each character in the play with individuals at court – *Hamlet* is not a *roman à clef*. Nevertheless, there is some correspondence of the action of the play with historical events. Prince Hamlet uses his sword to kill the well-meaning busybody Polonius who is spying on him from behind a curtain. The parallels with Robert Cecil concealing himself behind an arras to listen to the proceedings at Essex's trial, and John Harington's report that in 1601 the distressed Elizabeth "thrust her rusty sword at times into the arras in great rage"[7] are pertinent. Another parallel can be found in Act 4 (scenes 5 and 7) in which Ophelia, after enduring Hamlet's appalling verbal abuse, loses her mind and drowns herself. This sequence of events leads one to recall the lines of sonnet 139, in which the Queen complains of the effects of Essex's unkindness on her:

> *Sonnet 139*
> O call me not to justify the wrong,
> That thy unkindness lays upon my heart,
> Wound me not with thine eye but with thy tongue,
> Use power with power, and slay me not by Art,
>   . . .
>   Yet do not so, but since I am near slain,
>   Kill me outright with looks, and rid [eliminate] my pain.

The havoc created by Hamlet (read 'Essex') continues. Ophelia's brother Laertes dies while defending his sister's honour. His mother (Gertrude) and the King are both poisoned. Hamlet himself finally dies as a result of Laertes' treachery. Then the country is overrun by forces invading from the north – possibly Elizabeth's acknowledgement of the inevitability of James VI of Scotland succeeding to the English throne.

The play's parallels with the personal history of Elizabeth and Essex at the turn of the century support the hypothesis of Elizabeth's authorship, but these parallels do not, in themselves, constitute proof of royal composition. It would be useful to have some independent evidence to support Elizabeth's authorship of the play. We may have it, in the form of Elizabeth's idiosyncratic spelling and orthography. Let's look at the spelling issue first.

Each of the three plays *Hamlet, Coriolanus* and *Anthony and Cleopatra* contain unusual spellings for Roman names: 'Sceneca' for 'Seneca' in *Hamlet* (Q2), 'Scicinius' for 'Sicinius' in *Coriolanus* (Q1) and 'Scicion' for 'Sicyon' in

Anthony and Cleopatra[8]. The 'sc' usage also occurs as 'scilence' for 'silence' in the draft *Sir Thomas More* manuscript segment attributed to 'Hand D'[9], in the anonymous Elizabethan play *Thomas of Woodstock*[10], and as 'Justice Scilens' for Justice 'Silence' in *Henry IV Part 2* (Q).

Both Elizabeth and William Cecil occasionally substituted 'sc' for 's' in their writings. Elizabeth writes "scince" for "since" in a prayer of 1597[11] and "sclaunderer" for "slanderer" in her 1593 translation of Boethius' *Consolation of Philosophy*[12]. William Cecil uses the spelling 'scilence' for 'silence' in a 1577 letter to the Earl of Oxford[13]. These unusual spellings may not be confined to Elizabeth and Cecil, but they do indicate that the odd "sc" spelling of words in *Hamlet*, *Coriolanus*, *Anthony and Cleopatra* and the draft of *Sir Thomas More* could be explained as coming from the hand of Elizabeth.

Secondly, let's examine the evidence related to handwriting and orthography, which is even more telling. It has been noticed by the literary analyst A. C. Partridge that in the parts of the *Sir Thomas More* manuscript attributed to Shakespeare and also in the 'good' quartos "there is a distinct tendency to write C as a capital"[14].

This tendency is notable in Hamlet Q2: I counted 55 instances of capitalised c (excluding occurrences in proper names or at beginnings of lines) in Q2, which, as mentioned above, is generally agreed to be based on the author's manuscript[15]. As an example of c capitalisation I reproduce below, in the original Q2 spelling but in modern type, an extract from the Q2 page[16] of the graveyard scene in which Ophelia's corpse is brought on stage:

> Imperious *Cæsar* dead, and turn'd to Clay,
> Might stoppe a hole, to keepe the wind away.
> O that that earth, which kept the world in awe,
> Should patch a wall t'expell the waters flaw.
> But soft, but soft awhile, here comes the King,
> The Queene, the Courtiers, who is this they follow?
> And with such maimed rites? this doth betoken,
> The corse they follow, did with desprat hand
> Foredoo it owne life, twas of some estate,
> Couch we a while and marke.
>   Laer. What Ceremonie els?
>   Ham. That is *Laertes* a very noble youth, marke.
>   Laer. What Ceremonie els?
>   Doct. Her obsequies have been as farre inlarg'd
> As we haue warrantie, her death was doubtfull,
> And but that great commaund ore-swayes the order,
> She should in ground unsanctified been lodg'd
> Till the last trumpet: for charitable prayers,
> Flints and peebles should be throwne on her:
> Yet here she is allow'd her virgin Crants [funeral garlands],
> . . .

It is significant, but overlooked by previous Shakespeare researchers, that capitalising the letter c is also a unique feature of Elizabeth's handwriting. For example, in her twenty-seven stanza French poem, written in her own hand around 1590, forty-one words beginning with c (not counting those at beginnings of lines) have a capitalised first letter[17] while only nine do not, i.e. 82% of words beginning with c are capitalised. (Figure 7 is a facsimile of the last three verses of this poem, in Elizabeth's own hand, in which seven out of eight words beginning with c are capitalised.) In a letter to Henri IV of France 94% of words beginning with c are capitalised[18]. And in Elizabeth's translations of the poems (called Meters) in Boethius' *Consolation of Philosophy*[19] the ratio of capital to lower case c is also 94% (ninety-eight versus six respectively).

If this evidence is not sufficient to convince readers of Elizabeth's unusual capitalisation habit, then a brief examination of her 1598 English translation of Erasmus' Latin version of Plutarch's *De Curiositate* reveals that in the first 12 lines of her blank verse the letter c is always capitalised[20].

We can be almost certain that the 55 occurrences of capital c in the second quarto of *Hamlet* are authorial and not inserted by the printer or an editor – a copyist, editor or printer would have no reason at all for inserting a capital c where none existed in the manuscript[21]. Unless research shows that another Elizabethan author habitually capitalised the letter c where it occurs as the first letter in a word, we must assume that this idiosyncrasy is unique to Elizabeth's writing. It is strong evidence that she wrote the *Hamlet* manuscript on which Q2 is based.

---

[1] Thompson and Taylor (2006).
[2] Thompson and Taylor (2006, p. 81) summarise the evidence.
[3] Some copies of Q2 were printed in 1605 and bear the 1605 date.
[4] Melchiori (1992)
[5] Jenkins (1982).
[6] Erne's (2013) conclusion also suggests that the play's author was more interested in mulling over issues than in presenting these issues on the stage.
[7] We are indebted to Sir John Harington for recording an historical incident which relates Elizabeth's behaviour after Essex's death to the text of *Hamlet*. In the play Polonius is killed when Hamlet thrusts his sword into an arras (curtain). Harington wrote that "Elizabeth walks much in her privy chamber, and stamps with her feet at ill news, and thrusts her rusty sword at times into the arras in great rage" (McClure 1930, p. 90).
[8] Brockbank (1976, pp. 3 and 4).
[9] Partridge (1964, p. 58).
[10] Partridge (1964, p. 62).
[11] Mueller and Marcus (2003, p. 104).
[12] Mueller and Scodel (2009, p. 92).
[13] Nelson (2003, p. 165).

14 Partridge (1964, p. 58).
15 Thompson and Taylor (2006, pp. 82–84) summarise the argument, which began with Dover-Wilson's study (Dover-Wilson 1934).
16 See wikimedia.org/wikipedia/commons/2/2c/Hamlet_Q2.pdf (image 49) for a facsimile; note also that in the description of the Vision scene in *Henry VIII* (this volume, p. 65) all words beginning with c are capitalised.
17 Mueller and Marcus (2003, pp. 85–94).
18 Mueller and Marcus (2003, pp. 94–95.
19 Mueller and Scodel (2009).
20 Mueller and Scodel (2009, p. 390).
21 The proportion of capitalised 'C' first letters in words is lower than in Elizabeth's hand-written texts, which could indicate some regularisation of the Q2 text before publication.

37. Othello and King Lear

I kiss'd thee ere I kill'd thee
— *Othello*, Act 5, scene 2

The first recorded performance of *Othello* (also known by the title *The Moor of Venice*) was in 1604. On 1 November of this year Edmund Tilney, Master of the Revels noted in his Accounts Book that on "Hallomas Day, being the first of November" . . . "the Kings Majesty's players" performed "A Play in the Banqueting House at Whitehall Called The Moor of Venice [by] Shaxberd". October of this year must be taken as the latest date that *Othello* could have been written.

The plot of *Othello* is derived from a story published by the Italian author Cinthio[1] in 1565 and translated into French by Gabriel Chappuys in 1583. There was no English translation of this book before the mid-eighteenth century. The researcher Michael Neill[2] asserted that "verbal parallels between *Othello* and Cinthio's Italian work "overwhelmingly favour the Italian version" [over the French version] as the source for *Othello*. Neill's assertion is interesting as William Shakespeare is not known to have been able to read Italian. In contrast, Elizabeth I both read and wrote the language fluently.

It has been suggested[3] that the earliest possible date of composition must be 1601 since the play draws geographical detail from Pliny's *History of the World* (*Naturalis Historia*) which first appeared in English translation in 1601. But this conclusion assumes that 'Shakespeare' was not able to read the Latin original. Other evidence for the date of composition of *Othello* comes from the first published version of *Hamlet* which appeared in 1603 and is known as the first Quarto (Q1). Q1 was printed from actors' recollections of the play and contains lines inadvertently transferred from *Othello*[4], showing that *Othello* must have been staged by this date, and possibly in 1602, when *Hamlet* was first entered in the *Stationers' Register*.

The information summarised above shows that Elizabeth I could have written the play in her last years, but are there other indications of her authorship? To answer this question we must look at *Othello*'s plot.

For a modern audience one of the least satisfactory elements of the plot is its dependence on a misunderstanding concerning a handkerchief. Othello's wife Desdemona loses her handkerchief in Act 3, scene 3. It is picked up by Emilia, wife of the manipulative villain Iago. Iago snatches the handkerchief from his wife and, in conversation with his boss Othello, uses it to imply that Cassio (Othello's Lieutenant) is having an affair with Desdemona. The credulous Othello, trusting his subordinate more than his devoted and faultless wife, becomes jealously enraged and murders Desdemona.

It's almost unbelievably contrived – we are asked to believe that a battle-hardened general accustomed to dealing with men of all backgrounds can be misled by a low-ranking aide into committing murder on the slightest evidence of unfaithfulness: a mislaid handkerchief.

When we consider the likely date of writing of *Othello* (1603 or earlier) we can see that what appears to be a weakness in the play's plot is actually paralleled by historic events. On 1 July 1598[5] the Privy Council was discussing who should be Lord Deputy of Ireland. Essex opposed the appointment of Sir William Knollys, the Queen's nominee, and insolently turned his back on his sovereign during a heated exchange of views. Elizabeth boxed his ears. In an instinctive response Essex put his hand on his sword as if to draw it but was restrained by other Privy Councillors present. Angry at being humiliated in front of colleagues, Essex retired to sulk at home in Wanstead where he was ill-advised by his supporters. After a cooling-off period (for both the Queen and Essex), Essex was given the Lord Deputy post and command of an army raised to quell the Irish rebels. However, his Irish campaign failed militarily and Essex disgraced himself by making peace with the rebel Tyrone and abandoning his troops. Trust between him and the Queen was never restored. The saga ended tragically with Essex's rebellion and execution in 1601.

The disagreement at the Privy Council meeting that initiated Essex's final demise began as a relatively minor exchange between two hotheads. It could have been readily resolved on-the-spot if rational discussion and goodwill had prevailed and apologies had been offered. But because of the temperaments of both Essex and the Queen it escalated into a prolonged personal stand-off, eventually leading to tragedy for one party and intense disillusion for the other.

Cinthio's Italian version of the Othello story is likely to have struck a chord with Elizabeth. In Cinthio's story a small incident is magnified out of proportion to its actual significance. Mistrust grows. Friendship turns to hate. Tragedy results. The handkerchief incident in *Othello*, which appears to modern audiences to be such a trivial basis for suspicion, moral outrage and murder, is not so contrived and trivial once it is put into its historical context. It is symbolic of a minor event which led to momentous personal and historic consequences for Elizabeth.

That the plot of *Othello* mirrors the final phase of Elizabeth's relationship with Essex does not, of course, prove that Elizabeth I wrote the play. But together with the likely time of composition of the play it is yet another indication that the possibility of royal authorship cannot be ignored.

* * *

King Lear was entered in the *Stationers' Register* on 26 November 1607. The entry refers to a production before King James at Whitehall on St Stephen's night (26 December) in 1606. The play may have been written earlier in the same year, or much earlier. How much earlier appeared to be established by Kenneth Muir who wrote this seemingly definitive statement:

On 16 March 1603 Samuel Harsnett's *Declaration of Egregious Popish Impostures* was entered in the *Stationers' Register*; and as Shakespeare makes considerable use of this book throughout the play [*King Lear*] we can be certain that it was not written until after that date.[6]

The eminent scholar Stanley Wells was equally confident: "The combined evidence, then, suggests that Shakespeare wrote all or most of *King Lear* in the later part of 1605"[7]. It is true that many phrases and words in *King Lear* (mainly in Act 3) are identical or similar to those in Harsnett's virulently anti-Catholic *Declaration*. Among the numerous examples[8] are the devils named by Edgar when he feigns madness: Modo, Mahu, Frateretto, Flibbertigibbet and Hoppedance, and the hysterical mental disorder Lear calls "the Mother" or *Hysterica passio*. The connection to Harsnett's 1603 publication is clear. So surely William Shakespeare must have written *King Lear* in late 1603 or subsequently? What could be more obvious?

But we need to pause and reflect. Let's return to *The Tempest* and consider the arguments used to support the proposition that when writing this play, first performed in 1611, Shakespeare depended on William Strachey's account of a shipwreck on the coast of Bermuda, which was first published in 1625. Virginia and Alden Vaughan wrote confidently[9]:

> There are also two documents on which Shakespeare surely drew for specific passages: William Strachey's 'True Reportory', for the opening scene and perhaps for a few later references to dissensions, conspiracies, and retributions . . .

and with similar confidence Frank Kermode wrote[10]:

> Shakespeare's knowledge of this unpublished work [William Strachey's *True Reportory*] makes it probable that he was deeply interested in the story.

There is no prize for detecting the logical inconsistency between the arguments for determining the date of composition of *King Lear* on the one hand and *The Tempest* on the other. In the case of *King Lear*, scholars insist that inclusion in the play of material available in a book first published in March 1603 means that Shakespeare wrote the tragedy *after* this date. In the case of *The Tempest*, they insist that inclusion in the play of material apparently derived from a shipwreck story first published in 1625 means that Shakespeare had access to an unpublished manuscript of the relevant account *before* its publication date.

Let's revisit Kenneth Muir's 1985 assertion that Shakespeare depended on Harsnett's 1603 publication for details contained in *King Lear*. This claim is repeated in all standard texts, for example, the Oxford Shakespeare edition published in 2000[11] and edited by Stanley Wells. However, it does not take into account Samuel Harsnett's position in London society. Harsnett was a man of strong opinions. He did not find ecclesiastical favour until he became friends with Richard Bancroft, who was appointed Bishop of London in 1597[12]. Bancroft employed Harsnett as his chaplain. In August 1598, by virtue of his association with Bancroft, Harsnett was installed as 'prebendary of Mapesbury'[13] in St. Paul's Cathedral, and from 11 October 1599 to 17 January 1603 Harsnett was vicar of St Margaret's parish church in Fish Street, London. This church was situated north of London Bridge near today's Monument underground station.

Bancroft and Harsnett had a semi-political role to play – their aim was to steer the church down a middle course, deflecting criticism and spiritual/political attacks by both extreme Catholics and extreme Protestants (Puritans)[14]. A major part of Harsnett *Declaration* concerns exorcists, miracles, superstition and abuse of women (possibly sexually) by Catholic priests in the parish of Denham in Buckinghamshire in the years 1585 and 1586, reported in later legal cross examinations (the transcripts of evidence date to 1599)[15]. The exorcism techniques used in 1585 and 1586 followed those written down in the so-called *Miracle Book*, which was found in the possession of Robert Barnes in 1598[16]. There is no reason to suppose that the legal proceedings were held in secret; the scandalous activities are likely to have been the subject of much gossip and speculation among the public. Some of the participants in the exorcisms were also involved in the 1586 Babington Plot, and Sir Francis Walsingham and Lord Burghley (William Cecil) were aware of their activities. We know that the Cecils were familiar with the shady goings-on because at least one of the exorcists, a Catholic gentleman named Robert Barnes, communicated with Robert Cecil in 1598[17].

It is highly likely that in about 1599 (or possibly earlier), with Bancroft's support, Harsnett began collecting material for his book published as *Declaration of Egregious Popish Impostures*. It is inconceivable that Harsnett's entertaining polemic was not first vetted by senior government administrators like Cecil before publication. And if Robert Cecil read the Harsnett manuscript or drafts of it before 1603, so might have Elizabeth I – the subject matter was probably raised by Robert Cecil during one of his regular meetings with the Queen.

As the information about devils and exorcisms was probably circulating prior to 1600, and Harsnett's book manuscript was probably checked by high-ranking officials such as Robert Cecil before publication, the case for *King Lear* being written after the 1603 publication of Harsnett's *Declaration* collapses.

Other possible sources influencing the writing of *King Lear* are discussed by Wells[18]. An earlier play, *The True Chronicle History of King Leir* is a certain source. It was performed in 1594 and entered in the *Stationers' Register* in the same year. Whether the entry resulted in publication is not known – no printed copy dating from around this time is extant. (The first known edition was published in 1605.) The phrase "these late eclipses of the sun and moon" in Act 2 of *King Lear* could refer to paired eclipses in either 1601 or 1605, or, alternatively, may not relate to any actual eclipses, so is not useful for dating the play[19].

Gary Taylor[20] argued for the influence of the play *Eastward Ho* (written in 1605, by Ben Jonson, John Marston and George Chapman) on *King Lear*, which would suggest that King Lear was written shortly after *Eastward Ho* appeared on stage. I haven't reviewed all Taylor's alleged evidence for the dependence of *King Lear* on *Eastward Ho* here, but it is sufficient to remark that some phrases in common, such as a reference to a "little dog" both in *Eastward Ho* and *King Lear* are insufficient to establish a chronological relationship between the two plays. Other evidence in the form of parallels appears to be stronger, for example the portrait of a favoured servant adopting the manners and vices of his master in Act 5, scene 3 of *Eastward Ho* and in Act 3, scene 4 of *King Lear*. But while the subject of the wayward servant is common to both plays, actual verbal parallels in these scenes are few. If we are convinced that borrowing occurred (and I am not), the question of who borrowed from whom is unresolved by such evidence.

At the end of his article Taylor's attention shifts from textual parallels to the issue of parody: he concludes that *King Lear* was written after *Eastward Ho* because the latter play parodies *Richard III* and *Hamlet* (recorded in the Stationers' Register in 1597 and 1602 respectively) but not *King Lear*:

> In short, if *Eastward Ho* does not parody *King Lear*, that can only be because *King Lear* did not yet exist when *Eastward Ho* was written.

Taylor seems to be unaware of the limitations of negative evidence. We should note that numerous 'Shakespeare' plays published or recorded before 1605 (see Table 3) were *not* parodied in *Eastward Ho*. Consequently, the fact that *King Lear* is not parodied in *Eastward Ho* is not proof that it was still to be written when the latter play appeared on stage. In addition, the joint authors Ben Jonson, John Marston or George Chapman may well have seen a public performance of *King Lear* before its performance at Whitehall in December 1606. Which is to say that these authors could have borrowed from 'Shakespeare', not *vice versa*. In this connection Foakes found Taylor's argument for *King Lear*'s dependence on *Eastward Ho* "not convincing"[21].

Taylor not only argued for *King Lear*'s dependence on *Eastward Ho*, but also for its dependence on George Wilkins' play *The Miseries of Enforced Marriage*, printed in 1607. As with the supposed parallels with *Eastward Ho*, there are similarities of subject matter in both plays, but little similarity of actual words and phrases. For example, there are riotous scenes in taverns in Wilkins' play, and Goneril complains that her father's followers are behaving in a manner that one might expect in an inn or brothel (Act 1, scene 4, line 238). But riotous scenes inevitably resemble each other. It is unlikely that an author who invented the boisterous and ale-loving Falstaff needed to refer to

Wilkins' text before describing the disorderly behaviour of Lear's "knights and squires".

Taylor also suggested that the final *King Lear* scene in which Lear comes on stage with the dead Cordelia in his arms is based on the scene in *The Miseries of Enforced Marriage* in which the father laments over the body of his dead daughter. The parallel is forced. In fact the mad Lear does not lament. His speech and actions are disjointed, as expected of someone who has lost his mind. With a feather he tests whether Cordelia is still breathing, then testily shoos Kent away, then describes Cordelia's voice as "ever soft, gentle and low, an excellent thing in a woman". In the next sentence he announces that he has killed the hangman who executed her.

In summary, the dependence of *King Lear* on Harsnett's *Declaration of Egregious Popish Impostures* (1603) is rejected for the reasons I give above. The confident assertions of Kenneth Muir and Stanley Wells that *King Lear* was not written until after 1603 must be rejected. As there is also considerable doubt as to whether either *Eastward Ho* or *The Miseries of Enforced Marriage* were sources for *King Lear*, these two plays are not useful for dating *Lear*'s composition.

Although William Shakespeare would have had ample opportunity to get to know Harsnett in his walks around London or after attending a church service at which Harsnett officiated, no records exist to show that they knew each other or exchanged information on matters of mutual interest. As there is historical evidence that senior figures at court were monitoring and documenting the strange activities of Catholic priests and others at Denham (and were probably keeping the Queen informed of their findings), let us consider the possibility that *King Lear* was written by Elizabeth.

In late 1599 Elizabeth I was sixty-six years old. She was facing years of decline and she knew it, while not admitting it. She was childless and estranged from her favourite. William Cecil, her rock of stability and trusted advisor since her accession to the throne, had died. She dared not name a successor who might become a magnet for discontents. It would have been natural for her thoughts to turn to frightening matters associated with her own mortality: decline of her mental powers, the fragility of her authority over her subjects, the hypocrisy of those who judge ("Robes and furr'd gowns hide all"), the declining respect for an out-of-touch and aged monarch, the issue of succession, and the dangers of factionalism and civil war.

King Lear is about all these matters. Perhaps the greatest writing in the play is its portrayal of the gradual descent of the King into madness. The key word here is gradual. Edgar is expertly portrayed as feigning madness, but his feigned madness is all at the same level. Lear *progressively* descends into madness – a much more difficult task for a playwright (and an actor) to portray. On first appearance on stage Lear seems normal and logical and in control of his faculties – he is arranging the distribution of his kingdom between his three daughters. The first hint of mental instability comes later in

Act 1 when he unreasonably over-reacts to Cordelia's truthful but unflattering answer to his question as to which of his daughters loves him the most. He is tipped further into outrage and madness when his two ungrateful daughters refuse to accommodate his entourage. His madness is most extremely expressed in the famous scene on the heath in Act 4 in which he rails against injustice while fantastically dressed with wildflowers ("matter and impertinency mix'd; Reason in madness"). Finally, near the end of his life (Act 5, scene 3), he reverts to childlike simplicity and clarity.

Above all *King Lear* is about a sovereign coming to terms with fear of declining mental acuity, fear of loss of authority, and fear of disintegration of her kingdom. Elizabeth may have begun writing it in the late 1590s, as she became painfully aware of her fading dominance.

---

[1] Cinthio was the nickname of Giovanni Battista Giraldi.
[2] Neill (2006, p. 22).
[3] Neill (2006, p. 399).
[4] Neill (2006, p. 401).
[5] The date is uncertain; the Privy Council meeting may have been on 30 June (Guy 2016, p. 307).
[6] Muir (1985, p. xvii).
[7] Wells (2001), p. 14.
[8] Listed by Muir (1985, pp. 239–242).
[9] Vaughan and Vaughan (2003, p. 287).
[10] Kermode (1964, p. xxvii).
[11] Wells (2001, p. 10); Wells allows for the possibility that Shakespeare may have read Harsnett's work in manuscript.
[12] In 1597 Bancroft was appointed Bishop of London. In this year he also took over the duties of the Archbishop of Canterbury because of Archbishop Whitgift's age and infirmity. He was present at Elizabeth's death.
[13] Prebendary clergy were those who were paid from church income typically derived from rents on church-owned property, in this case from properties in Mapesbury.
[14] Puritans were tolerated (and supported by Essex) during the 1580s and early 1590s, but the country's mood changed after Bancroft preached an anti-Presbyterian sermon on 9 February 1589, after which Essex moderated his support for this radical religious group.
[15] Brownlow (1993, p. 23).
[16] Brownlow (1993, p. 22) suggests that the Miracle Book came into Robert Cecil's hands in about 1598, and that he passed it on to Bishop Bancroft. The Miracle Book and the original transcripts referred to by Harsnett disappeared in the Civil War.
[17] Brownlow (1993, p. 21).
[18] Wells (2001), pp. 10–14.
[19] Wells (2001, pp. 12–13.
[20] Taylor (1982).
[21] Foakes (2004).

38. Two early plays: *Romeo and Juliet* and *The Taming of the Shrew*

'Tis since the earthquake now eleven years
— *Romeo and Juliet*, Act 1, scene 3

Before we return to the later sonnets, I would like to look at two early plays in which a love story is the dominant theme, to learn whether they too are relevant to the Elizabeth-Essex hypothesis.

We cannot be sure that *Romeo and Juliet* was the first 'Shakespeare' play written, because what Table 3 presents as a sequence is only a list of the latest possible dates of composition of each play. But in the case of *Romeo and Juliet* we know when the author probably began writing the play from internal evidence: in an exchange concerning Juliet's age in Act 1, scene 3 the garrulous wet-nurse refers to an earthquake on the day, eleven years earlier, when she weaned Juliet off her breast:

> On Lammas Eve at night shall she be fourteen,
> That shall she, marry! I remember it well.
> 'Tis since the earthquake now eleven years,
> . . .
>
> 'Shake,' quoth the dovehouse. 'Twas no need, I trow,
> To bid me trudge.
> And since that time it is eleven years

The earthquake referred to by the nurse must be the English earthquake of 6 April 1580, which is the largest earthquake known to have occurred in Britain, felt throughout the south of the country (especially in Kent), as well as in northern France and the low countries. It was commented on by several writers including William Camden[1]. The shaking, which lasted for a minute, toppled chimneys and damaged churches and towers. Falling debris from a church roof killed two children in London.

Mention of the 1580 earthquake is clever. It is not required by the plot, but it brings the play into the real world. It would have elicited from the audience the reaction 'I remember that too'. Attempts to link the nurse's comments to a landslide in Kent[2] are disingenuous: a landslide is not an earthquake, and although a landslide might demolish a dovecote it would not shake it. Likewise, a reference to an earthquake in Verona, the Italian town where the play is set, is unlikely. Mention of such a distant occurrence would be irrelevant to an English audience. It is much more likely that it is the 1580 'English' earthquake that is referred to, and that at least the first act of the play was written in 1591. However, it is possible that the author was writing this part of the play later, and deliberately introduced the text implying a 1591 date for the nurse's speech. But there seems to be nothing in the play that compels such an adjustment, so a 1591 date of composition for Act 1 is retained.

The emphasis on chronology in *Romeo and Juliet* is curious and suggests that the author had a reason for drawing attention to dates and emphasising age relationships. Juliet's tender age seems to matter to the author although it matters little to the plot. All that matters to the audience is that she is young, beautiful, ripe for the picking and eager to be picked. If Juliet is thirteen years old in the play and about to turn fourteen on Lammas Eve of 1591 (as the earthquake reference apparently tells us) then she was born in 1577, the same year in which the "lovely Boy" (then also aged thirteen) first appeared at court and met the Queen.

Is the selection of the Lammas Eve date (31 July) also significant? It may well be: in August 1591 Essex was away campaigning in France, and he and Elizabeth were exchanging affectionate letters. It would be logical to assume that she began writing the play at about this time in 1591 when her passion for Essex was perhaps at its most intense and the dark clouds of doubt which gathered in the mid- and late 1590s were not evident. Up to and including Act 2, scene 4 the text contains several sonnets and sonnet-like 14-liners. The play actually begins with a prologue in the form of a sonnet. The vocabulary in the beginning of the play in places is also reminiscent of that in the sonnets, as the following couplets illustrate:

> O she is rich in beauty, only poor
> That when she dies, with beauty dies her store.
>
>> Compare to Sonnet 67:
>> *O him she stores, to show what wealth she had,*
>> *In days long since, before these last so bad*
>
> Let two more summers wither in their pride
> Ere we may think her ripe to be a bride
>
>> Compare to Sonnet 104:
>> *. . . Three Winters cold,*
>> *Have from the forests shook three summers' pride*
>
> Such comfort as do lusty young men feel
> When well-apparelled April on the heel
> Of limping winter treads . . .
>
>> Compare to Sonnet 98:
>> *When proud pied April (dressed in all his trim)*
>> *Hath put a spirit of youth in every thing*

What's in a name? That which we call a rose
By any other name would smell as sweet.

> Compare to Sonnet 54:
> . . . *Sweet Roses do not so,*
> *Of their sweet deaths, are sweetest odours made:*

And where the worser is predominant
Full soon the canker death eats up that plant.

> Compare to Sonnet 70:
> *For Canker vice the sweetest buds doth love*

The text after Act 2, scene 4 is less indebted to the sonnet form and there is evidence that it borrows words from Thomas Nashe's *Have With You to Saffron Walden* published in 1596[3]. Taken together, the reference to the earthquake, the lines with links to those in the sonnets, and the borrowings from Nashe indicate that the play may have been worked on by Elizabeth over at least six years.

Today we take *Romeo and Juliet* rather seriously as the archetypal love story, but it can also be seen or read as an ironic commentary and comedy about the foolishness of people in love – how common sense is set aside when emotions rule. For example, in Act 1, scene 2 Romeo is desperately in love with a young lady called Rosaline: he "Ne'er saw her match since the first the world began". But when he catches sight of Juliet in scene 5 of the same act the hyperbole is suddenly transferred to her: "I ne'er saw true beauty till this night".

The graveyard scene in Act 5 is pure pastiche – star-struck lovers losing all reason. Juliet drinks a sleeping potion and allows herself to be buried in a tomb to avoid a bigamous marriage to Count Paris. (Why doesn't she just run away with Romeo?) Count Paris, suitor to Juliet, blames Romeo for her death. He disturbs Romeo while the latter is prising open Juliet's tomb. They fight a duel. Paris is mortally wounded, and asks Romeo to bury him with Juliet.

On opening the tomb Romeo sees Juliet's apparently dead body and kills himself by drinking a lethal concoction which he purchased en-route (and after-hours) from a poor apothecary – good planning! Juliet wakes from her death-like slumber, but just too late for a happy ending – she sees Romeo's body and stabs herself dead with his dagger. (If Romeo was carrying a dagger, why did he need to buy poison?) We must ask ourselves, is this really tragedy or is it burlesque?

As noted in the discussion concerning *Othello*, there are parallels between the plot of the play and happenings at court. In 1591 Elizabeth was taking a serious interest in Essex. Sonnet 43 refers to the poet seeing her lover in her dreams. It is likely to have been written in August 1591 when Essex was campaigning in France (Appendix 3). Elizabeth was probably both amused, amazed and annoyed to observe lustful Essex (like Romeo) rapidly transferring his attention from one attractive woman to another. He had only just married Frances Walsingham when he started consorting with the Queen. At about the same time he was seducing Elizabeth Southwell, who later bore his child.

We can conclude that this play, ridiculing those governed by passions, was begun during this time of raised hormone levels around the court (together with the mildly erotic poems *Venus and Adonis* and *The Rape of Lucrece*). It was an expression not only of the ageing monarch's wry observations of the more personal goings-on at court, but of her own frustrated sexual desires.

* * *

Discussion about the date of composition of *The Taming of the Shrew* has been dominated by two complications. Firstly, the play appeared in London almost at the same time as another play with a very similar plot and title: *The Taming of a Shrew* (probably not written by 'Shakespeare', although researchers are not be certain on this point). Contemporaries may not have distinguished the two plays. Secondly, Francis Meres in 1598 mentioned a Shakespeare comedy entitled *Love's Labours Won*. A printed copy of this play has never come to light. The play has either been lost to posterity or it is known by another name. *Love's Labours Won* is an ideal alternative title for *The Taming of the Shrew*, for Petruchio labours relentlessly to win Kate. That the 1603 accounts of an Exeter Stationer (Christopher Hunt) list both "taming of a shrew" as well as "loves labor won" does not, as Barbara Hodgdon suggests[4], make a link of *The Taming of the Shrew* to *Love's Labours Won* "unlikely". Rather, it confirms only that the (probably) non-'Shakespearean' *The Taming of a Shrew* was not known by the title of *Love's Labours Won*.

Hodgdon remarked that "*The Taming of the Shrew* is most certainly about courtship and marriage – the social ritual of wooing, winning and wedding"[5]. Or is it? Although *The Taming of the Shrew* undoubtedly uses "wooing, winning and wedding" as a structure for an entertaining tussle between Katherina (Kate) and Petruchio, I suggest that its fundamental theme is neither a formulaic conflict between genders nor a commentary on the nature of courtship and marriage. Instead, it is a playful reflection on the difficulties experienced by two persons of combative temperaments trying to make a relationship work, with each aiming to be the dominant partner.

Most of the play mirrors the early Elizabeth-Essex relationship. It is hard to imagine that William Shakespeare would take the risk of writing a play that could be interpreted as referring to the antics of the Queen and her favourite. However, if we assume royal authorship the clash of personalities can be explained. Although the beginning of the Elizabeth-Essex association was based on friendship and mutual interests it soon developed into a clash of wills. The royal author was perceptive enough to realise that the bond between two people vying for dominance could never be stable: in the long term the relationship would only work if one partner was content to give way. Elizabeth was Queen and there was no chance of her ever allowing herself to be dominated by a male courtier. Essex was not smart enough to keep his emotional need to dominate in check. In 'Shakespeare's' usual manner the male and female roles are thinly disguised by being reversed – so in the play it is Katherina who has to modify her behaviour, not Petruchio.

The plot may reflect Elizabeth's early hope that her hot-headed favourite would mature and take his expected place at her side. Essex didn't modify his behaviour and it cost him his head.

---

[1] Mussen (2008) lists contemporary accounts and provides references.
[2] Weis (2012) quotes the texts supporting this theory.
[3] Weis (2012, p. 35).
[4] Hodgdon (2010, p. 13).
[5] Hodgdon (2010, p. 1).

PART FOUR. NEW LIGHT ON THE DARK LADY

39. Are We There Yet?

O cunning love, with tears thou keep'st me blind,
Lest eyes well seeing thy foul faults should find.
– Sonnet 148

There is a remarkable match between what is described in the first group of sonnets (1–126) and the course of Essex's career after 1587, when he became lovingly and later tragically associated with the ageing Queen. The match applies to all the important historical and personal events in which Essex (and sometimes the Queen) were involved, for example Essex's attendance at court, his marriage, his affairs, his voyages and military adventures, his campaign in Ireland and his revolt and execution (Appendix 3). Even Elizabeth's private experiences, such as disagreements with Essex, her sorrow over the death of friends and lovers, her reaction to Essex's marriage and his amorous liaisons, and concern about his being in peril at sea are recorded. Royal authorship explains the sonnets' subject matter (which is unrelated to *anything* we know about the historical Shakespeare) and explains why the youth's identity is carefully concealed.

Elizabeth's authorship of *Sonnets* is supported not only by these abundant references to Essex (the fair youth), but also by the analysis of the Dedication, which reveals her name as the "ever-living" poet. William Shakespeare would have had no motive for hiding identities by writing an obscure Dedication, for had he had qualms about offending those in positions of power and influence by publishing a book that strongly suggested he had a homosexual relationship with an aristocrat, he would simply have arranged for it to be published anonymously or posthumously.

In contrast Elizabeth had a reputation to protect, even after her death. She would not have wanted her secret to be revealed too quickly, although she probably was not thinking in terms of a delay of more than 400 years. We can assume that being proud of her work, she would have desired publication of

Sonnets and eventual recognition of her authorship. So she had a motive for providing an obscure but decipherable riddle in the unique Dedication.

As detailed in Part 3 of this book and summarised in chapter 44, the generally accepted dates of composition of the so-called 'late' plays are not as sound as scholars have assumed. There is no evidence that 'Shakespeare' was writing plays after 1603 or was actively cooperating with co-authors, but there is strong evidence that other writers edited or added to 'Shakespearean' texts after this date. In addition, there is a strange hiatus in 'Shakespearean' publications after 1603.

But before we decide, once and for all, that *Sonnets* must have been written by Elizabeth, we need to do some more detective work. If a new theory is correct, it will not only explain the more obvious observations (such as the correlation of the events in Essex's life with those we read about in the sonnets) but will also explain peripheral detail. For an example outside English literature we can turn to Charles Darwin's theory of evolution. This theory not only provides a mechanism (natural selection) for genetic adaptation to environmental changes, but also explains why different species occupy similar ecological niches on different continents, for example pumas in the Americas and tigers in India and southeast Asia; hares and badgers in Europe and wallabies and wombats in Australia.

Can authorship by Elizabeth explain many intriguing contemporary references to 'Shakespeare's' works that have never ceased to perplex scholars? Or are we left with a lot of 'loose ends' which just don't fit the theory? And what about the sonnets we have not yet considered (127–154) including those about the 'Dark Lady'? Did Elizabeth I write these too, and who was this mysterious woman?

Let's consider the 'Dark Lady' issue first. (The 'loose ends' are discussed in chapter 44.) Sonnet 127 introduces readers to this enigmatic woman. Most readers familiar with the sonnets probably accept that the 'Dark Lady' was a real person – after all, nearly all academic commentators assume she was. However, we must remember that the Dark Lady label is a scholarly invention – this moniker does not appear in the sonnets. Nevertheless, the traditional and universal interpretation of sonnet 127 and the following sonnets is that Shakespeare periodically transferred his affection from his youthful male friend (and his wife) to a dark-complexioned woman.

If Elizabeth I wrote *Sonnets*, the 'Dark Lady' sonnets have the potential to be a major problem. Should we conclude that she was infatuated with a woman as well as with Essex? It seems hard to believe. These sonnets clearly need further scrutiny.

40. The Dark Lady Sonnets

For I have sworn thee fair, and thought thee bright,
Who art as black as hell, as dark as night
– Sonnet 147

In contrast to the convincing chronology of sonnets 1–112 and the retrospective perspective of sonnets 113–126, the 'Dark Lady' sonnets form no obvious sequence. The passage of time is not a theme. In fact, the word "time", so common in sonnets 1–126, is not mentioned.

The sonnets form a mixed bag – the subject matter varies. They have been described by the Cambridge scholar Kerrigan as being "trapped in a chaos of inescapable passion"[1]. (The passion is certainly present but Kerrigan may have overestimated the chaos.) Many sonnets are critical and some are satirical.

Those who have generalised that these sonnets "are chiefly about a mistress with dark hair and dark eyes"[2] or written "with sonnet 126 our attention switches from the lovely Boy to a dark favoured mistress"[3] have misrepresented their subject matter. Only six of the twenty-eight sonnets actually allude to a woman with dark characteristics, the legendary Dark Lady (Table 9). Four sonnets mention that the youth is not as fair as he appears to be. Four complain of the youth's attraction to a pretty woman. Seven complain about the youth's character deficiencies, with no mention of a female, dark or otherwise. One sonnet flirtingly makes fun of the image of a lover's hands on a keyboard instrument and six have other sexual themes, including the last two in the sequence which appear, on first reading, to be conventional sonnets on the theme of Cupid's charms.

Table 9. Subject matter in the 'Dark Lady' sonnets.

Subject matter	Sonnet numbers	Total
Woman with dark characteristics	127, 130, 131, 132, 144, 147	6
Youth is not as fair as he appears	137, 138, 148, 152	4
Youth's attraction to a woman	133, 134, 139, 145	4
Youth's deficiencies	140, 141, 142, 143, 146, 149, 150	7
Flirting/eroticism/sex	128, 129, 135, 136, 151, 153, 154	7

Scholars characterising all sonnets 127–154 as 'Dark Lady' sonnets have not paid attention to detail. The uncritical follow-the-leader approach of successive academic commentators has led to these sonnets being misinterpreted. Careful reading and analysis are required if we are to interpret them correctly.

Let's begin with sonnet 127, in which the infamous Dark Lady of literary legend first strides onto the stage. There is nothing subtle about her entrance. The audience gets a blast of blackness. The words are forthright and negative. Black has replaced beauty. Black has slandered beauty with "bastard shame". Black has profaned (soiled) beauty. The black mistress is slandering creation. Not a pretty speech, but what does it all mean?

Sonnet 127
In the old age black was not counted fair,
Or if it were it bore not beauty's name:
But now is black beauty's successive heir,
And Beauty slander'd with a bastard shame,
For since each hand hath put on Nature's power,
Fairing the foul with Art's false borrow'd face,
Sweet beauty hath no name no holy bower,
But is profan'd, if not lives in disgrace.
Therefore my Mistress' eyes are Raven black,
Her eyes so sooted[4], and they mourners seem [seem to mourn],
At such who not born fair no beauty lack [others who are dark and beautiful],
Sland'ring Creation with a false esteem [her eyes devalue Creation by their pretence],
    Yet so they mourn becoming of their woe [mourn so convincingly],
    That every tongue says beauty should look so.

Scholars have long recognised that sonnet 127 has affinities to sonnet 7 of Philip Sidney's *Astrophel and Stella*, published in 1591, and probably written in 1582, four years before Sidney's death at the Battle of Zutphen. For comparative purposes I have reproduced Sidney's sonnet[5] below.

Sir Philip Sidney's Sonnet 7, from Astrophel and Stella
When Nature made her chief work, *Stella's* eyes,
In colour black why wrapped she beams so bright?
Would she in beamy Black, like painter wise,
Frame daintiest lustre, mixed of shades and light?
Or did she else that sober hue devise
In object best to knit and strength our sight,
Lest if no veil these brave gleams did disguise,
They sun-like should more dazzle than delight?
Or would she her miraculous power show,
That whereas black seems Beauty's contrary,
She even in black doth make all beauties flow?
    Both so and thus: she minding Love should be
    Placed ever there, gave him this mourning weed,
    To honour all their deaths who for her bleed.

Sidney's sonnet is a straightforward creation about his unrequited love for Stella. (Stella represents Penelope Rich, Essex's sister.) No schoolboy or schoolgirl could misunderstand it. Stella has dark eyes that "make all beauties flow" and enhance her beauty, just as a painter achieves a beautiful effect in a painting by contrasting light and shade. Her lovely eyes make men die for her. It is written in the traditional language of chivalrous love.

In contrast, sonnet 127 develops an argument: (1) blackness was not considered to be beautiful in past times; (2) blackness has supplanted beauty as a desirable quality; (3) beauty has been spoilt with a dark colouration; (4) blackness appears fair because of artistry; (5) true beauty has been desecrated and is no longer recognised; (6) my mistress' eyes are so black that she pretends she is superior to those who are less black than she is; (7) she acts so convincingly that everyone says black is beautiful.

Sonnet 127 borrows words and concepts from Sidney but is obviously no love poem. Nor is it a parody of Sidney's poem – it's not written to raise a laugh. The words "foul", "profan'd", "disgrace", "sland'ring" and "false esteem" clearly indicate a more serious intent: the sonnet is a devastating character analysis. Line 6 is the clue: the character previously considered fair is now considered to be a counterfeit resulting from "Art's false borrowed face". By "fairing the foul" this person has deceived the poet and profaned beauty itself (lines 7 and 8).

As the beautiful fair youth who ended up disgracing himself is the dominant subject of the previous 126 sonnets, and sonnet 127 refers to the fair being fouled, there can be no doubt that the "slander'd" beauty referred to is the fair youth himself, i.e. Essex. He only appeared fair because he "put on . . . Art's false borrowed face". The significant conclusion is that in sonnet 127 *the fair and the dark images refer to the same person.* Essex presented himself as fair, noble and beautiful, and many were convinced by his artistry, but in fact his true character was as black as black could be.

It follows that the so-called Dark Lady (traditionally identified with the "Mistress" of line 9), is not another real lover but a metaphorical representation of the dark (and concealed) side of Essex's personality. (The idea that the 'Dark Lady' represents the fair youth of the earlier sonnets was first put forward by S. Campbell in 1978[6], but without good supporting evidence.) In describing the youth in these uncomplimentary terms, Elizabeth has the youth swap genders.

This gender swap has fooled commentators and academics for centuries and led to the Dark Lady legend. But we must remember that gender-swapping is a common device in many of 'Shakespeare's' works, including *Sonnets*. In an early sonnet (20) the youth was described as having "a woman's face" and "a woman's gentle heart". The youth was also described as "the Master Mistress of my passion". Given this deliberately ambiguous use of gender in the early sonnets, the gender swap in sonnet 127 should come as no surprise. And recalling the number of cross-dressing scenes in 'Shakespeare's' plays, we would be naïve to argue that the specified genders in the sonnets should always be taken at their face value. It is also significant that Elizabeth herself used gender concepts loosely – her French poem[7] refers to her "inner man" (see chapter 47) and she frequently referred to herself as a prince.

The so-called Dark Lady is referred to in five other sonnets. It is important to establish whether the above interpretation of sonnet 127 as describing a fair person who has become "foul" and "slander'd with a bastard shame" also applies to the other five. Sonnet 130 is the next to describe an apparently dark female character.

> *Sonnet 130*
> My Mistress' eyes are nothing like the Sun,
> Coral is far more red, than her lips red,
> If snow be white, why then her breasts are dun:
> If hairs be wires, black wires grow on her head:
> I have seen Roses damasked, red and white,
> But no such Roses see I in her cheeks,
> And in some perfumes is there more delight,
> Than in the breath that from my Mistress reeks.
> I love to hear her speak, yet well I know,
> That Music hath a far more pleasing sound:
> I grant I never saw a goddess go,
> My Mistress when she walks treads on the ground.
>   And yet by heaven I think my love as rare,
>   As any she beli'd with false compare.

Is this a love poem? If so, it is very unconventional. The poet is telling us that his (her?) mistress doesn't have bright eyes, her lips aren't red, her breasts aren't white, her hair is wiry, her breath doesn't smell of perfume, her speech is not musical, and she doesn't walk like a goddess. Is the poet really giving us an accurate portrait of his ugly mistress, or is this some sort of jest?

A love poem by the minor poet Thomas Watson provides the essential clues. (Watson wrote works of pedantic mediocrity[8], some of which probably refer to Elizabeth I, which he published in his collection *Hekatompathia* in 1582.) It is full of superlatives and hackneyed similes which sound ridiculous to the modern reader. They may have sounded equally ridiculous to discerning Elizabethans.

> *Thomas Watson's poem*
> Hark you that list to hear what saint I serve:
> Her yellow locks exceed the beaten gold;
> Her sparkling eyes in heaven a place deserve;
> Her forehead high and fair of comely mould;
> Her words are music all of silver sound;
> Her wit so sharp as like scarce can be found:
> Each eyebrow hangs like Iris in the skies;
> Her Eagle's nose is straight of stately frame;
> On either cheek a Rose and Lily lies;

Her breath is sweet perfume, or holy flame;
Her lips more red than any coral stone;
Her neck more white than aged swans that moan;
Her breast transparent is, like crystal rock;
Her fingers long, fit for Apollo's lute;
Her slipper such as Momus dare not mock;
Her virtues all so great as make me mute:
> What other parts she hath I need not say,
> Whose face alone is cause of my decay.

After reading the line "Her breast transparent is, like crystal rock" we must be eternally thankful that the less-than-subtle Watson was not persuaded to describe the "other parts" of the saint he served. But, facetiousness aside, when we compare sonnet 130 with Watson's it is obvious that sonnet 130 is a parody of Watson's poem.[9] The woman's eyes, voice, cheeks, breasts, lips, breath, and feet are mentioned in both poems. Perhaps sonnet 130 was written when Elizabeth, in a light-hearted mood and among her court friends, was having a cosy literary evening writing amusing parodies at Thomas Watson's expense.

If we investigate further by carefully reading the other sonnets of the 'Dark Lady' group, we find more indications that we should not take the Dark Lady legend seriously. Sonnet 131 is an interesting link between sonnets 1–112 and the 'Dark Lady' group. Elizabeth begins by addressing her lover as her "fairest and most precious Jewel" – words that could have been applied to Essex when their relationship was blossoming . . .

Sonnet 131
Thou art as tyrannous, so as thou art,
As those whose beauties proudly make them cruel;
For well thou know'st to my dear doting heart
Thou art the fairest and most precious Jewel.
Yet in good faith some say that thee behold,
Thy face hath not the power to make love groan;
To say they err, I dare not be so bold,
Although I swear it to myself alone.
And to be sure that is not false I swear
A thousand groans but thinking on thy face,
One on another's neck do witness bear
Thy black is fairest in my judgement's place.
> In nothing art thou black save in thy deeds,
> And thence this slander as I think proceeds.

. . . but she ends the sonnet with the couplet beginning with the words "In nothing art thou black save in thy deeds" (line 13), indicating that Essex has committed some misdemeanour. The sonnet must have been written early in their relationship, for Elizabeth expresses that she is prepared to forgive him (i.e., to believe that Essex is "fair" rather than "black"). The final couplet makes clear that the blackness she writes about does *not* refer to the complexion of Essex (or of another lover, or of a 'Dark Lady'), it refers to actions; and the earlier lines referring to a fair person ("the fairest and most precious Jewel") make clear that the black deeds (evil actions) mentioned are those of the fair youth himself.

In modern English, the poet might have written 'I could have sworn that you were fair, but I was very much mistaken; your appearance is fair, but by your evil actions you have shown your true character'. As in sonnet 127, *blackness and fairness apply to the same person.*

The words "swear", "false", "witness", "judgement" and "slander" in sonnet 131 would not be out of place in a courtroom. The terminology in sonnet 87 (considered in chapter 20), having the first line "Farewell thou art too dear for my possessing", is similarly legal. Perhaps both sonnets were written at about the same time, in mid-1598.

The final couplet of sonnet 147 make another strong assertion about the nature of the youth's blackness:

> For I have sworn thee fair, and thought thee bright,
> Who art as black as hell, as dark as night.

and equally categorically sonnet 152 proclaims that the image of fairness projected by the youth is a lie:

> For I have sworn thee fair: more perjured eye,
> To swear against the truth so foul a lie.

Without a doubt these sonnets too are about a fair person who, over time, has revealed or acquired an evil (black) personality trait. This inference is confirmed by the distressed and disdained poet's lines in sonnet 132 "Thine eyes I love, and they . . . *Have put on black*" [my italics]:

> *Sonnet 132, lines 1–4*
> Thine eyes I love, and they as pitying me,
> Knowing thy heart torment me with disdain,
> Have put on black, and loving mourners be,
> Looking with pretty ruth upon my pain.

Similarly, in sonnet 137 the poet admits that she has been misled by blind love (lines 1–4). She then asks: why have Essex's corrupt eyes, which are "anchor'd in the bay where all men ride" (i.e., between a woman's thighs), tied him to her heart as if by hooks and distorted her judgment (lines 5–8)? And why has she convinced herself that they had a special relationship when she knew he was promiscuous (as is well documented) (lines 9 and 10)? And how is it that her eyes have portrayed an image conflicting with reality, misleading her into thinking that what is actually foul is fair (lines 11 and 12)? In the sonnet's final couplet she concludes that her heart and eyes must be playing tricks because they are diseased; it can be modernised to: 'I have always thought you fair, but my diseased heart and eyes have falsified the truth'.

> *Sonnet 137*
> Thou blind fool love, what do'est thou to mine eyes,
> That they behold and see not what they see:
> They know what beauty is, see where it lies,
> Yet what the best is, take the worst to be.
> If eyes corrupt by over-partial looks,
> Be anchored in the bay where all men ride,
> Why of eyes' falsehood hast thou forged hooks,
> Whereto the judgement of my heart is tied?
> Why should my heart think that a several plot[10]
> [Why should my heart think we have a special private relationship],
> Which my heart knows the wide worlds' common place
> [When my heart knows that you spread your favours around]?
> Or mine eyes, seeing this, say "this is not"
> To [So that I] put faire truth upon so foul a face.
>   In things right true my heart and eyes have erred,
>   And to this false plague are they now transferred.

Yet again, in sonnet 148 we read "If that be fair whereon my false eyes dote, What means the world to say it is not so?" which can be modernised to: 'If what I see looks fair, why does everyone insist it isn't?' And the concluding lines blame love itself for blinding the author to the fair person's "foul faults".

> *Sonnet 148*
> O me! What eyes hath love put in my head,
> Which have no correspondence with true sight,
> Or if they have, where is my judgement fled,
> That censures falsely what they see aright?
> If that be fair whereon my false eyes dote,
> What means the world to say it is not so?
> If it be not, then love doth well denote,
> Love's eye is not so true as all mens': no,
> How can it? O how can love's eye be true,
> That is so vexed with watching and with tears?
> No marvel then though I mistake my view,
> The sun it self sees not, till heaven clears.
>   O cunning love, with tears thou keep'st me blind,
>   Lest eyes well seeing thy foul faults should find.

The metaphorical use of the Dark Lady concept to describe the black side of Essex's character is brilliantly summed up in sonnet 144, which describes in essentially modern psychological terms Essex's unstable split personality –

he can be alternately loving and fair (a "better angel" or "a man right fair") or proud and evil (a "bad angel" or "a woman colour'd ill").

> *Sonnet 144*
> Two loves I have of comfort and despair,
> Which like two spirits do suggest [influence] me still,
> The better angel is a man right fair:
> The worser spirit a woman colour'd ill.
> To win me soon to hell my female evil,
> Tempteth my better angel from my sight[11],
> And would corrupt my saint to be a devil:
> Wooing his purity with her foul pride.
> And whether that my angel be turn'd fiend,
> Suspect I may, yet not directly tell,
> But being both from me both to each friend,
> I guess one angel in an other's hell.
> Yet this shall I ne'er know but live in doubt,
> Till my bad angel fire my good one out.

The final couplet reveals Elizabeth's chilling and prophetic conclusion: ultimately all will become clear when the youth's pride and dark characteristics dominate his pure and good traits ("Till my bad angel fire my good one out"). Good won't triumph over evil – the opposite will occur.

How is it that Shakespeare scholars have missed such obvious statements? The six sonnets referring to a woman with dark characteristics (Table 9) and sonnets 144, 148 and 152 considered above all tell us clearly and unequivocally that the character that the poet loved, that appeared to be good and fair, was really quite the opposite. They confirm the initial conclusion, based on analysis of sonnet 127, that blackness (or, if you like, the traditional Dark Lady concept) is a metaphor for the dark character traits of Essex, the fair youth the poet has loved and the "lovely Boy" of sonnets 1–112.

There is no doubt that Elizabeth was infatuated with Essex and fascinated by his charm, petulance, energy and boyish good looks. But around the time of Essex's rebellion, and after his execution, she must have wondered how she had been so deceived by him. The character analysis in sonnet 127 and the succeeding sonnets in the 'Dark Lady' group, some of which were probably written after Essex's execution, would be expected of Elizabeth, given the dramatic and personally heart-breaking events of 1599–1601.

To undertake rigorous scrutiny of her disastrous relationship with Essex would have been quite natural for the highly intelligent and analytical Queen. What were Essex's good points? What were his bad points? How was it that she did not recognise his evil side sooner? How did the man's mind work? Was he a charlatan? Who, in fact, was the 'real' Essex?

[1] Kerrigan (1986, p. 57).
[2] Burrow (2002, p. 634).
[3] Kerrigan (1986, p. 352).
[4] An alternative reading for the original "suted" is "suited", meaning "attired".
[5] Ringler (1962).
[6] Campbell (1978).
[7] Marcus et al. (2002, p. 417).
[8] Maurice Evans (Evans 1977, p. x) described Thomas Watson as "one of the earliest and dullest of the tribe" [of Elizabethan sonneteers].
[9] Sonnet 130 uses images that were the stock-in-trade of Elizabethan sonneteers. Taken as a whole the vocabulary of Thomas Watson's poem closely matches that of sonnet 130, so Watson's poem was probably the primary target, but similar second-rate poems by other Elizabethans may also have been in the author's mind (Burrow 2002, p. 640).
[10] "Several plot" (private plot) could also be a euphemism for the youth's private parts.
[11] Most editions (including that of Martin Seymour-Smith (1963)) substitute "side" for "sight", but "sight" is retained here as it makes sense. It is interesting to note that in *Othello* the words "side" and "sight" are used in the same sentence and in a similar context. In this play the idea that a man consists of two competing spirits (angels), one good and one evil, appears in Act 5, scene 2, lines 208–210. These lines follow those relating Desdemona's murder by Othello. Gratiano suggests that the sight of the murder would make Desdemona's father (Brabantio) cast aside his good nature [better angel] and commit a desperate act (the context suggests an allusion to suicide): "This sight would make him do a desperate turn, Yea, curse his better angel from his side, and fall to reprobation [damnation]". Act 5 of *Othello* and sonnet 144 were probably written at about the same time.

41. Heart of Darkness

Therefore I lie with her, and she with me,
And in our faults by lies we flattered be.
– Sonnet 138

Sonnet 137 (considered in the previous chapter) and sonnets 138, 148 and 152 do not refer specifically to a woman of dark complexion but are related to the six 'Dark Lady' sonnets previously considered (Table 9). Their common theme is that the youth is not as fair (i.e., upright, truthful and straightforward) as he appears.

Essex's Jekyll-and-Hyde personality is brilliantly portrayed in sonnet 138, reproduced below. He presents himself as upright and honest, but the poet knows from experience that this image does not represent the true Essex: "When my love swears that she [he] is made of truth, I do believe her [him] though I know she [he] lies". The royal poet has lost her naïvety, she is no longer "some untutor'd youth, Unlearned in the world's false subtleties". Essex's disloyalty has shattered her confidence and exposed her self-deception of being eternally young.

This sonnet must have been written by 1599, when it appeared in a slightly different form in *The Passionate Pilgrim* miscellany published by William Jaggard, who had probably picked up a circulating manuscript version of the poem that the Queen presumably had arranged to be 'leaked'. Perhaps she was deliberately testing the response of the literary market. Altering the sex of the sonnet's subject to female was probably intentional – it made the poem conventional and safe for public release.

The sonnet is purportedly about the love between an old man and a young woman, and the white lies these lovers tell each other to keep their relationship alive. The puns on the word "lie" indicate that the relationship was not platonic. There is no mistaking the poet's advanced years – the sonnet is insistent and explicit on this subject: "vainly thinking that she thinks me young" (line 5); "my days are past the best" (line 6); "wherefore say not I that I am old?" (line 10); "age in love, loves not t'have years told" (line 12). We should remember that William Shakespeare was only in his mid-thirties in 1599, and the sonnet makes no sense at all if we consider it as a poem describing Shakespeare's younger lover (whoever that might be) and their love-life together.

The version published in 1609 is reproduced below. ("She" should be read as "he" and "her" as "him".) The 1599 version follows.

Sonnet 138 (1609 version)
When my love swears that she is made of truth,
I do believe her though I know she lies [is dishonest, sleeps around],
That she might think me some untutor'd youth,

Unlearned in the world's false subtleties.
Thus vainly thinking that she thinks me young,
Although she knows my days are past the best,
Simply I credit [excuse] her false speaking tongue,
On both sides thus is simple truth suppress'd:
But wherefore [why] says she not she is unjust [deceitful or unfaithful]?
And wherefore [why] say not I that I am old?
O love's best habit is in seeming [pretending] trust,
And age in love [an old person in love], loves not t'have years told.
    Therefore I lie with her, and she with me,
    And in our faults by lies we flattered be.

Sonnet 1 (from *The Passionate Pilgrim*, 1599)[1]
When my love swears that she is made of truth,
I do believe her (though I know she lies),
That she might think me some untutor'd youth,
Unskilful in the world's false forgeries.
Thus vainly thinking that she thinks me young,
Although I know my years be past the best:
I, smiling, credit her false-speaking tongue,
Outfacing faults in love with love's ill rest [uneasy agreement].
But wherefore says my love that she is young?
And wherefore say not I that I am old?
O, love's best habit is a soothing tongue,
And age in love loves not to have years told.
    Therefore I'll lie with love, and love with me,
    Since that our faults in love thus smothered be.

There are significant differences between the versions. (Poets cannot resist revising their poems in order to express their changing thoughts, feelings and experiences.) The differences are shown in italics in the 1609 version in the parallel extracts below.

1599 version	1609 version
Unskilful in the world's false forgeries	*Unlearned* in the world's false *subtleties*
Although I know my years be past the best:	Although *she knows my days* are past the best,
I, smiling, credit her false-speaking tongue Outfacing faults in love with love's ill rest. But wherefore says my love that she is young?	*Simply I* credit her false speaking tongue, *On both sides thus is simple truth suppress'd:* But wherefore says *she not she is unjust*?
O love's best habit's in a soothing tongue,	O love's best *habit is in seeming trust*,
Therefore I'll lie with love, and love with me, Since that our faults in love thus smother'd be.	Therefore *I lie with her, and she with me,* *And in our faults by lies we flattered be.*

In the 1599 version the poet is confident love can conquer differences: she smilingly excuses (credits) the "false-speaking tongue" of the young admirer (line 7) and is prepared to ignore faults in the interests of maintaining the relationship, however fragile it might be (line 8). But in the 1609 version the response is dry and analytical: mutual admiration is seen for what it is: "simple truth suppress'd".

In the 1599 version the age difference of the lovers ("wherefore says my love that she is young?") is innocently questioned. But in the 1609 version the question is altered to an accusation of insincerity ("wherefore says she not she is unjust [why doesn't he admit he is deceitful]?").

In the 1599 version lovers' talk that downplays differences ("a soothing tongue") is considered positive. But in the 1609 version expressions of love are seen as a cynical ploy for inducing an illusion of trust ("O love's best habit is in seeming trust").

Finally, in the sexually loaded double meanings of the final couplet, we read in the 1599 version that love smothers faults (love is mentioned three times), but in the 1609 version the word love has been deleted. Instead lies are seen for what they are – flattery ("by lies we flattered be").

These textual differences reveal the poet's greater cynicism in the later version. The sentimental ideas of love conquering faults and smothering differences are replaced by harsher conclusions: being in love obscures truths, and flattery by one partner is simply lying.

Clearly Elizabeth wished the final version of sonnet 138 to express a more negative assessment of her relationship with Essex than the conciliatory assessment published in 1599. This change was an inevitable consequence of the breakdown of their relationship after his return from Ireland. A similar negative assessment is found in sonnet 152.

Sonnet 152
In loving thee thou know'st I am forsworn [I have not told the truth],
But thou art twice forsworn to me love swearing
[In saying that you love me you have told two lies],
In act thy bed-vow broke [you have slept around] and new faith torn,
In vowing new hate after new love bearing:
[By pretending that you hate those you have seduced]
But why of these two oaths' breach do I accuse thee,
When I break twenty: I am perjur'd most [I am more of a liar],
For all my vows are oaths but to misuse [misrepresent] thee:
And all my honest faith in thee is lost.
For I have sworn deep oaths of thy deep kindness:
Oaths of thy love, thy truth, thy constancy,
And to enlighten thee gave eyes to blindness [ignored your faults],
Or made them swear against the thing they see.
  For I have sworn thee fair: more perjured eye [I?]
  To swear against the truth so foul a lie.

Elizabeth twice accuses Essex of lying: firstly, for swearing that he loves her, while seducing others (which is well documented); and secondly, for saying that he does not really love those women he has seduced, but he loves Elizabeth only. Recall sonnets 109 and 110 (discussed in chapter 22) in which the young man initially proclaims his "Rose" is "my all" (109) while admitting being attracted to other women, then argues defensively and unconvincingly that these unsatisfactory relationships with others only served to prove Elizabeth was his true love: "worse assays prov'd thee my best of love . . . Mine appetite I never more will grind On newer proof, to try an older friend, A God in love, to whom I am confined" (110).

As suggested in chapter 22, these two earlier sonnets by Essex were probably written in February 1600, when he was desperately trying to regain the Queen's trust. Sonnet 152 is likely to be Elizabeth's reply to him, though whether it was ever sent to him is doubtful – it probably was just her way of organising her thoughts about Essex's preposterous and self-serving argument. She admits that although she has sworn that Essex is kind, loving, true and constant (i.e. fair), she has perjured herself (line 8) because he is none of these – she has also told a foul lie.

In sonnet 140, probably written during one of their emotional stand-offs, Elizabeth realises that she has been so infatuated with Essex that her own mental stability will be threatened if she starts speaking ill of him:

Sonnet 140, lines 9–14
For if I should despair I should go mad,
And in my madness might speak ill of thee,
Now this ill wresting world [deformed/crooked world] is grown so bad,
Mad slanderers by mad ears believed be
    That I may not be so [don't go mad], nor thou belied [slandered],
    Bear thine eyes straight, though thy proud heart go wide
    [Improve your conduct, even if your ego resists].

She makes clear that one of Essex's less admirable qualities among his "thousand errors" (141) is his "proud heart" (read 'big ego') (140). She is no longer delighted to see him or hear his voice. She doesn't like to be touched by him and rejects any "sensual feast" of taste or smell "with thee [the youth] alone" (141).

Sonnet 141
In faith I do not love thee with mine eyes,
For they in thee a thousand errors note,
But 'tis my heart that loves what they despise,
Who in despite of view is pleased to dote.
Nor are mine ears with thy tongue's tune delighted,
Nor tender feeling to base touches prone,
Nor taste, nor smell, desire to be invited
To any sensual feast with thee alone:

But [But neither] my five wits, nor my five senses can
Dissuade one foolish heart from serving thee,
Who leaves unswayed the likeness of a man[2],
Thy proud heart's slave and vassal wretch to be:
    Only my plague thus far I count my gain,
    That she [he] that makes me sin, awards me pain.

Whether the "sensual feast" (line 8) is a shared meal or a sexual dalliance is unclear, but the sonnet's last line mentions the author's "sin" and in the next sonnet (142) the poet writes of "sinful loving" which has induced a sense of hate in Essex (lines 1 and 2). So something a little more intimate than a dinner for two can be assumed.

Sonnet 142
Love is my sin, and thy dear virtue hate,
Hate of my sin, grounded on sinful loving,
O but with mine, compare thou thine own state,
And thou shalt find it merits not reproving [doesn't deserve criticism],
Or if it do, not from those lips of thine,
That have profan'd their scarlet ornaments,
And seal'd false bonds of love as oft as mine,
Robb'd others' beds revenues of their rents.
Be it lawful I love thee as thou lov'st those,
Whom thine eyes woo as mine importune thee,
Root pity [Plant compassion] in thy heart that when it grows,
Thy pity may deserve to pitied be.
    If thou dost seek to have what thou dost hide
    [If you ask to receive compassion which you yourself don't give],
    By self example may'st thou be denied
    [I'll refuse it because of your own example].

Elizabeth regrets "sinful loving" but points out that Essex has slept around ("Robb'd others' beds revenues of their rents"), so he has no right to criticise her. Lines 3 and 4 reminds one of a married couple arguing; they can be paraphrased: 'don't criticise me – look at yourself – you're not so perfect!' In the final couplet Elizabeth makes it plain that if he doesn't show compassion, he can't expect it from others, i.e., she's not going to make allowances for him anymore.

Hate is the subject of the first line of sonnet 142 and also of sonnet 145. The latter sonnet is an oddity. It has four 'beats' to the line rather than five (tetrameters rather than pentameters) which emphasise its simplicity. In reproducing the sonnet I have taken the liberty of enclosing the words 'I hate' and 'not you' in inverted commas.

Sonnet 145
Those lips that Love's own hands did make,
Breath'd forth the sound that said 'I hate',
To me that languish'd for her sake:
But when she saw my woeful state,
Straight in her heart did mercy come,
Chiding that tongue which ever sweet,
Was used in giving gentle doom:
And taught it [her tongue] thus anew to greet:
'I hate' she alter'd with an end [a final phrase],
That follow'd it as gentle day,
Doth follow night who like a fiend
From heaven to hell is flown away.
 'I hate', from hate away[3] she threw,
 And sav'd my life saying 'not you'.

If we read this poem in isolation, we might conclude that it was written by a man about a woman who has announced that she hates him (lines 1–3). Lines 4–14 tell us that the woman modified her words once her heart had gained control of her tongue and said "not you", effectively cancelling her original statement (line 13). But these lines can also be read as a suggestion from a man to a woman that she should consult her heart and withdraw her statement, to save his life (line 14).

The sonnet's vocabulary suggest strongly that it was written by someone in a spot of bother and deeply distressed – someone languishing in a state of limbo (lines 3–5), whose life can be saved if the woman addressed says that she does not hate him after all.

The scholar Stephen Booth suggested that the sonnet is not by Shakespeare on account of its simple form[4]. Kerrigan called it a "pretty trifle which has been much abused" and "a piece of juvenilia" that might have been inserted into the sonnet sequence by a person who "had a knowledge of the [sonnet] sequence superior to anything that an average scribe . . . might be likely to possess"[5]. The opinions expressed by both the above commentators can be accommodated by the Elizabeth-Essex hypothesis. Sonnet 145 is undoubtedly of inferior quality, competently written, but not well written. It is indeed likely to be a piece of juvenilia. However, 'Shakespeare's' early works are remarkably polished: witness 'his' first published work, the narrative poem *Venus and Adonis* (1593).

I agree with Kerrigan that it probably has been inserted into the sonnet sequence by someone who was very conscious of its rightful place, but suggest that this 'someone' was Elizabeth I. I also agree that the poem itself is a piece of juvenilia, but written by Essex. If we take the alternative view that the sonnet is Shakespearean we have to invent a scenario of intense distress between Shakespeare and an unknown lover and make excuses for the poet's lapse into near-doggerel.

We don't have to look far to find the relevant historical context. It is likely that this sonnet refers to fallout from the bad-tempered Privy Council debate of 1 July 1598, when Elizabeth boxed Essex's ears, prompting him to put his hand on his sword as if to draw it. Being proud and pig headed he refused to apologise immediately and there was a painful stand-off, followed (after several months) by Essex's ineffective and (finally) disastrous military performance in Ireland. Essex was in desperate straits in the months of February to August 1600. His entire future depended on his regaining Elizabeth's affection and trust – which explains why he wrote sonnet 145 imploring the Queen to renew her fondness for him. Nothing in Shakespeare's life suggests a credible alternative to this scenario.

In contrast to the simple lines of sonnet 145, sonnets 149 and 150, in which the word hate is also prominent, are definitely written by a superior poet. They are likely to be Elizabeth's rejoinder to Essex's appeal (sonnet 145). Sonnet 149 appears to describe the complex and conflicting thoughts running through Elizabeth's mind. We can link these thoughts to the distressing emotional upheavals she must have experienced in the year 1600. One part of her wants to believe Essex is good and noble despite his defects (line 11). Another part believes that his affection has turned to hate, and that she hates him too (line 5).

> *Sonnet 149*
> Can'st thou O cruel, say I love thee not,
> When I against my self with thee partake:
> Do I not think on thee when I forgot
> Am of my self, all tyrant [illogical] for thy sake?
> Who [One part of me] hateth thee that I do call my friend,
> On whom frown'st thou that I do fawn upon,
> Nay if thou lour'st on me do I not spend
> Revenge upon my self [blame myself] with present moan?
> What merit do I in my self respect [How can I respect that part of myself],
> That is so proud thy service to despise [that despises you],
> When all my best [my best part] doth worship thy defect,
> Commanded by the motion of thine eyes.
>   But love, hate on for now I know thy mind,
>   Those that can, see thou lov'st [see that you love me], and I am blind.

In the final couplet (in which I have inserted two commas for clarity) she accepts that Essex hates her ("But love, hate on"), and although she recognises that others can see that he loves her, she can't: "I am blind".

Sonnet 150 appears to have been written when Essex, with the desperate expertise of someone on the brink of disaster, was trying to manipulate Elizabeth's thoughts in order to regain her favour. She asks how it comes to pass "That in the very refuse of thy deeds, There is such strength and warranties [evidence] of skill, That in my mind thy worst all best exceeds?"

(lines 6–8). Apparently impressed by the workings of his unbalanced mind she chooses to see the character she used to admire despite "The more I hear and see just cause of hate" (line 10). She then ends the sonnet with the hope that if his unworthiness and faults make her love him, then she in turn must be worthy of his love (lines 13 and 14).

> *Sonnet 150*
> Oh from what power hast thou this powerful might,
> With insufficiency [your personal inadequacy] my heart to sway,
> To make me give the lie to my true sight,
> And swear that brightness doth not grace the day?
> Whence hast thou this becoming [appearance] of things ill,
> That in the very refuse of thy deeds,
> There is such strength and warranties of skill,
> That in my mind thy worst all best exceeds?
> Who taught thee how to make me love thee more,
> The more I hear and see just cause of hate,
> Oh though I love what others do abhor,
> With others thou should'st not abhor my state.
>   If thy unworthiness rais'd love in me,
>   More worthy I to be belov'd of thee.

---

[1] Two versions were printed in 1599, identified as o1 and Q by Burrow (2002). (o1 may in fact have been printed in late 1598.) The text reproduced here is o1.

[2] The meaning of this line is unclear.

[3] Gurr (1971) suggested that the line "I hate, from hate away she threw" puns on the name of Shakespeare's wife, Anne Hathaway. Regardless of authorship questions, there are two reasons why this is unlikely. Firstly, it would be most insensitive of Shakespeare, even if he had tired of his wife (and there is no evidence of this) to publicly associate her with hate. Secondly, Shakespeare's marriage certificate gives Anne's surname as Hathwey, not Hathaway, so presumably it was pronounced Hathwey, and this pronunciation does not support a pun.

[4] Booth (2000).

[5] Kerrigan (1986, pp. 376–377).

42. Psychoanalysis, Elizabethan Style

Her pretty looks have been mine enemies
— Sonnet 139

The psychological complexity of the 'Dark Lady' sonnets increases in sonnets 133 and 134. Most commentators have concluded that these sonnets indicate that a new competitor (usually identified with the 'Dark Lady') has upset the relationship between the poet and the youth.

> *Sonnet 133*
> Beshrew that heart that makes my heart to groan
> For that deep wound it gives my friend and me;
> Is't not enough to torture me alone,
> But slave to slavery my sweet'st friend must be.
> Me from my self thy cruel eye hath taken,
> And my next [other] self thou harder hast engrossed,
> Of him, my self, and thee I am forsaken,
> A torment thrice three-fold thus to be crossed:
> Prison my heart in thy steel bosom's ward [Enclose me in thy heart],
> But then my friend's heart let my poor heart bail
> [Then let my friend's heart bail mine],
> Who e'er keeps me, let my heart be his guard [so I can be his guard],
> Thou cans't not then use rigour in my Jail [Then I won't be hurt in jail].
> > And yet thou wilt, for I being pent in thee
> > [But I will get hurt, because as I am trapped in you],
> > Perforce am thine and all that is in me [All of me is part of you].

The first four lines of the sonnet do indeed support the inference that the youth has been attracted to another woman. However, there is no need to postulate that this woman is the so-called Dark Lady. Ockham's razor applies: there is a much simpler way of interpreting this sonnet, which on first reading appears to be so obscure.

No woman with a dark complexion is mentioned, so we should not complicate an already difficult sonnet by jumping to an unwarranted conclusion. As the young friend is described as being a "slave to slavery" (line 4), we could conclude that the friend has got married. (Elizabeth was notorious for her angry outbursts after finding that her courtiers and favourites had love interests other than her.) As noted in chapter 13, the early sonnets 33–36 express disappointment about the youth's "sensual fault" and were probably written at the time of Essex's marriage to Frances Walsingham in 1590 (see Appendix 3). It is logical to assume that sonnets 133 and 134 also refer to Essex's temporary fall from grace at this time. When Essex married Frances he received the same verbal treatment and temporary banishment from court as other frisky males before and after him.

Examining sonnet 133 carefully, we find that lines 5–14 contain a psychological analysis similar to that in sonnet 144 (chapter 40). In the latter sonnet Elizabeth divided the youth's personality into two parts, to which she assigned male and female (good and evil) genders. But in sonnet 133, instead of imagining the *youth's* personality as being split in two, she scrutinises the two parts of *her own* personality. After complaining in lines 1–4 of the "deep wound" Essex has given her by turning his attention elsewhere (most probably to Frances) she explains in lines 5–8 how Essex's defection has affected her: "Me from my self thy cruel eye hath taken, And my next [other] self thou harder hast engrossed, Of him [i.e. "my next self"], my self, and thee I am forsaken." Modernised, these words might be written: "your cruelty in deserting me has alienated me from my other self, my creative part, and this part of myself has been so affected that I have lost my own identity and my creativity, as well as you".

Elizabeth used this literary and psychological device of separating two parts of her own personality previously, in sonnet 89. In this sonnet, when describing an estrangement, she writes: "For thee, against myself I'll vow debate, For I must ne'er love him [part of herself] whom thou dost hate". In modern English the lines could be paraphrased: 'For your sake I'll argue against myself, for I couldn't bear to think highly of myself if you dislike me'. She is undoubtedly speaking about her divided self. It follows that "him" in the last line does not refer to a third person, it refers to the poet.

> *Sonnet 89*
> Say that thou did'st forsake me for some fault,
> And I will comment upon that offence,
> Speak of my lameness, and I straight will halt [walk]:
> Against thy reasons making no defence.
> Thou can'st not (love) disgrace me half so ill,
> To set a form upon desired change,
> As I'll my self disgrace, knowing thy will,
> I will acquaintance strangle and look strange:
> Be absent from thy walks and in my tongue,
> Thy sweet beloved name no more shall dwell,
> Lest I (too much profane) should do it wrong:
> And haply [by chance] of our old acquaintance tell.
>   For thee, against my self I'll vow debate,
>   For I must ne'er love him whom thou dost hate.

An exchange between Beatrice and Benedict in *Much Ado about Nothing* (Act 5, scene 2) uses almost identical words and concepts. Referring to her heart, Beatrice declares: "If you spite it for my sake, I will spite it for yours, for *I will never love that which my friend hates*"[1] [my italics].

Let's now return to sonnet 133. In lines 9–12 Elizabeth writes some charming poetic nonsense, paraphrased as 'enclose me in your heart, then let me out on bail, so I can be your guard, rather than be tortured in jail'. But in the final couplet she recognises this argument for the nonsense it is and admits that she is totally committed to (besotted with?) Essex and she will suffer by his actions anyway.

Sonnet 134 repeats the argument of sonnet 133 in different terms. The first line takes us back to the woman causing all the upset (probably Frances): "So now I have confessed that he is thine" (i.e., she accepts that Essex 'belongs' to Frances). Then the psychological analysis gets really complex. This is because the poem is written in a kind of condensed pseudo-legal shorthand describing emotional transactions between Essex and herself, who she again splits into two parts consisting of her day-to-day self and her creative (writing) self, on which her poetic inspiration depends.

> *Sonnet 134*
> So now I have confessed that he is thine,
> And I my self am mortgag'd to thy will,
> My self I'll forfeit, so that other mine,
> Thou wilt restore to be my comfort still:
> But thou wilt not, nor he will not be free,
> For thou art covetous, and he is kind,
> He learn'd but surety-like to write for me,
> Under that bond that him as fast doth bind.
> The statute of thy beauty thou wilt take,
> Thou usurer that put'st forth all to use,
> And sue a friend, came debtor for my sake,
> So him I lose through my unkind abuse.
>   Him have I lost, thou hast both him and me,
>   He pays the whole, and yet am I not free.

She knows she has lost Essex's affections ("he is thine") and any residual friendship depends on Essex's attitude ("I my self am mortgag'd to thy will") but she will give up part of herself ("My self I'll forfeit") if she can keep her creative part which is her comfort ("that other mine", equivalent to "my next self" in sonnet 133). But she has struck a problem: her creative part can only write when it has the assurance ("surety-like") that the old relationship of free exchange of affection is working. This is no longer the case: Essex has effectively (so it seems to Elizabeth) put up his beauty for sale like a "usurer that put'st forth all to use" and writing about her love is no longer the spontaneous and cost-free activity it used to be; it is now one-sided and drains her resources (her creative part "[be]came debtor for my sake"). So she has not only lost her affection for Essex, but also her poetic inspiration and creativity. Figuratively speaking, Essex has called in his debts (line 14). Although these transactions should generate clarity and closure she does not feel happy: "and yet am I not free".

Sonnet 139 has a much simpler psychological structure. It tells us about a woman (who is certainly not ugly or dark) in competition with the poet for the youth's attention ("Her pretty looks have been mine enemies") and the youth's perceived unkindness in being drawn to her. The words "pretty looks", like the words "sweet thief" in sonnet 35, indicate Elizabeth's apparent affection for this competitor. It is logical to conclude that this is another reference to Frances Walsingham, so again we have a specific link between sonnets of the first and second groups – both refer to the same subject matter, which is Elizabeth's unhappiness resulting from Essex's marriage. Sonnets 35, 133, 134 1nd 139 were probably all written at about the same time.

Sonnet 139
O call me not to justify the wrong,
That thy unkindness lays upon my heart,
Wound me not with thine eye but with thy tongue,
Use power with power, and slay me not by Art,
Tell me thou lov'st elsewhere [Just say you love someone else]; but in my sight,
Dear heart forbear to glance thine eye aside [give me full attention],
What need'st thou wound with cunning when thy might
Is more than my o'er-press'd [besieged] defence can bide?
Let me excuse thee, ah my love [Essex] well knows,
Her pretty looks have been mine enemies [have worked to my disadvantage],
And therefore from my face she turns my foes [my foes are distracted],
That they else-where might dart their injuries [can disappoint others]:
    Yet do not so, but since I am near slain,
    Kill me out-right with looks, and rid [eliminate] my pain.

In this sonnet Elizabeth is still prepared to excuse Essex for his treatment of her. She stills needs his affection. We can conclude that if the woman referred to as having "pretty looks" is Frances, this must be a relatively early sonnet, probably written in 1590. But we cannot be sure, since Essex had a number of sexual liaisons.

---

[1] Elizabeth may have acquired the literary trick of dividing her personality into two or more parts, each having its own thoughts and desires, from one of her favourite books, Anicus Boethius' *Consolation of Philosophy* (Watts 1969) which she translated from the Latin. Boethius, a scholar and former consul at Rome, was imprisoned in Pavia in about 524 A.D. and wrote down his imagined conversations with a character called Philosophy. This device enabled him to present two sides of his own philosophical musings in personalised form. Elizabeth's tutor Roger Ascham used the same device: writing to Elizabeth in 1567 he light-heartedly asked her to divide her personality into two so that one part (his friend) might intercede with the other (the Queen) to grant him a favour (Giles 1864, p. 152).

43. Flirting sonnets

Since saucy Jacks so happy are in this,
Give them thy fingers, me thy lips to kiss.

– Sonnet 128

I suggested in chapter 40 that sonnet 130 is a spoof of a poem by Thomas Watson. There are other light-hearted verses among the so-called Dark Lady sonnets. In sonnet 128 the poet describes how observing the touch of her lover's fingers on the keyboard of the virginals makes her wish that she could kiss the player's lips. The style is playful and flirtatious. The sonnet seems to belong to the carefree first flowering of the Elizabeth-Essex relationship, although we have no way of knowing for certain to whom it is addressed.

Sonnet 128
How oft when thou my music music play'st,
Upon that blessed wood whose motion sounds
With thy sweet fingers when thou gently sway'st,
The wiry concord that mine ear confounds,
Do I envy those Jacks [keys] that nimble leap,
To kiss the gentle inward of thy hand,
Whilst my poor lips which should that harvest reap,
At the woods' boldness by thee blushing stand.
To be so tickled they would change their state,
And situation with those dancing chips,
O'er whom thy fingers walk with gentle gait,
Making dead wood more blest than living lips,
 Since saucy Jacks so happy are in this,
 Give them thy fingers, me thy lips to kiss.

In contrast sonnets 135 and 136 are humorous in a rather self-conscious and laboured manner. They pun relentlessly on the name Will, which had several meanings in Elizabethan England, some of them sexual and denoting both the male and female reproductive organs[1]. One can imagine that these poems were written at court in a spirit of competition: how many times can the naughty word Will be included in a sonnet, while still retaining grammatical sense? Sonnet 135 wins with thirteen mentions, while sonnet 136 comes a poor second with only seven. The choice of William Shakespeare as Elizabeth's 'front' man would have made this poetic exercise particularly amusing to those in the know.

Both sonnets appear to have been written by a man, or as if by a man. The poet addresses a person whose will (vagina) is large and spacious (line 5) and wants the woman "to hide my will [penis] in thine" (line 6). In lines 11 and 12 he repeats the request: "add to thy *Will*, One will of mine to make thy large *Will* more." Whether the man's will was satisfied we will never know.

Sonnet 135
Who ever hath her wish, thou hast thy *Will*,
And *Will* to boot, and *Will* in over-plus,
More than enough am I that vex thee still,
To thy sweet will making addition thus.
Wilt thou whose will is large and spacious,
Not once vouchsafe to hide my will in thine,
Shall will in others seem right gracious,
And in my will no fair acceptance shine:
The sea all water, yet receives rain still,
And in abundance addeth to his store,
So thou being rich in *Will* add to thy *Will*,
One will of mine to make thy large *Will* more.
    Let no unkind, no fair beseechers kill,
    Think all but one, and me in that one *Will*.

The next sonnet begins by asking the addressee to imagine that if "I come near" think of me as thy Will – presumably this is a joke on Shakespeare's name. It would of course be no joke at all if the person coming close really was called Will.

Sonnet 136
If thy soul check thee that I come so near,
Swear to thy blind soul that I was thy *Will*,
And will thy soul knows is admitted there,
Thus far for love, my love-suit sweet fulfil.
Will, will fulfil the treasure of thy love,
I fill it full with wills, and my will one,
In things of great receipt with ease we prove,
Among a number one is reckon'd none.
Then in the number let me pass untold,
Though in thy store's account I one must be,
For nothing hold me, so it please thee hold,
That nothing me, a some-thing sweet to thee.
    Make but my name thy love, and love that still,
    And then thou lovest me for my name is *Will*.

The sexual innuendos in this sonnet are not subtle and would be immediately perceived by any Elizabethan or Jacobean. The poet not only plays on the meanings of the word "will" but also on the word "fulfil," giving the latter the sexual sense of "fill full". Lines 3 – 6 could be rewritten "my will [penis] is admitted as far as it can go, fulfilling my desire ('love-suit') but in doing so my penis will also fill full ('fulfil') your vagina ('the treasure of thy love'); I fill it full with desire ('wills') and my penis ('will')". In lines 8 and 9 there is further sexual word play with the words "none" and "nothing", meaning nought ("o") representing the vagina: "Then in the number [vagina] let me pass untold". And again in lines 11 and 12: "For nothing hold me . . . a some-thing sweet to thee". (The reader's imagination will supply the missing details.) Pretentious scholarly comment on these lines such as "they multiply the figures of multiple sense, paronomasia and antanaclasis, the more frenziedly the closer they get to sexual activity"[2] is amusing but unhelpful.

Whether these two sonnets about sexual intimacy were based on personal experience or were simply written for fun and stimulated by the excesses of erotic imaginations and a love of puns by the court intelligentsia cannot of course be decided. The reader must come to his or her own conclusion. If the two sonnets are playful exercises caution is required before assigning genders to their author or authors. We note, however, that there is nothing in these sonnets that can be interpreted as referring to a 'Dark Lady'.

Another erotic sonnet is sonnet 151. This is a decidedly male invention, with its reference to rising flesh: "rising at thy name doth point out thee, As his triumphant prize". It may have been written by Essex in the heady days when he was the Chosen One. Male authorship is indicated by the words of the last couplet: "I call, Her love, for whose dear love I rise and fall". The sonnet bears the hallmark of other poems attributed to Essex (sonnets 26, 109, 110 and 145): a succession of simple one- or two-line statements with predictable rhymes. We can conclude that this sonnet is an early effort by Essex, who in line 1 excuses sexual play on the grounds of his immaturity, and in line 8 brags that his noble inclinations ("nobler part") can't control his body's treason. This is further evidence that the relationship between Elizabeth and Essex may have been based on rather more than platonic admiration[3].

Sonnet 151
Love is too young to know what conscience is,
Yet who knows not conscience is borne of love,
Then gentle cheater [illicit partner] urge not my amiss [poor behaviour],
Lest guilty of my faults thy sweet self prove.
For thou betraying me, I do betray
My nobler part [principles] to my gross body's treason,
My soul doth tell my body [private parts] that he may,
Triumph in love, flesh stays no farther reason [doesn't respond to reason],
But rising at thy name doth point out thee,
As his triumphant prize, proud of this pride,
He is contented thy poor drudge to be
To stand in thy affairs, fall by thy side.
    No want of conscience hold it [It's not from lack of principles] that I call,
    Her love, for whose dear love I rise and fall.

In contrast to these amusing erotic sonnets, sonnet 129 stands alone as a diatribe against lust. For "lust" read 'sex'. Like the parody (sonnet 130) of Thomas Watson's poem, sonnet 129 is anti-romantic, but differs in being written in a heavy brutal style. There is no attempt to be humorous. The poet tells the reader that expenditure of "spirit" (the word may be read to mean both energy and semen) is wasteful (line 1). Lust is "Savage, extreme, rude, cruel, not to trust" (line 4). Lust is no sooner enjoyed than it is despised (line 5). Lust has no basis in reason (line 6): it produces bliss, but once achieved ("prov'd"), bliss is immediately followed by woe (line 11). Anticipation brings joy, but once the sexual act is over its joy is like the passing of a dream (line 12).

Sonnet 129
Th'expense of Spirit in a waste of shame
Is lust in action, and till action, lust
Is perjur'd, murd'rous, bloody full of blame,
Savage, extreme, rude [brutal], cruel, not to trust,
Enjoy'd no sooner but despised straight,
Past reason hunted, and no sooner had
Past reason hated as a swallowed bait,
On purpose laid to make the taker mad.
Mad in pursuit and in possession so,
Had, having, and in quest, to have extreme,
A bliss in proof [in the having] and prov'd [afterwards] a very woe[4],
Before a joy propos'd [anticipated] behind [but afterwards] a dream,
   All this the world well knows yet none knows well,
   To shun the heaven that leads men to this hell.

In this sonnet Elizabeth is apparently looking back with regret and disgust on episodes of physical lovemaking. These sexual adventures may have involved Essex, or possibly his stepfather, Robert Dudley, Earl of Leicester, who was thought by many contemporaries to be her youthful lover.

The final two poems in *Sonnets* are strangely impersonal. They are ostensibly based on ancient myths about the love-god Cupid and his helpful nymphs. Sonnet 154, the final poem, is reproduced below.

Sonnet 154
The little Love-God [Cupid] lying once a sleep,
Laid by his side his heart inflaming brand,
Whilst many Nymphs that vow'd chaste life to keep,
Came tripping by, but in her maiden hand,
The fairest votary took up that fire,
Which many Legions of true hearts had warm'd,
And so the General of hot desire [Cupid],
Was sleeping by a Virgin hand disarm'd.
This brand[5] she quenched in a cool Well by,
Which from love's fire took heat perpetual,
Growing a bath and healthy remedy,
For men diseased, but I my mistress' thrall [slave],
   Came there for cure and this by that I prove,
   Love's fire heats water, water cools not love.

These two highly stylised sonnets are more erotic than might appear on casual reading. The scholar Katherine Duncan-Jones (2010) pointed out that they are based on a six-line epigram in Greek by Mariano Scholasticus (a sixth century Byzantine poet) that appeared in a Latin publication in 1603[6]. But Duncan-Jones also noted that the two sonnets "seem closer to the Greek original than to any of the Latin or vernacular adaptations of it" so it seems likely that they were written before the appearance of the Latin publication, by someone acquainted with ancient Greek. Presumably Elizabeth enjoyed the challenge of writing two English versions of the Greek epigram.

* * *

Sonnets 127–154 have varied subject matter but, in contrast to those of the first group (1–126), they are mostly introspective and concerned with analysing the poet's thoughts and feelings about the darker side of Essex's character rather than analysing her changing relationship to Essex over time. They must have been written concurrently with many of the sonnets of the first group but are not in chronological order. It follows that the sonnets of the first group were deliberately selected to form a coherent chronological sequence, in order to describe the emotional history of the relationship, while those in the second, containing more intimate and introverted reflections, as well as several miscellaneous sonnets (some playful, some erotic, and some by Essex), were assembled in no apparent order as part two of the manuscript submitted to the printer, with the last two being deliberately placed to bring the sonnets to an apparently respectable and conventional close.

This interpretation of the so-called Dark Lady sonnets as poems describing the dark side of Essex's character is contrary to a long tradition. Over four centuries the Dark Lady has become a literary legend. That William Shakespeare, married to a woman eight years older than himself, to whom he left his second-best bed, lusted after a swarthy woman of dark complexion who was visually unattractive but who could satisfy his sexual urges seems to appeal to scholarly (and mostly male) imaginations. Who was this seductive dark and apparently ugly woman to whom the poet transferred his affections? Was she one of the Negro prostitutes known to be working in London in Shakespeare's time? Was she a dark-haired lady-in-waiting of the Queen? Or was she the Earl of Pembroke's mistress, Mary Fitton, possibly lampooned as Mistress Mal in *Twelfth Night*?[7]

The analysis presented here shows that these entertaining speculations are academic inventions with no basis in the sonnet texts. Scholars have been misled by Elizabeth's penetrating psychological analysis of her relationship with Essex, and her cleverness in disguising both her and his identity. For Queen Elizabeth blackness, personified as evil and female, symbolised all that was negative about Essex's flawed character. To interpret these sonnets correctly we must swap the gender of the poet's subject and pay attention to detail. The inescapable conclusion is that the Dark Lady so beloved by Shakespeare scholars never existed. 'Shakespeare's' legendary Dark Lady is just that – a myth.

---

[1] Partridge (1969, pp. 218–219).
[2] Burrow (2002, p.131).
[3] Devereux (1853a, p. 293) expressed similar thoughts in charmingly restrained language: "We have no way of showing how far the Earl was indebted to the passion of love for the influence he obtained over Elizabeth: but unquestionably her contemporaries did not consider her purity as quite unspotted".
[4] This line has been much discussed in the literature. Orgel (2002) provides a summary of editors' amendments. However, I suggest that the problem has been overstated. All that is required is an apostrophe in "proud" to ensure that it reads as "prov'd", which is almost certainly the correct reading (rather than "proud") because it links to "proof" earlier in the line. With this small clarification this and the following line can be read as considering both the before- and after-effects of yielding to lustful desire.
[5] Cupid's brand is quenched in a cool well, which doesn't extinguish it. In fact the brand causes the well to seek "heat perpetual", i.e., more of the same. The sexual innuendo is clear.
[6] Duncan-Jones (2010), p. 422.
[7] Burgess (1972), p. 148.

PART FIVE. THE BIG PICTURE

44. The "Heaven-Born Goddess"

All great truths begin as blasphemies.
— George Bernard Shaw

In Part 3 of this book I demonstrated that the plays traditionally assigned dates of composition after 1603, the year of Elizabeth's death, have been incorrectly considered as 'late' (i.e. Jacobean) creations by generations of commentators. Careful analysis of these so-called late plays shows that, contrary to centuries of assumptions, there is no evidence of 'Shakespeare's' hand in any play after 1603.

Some of the 'late' plays were originally short or unfinished (*Pericles*, *Henry VIII*, *Timon of Athens* and *The Two Noble Kinsmen*) and were added to by other authors. Others were complete but contain late (Jacobean) additions or modifications by another hand (*Macbeth* and *Measure for Measure*) but show no evidence of being worked on by 'Shakespeare' after 1603. *The Tempest*, long considered to be 'Shakespeare's' last play, is not sourced from William Strachey's unpublished account of a wreck on the coast of Bermuda. It is closer to sources available in the late 1580s, which also contain links to the play's South American references. *The Winter's Tale* also draws on sources available in the late sixteenth century.

The traditional arguments presented for the dependence of *Coriolanus* on William Camden's *Remaines of a Greater Work Concerning Britaine* (published in 1605) are flawed – the text and words in *Coriolanus* apparently derived from *Remaines* were available in earlier sources, and even if it is assumed that *Remaines* was a source, it should be noted that Camden was a teacher and his notes or drafts for *Remaines* are likely to have circulated before his book was published.

Sources, style and word choice all date *Cymbeline* to the sixteenth century rather than the early seventeenth. Although first published in 1609, *Troilus and Cressida* was listed in the *Stationers' Register* in 1603, and the sources used for the play indicate it was written around the turn of the century.

All's Well that Ends Well has a similar sombre tone to *Troilus and Cressida* and *Measure for Measure*. It contains no evidence of having been written in Jacobean times.

The short play *Timon of Athens* contains themes in common with *King Lear* and is likely to have been written before the latter play and then abandoned. All sources used in *Anthony and Cleopatra* were available in the late sixteenth century and the widely-held assumption that the play was written in the years 1606–1607 has no firm foundation.

Several of the texts of the so-called 'late' plays (e.g., *All's Well that Ends Well*, *Anthony and Cleopatra*, and *Timon of Athens*) are in a state unsuited for stage production. They either have ambiguous speech prefixes, or plot notes apparently inserted by the author, or vague stage directions, or entrances for 'ghost' characters who say nothing and are superfluous to the plot. These deficiencies make the plays unstageable in their First Folio form and indicate that they are unlikely to have been written by a professional actor or to have been staged before 1623.

Why a playwright, who depended for his living on not only writing but staging plays, would have taken the trouble to write but then hold back plays from the stage has never been satisfactorily explained. Equally puzzling is 'Shakespeare's' apparent willingness to cooperate with second-rate authors such as Thomas Middleton and George Wilkins to complete plays, shortly after writing masterpieces such as *Hamlet* and *King Lear*. These troubling issues, studiously ignored by orthodox academic commentators, disappear if Elizabeth's authorship is assumed. We can conclude that at her death she left behind a collection of plays, some already published, some short but complete, some unfinished, and some completed but not released for staging because of their sensitive subject matter. These plays were released (possibly on her instructions) in about 1608 or 1609, along with the *Sonnets* manuscript. Minor authors attempted to 'complete' the shorter plays and edit others, with variable success. Some editors inserted topical references likely to appeal to King James and Jacobean audiences.

Hamlet is undoubtedly an Elizabethan play. But it is of special interest because an early printed edition, known as Q2, contains signs of being based on Elizabeth's manuscript: words beginning with c are frequently capitalised, and it is significant that the capitalisation of c where this letter begins a word within a line of poetry or text is a unique feature of Elizabeth's handwriting.

Importantly, much of the subject matter of the apparently 'late' plays mentioned above and considered in detail in Part 3 corresponds in many ways with the ups and downs of the Elizabeth-Essex relationship, or other historical Elizabethan (rather than Jacobean) events, as does the subject matter of the truly late plays like *Hamlet* and *King Lear*, and earlier plays such as *Romeo and Juliet* and *The Taming of the Shrew*.

* * *

If a new theory is correct, it will explain a multitude of minor details as well as major observations. If, on the contrary, we find that the minor details cannot be accommodated, the new theory may be invalid or require revision. Likewise, the Elizabeth-Essex hypothesis, if correct, should help explain all sorts of curious observations about Shakespeare and his works that have puzzled academics for decades, if not centuries.

A minor example, noted in the previous chapter, is the closeness of the last two sonnets to the Greek text on which they are based[1]. William Shakespeare probably did not know Greek, at least not well enough to bother to translate the Greek of a sixth century poet. (Ben Jonson remarked on Shakespeare's "small Latin and less Greek".) If we believe that William Shakespeare wrote the last two sonnets, we need to construct a train of speculation: a colleague of Shakespeare's brought the Greek originals to his attention; then someone translated them for him; and then he wrote sonnets in a formal antique style, incorporating their ancient ideas. All of this could have happened, but there is absolutely no proof that any of it did.

There is no problem in explaining how sonnets 153 and 154 were written if we assume royal authorship – Elizabeth had been writing and reading Greek since her early teens. Of course, this example, in isolation, does not carry much weight. It does not prove that Elizabeth wrote *Sonnets*. But it is just one of many pointers indicating that the theory propounded in this book may have merit.

When many unexplained issues (like the above issue concerning Shakespeare's knowledge of Greek) can be resolved by adopting a new theory or way of thinking the *principle of cumulative evidence* becomes relevant. In 1876 the Shakespeare scholar W. Spalding was the first to apply this principle to authorship issues: "numerous probabilities all tending the same way are sufficient to generate positive certainty"[2]. Put simply, the principle states that many small pieces of evidence, all indicative of the same interpretation, acquire significance even though individually they appear to have slight importance. This principle may seem commonplace and obvious now but has not always been accepted.

Let's explore the application of this principle to *Sonnets*, using vocabulary as our example. Every author uses vocabulary and images that reflect his or her background and experience. Jane Austen's vocabulary reflects her close acquaintance with the way of life of the lesser landed gentry in early nineteenth century England; Joseph Conrad's his knowledge of ships and seafaring; Robert Frost's his immersion in New Hampshire country life; and A. B. 'Banjo' Patterson's his close acquaintance with the Australian bush. It is almost impossible to fake such personal experience.

If we cast aside what we have learnt about Shakespeare and what innumerable biographers have written (and endlessly repeated), and imagine we are reading *Sonnets* for the very first time, what would we conclude about their author? Undoubtedly, we would conclude that the poet was exceedingly well read in classical literature. Not only is the form of the poems based on a tradition beginning with Petrarch, but the poems also contain numerous references and allusions to the works of Homer, Ovid, Plutarch and other classical authors, as well as to the works of Elizabethan poets.

Without a doubt we would also guess that the poet was an aristocrat – most of the subject matter concerns members of the privileged class, their activities, associates, pastimes and possessions. We read of stringed instruments (8), the virginals (a precursor of the harpsichord) (128), hawks, hounds and hunting (91), paintings (16, 24, 46, 47 and 48), jewels (48, 52 and 96), other poets (21, 32, 78, 79, 80, 82, 83, 85, 86 and 106), lawyers and legal procedures (4, 35, 49, 125 and 126), and above all lords, knights, ladies, queens, kings and princes (25, 29, 55, 63, 78, 87, 94, 96, 106 and 114). The words sovereign, crown, majesty and monarch are frequently used (33, 57, 107, 114, 115, 126 and 153). We also read of travel on horseback, overseas journeys, personal danger, mistresses and sexual liaisons. It was only the very rich elite (the aristocrats of Elizabethan England) who could afford hawks and hounds, paintings, mistresses, jewels and musical instruments, and had the leisure to enjoy them.

A stringed instrument, generally agreed to be the lute, is mentioned in sonnet 8. The phrase "one string, sweet husband to another" probably refers to the paired strings of this instrument vibrating sympathetically. In sonnet 128 the poet refers to the action of the jacks and keys when playing the virginals.

Elizabeth was musical and played both the lute and the virginals. On one occasion in 1559, when on the Thames in her barge, she spied Baron Breneur, ambassador of the Archduke Charles in another boat and had her boat draw alongside his so that she could serenade him with her lute playing. On another occasion the Scottish ambassador, Sir James Melville, was permitted to listen to her playing the virginals. She remarked to him that "she used not to play before men, but when she was solitary, to shun melancholy"[3].

The mention in the sonnets of two instruments that Elizabeth played could of course be coincidental, but on the other hand, it would be perfectly natural for Elizabeth to include in her poems metaphors and images based on instruments with which she was familiar, and which she loved playing. There is no evidence that Shakespeare possessed, or was familiar with, these instruments. We can therefore add this observation to our inventory of relatively minor evidence supporting Elizabeth's authorship.

There are references to the seasons, weather and flowers in the sonnets, but these are no more than those expected from any Elizabethan, for even in big cities like London the bigger houses had gardens (as they still do), and the countryside could be reached in a morning stroll. With rare exceptions, such as the reference to a housewife chasing chickens in sonnet 143, and the hand of the dyer in sonnet 111, there are no allusions to everyday work.

One might argue that courtly vocabulary does not prove royal authorship. But it is significant that this vocabulary is dominant and seems to flow naturally from the poet's pen – there is no evidence to suggest that courtly references have been 'dropped into' sonnets in an attempt to give them aristocratic colour. The vocabulary of the country farmhouse and rural trades is all but absent, which strongly suggests that the sonnets were not written by a provincial Warwickshire countryman.

Also intriguing is the absence in the historical record of communications between Shakespeare and other literary or theatrical colleagues, or between him and courtly associates with literary interests. When a commoner gains high status, state papers normally provide some sort of record – witness the documented rise of Chaucer or that of Thomas Wolsey, later Cardinal Wolsey. In the case of Shakespeare there is no record that he moved in aristocratic social circles, or indeed (surprisingly) that he moved in literary circles. Such a total absence of evidence of literary communications with colleagues or officials is almost beyond belief.

Aristocrats or royalty have much greater opportunity and power than commoners to conceal facts from the public. Diana Price[4] explained how a privileged author (whom she insists on describing as a "gentleman"), by depending on a combination of discretion and respect from his circle of acquaintances, might keep the secrets of his personal life hidden. To illustrate the point, she described how President Kennedy's numerous sexual liaisons and Roosevelt's severe physical disability were concealed from the public:

> Just as the Secret Service and the press corps did not broadcast the facts about Kennedy or Roosevelt, Shakespeare's professional colleagues did not write explicitly about a gentleman [sic] dramatist in their midst. Their discretion suggests that they held Shakespeare at a respectful distance, safe from the taint of the literary, theatrical and publishing professions.

Although Elizabeth could depend on her close acquaintances and advisors to keep confidences, her power to control the flow of information was no doubt less outside the confines of the court, in the publishing world of people seeking a saleable story, exchanging news and gossip, and not averse to poking fun at the establishment. Getting her poems printed and published risked revealing her authorship, for she required the cooperation of middlemen outside her normal aristocratic circle: a scribe to make a fair copy; a plausible and trustworthy 'front man' (Shakespeare); a publisher; a courier to negotiate with the publisher and deliver a manuscript; a typesetter and printer; and a bookseller.

During or after publication artisans, actors and literary people outside the court may have known or guessed from whose head, heart and hand the words of *Shakespeare's Sonnets* were coming. They may have had a shrewd idea that the actor, theatre shareholder, landowner and tax-evader

Shakespeare, who they might have met backstage, on London's streets, or in a tavern, was incapable of writing the immortal lines published by Thomas Thorpe. The disparity between the portrayal of the poet in the sonnets as a passionate old person obsessed with a beautiful young man and their actual knowledge of Shakespeare as a staid middle-aged businessman chiefly concerned with turning a profit[5] may have also encouraged authorship speculation.

Price[6] suggested that several literary Elizabethans did know the Shakespeare secret, and among these were the writers Thomas Edwardes, John Weever, John Davies and Henry Chettle.

In 1595 Thomas Edwardes wrote rather clumsily written verses praising several Elizabethan poets. Each poet is introduced by a nickname or a recognisable character in his poems: for example, *Collyn* refers to Edmund Spenser, *Rosamund* to Samuel Daniel, *Amintas* to Thomas Watson, *Leander* to Marlowe and *Adon* (*Adonis*) to Shakespeare. Edwardes' stilted lines[7] about Shakespeare (in modernised spelling) read as follows:

> Adon [Adonis] deftly masking through
> Stately troupes rich conceited,
> Show'd he well deserved to
> Loves delight on him to gaze
> And had not love herself entreated,
> Other nymphs had sent him bays [bay-leaf garlands].
>
> Eke[8] [also] in purple robes distain'd [displayed],
> Amidst the Centre of this clime,
> I have heard say doth remain,
> One whose power floweth far,
> That should have been of our rhyme
> The only object and the star.
>
> Well could his bewitching pen,
> Done the Muses objects to us
> Although he differs much from men,
> Tilting under Friaries,
> Yet his golden art might woo us
> To have honoured him with bays.

The mention of *Adon*[is] in the first verse refers to 'Shakespeare's' popular publication *Venus and Adonis* and demonstrates that Edwardes is indeed referring to 'Shakespeare'. Some commentators, perplexed by verses two and three, suggest that these verses refer to another author, but the fact that no other author is named, and that these verses are linked to verse one by the word "eke" [also], tells us that all three verses refer to the same poet, the *Adon* or *Adonis* of the first verse. Several phrases in these verses make us suspect that Edwardes knew something unusual about 'Shakespeare', but was only able to refer to it obliquely:

- Adonis is described as being dressed in *purple*, a royal colour[9].
- "Love herself" entreated that Adonis should not be honoured. (Note the choice of words: "herself" not "itself".)
- 'Shakespeare' is described as being at the *Centre of this clime* (the centre of this country or region or universe).
- Edwardes writes that a powerful person whom he cannot mention by name should have received his praise: *One whose power floweth far, That should have been . . . The only object and the star* of his adulatory verses.
- He writes that 'Shakespeare' *differs much from men Tilting under Friaries*. (As the hall at Blackfriars was in use as a theatre in 1595, these lines can be interpreted to mean either that 'Shakespeare' is not a man, or that he differs in some respect from actors on the stage ("men tilting") at Blackfriars, or that both interpretations apply, i.e., 'Shakespeare' is neither a man nor an actor.)
- Edwardes implies that there seems to be some doubt about whether Shakespeare is actually the appropriate subject for his praise: his golden art *might* make us honour him with garlands of bay leaves.

In relation to what we know about Shakespeare the actor, the above six references make no sense at all, and academic commentators quietly ignore the issues they raise. But we have to ask the question, why should Edwardes deliberately have written gobbledygook about the man who was, at the time, apparently in the process of establishing a successful literary and stage career and beginning to dominate the London literary scene? If the lines seem to be gobbledygook when applied to our traditional image of the man Shakespeare the obvious conclusion is that either they refer to someone else, or Edwardes just enjoyed stringing together words to construct lines without meaning. Assuming that no serious poet would do the latter, do Edwardes' lines make sense if applied to someone else?

The answer is yes, they make very good sense. If they are applied to Elizabeth I the meaning of all the references becomes clear. (Remember the notion previously presented, that if a new idea is correct, annoying 'loose ends' that have defied explanation will often be tidied up.) While perusing Edwardes' six dot points above we should note that:

- Elizabeth was royal, therefore the reference to *purple robes* is appropriate.
- Elizabeth undoubtedly was happy for her poems to be attributed to Shakespeare, but through official channels probably discouraged any

fêting of him as a distinguished author – too much attention might have revealed inconsistencies which would have blown her cover.
- The court in London was, without a doubt, the political heart of England, and London was just beginning its growth into an international commercial centre. If an Englishman (or woman) in Elizabethan England had been asked 'who would you nominate for the honour of being at the *Centre of this clime* [country]?' undoubtedly the answer would have been Elizabeth I.
- Elizabeth's power and influence were strong and firmly established after the defeat of the Spanish Armada in 1588, so the description *One whose power floweth far* was an appropriate and accurate description to apply to her.
- Elizabeth was a woman and from a superior social class to the actors at Blackfriars, so the phrase *differs much from men Tilting* [acting] *under Friaries* is also appropriate.
- And lastly, there was a good reason why people might not present Shakespeare with the garlands of bays traditionally presented to outstanding poets – he was an actor and a businessman, not a poet – he did not deserve the honour.

Let's now look at John Weever's contribution. John Weever also wrote a poem in 1595. It was an epigram entitled *Ad Gulielmum* [William] *Shakespeare*. The first four lines of his fourteen-line poem[10] are:

Honey-tongu'd *Shakespeare*, when I saw thine issue [poems],
I swore *Apollo* got [begot/created] them and none other,
Their rosy-tainted [tinted] features cloth'd in tissue,
Some heaven-born goddess said to be their mother.

The lines are ambiguous, and probably deliberately so. Notice the points that Weever makes: a goddess is the mother of Shakespeare's works[11] and the works are rose tinted and "cloth'd in tissue", suggesting concealment and disguise.

In 1595 there was only one woman in England who people described as a goddess and associated with roses and that was Elizabeth I[12], who was variously identified with the goddesses Diana and Cynthia. Then we have the phrase "honey-tongu'd Shakespeare" to consider. As I explain below, honey-tongued was a pejorative term widely used to denote insincerity or dishonesty in Elizabethan writing and in court circles.

John Davies of Hereford is the third author mentioned by Diana Price. In 1610 Davies published his book *The Scourge of Folly* containing an epigram about Shakespeare, entitled *To our English Terence Mr. Will. Shake-speare*:

Some say (good *Will*) which I, in sport, do sing
    Had'st thou not played some Kingly parts in sport,
Thou had'st been a companion for a *King*;
And, been a King among the meaner sort.
Some others rail; but, rail as they think fit,
Thou hast no railing, but a reigning Wit:
    And honesty *thou sow'st, which they do reap,*
    So, to increase their Stock *which they do keep*[13].

This epigram is yet another example of an author pretending to pay a compliment, but actually sending his readers an obscure message. Let's look at the intended (cryptic) meaning. In the epigram's title Davies compares Shakespeare to Terence, a Roman dramatist suspected of taking the credit for others' works. He writes that he is only addressing "good Will" in sport, i.e. he is only jesting. So we must conclude that his comments are really directed at someone else. Davies also says that his good Will has been (or could have been?) a companion for a King. The three references to royalty and the mention of "reigning wit" are the clues enabling readers to identify the true addressee. Then we have the last two lines to consider. In modern English they could be written 'Shakespeare has produced and publicised ("sow'st") the texts attributed to him, but the credit ("Stock") for these belongs elsewhere'.

Let's now look again at the writings of Henry Chettle whom we first met in chapter 3 in which I described the skirmish he had with authority as a result of his publishing Robert Greene's *Groatsworth of Wit*. Henry Chettle wasn't the sort of person to be cowed by the establishment. After Elizabeth's death on 24 March 1603 he wrote these lines[14] complaining that Shakespeare had not written any tribute to his late sovereign:

Nor doth the silver-tongued *Melicert*,
Drop from his honeyed muse one sable tear
To mourn her death that graced his desert,
And to his lays penned her Royal ear
Shepherd [Poet], remember our *Elizabeth*,
And sing her Rape, done by that *Tarquin*, Death.

That Chettle wrote this complaint at all is curious – why didn't he just drop by at Shakespeare's lodgings and remind the busy actor of his obligations to his late sovereign? I conclude that he wanted to score a point – he wanted to embarrass Shakespeare in public. I suggest that Chettle was taking an opportunity to poke fun at the establishment (a favourite occupation of his) because he knew that Shakespeare was only a front man for the royal author, and not up to the job of writing a decent eulogy.

Chettle was a master of innuendo. The reference to Tarquin of *The Rape of Lucrece* tells us that the name Melicert stands for Shakespeare, but why did Chettle choose this obscure name from Greek mythology to describe the man supposed to be England's premier writer? C. Ingleby[15] suggested that Chettle's reason was that Melicert rhymed with desert. This suggestion is naïve. Previous use of the name Melicert in contemporary literature indicates that Chettle had more reason than rhyme in mind. For example, the author Robert Greene used the mythological name Melicert to describe a poet who is in dispute with Menaphon (probably representing Greene himself) for the leadership of the shepherds (poets). In his romance *Menaphon* (1589) Greene wrote:

> "What needs that question?" quoth Menaphon, "am I not the King's shepherd [poet], and chief of all the bordering swains [poets] of Arcadia [the literary community]?" "I grant [I agree with you]" quoth Melicertus, "but am I not a Gentleman, though attired in a shepherd's [poet's] skincoat [rough clothing]; superior to thee by birth, though equal now in profession?"

Greene's Menaphon boasts that he is the King's poet, to which Melicert replies that he himself (Melicert) is a gentleman, although he is disguised as a poet; and although he is superior to Menaphon by birth, professionally they are equals. Chettle in 1603 has essentially reiterated Greene's 1589 assertion that the poet Melicertus is a disguised gentleman. I suggest that Chettle has re-used Greene's character Melicert quite deliberately, to imply that the name Shakespeare masks the identity of a poet from a superior class.

But the name Melicert is also intrinsically significant. Literally it means "honey cutter". The association of Shakespeare's name with honey or sweet things is surprisingly common in Elizabethan literature. Several contemporary writers referred to Shakespeare's honeyed or sugared writings. The student play sequence *The Return from Parnassus* lampoons Shakespeare (and other poets) and refers to "sweet Mr. Shakespeare" or "sweet Master Shakespeare" three times[16]. Francis Meres wrote in 1598 that "the sweet and witty soul of Ovid lives in mellifluous and honey-tongued Shakespeare". And as mentioned above, in 1595 John Weever wrote of Shakespeare's "honey-tongu'd" poetry.

Without knowledge of Elizabethan vocabulary, one might assume that the term honey-tongued and similar phrases were intended to be complimentary. But to describe someone as honey-tongued in Elizabethan times was equivalent to describing them as a "sweet talker" today – the phrase denoted insincerity, dissemblance or even lying. For example, in *The Winter's Tale* (Act 2, scene 2) Paulina says "If I be honey-mouth'd, let my tongue blister" [If I'm not telling the truth, let my tongue blister][17]; in *Love's Labours Lost* (Act 5, scene 2), the King of Navarre, referring to a nobleman described as "honey-tongued Boyet", exclaims "A blister on his sweet tongue!"[18] [Damn his insincere talk!]; and Philip Sidney, in his *Apology for Poetry*, described "honey-flowing eloquence" as being an affectation.

We can conclude that when Chettle associated the name Melicert with Shakespeare and described Shakespeare's muse as "honeyed" he was not being complimentary. Far from it. Like Weever and the anonymous author of the Parnassus plays (and probably Meres too) he was implying that Shakespeare was a fraud.

Finally let us turn the clock back to the events described in chapter 3 and 'Shakespeare's' unplanned public debut in the literary dispute of 1592, which involved Henry Chettle in his publishing role.

In 1592 Chettle published Robert Greene's *A Groatsworth of Wit*, a pamphlet purporting to be the writings of the dying and destitute author and playwright. In chapter 3 I quoted Greene's famous but ambiguous attack on rival actors/authors. Most scholars agree that this is the first reference to Shakespeare (the "Shake-scene" mentioned in the pamphlet) by a jealous literary colleague.

The pamphlet contains the phrase "Tiger's heart wrapped in a Player's hide", which is Greene's parody of 'Shakespeare's' line "O tiger's heart wrapped in a Woman's hide" uttered by Richard, Duke of York in the play now known as *Henry VI Part 3*:

> Base-minded men all three of you, if by my misery you be not warned . . . for there is an upstart Crow, beautified with our feathers, that with his *Tiger's heart wrapped in a Player's hide*, supposes he is as well able to bombast out a blank verse as the best of you: and being an absolute *Johannes factotum* [Jack-of-all-trades], is in his own conceit the only Shake-scene in a country.

Conventional academic wisdom regards Greene's outburst as an attack on actors like Shakespeare who considered they could write, and who put qualified academics like Greene himself out of a job. Researchers cite the outburst as evidence that by 1592 Shakespeare had made his mark in the London theatre and ruffled the feathers of existing writers. This interpretation, repeated in countless standard biographies, plays on our romantic desire to identify with an underdog hero who beats the odds – in this case a bright young man from the country who takes on the literary establishment in London and wins.

However, a question conveniently ignored by biographers is why Greene's statement about a nonentity from the provinces should have caused such a stir. For in 1592 neither *Venus and Adonis* nor *The Rape of Lucrece* had been published and Shakespeare's name had not appeared in print on any of his works. By this date Shakespeare had only just begun his career as an actor/playwright in the crowded London theatre scene and was unlikely to have been widely known.

I suggest the significance of Greene's words, and the reason why they caused such a stir at the time (to the extent that Chettle had to apologise to persons of high rank), is not that they constituted an attack on Shakespeare as an upstart actor who thought he could write, but that they constituted an attack on Shakespeare as an actor fronting for the writings of someone else.

The key words supporting this interpretation are contained in Greene's deliberate misquote "Tiger's heart wrapped in a Player's hide" for the original "Tiger's heart wrapped in a Woman's hide". Significantly, Greene has chosen a 'Shakespearean' line insinuating subterfuge and disguise. And, highly significantly, he also equates his word "player" to the original word "woman": *player* equals *woman*. Did Greene know, or had he guessed, that the actor Shakespeare was a front man for a woman writer? Had someone informed him of the new writer's true identity?

We can be pretty sure that Greene knew that Shakespeare was a fraud, because three years earlier, in *Menaphon* (see discussion above) he had already indicated that Melicertus was a gentleman disguised as a shepherd (read 'poet'). In his "upstart Crow" text Greene had touched upon the truth and his inflammatory diatribe, published by Henry Chettle, produced an instant reaction at court. Elizabeth I would have been furious that her carefully prepared cover was at risk of being revealed to all and sundry. How ignominious it would have been for a monarch to be associated with playwriting, and exposed by the dissolute author Greene to boot! She would have pulled rank immediately. Court officials or their delegates acting on instructions (the "divers of worship" mentioned in Chettle's apology) are likely to have sprung into action and to have ordered the publisher Henry Chettle, in no uncertain terms, to retract Greene's offensive insinuation.

We can conclude that Chettle didn't apologise because Greene's attack had offended Shakespeare. Who in court would have cared a jot whether the unknown Warwickshire countryman was offended? He apologised because he had offended the Queen – an infinitely more serious offence. The court, and by implication Elizabeth, reacted strongly in order to quash damaging speculation about royal authorship once and for all.

But Chettle had the last laugh. It seems that he could not resist a chance to needle the establishment and annoy William Shakespeare in the process. In 1603, under the guise of writing a tribute to his late sovereign, he cheekily pointed out to Shakespeare and the world that the supposedly great author had not written the expected eulogy in praise of the recently deceased queen: "Shepherd, remember our Elizabeth".

As far as we know Shakespeare never did write the expected eulogy. We can assume that he didn't have the ability. So Chettle made his point. But his contemporaries didn't notice, or didn't care – the glorious Elizabethan age was over.

---

[1] Duncan-Jones (2010, p. 422).
[2] Spalding (1876).

3 Donaldson (1969, p. 68).
4 Price (2001).
5 This is the impression one gains from reading about the activities of Shakespeare in Stratford, as documented by Schoenbaum (1981).
6 Price (2001, p. 226).
7 For an accessible version in the original spelling see Ingleby et al. (1932, p. 25).
8 Eke is an old English word for additional or also, as in ekename (nickname); cf. Dutch *ook*.
9 Following the royal tradition, Elizabeth wore purple velvet when she rode into London on 28 November 1558 to assume power after the death of Queen Mary.
10 Ingleby et al. (1932, p. 24).
11 The writer of the preface to *Troilus and Cressida* expressed a similar sentiment: 'Shakespeare's' comedies "seem . . . to be born in that sea which brought forth *Venus*" (chapter 28).
12 Strong (1987).
13 Ingleby et al. (1932, p. 219).
14 Ingleby et al. (1932, p. 123).
15 Ingleby et al. (1932, p. 123). These authors point out that the poem is technically anonymous and undated, but it is printed with an account of Elizabeth's funeral (1603) signed "Hen: Chetle".
16 Ingleby et al. (1932, pp. 67–68). The Parnassus plays were performed by students of St John's College, Cambridge between 1598 and 1602 (Edmondson and Wells (2013, p. 77). They were printed by George Eld for John Wright in 1606.
17 Pafford (1963, p. 42). See also note 18 below.
18 Although, according to Hunter (2009, p. 37), the word 'sweet' was "one of the most generally ridiculed affectations of courtly language", in the sonnets the adjective is used numerous times (one could say over-used) to describe persons, almost invariably as a term of endearment (e.g. "sweet self" (1, 4, 13), "sweet husband" (8), "sweet love" (29, 76), "sweet graces" (78) etc.). In 'Shakespeare's' other works it is used in a negative sense chiefly when referring to insincere talk. Clearly its meaning depends strongly on context: contrast our present usage of sweet in "she's a sweet little girl" and "he's a really sweet talker".

45. A Lover's Complaint

Some beauty peeped through lattice of sear'd age
– A Lover's Complaint, stanza 2

At this point I would like to divert readers' attention to the lesser-known and little-studied work by 'Shakespeare' that was published with *Sonnets*, entitled *A Lover's Complaint*. Is this neglected poem also relevant to the Elizabeth-Essex hypothesis?

In Thorpe's 1609 publication *A Lover's Complaint* follows *Sonnets*. It is a pseudo-pastoral narrative[1] of forty-seven verses about a woman of "sear'd age", still showing signs of past beauty, who has been deceived by (and lost her virginity to) a young man of fair complexion, whose "qualities were as beauteous as his form". Because of its narrative structure and apparently lower quality than the sonnets several commentators have doubted that the poem was written by 'Shakespeare'. The most recent dissenting voice was that of Brian Vickers[2] who argued that vocabulary similarities of *A Lover's Complaint* and the writings of John Davies of Hereford prove that Davies was *Complaint*'s author. In a short but comprehensive review Jackson[3] acknowledged that there are some apparent links to Davies' works if *Complaint* and Davies' work are considered in isolation. However, Jackson showed that the links between *Complaint* and 'Shakespeare's' other works that he considered as belonging to the same period of composition (especially *Cymbeline*, but also *Coriolanus* and *Measure for Measure*)[4] are much stronger. Readers may read Jackson's review for the detailed evidence. His summary statement on the last page of his review is worth quoting, because it clinches the argument that 'Shakespeare' wrote the *A Lover's Complaint*:

> . . . altogether at least fifteen [rare] words link the *Complaint* to Shakespearean plays first published/performed 1598/1614 or to sonnets in the Quarto entitled *Shakespeare's Sonnets* (1609) and to not more than one non-Shakespearean work. These fifteen words are used thirty-one times by Shakespeare within this period and only six times by all the other writers of poetry, drama or prose [in the same period], and never by John Davies of Hereford.

Here is it sufficient to say that Jackson's argument that 'Shakespeare' wrote *A Lover's Complaint* is overwhelming – we can rest assured that this poem is part of the 'Shakespeare' canon. A synopsis of the story told in *A Lover's Complaint* (see below) will establish whether the poem has any relevance to interpreting *Shakespeare's Sonnets*.

* * *

Sitting on a riverbank an old woman tells her tale of woe to a country parson. Their conversation is overheard by a third person who notes down what he/she hears. (One never knows who might be loitering on riverbanks with a pencil and notepad.)

On reading the first few stanzas Jacobean readers might have been surprised to discover that the complaining lover is female, not male – overturning the poetic convention of the times. Although the poem purports to be a simple country tale (the woman is described as wearing a straw hat), it is actually about courtly love. The woman has received numerous letters, jewels and rings of ivory and gold from her seducer – not the usual gifts one would give to a shepherdess. Sitting by the river she tears up his letters and throws the fragments and his costly gifts into the water.

Lines 36–49
A thousand favours from a maund [basket] she drew,
Of amber, crystal and of beaded [inlaid] jet,
Which one by one she in a river threw,
Upon whose weeping margin she was set;
Like usury applying wet to wet,
Or monarch's hands that let not bounty fall
Where want cries some, but where excess begs all.

Of folded schedules [written sheets] had she many a one,
Which she perused, sighed, tore and gave the flood,
Crack'd many a ring of posied gold and bone [ivory],
Bidding them find their sepulchres in mud;
Found yet more letters sadly penn'd in blood,
With sleided [threads of] silk feat and affectedly
Enswath'd and seal'd to curious secrecy.

In the following stanzas she recalls that the young man told her he had received "deep-brained sonnets" as well as pearls, rubies, diamonds, emeralds, sapphires and opals from many other admirers, but he swore his other conquests only resulted from lust ("errors of the blood"), not love. He stated that even a nun gave him gifts:

Lines 232–233
Lo, this device was sent me from a Nun,
Or Sister sanctified, of holiest note;

Although this holy woman initially "kept cold distance" from the young man he persisted to his own advantage:

Lines 247–249
The accident which brought me to her eye
Upon the moment did her force [resistance] subdue;
And now she would the caged cloister fly:

Did she fly from the cloister into his arms? Lines 260–264 tell us:

My parts had power to charm a sacred Sun [Nun?],
Who disciplin'd, ay, dieted in grace,
Believ'd her eyes when they [the man's parts] t'assail begun,
All vows and consecrations giving place [way]:

Such a story might have been a warning to a less susceptible woman. But the riverbank woman was very susceptible: the young man implored her to take the jewels he has received from other women, if she will give him her hand (and more). Enticed either by the precious stones or starved of sex, and despite his bragging about seducing a nun, she succumbs. She describes how she relented (took off "her white stole of chastity" and "sober guards") and gave in to his desires:

Lines 295–301
For, lo, his passion, but an art of craft,
Even there resolv'd my reason into tears;
There my white stole of chastity I daff'd [doffed, took off],
Shook off my sober guards and civil fears;
Appear to him, as he to me appears,
All melting; though our drops this diff'rence bore,
His poison'd me, and mine did him restore.

He abandons her. She sums up how she was deceived:

Lines 316–329
Thus merely with the garment [appearance] of a Grace
The naked [brazen] and concealed fiend he cover'd,
That th'unexperient [So that the naïve person] gave the tempter place,
Which, like a Cherubin, above them hover'd.
Who, young and simple, would not be so lover'd?
Ay me! I fell; and yet do question make
What I should do again for such a sake [If I could have reacted differently].

'O, that infected moisture of his eye,
O, that false fire which in his cheek so glow'd,
O, that forced thunder from his heart did fly,
O, that sad breath his spongy lungs bestow'd,
O, all that borrow'd motion, seeming ow'd,
Would [Could] yet again betray the fore-betray'd [betray me again],
And new pervert a reconciled [acquiescent] maid.'

Here the tale ends, without resolution. The poet makes no moral judgement. We are not told what happened to the seducer or the seduced.

* * *

In isolation the poem seems unremarkable. It is written in an archaic pastoral style reminiscent of the poems of Spenser and seems contrived and conventional[6]. It is ignored by some orthodox Shakespeareans as it seems to be of inferior quality to *Sonnets* and to bear little relevance to it. Few scholars have directly linked its subject matter to that of *Sonnets*, treating it only as a literary curiosity that has, for some reason, been published in the same book.

In the light of the Elizabeth-Essex hypothesis its significance is obvious – it sums up and repeats the message of *Sonnets* in beguiling simplicity and with no swapping of genders: an older woman has been wronged, when younger, by a fair young man who has seduced other women of rank or virtue. Like Essex, the young man is a good horseman: "Well could he ride and often men would say That horse his mettle from his rider takes". He is essentially a con artist – he presents himself as fair and true but is actually evil. The woman on the riverbank has been deceived by his charming manner and persistence (like the nun before her). Although she is aware of his previous amorous conquests she cannot resist his advances.

A point of difference is that in *A Lover's Complaint* the loss of the woman's virginity is described as explicitly as the mores of the time allowed, but in the sonnets the references to having sex are ambiguous, if we accept that the 'Will' sonnets (135 and 136) were written as humorous poetic exercises. In both *Sonnets* and reason prevails too late to prevent personal tragedy, and regret follows. In both texts there is no personal resolution and no decisive emotional judgement. In *A Lover's Complaint* there is no analysis and we are left with the impression that the author is simply content to report observations: this is the way of the world and how men and women relate; how love and seduction work; how pleasures experienced lead to feelings of regret.

In literary terms the poem is a coda to *Sonnets*. The subject matter indicates a link to the Elizabeth-Essex relationship, and the validity of this link is strengthened by the c. 1600 date for the poem deduced from vocabulary studies[7]. The date links the composition of *A Lover's Complaint* to sonnets 113–126: like *A Lover's Complaint* these late sonnets reassess Elizabeth's affection (love?) for Essex. Because *A Lover's Complaint* relates the story of the Elizabeth-Essex relationship in relatively simple language obscured by an archaic poetic structure and style scholars have overlooked its significance.

1 In 1591 Edward Spenser published a contrived pastoral poem about a woman "sorrowfully wailing" beside a riverbank in his volume *Complaints*. Like *A Lover's Complaint*, Spenser's poem consists of seven-line stanzas, and the later poem may have copied the structure and some of the conventions of the earlier one.
2 Vickers (2007).
3 Jackson (2008) summarises the debate. Among the distinguished scholars who find evidence that 'Shakespeare' did not author *Complaint* are Tarlinskaja (2005) and Vickers (2007). The latter's arguments are the most detailed of the negative school, though not the most comprehensive. Among those who find evidence that 'Shakespeare' did author *Complaint* are Kerrigan (1996), Duncan-Jones (2010), Burrow (2002) and Jackson (2008) himself. Jackson's detailed analyses based on a variety of vocabulary-based approaches to authorship issues are comprehensive and convincing.
4 *Cymbeline* is likely to have been written at about the turn of the century, and probably before 1600 (chapter 30); *Coriolanus* was written at about the same time (chapter 27); 'Shakespeare's' contribution to *Measure for Measure* was written in the late 1580s or the 1590s, but probably later rather than earlier in this time range (chapter 29).
5 The meaning here is 'just as when one is paid interest, money is added to the capital, so her tears added water to the river'.
6 Kerrigan (1986, p. 432) considered that 'Shakespeare' wrote in an archaic style in an apparently deliberate attempt to create a formal atmosphere of antique quaintness.
7 Slater (1975).

46. *The Phoenix and the Turtle*

he was my self and was someone else
— Rainer Maria Rilke[1]

Sonnets and *A Lover's Complaint* were not the only late poems published by 'Shakespeare'. Let's return to 1601, the year of Essex's execution. In this year the little-known Elizabethan writer Robert Chester published a miscellany of his own poems and included in his publication, entitled *Love's Martyr, or Rosalin's Complaint*, a poem by "William Shake-speare". This poem is normally referred to as *The Phoenix and the Turtle*, although this title does not appear in the publication. (Turtle in this context means Turtle Dove.)

The Phoenix and the Turtle[2]

Let the bird of loudest lay,
On the sole *Arabian* tree,
Herald sad and trumpet be:
To whose sound chaste wings obey.

But thou shrieking harbinger,
Foul precurrer of the fiend,
Augur of the fever's end,
To this troupe come thou not near.

From this Session interdict
Every fowl of tyrant wing,
Save the eagle, feath'red King,
Keep the obsequy so strict.

Let the Priest in surplice white,
That defunctive Music can,
Be the death-divining Swan,
Lest the *Requiem* lack his right.

And thou, treble-dated Crow,
That thy sable gender mak'st
With the breath thou giv'st and tak'st,
'Mongst our mourners shalt thou go.

Here the Anthem doth commence,
Love and Constancy is dead,
Phoenix and the *Turtle* fled,
In a mutual flame from hence.

So they loved, as love in twain,
Had the essence but in one,
Two distincts, Division none,
Number there in love was slain.

Hearts remote, yet not asunder;
Distance, and no space was seen,
'Twixt the *Turtle* and his Queen;
But in them it were a wonder.

So between them Love did shine,
That the *Turtle* saw his right,
Flaming in the *Phoenix*' sight;
Either was the other's mine.

Property was thus appalled[3],
That the self was not the same:
Single Natures, double name,
Neither two nor one was called.

Reason, in it self confounded,
Saw Division grow together,
To themselves yet either neither,
Simple were so well compounded.

That it cried, how true a twain,
Seemeth this concordant one,
Love hath Reason, Reason none,
If what parts can so remain.

Whereupon it made this *Threne*,
To the *Phoenix* and the *Dove*,
Co-supremes and stars of Love,
As chorus to their tragic scene.

Threnos
Beauty, Truth, and Rarity,
Grace in all simplicity,
Here enclosed in cinders lie.

Death is now the *Phoenix*' nest,
And the *Turtle*'s loyal breast
To eternity doth rest.

Leaving no posterity,
'Twas not their infirmity,
It was married Chastity.

Truth may seem, but cannot be,
Beauty brag, but 'tis not she;
Truth and Beauty buried be.

To this urn let those repair,
That are either true or fair,
For these dead Birds, sigh a prayer.

William Shake-speare

Robert Chester may have been an employee of a distant relative of the Queen, Sir John Salusbury, whom the Queen knighted in 1601. The miscellany may have been written to celebrate this important occasion for Sir John.

The Phoenix and the Turtle is written in a compressed style, with many classical references. To understand it we need to appreciate the story of the Phoenix, a mythical bird which, legend had it, lived in Arabia and re-incarnated itself by building a nest to which it set fire, afterwards arising newborn out of the ashes. Elizabeth was named a Phoenix in her lifetime, presumably because of her longevity and survival despite dangers and difficulties.

The first five verses introduce a bird acting as herald of a requiem and list those birds that are allowed to attend as mourners, or excluded. Tyrant birds are specifically excluded. The anthem (verse six) signals the beginning of the requiem. Reading line 3 of verse 6 ("*Phoenix* and the *Turtle* fled") we can't be sure whether the Requiem is for one of these birds or both, but the final line ("For these dead Birds, sigh a prayer") resolves this issue. Verses seven and eight provide clues as to how the poem should be interpreted:

> So they loved as love in twain,
> Had the essence but in one,
> Two distincts, Division none,
> Number there in love was slain.
>
> Hearts remote, yet not asunder;
> Distance, and no space was seen,
> 'Twixt the *Turtle* and his Queen;
> But in them it were a wonder.

The Phoenix and the Turtle has been of particular interest since 1839 when A. B. Grosart related its subject matter to the friendship of Essex and the Queen. P. Hyland[4] summarised the arguments in favour of Grosart's interpretation, but in true academic fashion Hyland hedged his bets and cautioned that "there are objections to a reading of the poem that tries to find parallels that are too specific". The weakness in this statement is the word "tries". Readers don't need to 'try' to find the parallels identified by Grosart: they are all obvious. Whether they are "too specific" is irrelevant.

When one reads *The Phoenix and the Turtle* in relation to the proposition that Elizabeth I wrote *Sonnets*, Grosart's argument is overwhelming. The lines could hardly be more explicit: the Turtle dove (Essex) was in love with the Queen (Elizabeth), and they seemed like one person ("Two distincts, Division none"). They were so united in love that one could not count them as two individuals ("Number there in love was slain"). But it was a "wonder" that two people with such different characters ("hearts remote") ever came together. The verses explore the paradox that the Phoenix and the Turtle were at the same time so close but remained two individuals ("distance, and no space between").

The first thirteen verses are positive. The love between the Phoenix and the Turtle defied reason ("Reason in it self confounded, Saw division grow together") – they were "Co-supremes and stars of Love". The threnos (lament) describes the tragedy: what seemed to be a beautiful relationship ("Grace in all simplicity") ended in ashes:

> Beauty, Truth and Rarity.
> Grace in all simplicity,
> Here enclosed in cinders lie.

The Turtle dove (Essex) is dead ("To eternity doth rest") and death is preparing its nest for the Phoenix (the Queen) ("Death is now the Phoenix' nest").

The third verse of the threnos points out that their love left nothing for posterity ("Leaving no posterity", i.e. no children), but the lack of offspring wasn't because of physical defects ("'Twas not their infirmity", i.e., it wasn't because they couldn't have sex) but because of a preference for "married Chastity". The unique characteristics of the two birds were beauty, truth and rarity. But the cynical and aged poet laments that beauty is not real ("Beauty [may] brag, but 'tis not she") and truth is an illusion ("Truth may seem, but cannot be"). The poem's sad and world-weary conclusion reflects the wording of sonnet 101 (probably written earlier, in 1599, when Essex was in Ireland, and Elizabeth was struggling to maintain faith in him), in which the poet questions whether truth and beauty should be best kept separate ("never intermix'd"):

> *Sonnet 101, lines 1–8*
> O truant Muse what shall be thy amends,
> For thy neglect of truth in beauty dyed?
> Both truth and beauty on my love depends:
> So dost thou too, and therein dignifi'd:

> Make answer Muse, wilt thou not haply say,
> Truth needs no colour with his colour fix'd [needs no embellishment],
> Beauty no pencil, beauty's truth to lay [beauty needs no extra layer of paint]:
> But best is best, if never intermix'd.

The Phoenix and the Turtle deviates from the phoenix legend. The phoenix is not reborn. In fact the conclusions reached are dismal: love and the meeting of minds are illusory; beauty, truth, grace and simplicity end in ashes; and those who are true and fair need to take note of these truths. (*A Lover's Complaint* has the same resigned tone – this is the way of all flesh.)

Such allusions would have been obvious to readers in 1601, when Essex's downfall was the news story of the year. It is impossible to believe that William Shakespeare, or any contemporary poet wishing to avoid royal wrath, would have had the audacity to write such sad and tactless lines on a subject so sensitive to the ageing queen, and publish them in 1601.

A simpler explanation for the appearance of the poem in 1601 is required: it was written by Queen Elizabeth I herself, after the execution of Essex. A. B. Grosart's 1839 interpretation is correct. The sixty-seven-year-old Queen has finally realised that she has been deceived by Essex. Like the later sonnets and *A Lover's Complaint*, published with *Sonnets*, *The Phoenix and the Turtle* is a lament for (and a penetrating analysis of) their relationship.

Lytton Strachey put into prose what Elizabeth wrote in poetry:

> Human relationships must either move or perish. When two consciousnesses come to a certain nearness the impetus of their interactions, growing ever intenser and intenser, leads on to an unescapable climax. The crescendo must rise to its topmost note; and only then is the preordained solution of the theme made manifest.[5]

Essex was dead. Elizabeth's spirit died with him. The poem anticipates her own death and summarises their personal tragedy: she and Essex were two very different individuals who for a time mistakenly believed that they were united by an inseparable bond.

---

[1] As reported by Maurice Betz (Hulse 2009, p. xxi)
[2] Punctuation in the original, as reproduced in the Elizabethan Club (1964) edition, has been retained, except that line 3 in verse 10 has been written "Single Natures, double name" as this seems to be the sense implied by line 4 of the same verse. Spelling has been updated to conform to modern British usage.
[3] "Property" is the principle that one person, or one pair, is a single entity. The line means 'The principle of distinctness of persons and/or pairs was flouted – they were neither individuals nor a pair'.
[4] Hyland (2003).
[5] Strachey (1971, p. 10).

47. The Royal Poet

No means I find to rid him from my breast,
Till by the end of things it be suppressed.
— Sonetto, Queen Elizabeth I

When looking at peripheral evidence that might support or disprove the proposition that Elizabeth wrote *Sonnets*, we should not ignore her own compositions, in her own handwriting. Her official correspondence is not the place to search. It is generally brisk and business-like, and sometimes carefully self-edited to present herself and her decisions in the best light. In contrast, in her personal correspondence, her candid assessments of individuals (including Essex, particularly when he was campaigning) could be devastating. In situations where she had nothing to lose her letters could be anything but diplomatic.

Elizabeth also wrote poems. Fortunately, one love poem by Elizabeth has survived. It is not in her hand, nor is it signed or dated, but scholars have never doubted its authenticity because of its provenance and context. It is preserved in chronologically arranged papers collected by the Bishop of St Asaph, Thomas Tanner (1674–1735). The papers are now preserved in the Bodleian Library, Oxford. The position of the poem in the collection indicates a date of about 1600–1601, the time of Essex's detention and trial, but it could relate to Elizabeth's earlier courtship of the Duke of Anjou[1]. The poem, entitled "Sonetto", although not actually a sonnet, is catalogued by the Bodleian Library as "A sonnet by Queen Elizabeth, relative to her passion for the Earl of Essex"[2].

Sonetto[3]
I grieve and dare not show my discontent;
I love and yet am forced to hate;
I do, yet dare not say I ever meant;
I seem stark mute, but inwardly do prate.
    I am, and not; I freeze and yet am burned,
    Since from myself another self I turned.

My care is like my shadow in the sun –
Follows me flying, flies when I pursue it,
Stands, and lies by me, doth what I have done;
His too familiar care doth make me rue it.
    No means I find to rid him from my breast,
    Till by the end of things it be suppressed.

Some gentler passion slide into my mind,
For I am soft and made of melting snow;
Or be more cruel, Love, and so be kind.

> Let me or float or sink, be high or low.
>> Or let me live with some more sweet content,
>> Or die and so forget what love e'er meant.

(Text from Bodleian Tanner 76, p. 162)

The resigned style of this poem is simpler than that of most of the sonnets. The message is clear and unambiguous and expressed in a straightforward manner: a woman has had to reject a man she loves or loved ("Since from myself another self I turned") and the only escape from her unhappiness seems to be death ("Or die and so forget what love e'er meant"). The texture of the poem is not as dense as that of the sonnets, giving the impression that the poem has not been much reworked. Like the sonnets, and like Elizabeth's prose so praised by Ascham, the poem is full of "comparisons of contraries well put together" – love/hate, mute/prate, freeze/burn, shadow/sun, cruel/kind etc. The poem's vocabulary and subject matter is similar to both Petrarch's sonnet 134 and the Earl of Oxford's poem *Winged with Desire*. One can speculate that both *Sonetto* and Oxford's poem were modelled on the earlier work.

> *Petrarch's sonnet 134*[4]
> I find no peace and have no arms for war,
> And fear and hope, and burn and yet I freeze;
> And fly to heaven, lying on earth's floor,
> And nothing hold and all the world I seize.
> My jailer opens not, nor locks the door,
> Nor binds me to her, nor will lose my ties;
> Love kills me not, nor breaks the chains I wear,
> Nor wants me living, nor will grant me ease.
> I have no tongue, and shout; eyeless, I see;
> And long to perish, and I beg for aid;
> And love another and myself I hate.
> Weeping I laugh, I feed on misery;
> By death and life so equally dismayed:
> For you, my lady, am I in this state.

Sonetto has interesting parallels to themes in the sonnets – the word hate is prominent, as it is in some sonnets. There are echoes of sonnet 90 in the request that love should be cruel to be kind. The metaphors of floating or sinking also occur in sonnets 45 and 80. The desire to die in order to escape from her grief is mentioned twice (lines 12 and 18).

Sonetto contains thirty words or derivatives in common with the sonnets: breast, burn, care, content, cruel, die, discontent, familiar, flies, follow, freeze, gentle, grieve, hate, inward, kind, lie, love, mute, passion, pursue, sink, slide, snow, soft, stand, sun, suppress, sweet and turn. On the other hand, the six words dare, force, prate, rue, stark and melting are not found in the sonnets.[5] The vocabularies of *Sonnets* and *Sonetto* are too different in size to compare meaningfully in a statistical manner, but their similarity indicates that common authorship must be suspected.

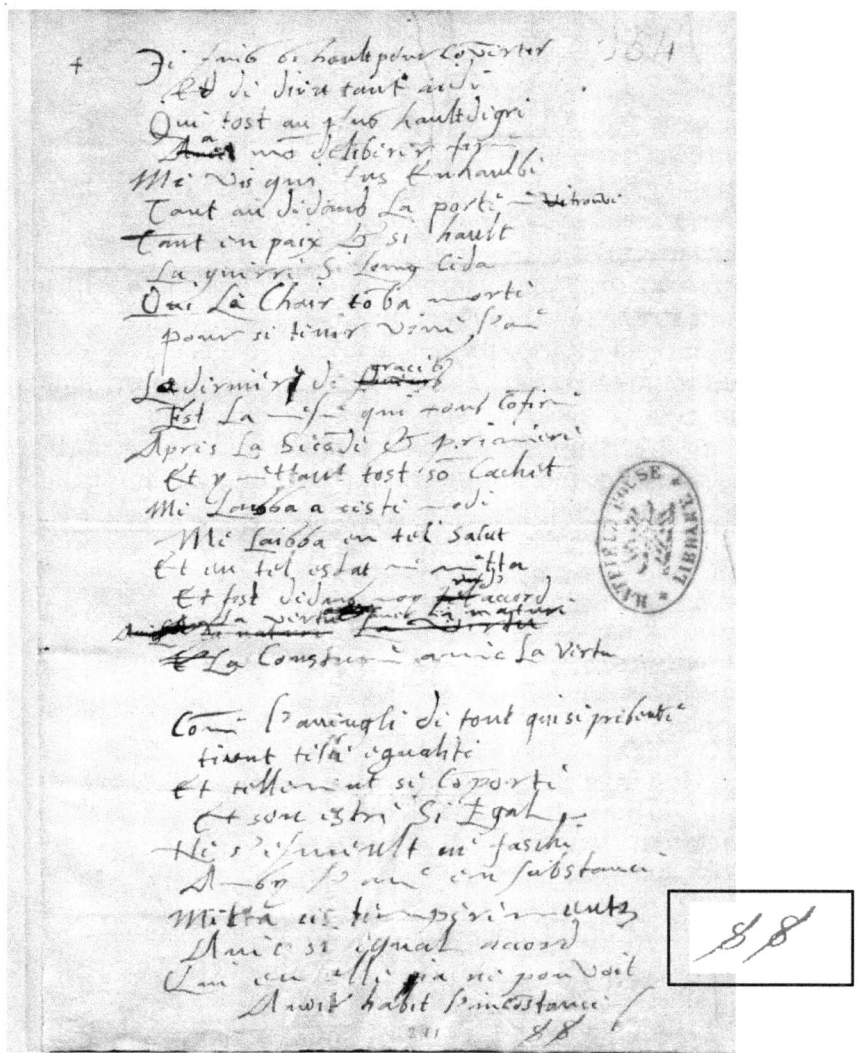

Figure 7. The last page of Elizabeth's poem in French that begins with the words "With the blinding so strange". For a printed version in the original French see Mueller and Marcus (2003, p. 85); for a translation see Marcus et al. (2002, p. 413). The 23 verses deal with Elizabeth's regaining of mental equilibrium after a spiritual or emotional crisis. The poem is signed with the initials SS (enlarged in inset). Reproduced with the permission of the Marquess of Salisbury, Hatfield House, U.K.

Another poem of the Queen's is an untitled and little-known poem in French having the first line "Avecq l'aueugler si estrange" [With the blinding so strange] (Figure 7). It is the longer of two poems written in her own hand, and includes her idiosyncratic use of the Greek letter φ (phi) to represent *ph*. It has been tentatively dated to about 1590[6] but the evidence is inconclusive. Although some editors[7] consider the poem to be Elizabeth's translation of a lost work by another author, such a work has never been found. Although deletions can be expected in a translation, the combination of many deletions and evidence of revised trains of thought following deletions indicate that the writer was developing ideas while putting pen to paper rather than translating a text, which supports the original composition conclusion[8].

We can be sure that Elizabeth clearly never intended this poem to be published. It is a rough draft and clearly composed when she was in a troubled state of mind and struggling through a personal crisis. Now kept among the Cecil papers at Hatfield House, it may have been collected by Robert Cecil from the Queen's rooms after her death, along with her other personal papers.

The poem is a remarkable self-analysis concerning the triumph of willpower over severe temptation. The deletions and the sprawling, loose handwriting are signs of rapid composition. One thought follows another, not always with grammatical connection, in a 'stream-of-consciousness' flow:

> *With the blinding so strange, first verse*[9]
> With the blinding so strange,
> So contrary to my name,
> Although every evil deceives me
> By this share in being man,
> I recognised how foolish
> This being in which I was born,
> So much was lost from all
> That appeared in me then
> Nothing that was mine
> So far was I from me

The poem mentions being deceived by evil ("Although every evil deceives me") and a happy state in the past ("the dream that grieved me – The dream that was past – seemed to torment me"). The later verses detail a struggle between Imagination ("Fantasy panting like a child"), Reason, Willpower and Memory in her "inner man".

The last verse, loosely translated, echoes the teachings of Boethius in his *Consolation of Philosophy*[10]:

> Like a blind man who maintains equilibrium, whatever is going on around him, and comports himself with equanimity, becoming neither agitated nor upset, so my soul has essentially balanced my opposing temperaments, and will not and cannot wear inconstancy for a garment.

It seems likely that the French poem relates to Elizabeth's infatuation and subsequent disillusion with Essex. Her other emotional entanglements were either too early and generally happy (for example, her friendship with the Earl of Leicester) or too superficial (her courtship of the Duke of Anjou)[11] to elicit such strongly worded tormented poetic outpourings.

The poem, however, has more significance than this likely subject matter, for the poem is signed, not with Elizabeth's usual ornate signature "Elizabeth" or "ER", but with the initials *SS*. Each initial is crossed through at an angle, like a modern dollar sign (Figure 7). It may be significant that when courting Elizabeth, the Duke of Anjou used $ symbols arranged singly around a capital E in a coded letter expressing his love for the Queen[12] but these symbols may simply represent the name of the Duke's go-between in his courtship of the Queen, Jean de Simier[13], for whom Elizabeth seemed to have some playful regard. Elizabeth herself never signed correspondence with the letters SS. Could the pair of initials be meant to represent "*S*hake-*S*peare"?

Before we conclude that we have evidence, in Elizabeth's own hand, linking her to Shakespeare, we must take account of previous use of 'SS' in a royal connection. The double or multiple S symbol was used on collars or chains of office symbolising royal allegiance in the early 1390s and may have denoted *sovereign* or *souveignez vous de moi* (remember me) or *soverayne souveignez*[14]. SS collars were worn by supporters of the Lancastrians during the Wars of the Roses[15] and Henry VII used the SS symbol to mark the union of the houses of Lancaster and York. In Holbein's portrait of Sir Thomas More, Henry VIII's chancellor wears a chain of office consisting of successive 'S' letters, two portcullises and a Tudor rose[16] and "Collars of Esses" are mentioned in the coronation scene (Act 4, scene 1) of *Henry VIII*. The double S symbol also occurs together with a Tudor rose in a surviving example of Elizabethan embroidery[17] and a "Collar of Esses" dating from 1545 is worn by present-day lord mayors of London[18].

Just why SS should be used as a symbol of allegiance to a Tudor king or queen is an interesting academic puzzle. However, the previous use of these initials by royal supporters does not explain why Elizabeth used SS to sign her French poem. Elizabeth owed allegiance to no one, so why should she sign a poem with letters that implied allegiance to herself? Although we can assume that Elizabeth was aware of the previous use of the initials SS by her subjects, this assumption has no relevance to her signing with these initials.

Elizabeth would have known that her personal papers would be preserved and were likely to be read by unknown eyes in the future. Did she deliberately sign her poem with initials providing a clue to her *alter ego*: 'for those that have eyes to see I am *S*hake*S*peare'?

[1] Francis, Duke of Alençon became Duke of Anjou in mid-1576. He was the youngest son of Henri II and Catherine de Medici. He courted Elizabeth I between 1578 and 1581.

[2] S. Tomlinson, Bodleian Library, Oxford, England (personal communication 27 August 2002). According to Marcus et al. (2000, p. 302) the Bodleian library copy (Tanner 76, folio 94r) is a late seventeenth century copy placed "erroneously among Essex materials . . . relating to the year 1601", but these editors provide no evidence to support the claimed erroneous placement. The title "On Monsieur's Departure" dates from a copy probably made in the 1630s (Marcus et al. 2000), i.e., 50 years after the Duke of Anjou's last meeting with Elizabeth in 1582. For this reason the title cannot be taken as evidence that the poem relates to Elizabeth's courtship of the Duke. However, Marcus et al. (2000) as well as other researchers (e.g. Bell 2010) assume, on the basis of the title, and without any independent supporting evidence, that the poem does indeed refer to Elizabeth's regard for the Duke.

[3] Text and punctuation as presented in Marcus et al. (2000).

[4] Translation of Mortimer (2002).

[5] The words "melting" and "force" occur in *A Lover's Complaint*, printed by Thomas Thorpe after *Sonnets*.

[6] Marcus et al. (2002, p. 413).

[7] May and Prescott (1994).

[8] Marcus et al. (2002, p. 413). These authors concluded "we find no features of the manuscript to invalidate our assumption that this poem is a complete, original composition by Elizabeth".

[9] Cecil Papers, Hatfield House 147, folios 207r–212r. For a typeset reproduction of the original French version with Elizabeth's deletions and corrections see Mueller and Marcus (2003, pp. 85–94). This translation is that of Marcus et al. (2002, p. 413).

[10] Watts (1969).

[11] Guy (2016, p. 48 and endnote 31) wrote that Elizabeth danced with glee around her bedchamber "for the very joy of getting rid of him [Anjou]" when he left court for the last time in 1582. Although she clearly enjoyed Anjou's company, her talk of marriage was probably play-acting to protect England's détente with France.

[12] Doran (2003, p. 90).

[13] Elizabeth seems to have had some playful affection for de Simier and gave him the nickname 'singe' (monkey).

[14] Mortimer (2007, appendix 7); see also illustrations of the effigies of Thomas of Lancaster, Duke of Clarence; Ralph Neville, Earl of Westmoreland; and John Beaufort, Earl of Somerset.

[15] Doran (2003, p. 55). In November 1592 Essex appeared before the Queen wearing a "collar of esses" (Hammer 1999, pp. 211–212).

[16] Portrait in the National Portrait Gallery, London.

[17] Doran (2003, p. 202).

[18] Doran (2003, p. 55).

48. Epilogue

Do you not know I am a woman? When I think, I must speak.
– As You Like It, Act 3, scene 2

Over one hundred years ago Lytton Strachey challenged the literary world to find "the key which shall unlock the mystery of *Shakespeare's Sonnets*". Readers of this book must judge for themselves whether the key has been found. Is there sufficient evidence to support the propositions that Elizabeth I wrote the book of poems traditionally attributed to Shakespeare; that she was "the greatest man who ever lived"; and that the sonnets refer to her infatuation with the Earl of Essex? While contemplating these questions readers must also consider whether there is sufficient evidence to support William Shakespeare's authorship of *Sonnets* and that the poems refer to his infatuation with a young man of fair complexion.

Let's summarise the main points supporting the Elizabeth-Essex hypothesis:

- The events described in the first group of sonnets (1–126) are paralleled precisely with the documented historical events in the lives of Elizabeth and Essex, including their first acquaintance, Essex's absences from court, military adventures, Elizabeth's loss of friends, praise by other poets, adulation by the public, Essex's campaign to quash the Irish rebellion and his execution. Not only are historical events relating to the lives of Elizabeth and Essex recorded in *Sonnets*, but they are also recorded in the correct historical order. Sonnets likely to represent the Queen's retrospective thoughts about their relationship conclude the sequence.
- None of the sonnets can be matched with events in Shakespeare's life.
- The sonnets traditionally considered to concern Shakespeare's association with a so-called Dark Lady do not represent a difficulty. Careful reading shows that these sonnets are a penetrating psychological analysis of the dark side of Essex's complex and flawed character by a distraught but perceptive and analytical Queen.
- The Dedication in *Sonnets*, when analysed using an approach that we might apply to a modern-day word game or cryptic crossword reveals the name ELISABETH as the "ever-living poet". The word ELISABETH occurs exactly where we would expect the author's name in the Dedication and replaces the word WISHETH.
- Style, imagery, vocabulary, metaphors and numerous peripheral allusions in *Sonnets* are consistent with royal authorship, but not with authorship by a Warwickshire countryman.

- A surviving poem of Elizabeth's, in French and in her own handwriting, is signed *SS*.
- Numerous literary 'loose ends' that have puzzled scholars for centuries can be explained neatly by the Elizabeth-Essex hypothesis. For example, published contemporary remarks by other poets, the subject matter of *A Lover's Complaint* and *The Phoenix and the Turtle*, and peculiar detail like the reference to Saturn laughing and leaping (in sonnet 98), fit perfectly with the Elizabeth-Essex hypothesis.
- Research shows that the so-called 'late' plays traditionally assigned post-1603 dates of composition can be confidently dated to 1603 or earlier, and that several plays assigned later dates of composition have been edited or added to by Jacobean authors; consequently, the plays do not present an impediment to the proposition that Elizabeth wrote the works normally attributed to Shakespeare.

We should also ask:
- What reason, other than Elizabeth being 'Shakespeare', can possibly explain the *SS* signature on Elizabeth's French poem?
- What other explanation can there be for Robert Greene substituting his own word "Player" for "Woman" in the quotation used in his apparently jealous attack on 'Shakespeare'?
- Why should obscure contemporary poems about Shakespeare link his work to royalty and poets in disguise?

Taken as a whole, these repeated indications of Elizabeth's authorship (and numerous others mentioned in the text of this book) are so unlikely to have arisen fortuitously that royal authorship must be considered highly probable. Spalding's principle, discussed briefly in chapter 44, applies: "numerous probabilities all tending the same way are sufficient to generate positive certainty"[1]. Which is to say that when many small pieces of evidence all indicate a certain interpretation, they acquire significance even though, when considered in isolation, they appear to have slight importance.

Some readers will insist that probability is not certainty. They are correct, but it must be pointed out that their argument is double-edged. Despite 'Shakespeare's' vast output, no signed manuscript of a poem or play by William Shakespeare exists, and exhaustive research (comprehensively summarised by Diana Price[2]) has not revealed any independent documentary evidence written during his lifetime linking Shakespeare the landowner, theatre investor and actor to 'Shakespeare' the writer. We have no indication that he ever owned a book, let alone a library. There is no doubt that William Shakespeare existed, but the hypothesis that he was also the man who wrote the works attributed to him requires proof, and this proof has not been forthcoming. In fact, the details of events recorded in the sonnets and presented in Part Two of this book bear no relationship to recorded events in William Shakespeare's life.

Elizabeth was arguably the most intellectual and best-educated monarch ever to have reigned in England and Wales. She was undoubtedly the most remarkable personality of her age, and one of the most remarkable women in European history. She was trained in classical and modern European languages by the best teachers of her time and could converse in French, Italian, Spanish, German, Welsh, Greek and Latin. From early childhood she was immersed in literature and history. She experienced power struggles in her teenage years and throughout her life and understood the intrigues and machinations of men and women driven by lust and the desire for control and influence.

We should note that many of 'Shakespeare's' heroines, for example, Rosalind, Viola, Beatrice, Katherine, Cleopatra, Lady Macbeth, Imogen and Portia, are portrayed as highly expressive strong women in control of their own destinies, to the extent that their lovers and assorted menfolk sometimes appear weak, pliable or just plain stupid by comparison. If William Shakespeare was so sympathetic to virtuous educated women and respected their leadership qualities, how is it that his own daughters could not write their names?

We should also remember that like many great leaders Elizabeth was a natural actor. She loved the stage, both the stage of the theatre (her troupe, the Queen's Men, staged over 20 plays at court in the 1580s) and her very own 'stage', the court:

> Elizabeth had made her court . . . a brilliant theatre in which she, as the leading actress, was constantly on stage. A natural-born actress, she played out a role, written by herself but embellished by the creations of her admirers. The performance was continuous and lasted to the end of her life.[3]

Her teachers remarked on her natural aptitude for learning and for expressing herself. We should note that some sources used by 'Shakespeare' in his plays were only available in untranslated French, Italian, Spanish, Greek and Latin texts. Apart from her intellectual interests, Elizabeth was also extremely sensitive, passionate, physically strong, and attracted and attractive to the opposite sex. It was a mark of her strong character and self-control that reason and intellect normally triumphed over passion, but the passion was always there, and strongly felt. Her infatuation for Essex is well documented.

It would be most surprising if a woman of her literary ability, education and passion had *not* expressed in writing her personal feelings for this brilliant but flawed courtier. I suggest that those who find the idea that a woman wrote *Sonnets* preposterous should put aside prejudice, legend, tradition and academic orthodoxy masquerading as fact and carefully consider the evidence and the evidence alone.

Clearly Elizabeth was proud of what she had written. Her pride is evident in the sonnets. They repeatedly assert that the poems will outlive the author's fame. We can guess that, before she died over four hundred years ago in 1603, she arranged with a trusted literary friend[4] for one of the most intense and tragic courtly love stories of the English Renaissance to be published posthumously under Shakespeare's name in a form in which royal authorship was decipherable but deniable.

The necessity to guard her good standing with her subjects would explain why the personal references in the sonnets are so obscure, why the Dedication's language is contrived, and why *Sonnets* was published in 1609. For had *Sonnets* been published in the Queen's lifetime, under her own name, the nation would have been scandalised, and her carefully cultivated reputation based on the 'Virgin Queen' image would have been destroyed.

---

[1] Spalding (1876).
[2] Price (2001).
[3] MacCaffrey (1993, p. 80).
[4] The Countess of Pembroke, who had edited and published Sir Philip Sidney's poems and was a close associate of the Queen, is a contender for the person who arranged publication of *Sonnets*.

Acknowledgements

I thank the Victoria and Albert Museum for permission to reproduce the Nicholas Hilliard miniatures (Figures 2 and 3); the Marquess of Salisbury, Hatfield House, for permission to reproduce the final page of Elizabeth's poem in French (Figure 7); Drs Brad Tucker and Bruce Peterson of the Mt Stromlo Observatory, Canberra for providing the information on the position and brightness of Saturn in late March and early April, 1599; and Miu Lee for designing the front and back cover and for technical support. Taylor and Francis, publishers of the journal *Colonial Latin American Review*, kindly allowed me to use parts of my 2011 article (in volume 20, issue 3) on sources of *The Tempest* within this book. The discussion on the sources and date of writing of *Coriolanus* is an edited version of my article published in *The Oxfordian* (volume 12) in 2010. I am grateful to Mercedes Duncan for translating the Spanish text on pages 192 and 193 into English. I thank my wife Els McIntosh for many useful discussions and for checking an advanced draft of the manuscript.

Literature cited

What's in the brain that Ink may character
— Sonnet 108

Akrigg, G. P. V. 1968. Shakespeare and the Earl of Southampton. Hamish Hamilton, London.

Anonymous 2006. The Chambers Dictionary, 10th Edition. Chambers Harrap. Edinburgh.

Austin, W. B. 1969. A computer-aided technique for stylistic determination. The authorship of Greene's Groatsworth of Wit. Report, U.S. Department of Health, Education and Welfare, Office of Education. Washington DC.

Bell, I. 2010. Elizabeth I. The Voice of a Monarch. Palgrave Macmillan, New York.

Bicheno, H. 2013. Elizabeth's Sea Dogs. How the English became the Scourge of the Seas. Conway, London.

Black, J. B. 1959. The Reign of Elizabeth 1558–1603. 2nd Edition. Clarendon Press, Oxford.

Bloom, H. 1998. Shakespeare: The Invention of the Human. Riverhead Books, New York.

Booth, S. (editor) 2000. Shakespeare's Sonnets. Yale University Press. New Haven, Conn. and London.

Bourus, T. and Taylor, G. 2014. Measure for Measure(s): Performance-testing the Adaptation Hypothesis. Shakespeare 10: 363–401. doi: 10.1080/17450918.2013.868508

Brault, G. J. 1978. The Song of Roland. An Analytical Edition. Volume 1. Penn State Press, State College, Pennsylvania.

Brockbank, P. (editor) 1976. Coriolanus. Arden Shakespeare. Methuen, London.

Brockbank, P. (editor) 1994. Coriolanus. Arden Shakespeare. Routledge, London and New York.

Brooke, N. 1998 (editor). Macbeth. The Oxford Shakespeare. Oxford University Press, Oxford.

Brownlow, F. W. 1993. Shakespeare, Harsnett, and the Devils of Denham. University of Delaware Press.

Bullough, G. 1964. Narrative and Dramatic Sources of Shakespeare. Vol. V. Routledge and Kegan Paul, London.

Bullough, G. 1966. Narrative and Dramatic Sources of Shakespeare. Vol. VI. Routledge and Kegan Paul, London.

Burgess, A. 1972. Shakespeare. Penguin, London. First published 1970.

Burrow, C. (editor) 2002. Shakespeare: the complete Sonnets and Poems. Oxford University Press, Oxford.

Burrow, C. (editor) 2008. Shakespeare: the complete Sonnets and Poems. Oxford University Press, Oxford.

Campbell, S. C. 1978. Only Begotten Sonnets. Bell and Hyman, London.

Capell, E. 1780. The Tempest. Notes and Various Readings to Shakespeare, Part III, Vol. II. Henry Hughs, London.

Chambers, E. K. 1930. The Problem of Chronology. Pp. 243–274 *in*: William Shakespeare: A Study of Facts and Problems, Volume I. Clarendon Press, Oxford.

Chaplin, C. 2003. My Autobiography. Penguin, London. First published 1964, by The Bodley Head, London.

Chettle, H. 1841. In (E. R. Rimbault and G. Smith, editors): Kind-Heart's Dream. Percy Society, London. First published December 1592, by William Wright.

Clark, S. and Mason. P. (editors) 2015. Macbeth. The Arden Shakespeare. Bloomsbury, London.

Clarke, B. R. 2016. The Virginia Company's role in The Tempest. In (Penda, P., editor): The Whirlwind of Passion: New Critical Perspectives on William Shakespeare. Cambridge Scholars Publishing, Cambridge.

Cohen, J. M. and Cohen, M. J. 1960. The Penguin Dictionary of Quotations. Penguin, London.

Colección Muñoz 1866. In: Colección de documentos inéditos, Luis Torres de Mendoza 5: 286–420. Frias y Campania, Madrid.

Cotgrave, R. 1611. A Dictionary of the French and English Tongues. London.

David, R. (editor) 1994. Love's Labour Lost. The Arden Shakespeare. Routledge, London.

Del Vecchio, D. and Hammond, A. (editors) 1998. Pericles, Prince of Tyre. New Cambridge Shakespeare. Cambridge University Press, Cambridge.

Devereux, W. B. 1853a. Lives and Letters of the Devereux Earls of Essex. Volume I. John Murray, London.

Devereux, W. B. 1853b. Lives and Letters of the Devereux Earls of Essex. Volume II. John Murray, London.

Dickinson, J. (translator), 1963. John of Salisbury's Policraticus. Russell and Russell, New York, N.Y. (http://www.constitution.org/salisbury/policrat456.htm)

Dille, G. F. (translator and editor) 2011. Misfortunes and Shipwrecks in the seas of the Indies, Islands, and Mainland of the Ocean Sea, 1513–1548. Book 50 of the General and Natural History of the Indies by Gonzalo Fernández de Oviedo y Valdéz. University of Florida, FL.

Dobson, M. and Wells, S. 2001. The Oxford Companion to Shakespeare. Oxford University Press, Oxford.

Donaldson, G. (editor) 1969. The Memoirs of Sir James Melville of Halhill. The Folio Society London. W. and J. Mackay Ltd, Chatham.

Donaldson, I. 2011. Ben Jonson. A life. Oxford University Press, Oxford.

Doran, S. (editor) 2003. Elizabeth. The Exhibition at the National Maritime Museum. Chatto and Windus, London.

Dover-Wilson, J. 1934. The Manuscript of Shakespeare's Hamlet. Cambridge University Press, Cambridge.

Duncan-Jones, E. E. 1961. Queen Katherine's vision and Queen Margaret's dream. Notes and Queries ns 8(4): 142–143. doi.org/10.1093/nq/8-4-142b.

Duncan-Jones, K. 1991. Sir Philip Sidney. Courtier Poet. Hamish Hamilton, London.

Duncan-Jones, K. 1995. Deep-dyed canker blooms: botanical reference in Sonnet 54. Review of English Studies 46: 521–525.

Duncan-Jones, K. (editor) 2010. Shakespeare's Sonnets. The Arden Shakespeare. Methuen, London.

Dunn, J. 2003. Elizabeth and Mary. Cousins, Rivals, Queens. Flamingo, Harper Collins. London.

Dutton, R. 1996. The Birth of the Author in Elizabethan Theater. Pp. 71–92 *in* (Parker R. B. and Zitner, S. P., editors): Essays in Honour of S. Schoenbaum. Associated University Presses, London.

Edmondson, P. and Wells, S. (eds) 2013. Shakespeare beyond Doubt. Cambridge University Press, Cambridge.

Elizabethan Club 1964. Shakespeare's Poems. Yale University Press, New Haven and London.

Erne, L. 2013. Shakespeare as a Literary Dramatist. Cambridge University Press, Cambridge.

Evans, M. (editor) 1977. Elizabethan Sonnets. Dent and Sons, London.

Fleay, F. G. 1876. On 'Pericles'. Shakespeare Manual, chapter 6: 209–223.

Florio, J. (translator) 1603. The Essayes, or Morall, Politicke and Millitarie Discourses of Lo: Michaell de Montaigne. Edward Blount, London.

Foakes, R. A. (editor) 1957. King Henry VIII. The Arden Shakespeare. Routledge, London and New York.

Foakes, R. A. (editor) 2004. King Lear. The Arden Shakespeare. Thomson Learning. London.

Force, P. (editor) 1844. Tracts and other papers relating principally to the origin, settlement, and progress of the colonies in North America, from the discovery of the country to the year 1776. Volume 3. Wm Q. Force, Washington.

Foster, D. 1987. Mr. W.H., R.I.P. PMLA 102: 42–54.

Freese, J. H., Church, A. J., Brodribb, W. J. 1904. Livy: *Ab Urbe Condita*, book II. http://ancienthistory.about.com/library/. Accessed 2010.

Furness, H. H. 1892. Shakespeare. The Tempest. A New Variorum Edition. Lippincott, Philadelphia and London.

Furness, H. H. 1928. Shakespeare. The Tragedie of Coriolanus. A New Variorum Edition. Lippincott, Philadelphia and London.

Gibbons, B. (editor) 1991. Measure for Measure. New Cambridge Shakespeare. Cambridge University Press, Cambridge,

Giles, J. A. 1864. The whole works of Roger Ascham. Volume II. John Russell Smith, London.

Green, N. 2005. David Kathman's false parallels between the Strachey letter, the Jourdain account, the anonymous *True Declaration* and Shakespeare's *The Tempest*'. http://www.oxford-shakespeare.com/documents.html. Accessed July 2019.

Greene, R. 1923. A Groatsworth of Wit, bought with a Million of Repentance; the repentance of Robert Greene. Bodley Head, London. First published 1592.

Grosart, A. B. 1878. Loves Martyr or Rosalins Complaint. New Shakespeare Society, London.

Gurr, A. 1971. Shakespeare's first poem: sonnet 145. Essays in Criticism 21: 221–226.

Guy, J. 2016. Elizabeth. The Forgotten Years. Viking, London.

Hadfield, A. 2013. The Oxford Handbook of English Prose, 1500–1640. Oxford University Press, Oxford.

Hamilton, C. 1985. In Search of Shakespeare. A Study of the Poet's Life and Handwriting. Robert Hale, London.

Hammer, P. E. J. 1999. The Polarisation of Elizabethan Politics. The Political Career of Robert Devereux, 2nd Earl of Essex, 1585–1597. Cambridge University Press, London.

Harrison, G. B. 1937. The Life and Death of Robert Devereux, Earl of Essex. Cassell, London.

Harrison, G. B. 1948. A note on Coriolanus. Pp. 239–240 in (MacManaway, J. G., Dawson, G. E. and Willoughby, G. E., editors): *Joseph Quincy Adams Memorial Studies*. Folger Shakespeare Library, Washington.

Harrison, G. B. (editor) 1966. Willobie his Avisa. Edinburgh University Press, Edinburgh. First published 1594.

Harrison G.B. and Jones R.A. (editors and translators) 1931 De Maisse; a Journal of all that was accomplished by Monsieur de Maisse, ambassador in England from King Henri IV to Queen Elizabeth. Nonesuch Press, London.

Hieatt, A. K., Hieatt, C. W. and Prescott, A. L. 1991. When did Shakespeare write *Sonnets* 1609? Studies in Philology 88: 69–109.

Hodgdon, B. (editor) 2001. The Taming of the Shrew. The Arden Shakespeare. A. and C. Black Publishers, London.

Hoeniger, F. D. (editor) 1963. Pericles. The Arden Shakespeare. Methuen, London.

Hoeniger, F. D. 1982. Gower and Shakespeare in Pericles. Shakespeare Quarterly 33: 461–479.

Holden, A. 1999. William Shakespeare. Little, Brown, London.

Hosington, B., 2000. The Early Modern Englishwoman: A Facsimile Library of Essential Works. Anne, Margaret and Jane Seymour: Printed Writings 1500–1640: Series I, Part Two, Volume 6 (2). Taylor & Francis, London.

Hotson, L. 1949. Shakespeare's Sonnets Dated, and other Essays. Rupert Hart-Davis, London.

Hotson, L. 1964. Mr. W.H. Rupert Hart-Davis, London.

Hotson, L. 1977. Shakespeare by Hilliard. University of California Press, Berkeley, California.

Hoy, C. 1960. The Shares of Fletcher and his Collaborators in the Beaumont and Fletcher Canon (V). Studies in Bibliography 13: 77–108.

Hulse, M. (translator and editor) 2009. Rainer Maria Rilke. The Notebooks of Malte Laurids Brigge. Penguin, London.

Humphreys, A. R. 1987. The Second Part of King Henry IV. Arden edition. Methuen.

Hunter, G. K. 1986. Shakespeare and the Traditions of Tragedy. Chapter 8 in (Wells, S., editor); The Cambridge Companion to Shakespeare Studies. Cambridge University Press, Cambridge.

Hunter, G. K. (editor) 2009. All's Well That Ends Well. The Arden Shakespeare. Bloomsbury, London.

Hyland, P. 2003. An Introduction to Shakespeare's Poems. Palgrave MacMillan, New York.

Ingleby, C. M., Toulmin-Smith, L. and Furnivall, F. J. 1932 The Shakspere Allusion-Book: a Collection of Allusions to Shakspere from 1591 to 1700. Volume I. Humphrey Milford and Oxford University Press, London.

Ingram, J. K. 1874. On the "weak endings" of Shakspere, with some account of the history of the verse tests in general. Transactions of the New Shakspere Society 1: 442–464.

Jackson, M. P. 1994. Another metrical index for Shakespeare's plays. Evidence for chronology and authorship. Neuphilogische Mitteilungen 95: 453–458.

Jackson, M. P. 2003. Defining Shakespeare: 'Pericles' as a test case. Oxford University Press, Oxford.

Jackson, M. P. 2008. A Lover's Complaint, Cymbeline, and the Shakespeare canon: interpreting shared vocabulary. Modern Language Review 103: 621–638.

Jenkins, H. (editor) 1982. Hamlet. The Arden Shakespeare. Methuen, London.

Jowett, J. and Taylor, G. 1993. With New Additions: theatrical interpolation in Measure for Measure. Pp. 107–236 and 248– 321 *in:* Shakespeare Reshaped 1606–1623. Clarendon Press, Oxford.

Karras, R. 1996. Common women; Prostitution and sexuality in medieval England. Oxford University Press, Oxford.

Kathman, D. 1996. Dating *The Tempest.* https://shakespeareauthorship.com/tempest.html (accessed June 2018).

Kells, S. 2018. Shakespeare's Library. Unlocking the Greatest Mystery in Literature. Text Publishing, Melbourne.

Kermode, F. (editor) 1964. The Tempest. The Arden Shakespeare. Routledge. London.

Kermode, F. 2000. Shakespeare's Language. Penguin, London.

Kerrigan, J. (editor) 1986. The Sonnets and A Lover's Complaint. Penguin, London.

Kimborough, R. 1983. Sir Philip Sidney. Selected Prose and Poetry. Second Edition. University of Wisconsin Press.

Klein, K. (editor) 2001. Timon of Athens. The New Cambridge Shakespeare. Cambridge University Press. Cambridge.

Lacey, R. 1971. Robert Devereux, Earl of Essex. An Elizabethan Icarus. Weidenfield and Nicolson, London.

Lever, J. W. 1965. Measure for Measure. The Arden Shakespeare. Routledge, London.

Littledale, H. 1885. The Two Noble Kinsmen. By William Shakspere and John Fletcher. Edited from the Quarto of 1634. Part II. General Introduction and List of Words. New Shakespeare Society, London.

Logan, T. P. and Smith, D. S (editors) 1975. The Popular School: A Survey and Bibliography of Recent Studies in English Renaissance Drama. University of Nebraska Press.

Loomis, E. A. 1956. The Master of the Tiger. Shakespeare Quarterly 7: 457.

Luce, M. (editor) 1901. The Tempest. Methuen, London.

Lyle, E. B. 1977. The "twofold Balls and treble scepters" in Macbeth. Shakespeare Quarterly 28: 516–519.

MacCaffrey, W. T. 1993. Elizabeth I. Edward Arnold, London.

MacCaffrey, W. T. 1994. Elizabeth I: War and politics 1588–1603. Princeton University Press, Princeton.

MacLure, M. 1966. George Chapman. A Critical Study. University of Toronto Press, Toronto.

Major, R.H. (editor) 1849. The Historie of Travaile into Virginia Britannia. Hakluyt Society, London.

Malone, E. (editor) 1790. Plays and Poems of William Shakespeare. Vol. I. Rivington, London.

Malone, E. 1808. An account of the incidents, from which the title and part of the story of Shakespeare's Tempest were derived; and its true date ascertained. C. and R. Baldwin, London.

Marcus, L. S., Mueller, J. and Rose, M. B. (editors) 2002. Elizabeth I. Collected Works. University of Chicago Press, Chicago and London.

Margetts, M. 1988. The birth date of Robert Devereux, 2nd Earl of Essex. Notes and Queries (n.s.) 35: 34–35.

Markham, A. H. 2017. The Voyages and Works of John Davis the Navigator. Routledge, for The Hakluyt Society, London. First published 1880.

Markham, C. (translator) 1895. Narratives of the voyages of Pedro Sarmiento de Gamboa to the Straits of Magellan. Hakluyt Society, London.

Martin, C. and Palmer, G. 1999. The Spanish Armada, Revised. Manchester University Press, Manchester.

Maxwell, J. C. (editor) 1968. Timon of Athens. Cambridge.

May, S. W. 1980. The poems of Edward de Vere, 17th Earl of Oxford and Robert Devereux, 2nd Earl of Essex. Studies in Philology 77 (Text and Studies Issue): 43–115.

May, S. W. and Prescott, A. L. 1994. The French verses of Elizabeth I. English Literary Renaissance 24: 9–43.

McClure, N. E. (editor) 1930. The letters and Epigrams of Sir John Harington. University of Pennsylvania Press, Philadelphia.

McIntosh, P. D. 2012. Storms, shipwrecks and South America: from Pedro Sarmiento de Gamboa's voyages to Shakespeare's *The Tempest*. Colonial Latin American Review 20: 363–379.

Melchiori, G. 1992. Hamlet: the acting version and the wiser sort. Pp. 195–210 *in* (Clayton, T., editor): The *Hamlet* First Published (Q1. 1603): Origins, Form, Intertextualities. University of Delaware Press, Newark.

Meres, F. 1598. Palladis Tamia: Wit's treasury. A Comparative Discourse of our English Poets, with the Greek, Latin and Italian Poets. London.

Minshaeus, J. 1617. Dictionary of Etymology. (Copy held in British Library, London.)

Mortimer, A. (translator) 2002. Petrarch. Canzoniere. Penguin Classics, London.

Mortimer, I. 2007. The Fears of Henry IV. The Life of England's self-made King. Jonathan Cape, London.

Mueller, J. and Marcus, L. S. (editors) 2003. Elizabeth I. Autograph compositions and foreign language originals. University of Chicago Press, Chicago and London.

Mueller, J. and Scodel, J. (editors) 2009. Elizabeth I: translations, 1592–1598. University of Chicago Press, Chicago and London.

Muir, K. 1957. Shakespeare's Sources. Methuen, London.

Muir, K. 1978. The Sources of Shakespeare's Plays. Yale University Press, New Haven.

Muir, K. (editor) 1984. Macbeth. Arden Shakespeare. Bloomsbury, London.

Muir, K. (editor) 1985. King Lear. Arden Shakespeare. Methuen, London.

Mumby, F. A. 1909. The Girlhood of Queen Elizabeth. Constable, London.

Mumby, F. A. 1914. Elizabeth and Mary Stuart. Constable, London.

Murphy, D. N. 2015. The Marlowe-Shakespeare Connection. Looking for William Hall. http://marlowe-shakespeare.blogspot.com.au/2015/03/looking-for-william-hall-by-donna-n.html (accessed 23 August 2015).

Musson, R. M. W. 2008. The seismicity of the British Isles to 1600. British Geological Survey Open Report, OR/08/049. 102pp.

Neale, J. E. 1949. The Elizabethan House of Commons. Jonathan Cape, London.

Neale, J. E. 1958. Essays in Elizabethan History. Jonathan Cape, London.

Neale, J. E. 1961. Elizabeth I. Pelican, London. First published 1934.

Neill, M. (editor) 1994. Anthony and Cleopatra. Oxford University Press, Oxford

Neill, M. (editor) 2006. Othello, the Moor of Venice. The Oxford Shakespeare. Oxford University Press, Oxford.

Nelson, A. 2003. Monstrous Adversary. The Life of Edward de Vere, 17th Earl of Oxford. Liverpool University Press, Liverpool.

Nichols, J. 1969. The Progresses and Public Processions of Queen Elizabeth. Volume 1. AMS Press, New York. First published 1823.

Nosworthy, J. M. (editor) 1969. Cymbeline. The Arden Shakespeare. Routledge, London.

Oehrli, A. E. and Carrandi, J. Z. 2016. Edition and Translation of the "Carta a lord Burghley" by Pedro Sarmiento de Gamboa. Hipogrifo (issn: 2328–1308), 4.1, 2016, pp. 23–42. http://dx.doi.org/10.13035/H.2016.04.01.03.

Ogburn, C. 1988. The Mystery of William Shakespeare. Cardinal (Penguin Books), London.

Oldys, W. and Birch, T. 1829. The works of Sir Walter Ralegh, Kt. Volume 1: The Lives. Oxford University Press, Oxford.

Oliver, H. J. (editor) 1959. Timon of Athens. The Arden Shakespeare. Methuen, London.

Orgel, S. 2002. Glossing over it: homoeroticism in Shakespeare's Sonnets. London Review of Books, 7 August 2002.

Padel, J. 1981. New poems by Shakespeare: order and meaning restored to the Sonnets. Herbert Press, London.

Pafford, J. H. P. (editor) 1963. The Winter's Tale. The Arden Shakespeare. Methuen, London.

Paige, P. S. (editor) 1969. The voyage of Magellan: the journal of Antonio Pigafetta. A translation by Paula Spurlin Paige from the edition in the William L. Clements Library, University of Michigan, Ann Arbor. Prentice-Hall, Englewood Cliffs, N.J. (Journal first published in 1525.)

Partridge, A. C. 1949. The problem of Henry VIII reopened: some linguistic criteria for the two styles apparent in the play. Bowes and Bowes, Cambridge.

Partridge, A. C. 1964. Orthography in Shakespeare and Elizabethan Drama. A Study of Colloquial contractions, Elision, Prosody and Punctuation. University of Nebraska Press, Lincoln.

Partridge, E. 1969. Shakespeare's Bawdy. Routledge and Paul, London.

Paul, H. N. 1950. The royal play of Macbeth: when, why, and how it was written by Shakespeare. Macmillan, New York.

Phillips, G. and Keatman, M. 1995. The Shakespeare Conspiracy. Arrow Books, London. First published 1994.

Picard, L. 2003. Elizabeth's London. Everyday Life in Elizabethan London. Weidenfield and Nicolson, London.

Pollard, A. W. 1909. Shakespeare Folios and Quartos: A Study in the Bibliography of Shakespeare's Plays 1594–1685. Oxford University Press, Oxford.

Potter, L. 2012. Pp. 86–105 in: The Life of William Shakespeare: a Critical Biography. *Wiley-Blackwell, Chichester.*

Price, D. 2001. Shakespeare's Unorthodox Biography. Greenwood Press, Westport, Connecticut.

Prior, R. 1972. The Life of George Wilkins. Shakespeare Survey 25: 137–152.

Purchas, S. 1905. Purchas his Pilgrimes. James MacLehose and Sons, New York, NY. First published 1625. https://babel.hathitrust.org/cgi/pt?id=uc1.b3510725&view=1up&seq=9 .

Rea, J. D. 1919. A Source for the storm in The Tempest. Modern Philology 17(5): 279–286.

Reedy, T. 2010. Dating William Strachey's 'A True Reportory of the Wracke and Redemption of Sir Thomas Gates': A Comparative Textual Study. Review of English Studies 6: 529–552. https://doi.org/10.1093/res/hgp107 .

Ringler, W. (editor) 1962. The Poems of Sir Philip Sidney. Oxford University Press, London.

Rollins, H. E. R. (editor) 1944. A New Variorum Edition of Shakespeare: The Sonnets, 2 vols. London. Lippincott, Philadelphia and London.

Rosenblat, A. (editor) 1950. Pedro Sarmiento de Gamboa, viajes al Estecho de Magellanes (1579–1584). 2 vols. Emece, Buenos Aires.

Rowse, A. L. 1973. Shakespeare, the Man. Harper and Rowe, New York.

Rowse, A. L. 1974. The Elizabethan Renaissance: The life of the Society. Sphere Books, London, 335 p. First published 1971.

Schoenbaum, S. 1966. Internal Evidence and Elizabethan Dramatic Authorship. An Essay in Literary History and Method. Northwestern University Press, Evanston.

Schoenbaum, S. 1981. William Shakespeare. Records and Images. Scolar Press, London.

Seymour-Smith, M. (editor) 1963. Shakespeare's Sonnets. Heinemann, London.

Slater, E. 1975. Shakespeare: word links between poems and plays. Notes and Queries 220: 157–163.

Slater, E. 1978. Word links between Timon of Athens and King Lear. Notes and Queries 223: 147–148.

Smith, H. 1974. The Two Noble Kinsmen. In (Blakemore Evans, G., editor): The Riverside Shakespeare. Houghton Mifflin, New York.

Smith, M. A. 1966. Metrical analysis in nineteenth-century English criticism of Shakespeare. Thesis, North Texas State University, Denton.

Somerset, A. 1991. Elizabeth I. Weidenfeld and Nicolson, London.

Spalding, W. 1876. Letter on Shakespeare's Authorship of "The Two Noble Kinsmen." Publications of the New Shakespeare Society (London) Series VIII, no. 1, p. 3. First published anonymously 1833.

Spedding, J. and Hickson, S. 1874. Spedding: On the Several Shares of Shakspere and Fletcher in the Play of Henry VIII; Hickson: A confirmation of Mr Spedding's Paper. Transactions of the New Shakespeare Society 1874, part 1, 1–22.

Spivack, C. 1967. George Chapman. Twayne, New York.

Stamp A. E. (editor) 1930. The Disputed Revels Accounts. Oxford University Press for the Shakespeare Association.

Steane, J. B. (editor) 1972. Thomas Nashe: The Unfortunate Traveller and other works. Penguin, Harmondsworth, England. 1972. (Pierce Pennilesse first published 1592.)

Stoll, E. E. 1927. Certain fallacies and irrelevancies in the literary scholarship of the day. Studies in Philology 24: 485–508.

Strachey, L. 1905. Shakespeare's Sonnets. Spectator 94 (4 February): 177–178.

Strachey, L. 1971. Elizabeth and Essex. A Tragic History. Penguin, London. First published 1928.

Stritmatter, R. and Kositsky, L. 2007. Shakespeare and the voyagers revisited. Review of English Studies 58: 447–472.

Stritmatter, R. and Kositsky, L. 2009. 'O Brave New World': The Tempest and Peter Martyr's De Orbo Novo. Critical Survey 21: 7–42. oi: 103167/c.2009.210202.

Strong, R. 1987. The Cult of Elizabeth. Thames and Hudson, London. First published 1977.

Stunz, A. H. 1942. The date of Macbeth. ELH 9: 95–105.

Tarlinskaja, M. 1987. Shakespeare's Verse: Iambic Pentameter and the Poet's Idiosyncrasies. P. Lang, New York.

Tarlinskaja, M. 2005. Who did NOT write 'A Lover's Complaint'. Shakespeare Yearbook 15: 343–382.

Taylor, G. 1982. A new source and an old date for King Lear. Review of English Studies 33 (132): 396–413.

Thompson, A. and Taylor, N. (editors) 2006. Hamlet. Arden Shakespeare, Methuen, London.

Tillyard, E. M. W. 1938. Shakespeare's Last Plays. Chatto and Windus, London.

University of Warwick (2022) Department of History. https://warwick.ac.uk/fac/arts/history/people/research_staff/marthamcgill/resources/astrology/

Vaughan, A. T. 2008. William Strachey's 'True Reportory' and Shakespeare: a closer look at the evidence. Shakespeare Quarterly 59: 245–73.

Vaughan, A. T. 2013. Foreword to the second edition. *In* (Wright, L. B., editor): A Voyage to Virginia. Two Narratives. Strachey's True Reportory and Jourdain's Discovery of the Bermudas. University of Virginia Press, Charlottesville, VA.

Vaughan, V. M. and Vaughan, A. T. (editors) 2003. The Tempest. Arden Shakespeare, Thomson Learning, London.

Vaughan, V. M. and Vaughan, A. T. (editors) 2011. The Tempest. Arden Shakespeare, Bloomsbury, London.

Vendler, A. 1997. The Art of Shakespeare's Sonnets. Harvard University Press, Cambridge, Massachusetts.

Vickers, B. 2002. Shakespeare, Co-author. A Historical Study of Five Collaborative Plays. Oxford University Press, Oxford.

Vickers, B. 2007. Shakespeare, A Lover's Complaint and John Davies of Hereford. Cambridge University Press, Cambridge.

Walpole, H. (Editor and Translator) 1797. Paul Hentzner's Travels in England during the Reign of Queen Elizabeth. Edward Jeffrey, London. https://www.elfinspell.com/HentznerModern.html

Wallis, H. 1984. The Cartography of Drake's Voyage. Pp. 121–163 in (Thrower, N. J. W., editor): Drake and the Famous Voyage, 1577–1580. Essays commemorating the Quadricentennial of Drake's Circumnavigation of the Earth, University of California Press, Los Angeles, CA.

Warren, R. (editor), 1998. Cymbeline. The Oxford Shakespeare. Oxford University Press, Oxford.

Warren, R. (editor), 2003. Pericles. The Oxford Shakespeare. Oxford University Press, Oxford.

Watts, V. E. (translator) 1969. Boethius. The Consolation of Philosophy. Penguin, Harmondsworth.

Weir, A. 1998. Elizabeth the Queen. Jonathan Cape, London.

Weis, R. (editor), 2012. Romeo and Juliet. The Arden Shakespeare. Bloomsbury Publishing, London.
Wells, S. 2001. King Lear. Oxford World's Classics. Oxford University Press. Oxford.
Wells, S., Taylor, G., Jowett, J. and Montgomery, W. (editors) 2005. The Oxford Shakespeare: The Complete Works. Oxford University Press, Oxford.
Wells, W. 1920. Timon of Athens. Notes and Queries (12th series) 6: 266–269.
Wilde, O. 1958. The Portrait of Mr. W.H. Butler and Tanner, Frome and London. First published 1889.
Wilders, J. (editor) 1995. Antony and Cleopatra. The Arden Shakespeare. Routledge, London.
Wilkes, G. A. 2006. 'Left to Play the Ill Poet in My Own Part': The Literary Relationship of Sidney and Fulke Greville. Review of English Studies 57: 291–309.
Wotton, H. 1651. Reliquiæ Wottonianeæ, or A collection of lives, letters, poems: with characters of sundry personages, and other incomparable pieces of language and arts by the curious pencil of the ever memorable Sir Henry Wotton. Marriot, Bedel and Garthwait, London.
Wyndham, G. (editor) 1999. The Poems of William Shakespeare. Tiger Books International, London. First published 1898.

Appendix 1

Summary of subject matter in sonnets 1–126.

No.	Key words/phrases	Subject matter
S1	From fairest creatures we desire increase	First expression of interest in youth by poet; youth is fair
S2	This fair child of mine	Youth urged to produce heir
S3	The lovely April of her prime	Youth urged to produce heir; mentions youth's mother being lovely when young
S4	Thy unus'd beauty must be tomb'd with thee	Youth urged to produce heir
S5	Never resting time leads Summer on	Youth urged to produce heir – he too will get old
S6	Thou art much too fair	Youth urged to produce heir; youth is fair
S7	Unless thou get a son	Youth urged to have a son
S8	Thou single wilt prove none	Youth urged to marry
S9	Thou no form of thee hast left behind	Youth urged to produce heir
S10	Thou art so possessed with murd'rous hate	Youth urged to produce heir; first argument?
S11	Thou should'st print more	Youth urged to produce heir
S12	Breed to brave him	Youth urged to produce heir
S13	You had a Father, let your Son say so	Youth urged to have a son; father dead
S14	Thy end is Truth's and Beauty's doom	Youth's death will be the end of truth and beauty
S15	War with Time for love of you	Ravages of time – restated love
S16	This bloody tyrant time	Ravages of time – restated love; pupil pen
S17	But were some child of yours alive	Youth urged to have a child
S18	Shall I compare thee to a Summer's day?	Love poem
S19	Do thy worst old Time	Ravages of time – restated love
S20	A woman's face	Subject has womanly character – bawdy references suggesting intimacy
S21	Every fair with his fair doth rehearse	Love poem
S22	Then look I death my days should expiate	Restated love; first mention of death and poet being old
S23	O learn to read what silent love hath writ	Poet not writing down all private thoughts
S24	Mine eyes have drawn thy shape	Mention of picture of youth
S25	Then happy that I love	Simple love poem
S26	Lord of my love	Simple love poem mentioning princes, favourites, vassalage and duty
S27	From far where I abide	Youth absent
S28	How far I toil, still farther off from thee	Youth absent
S29	I all alone beweep my out-cast state	Poet lonely; love poem; youth absent
S30	Precious friends hid in death's dateless night	Poet lonely; refers to misfortune and deaths of friends and past lovers
S31	The trophies of my lovers gone	Poet lonely; refers to misfortune and deaths of friends and past lovers

S32	Death my bones with dust shall cover	Love poem; poet old; lines "outstripped by every pen"
S33	He was but one hour mine	Youth has another lover; poet is jealous
S34	I have still the loss	Youth has another lover; poet is disappointed
S35	Thy sensual fault; sweet thief	Youth has another lover
S36	We two must be twain	Argument and separation; public image to protect
S37	Best I wish in thee	Reconciliation
S38	If my slight Muse	Reflective poem mentioning Muse
S39	Let us divided live	Poet and youth separated
S40	Kill me with spites; Lascivious grace	Youth has another lover
S41	Beauteous thou art, therefore to be assailed	Youth has another woman lover
S42	I lov'd her dearly	Youth attracted to a woman who is known to the poet
S43	Dreams do show thee me	Youth present in poet's dreams; youth absent
S44	From limits far remote; thought can jump both sea and land	Youth journeys over the sea; youth and poet separated
S45	Those swift messengers return'd	Youth absent; youth and poet correspond
S46	Thy picture's sight	Poet has a picture of the youth; youth absent
S47	With my love's picture . . . thy self away	Poet has a picture of the youth; youth absent
S48	Within the gentle closure of my breast	Poet has a miniature picture of the youth; youth absent
S49	My defects; to leave poor me	Poet lonely; youth absent
S50	My grief lies onward and my joy behind	Poet journeys away from youth; youth absent
S51	From thee I speed	Poet journeys away from youth; youth absent
S52	Up-locked treasure; make some special instant special blessed	Poet argues that occasional meetings make youth special; youth absent
S53	Millions of strange shadows on you tend	Youth is being flattered by crowds
S54	When that shall fade	Reflective sonnet; ravages of time; youth will live on in the *Sonnets*; youth absent?
S55	Wasteful war; 'gainst death . . . shall you pace forth	Reflective sonnet; ravages of war; youth will live on in the *Sonnets*; youth absent
S56	Sad *Interim* like the Ocean	Separation; reference to ocean separating two shores; youth overseas
S57	I . . . watch the clock for you	Youth flattered; youth has no time for the poet
S58	Your charter is so strong	Youth flattered by populace
S59	Five hundred courses of the Sun	Reference to idealized image of youth 500 years ago
S60	Waves make towards the pebbled shore	Reflective sonnet; sea mentioned; youth overseas?
S61	From me far off	Reflective sonnet; youth absent
S62	Beated and chopped with tanned antiquity	Poet old
S63	He in them still green	Youth will be remembered as young, not old; poet is old

S64	Hungry Ocean	Sonnets mentioning the sea; fear youth will be lost; youth absent
S65	In black ink my love may still shine bright	Fear youth will be lost; youth absent but poet's love for him will be remembered in the *Sonnets*
S66	Tir'd with all these for restful death I cry	Poet ageing
S67	Wherefore with infection should he live?	Youth in bad company
S68	Bastard signs of fair	Youth is not as fair as he appears
S69	Thy odour matcheth not thy show	Youth misbehaving
S70	Slander's mark was ever yet the fair	Youth being slandered and suspected of ill intent
S71	When I am dead	Poet near death; youth will survive him
S72	After my death	Poet ageing; youth will survive him
S73	The ashes of his youth	Poet ageing; youth will survive him
S74	My body being dead	Poet ageing; youth will survive him
S75	Gluttoning on all, or all away	Poet complains of feast or famine; youth comes and goes
S76	I always write of you	Love poem
S77	The wrinkles which thy glass will truly show	Youth is ageing
S78	Double Majesty	Rival poets write fulsomely about youth
S79	Travail of a worthier pen	Rival poets praise youth; Shakespeare is modest about his ability
S80	A better spirit doth use your name	Rival poets praise youth; Shakespeare is modest about his ability
S81	You survive when I in earth am rotten	Youth younger than poet; youth will be immortalized in poetry
S82	Their fair subject, blessing every book	Rival poets dedicate works to youth; youth is fair
S83	Fair eyes	Rival poets praise youth; youth is fair
S84	Being fond on praise	Rival poets praise youth; youth is vain
S85	Other write good words	Rival poets praise youth
S86	That affable familiar ghost	Rival poet (Chapman?) praises youth
S87	Farewell thou art too dear for my possessing	Poet is exasperated and bids farewell to youth; disagreement
S88	Place my merit in the eye of scorn	Poet feels scorned; poet will take blame
S89	Thou dost hate	Youth hates poet; poet will take blame
S90	Then hate me	Painful estrangement; sonnet describes hate
S91	Me most wretched make	Painful estrangement; poet feels wretched
S92	Steal thy self away; thy revolt	Painful estrangement; youth sulking, in revolt and false
S93	In thy face sweet love should ever dwell	Painful estrangement; but poet still in love
S94	Lilies that fester, smell far worse than weeds	Poet accepts youth has faults
S95	What a mansion have those vices got	Youth is fair but has vices; sonnet on the youth's faults
S96	Thy fault is youth	Sonnet on the youth's faults
S97	Yet this time remov'd was summer's time	Youth absent in summer and autumn

S98	From you have I been absent in the spring; a spirit of youth . . . *Saturn* laughed and leapt	Youth absent in April and spring; Saturn mentioned as dancing
S99	From my love's breath	Reflective sonnet; youth absent
S100	Give my love fame	Reflective sonnet; muse mentioned; youth absent
S101	Long hence, as he shows now	Reflective sonnet; youth absent
S102	Sweets grown common lose their dear delight	Reflective sonnet; youth absent; familiarity breeds contempt
S103	What poverty my Muse brings forth	Reflective sonnet; muse mentioned; poetry cannot describe the youth; youth absent
S104	Like a Dial hand	Reflective sonnet; youth absent; poet has known youth nine years
S105	Fair, kind, and true	Reflective sonnet; poet still in love; youth absent
S106	Such a beauty as you master now	Reflective sonnet; poet still in love; youth absent
S107	He insults o'er dull and speechless tribes	Youth and/or death is dominating tyrants and uneducated people
S108	Time and outward form would show it dead	Poet still feels love for youth, but can't show it openly?
S109	My soul which in thy breast doth lie	Sonnet from youth to the poet?
S110	I have gone here and there	Apologetic sonnet from youth to poet?
S111	Correction	Youth receives a public sanction
S112	Vulgar scandal; all the world besides me thinks y'are dead.	Scandal; youth dead
S113	Since I left you	Retrospective analysis
S114	If it be poison'd	Sonnet of retrospective love; reference to poisoned relationship
S115	Those lines that I before have writ do lie	Retrospective analysis
S116	The edge of doom	Retrospective analysis
S117	Accuse me thus	Sonnet from youth to the poet?
S118	To bitter sauces did I frame my feeding	Poet disassociates himself from the youth
S119	Wretched errors . . . ruin'd love	Poet regrets past
S120	I suffered in your crime . . . night of woe	Youth has committed a crime
S121	They that level at my abuses, reckon up their own	Poet cannot be judged by others who are evil
S122	Nor need I tallies thy dear love to score	Poet has given away mementoes
S123	Time, thou shalt not boast that I do change	Poet says he will not change despite things changing around him
S124	Fools of time, Which die for goodness, who have liv'd for crime	Youth lived for crime
S125	Dwellers on form and favour lose all; suborn'd *Informer*	Youth has put too much emphasis on show; has committed crime
S126	Her *Quietus* is to render thee	Nature surrenders youth to Time

Appendix 2

Sequence of events in Essex's life.

Date	Event in Essex's life
10 Nov 1565	Born
1581	Graduates from Cambridge
1585	Formal presentation to Queen
Dec 1585	To Netherlands with Earl of Leicester
Sep 1586	At Battle of Zutphen; Sir Philip Sidney dies
Oct 1586	Back at court
Jun 1587	Made Master of the Horse
Jul 1587	1st argument with Queen
Aug 1587	Reconciliation; later made Knight of the Garter
1587/88	Miniatures, probably of Essex, by Nicholas Hilliard
Early Apr 1589	Rides to Plymouth; departs from Falmouth for Corunna and Lisbon raids
18 Apr 1589	Re-embarks from Plymouth
End Jun 1589	Fleet returns
1590	Marries Frances Walsingham, widow of Sir Philip Sidney;
Oct 1590	Queen expresses displeasure; Essex banned from court temporarily
1590/1591	Essex's affair with Elizabeth Southwell
2 Aug 1591	Commands forces in Normandy
8 Oct 1591	Returns to England briefly
18 Oct 1591	Resumes duties in Normandy
10 Jan 1592	Returns to Normandy for the third time; back with Queen on 14 Jan
25 Feb 1593	Sworn to Privy Council
Winter 1593	Lopez affair; Essex disappears from court in a sulk for two days when Queen fails to take him seriously
Jan 1594	Returns to court; with Queen at Twelfth Night celebrations
Dec 1595	Absent from court in north of England
Apr 1596	Preparations for Calais relief
31 May 1596	Fleet for Cadiz raid sails; driven back to port
3 Jun 1596	Fleet sets out again
20 Jun 1596	Cadiz raided
Aug 1596	Returns as conquering hero
Feb–Mar 1597	Leaves court in a huff
10 Mar 1597	Made Master of the Ordnance
Easter 1597	Has an affair with Lady Derby
10 Jul 1597	The Islands Voyage; Queen and Essex exchange loving letters
12 Jul 1597	Ships dispersed by storm; rumours that Essex had perished at sea; Essex returns to Plymouth
1 Aug 1597	Consults with Queen at Court
17 Aug 1597	Ships set out again for Spain and the Azores
26 Oct 1597	Fleet returns; Queen greets Essex coolly
Nov–Dec 1597	Retires to Wanstead to sulk over favour given to Lord Howard
Late 1597	Affair with Lady Derby made public
28 Dec 1597	Returns to court; made Earl Marshal
Jan–Jun 1598	Philandering with court ladies

1598	Chapman compares Essex to Achilles and praises Essex's "royal humanity." Other poets to praise Essex were Edmund Spenser, George Peele, John Mundy and Thomas Watson.
1 Jul 1598	Has his ears boxed by Queen
Aug 1598	Keeps away from court
Sep 1598	Ill; away from court
12 Mar 1599	Receives commission of C-in-C in Ireland
27 Mar 1599	Leaves for Ireland
Apr–Sep 1599	Irish campaign
24 Sep 1599	Irish campaign fails; leaves Dublin
27 Sep 1599	Reaches London
28 Sep 1599	Bursts in on Queen at Nonesuch Palace
1 Oct 1599	Imprisoned in York House
Early Dec 1599	Ill; Queen sends her doctors and broth, and a message
Jan 1600	Recovers
Feb 1600	Writes conciliatory letter to Queen expressing his loyalty
Mar 1600	Transferred to house arrest
5 Jun 1600	Appears before special commission of councilors; further messages of conciliatory submission to Queen
26 Aug 1600	Receives liberty; writes many letters to Queen; thrust from her presence
Oct 1600	Queen refuses to renew Essex's monopoly on sweet wines
25 Dec 1600	Essex writes to James VI complaining of Cecil's corruption
2&3 Feb 1601	Essex and Southampton plan coup, but no agreement
7 Feb 1601	Essex summoned to privy Council; refuses to attend
7 Feb 1601	Essex and Southampton have meal with Essex's sister Lady Rich
8 Feb 1601	Treason and rebellion: Essex attempts to raise the London mob; fails; returns to Essex House by river; Essex House besieged
17 Feb 1601	Indictment against Essex for conspiracy, attempting to slay Queen and subvert government
19 Feb 1601	Trial in Westminster Hall
25 Feb 1601	Executed

Appendix 3

The sequence of events in Essex's life and at court, compared to the sequence of events described in sonnets 1–126.

Date	Events in Essex's life and at court	Sonnet no.	Subject matter	Interpretation
7 Sep 1533	Elizabeth born			
10 Nov 1565	Robert Devereux born			
1577	Presented at court			
1581	Graduates from Cambridge			
1585	Formal presentation to Queen			
Dec 1585	To Netherlands campaign			
Sep 1586	Battle of Zutphen			
Oct 1586	Back at court	1–9	First expression of interest in fair youth by poet	Elizabeth's attention captured by Essex's charm and grace
Jun 1587	Made Master of the Horse			
		3	Mentions youth's mother being lovely when young	Catty comment about Lettice Knollys, who Elizabeth disliked
Jul 1587	1st argument with Queen	10	Youth is capable of "murd'rous hate"	Elizabeth detects flaw in youth's character
Aug 1587	Reconciliation	11–23	Restated love	
	Late night games with the Queen	20	Bawdy sonnet implying intimacy	Elizabeth and Essex become lovers?
Late 1587		22	First mention of death and poet being old	Elizabeth is 53 or 54 years old
1587/88	Miniatures, probably of Essex, by Nicholas Hilliard	24	Mention of picture of youth; youth absent	Essex probably commissioning miniatures by Hilliard for himself and the Queen
Early Apr 1589	Rides to Plymouth; departs from Falmouth for Corunna and Lisbon raids	25	Disregard for military honours	Love more important than honours
		26	Simple love poem about princes, duty, and vassalage	Youth absent; sonnet by Essex?
18 Apr 1589; June 1589	Re-embarks from Plymouth; Fleet returns	27, 28	Youth "from far where I abide"	Essex absent from court

1588–1590	Seven friends of the Queen die: 1588; Earl of Leicester; 1589: Sir Walter Mildmay, Chancellor of the Exchequer; 1590: Blanche Parry, Chief Gentlewoman of the Privy Chamber; Sir Francis Walsingham, Secretary of State and Lord Treasurer; Sir James Croft, Comptroller of the Queen's Household; Ambrose Dudley, Earl of Warwick; Earl of Shrewsbury	29, 30	Poet refers to misfortune and deaths of friends and past lovers	Elizabeth devastated by the deaths of her friends and courtiers and particularly by the death of (her lover?) Robert Dudley, Earl of Leicester
		31	Youth considered to be a reminder of a past love	Essex reminds Elizabeth of Leicester
		32	Love poem; poet refers to his/her own death	Elizabeth is depressed
Oct 1590	Marriage to Frances Walsingham, widow of Sir Philip Sidney revealed at court; Queen's displeasure;	33	Poet is jealous	Elizabeth is jealous
		34–36	Youth commits an offence; his straying affections	
	Essex banned from court	37, 38	Reflective poems	Essex absent
	Essex banned from court Affair with Elizabeth Southwell	39	Poet and youth separated	
		40, 41	Youth has another lover	Elizabeth Southwell was the Queen's Maid of Honour
		42	Youth attracted to a woman who is known to the poet	
	Essex commands forces in Normandy	43	Youth present in poet's dreams	Essex absent
2 Aug 1591	Queen visits Cowdray, Petworth, Chichester, Portsmouth, Titchfield Abbey and Portsmouth (26–29 August), all on or near the south coast ...	44, 45	Youth journeys to a far-off place overseas; youth and poet correspond	Elizabeth and Essex correspond while Essex is in Normandy; Queen waits for Henri IV and Essex in Portsmouth
Aug 15–21 1591		46–48	Poet has (miniature?) pictures of the youth beside her bed and on his/her chest	Essex absent; the pictures remind Elizabeth of him
		49	Poet worried he/she will lose youth's love	Elizabeth fears for future
	... then travels north to Oxford	50, 51	Poet fears rejection and with a heavy heart, journeys away from youth on horseback	On leaving and travelling northwards Elizabeth was travelling further from Essex in Normandy

Date	Event	Sonnet	Content	Context
2 Sep 1591		52	Poet argues that occasional meetings make youth special	Elizabeth reconciling herself to Essex being away
	Returns to England; consults with Queen	53	Youth is being flattered by crowds	Essex seen as the champion of the Protestant cause
Early Oct 1591	Resumes duties in Normandy	54?	Reflective sonnet	Essex absent again
18 Oct 1591	Last visit to Normandy; returns to London on 14 Jan			
10 Jan 1592	Sworn to Privy Council		No sonnets.	Essex active in State affairs and in regular personal contact with the Queen
25 Feb 1593	Lopez affair; disappears from court in a sulk for two days when Elizabeth fails to take him seriously			
Winter 1593/4	Returns to court; Twelfth Night celebrations			Essex and Queen attend Twelfth Night celebrations
Jan 1594	Absent from court in north of England	54?	Reflective sonnet	Essex absent
Dec 1595	Preparations for Calais relief			
Apr 1596	Fleet for Cadiz raid sails; driven back	55	Reflective sonnet; wasteful war and death	Essex away on a military mission
31 May 1596	Fleet sets out again	56	Separation ("sad Interim"); reference to ocean separating two shores	Essex away at sea
Jun 1596	Cadiz raid			
Aug 1596	Returns as conquering hero	57, 58	More flattery: "your charter is so strong"; poet not getting attention	Adulation of Essex by the populace and poets; Queen jealous and missing Essex
Feb–Mar 1597	Arguments; leaves court in a huff	59	Reference to happier times	Queen writes of Essex's faults
10 Mar 1597	Made Master of the Ordnance			Reconciliation
Easter 1597	Affair with Lady Derby			
10 Jul 1597	The Islands Voyage; loving letters between Queen and Essex	60, 62	Reflective sonnets; sea mentioned	Essex away at sea
		61	Youth still far from home	
12 Jul 1597	Ships dispersed by storm; rumours that Essex had perished at sea; Essex returns to Plymouth	63	Fear of youth's death	Elizabeth fears death of her favourite at sea
		64, 65	Mention of the sea; fear youth will be lost	

Date	Event	Sonnets	Sonnet content	Historical parallel
1 Aug 1597	Consults with Queen at Court			
17 Aug 1597	Ships set out again for Spain and the Azores			
23 Oct 1597	Lord Howard made Earl of Nottingham	66	Despair; poet ageing	Queen is almost 64 years old
26 Oct 1597	Fleet returns; Queen greets Essex coolly	67, 68	Reference to a painting of the youth	Queen has a painting of Essex?
Late 1597	Affair with Lady Derby made public	69–74	Youth not as fair as he appears; youth misbehaving and being slandered; poet ageing; youth will survive him	Elizabeth has heard of Essex's affair with Lady Derby and the gossip. Essex receives bad advice from friends at Wanstead
Nov–Dec 1597	Retires to Wanstead to sulk over favour given to Lord Howard			
28 Dec 1597	Returns to court; made Earl Marshal	75, 76 77	Love poems Youth is ageing too	Reconciliation
Jan–June 1598	Philandering with court ladies; in 1598 the poet George Chapman compares Essex to Achilles	78–86	Rival poets praise youth: "double Majesty" and "royal humanity"	Elizabeth finds praise of Essex by rival poets irksome and unsettling
1 Jul 1598	Has his ears boxed by the Queen; Essex makes as if to draw his sword; withdraws from court	87	Poet is exasperated and bids farewell to youth	Elizabeth believes this incident has ended the relationship with Essex for ever
		88, 89	Youth has forsaken the poet; poet will take blame	Stand-off, but Elizabeth hopes for reconciliation
		90–94	Painful estrangement; sonnets describe hate, revolt and wretchedness	Elizabeth still prepared to make allowances for her favourite
Aug 1598	Keeps away from court	95, 96	Sonnets on the youth's faults	Essex behaving badly
Sep 1598	Ill; still away from court	97	Youth absent in summer and autumn	Essex absent from court, Jul–Sep 1598; Queen misses him
27 Mar 1599	Leaves for Ireland	98	Youth absent in April and spring; Saturn mentioned as leaping	Essex left for Ireland in late March; Saturn is paired with star Spica
		99–106	Reflective sonnets	Youth absent

Date	Event	Sonnet	Sonnet content	Commentary
		107	"Uncertainties now crown themselves assur'd"; youth is dominating "o'er dull and speechless tribes"	1599 rumours of Queen's death prove unfounded; Essex is fighting Tyrone's rebels
24 Sep 1599	Irish campaign fails; Essex leaves Dublin			
28 Sep 1599	Essex arrives at Nonesuch Palace and meets Queen	108	"Time and outward form would show it [love] dead"	Essex in disgrace; poet still feels love for youth, but can't show it openly; Elizabeth separates private emotions from her public attitude
1 Oct 1599	Imprisoned in York House			
Early Dec 1599	Essex ill; Elizabeth sends her doctors, broth, and a message			Elizabeth still cares for Essex
Jan 1600	Essex recovers			
Feb 1600	Writes conciliatory letter to Elizabeth expressing his loyalty	109, 110	Two sonnets from youth to poet?	Essex admits faults but professes love
Mar 1600	Transferred to house arrest at Essex House			
5 June 1600	Appears before commission of councillors; further submissive messages sent to Elizabeth	111	Youth receives a public sanction from the poet	Elizabeth is requesting his forgiveness for having to treat him so harshly in public
Aug 1600	Receives liberty; writes many letters to the Queen; thrust from her presence	112	Poet writes that the youth forgives the poet for the latter's harsh actions	Increasing dichotomy between Elizabeth's public and private attitude to Essex
8 Feb 1601	Essex rebellion			
25 Feb 1601	Essex executed	112	"All the world besides me thinks y'are dead"	Essex dead but Elizabeth still thinking of him
1600–1603		113–126	Several sonnets on retrospective love; reference to youth's crime	Elizabeth still clinging to the idea that she loves her "lovely Boy"
24 Mar 1603	Elizabeth dies			

www.ingramcontent.com/pod-product-compliance
Lightning Source LLC
Chambersburg PA
CBHW060526010526
44107CB00059B/2611